D1525243

FROM
SPEAR
TO
FLINTLOCK

FROM
SPEAR
TO
FLINTLOCK

*A History of War in Europe
and the Middle East to
the French Revolution*

FREDERIC J. BAUMGARTNER

New York
Westport, Connecticut
London

Library of Congress Cataloging-in-Publication Data

Baumgartner, Frederic J.
   From spear to flintlock : a history of war in Europe and the
  Middle East to the French Revolution / Frederic J. Baumgartner.
     p. cm.
   Includes index.
   ISBN 0-275-93955-3 (alk. paper)
   1. Europe—History, Military. 2. Near East—History, Military.
  I. Title.
  D25.5.B3 1991
  355'.0094—dc20   91-10421

British Library Cataloguing in Publication Data is available.

Library of Congress Catalog Card Number: 91-10421
ISBN: 0-275-93955-3

First published in 1991

Praeger Publishers, One Madison Avenue, New York, NY 10010
An imprint of Greenwood Publishing Group, Inc.

Printed in the United States of America

The paper used in this book complies with the
Permanent Paper Standard issued by the National
Information Standards Organization (Z39.48—1984).

10 9 8 7 6 5 4 3 2 1

Contents

Illustrations

Maps

Preface

The study of the history of war and the military has undergone a profound change in the 1980s. It has become for the first time a legitimate area of professional expertise for academic historians. Prior to 1960, military history was regarded primarily as the domain of a small number of historians associated largely with military academies. Their purpose was to teach future officers the strategy and tactics of past wars and battles in order to prepare them for military careers. Outside of the military academies there was a small number of historians working in military history, who were regarded by their colleagues as antiquarians. Indeed they often were antiquarians, consumed with the desire to learn the smallest details of the tactics of battle, old weaponry, and so forth.

As a result of both the Vietnam War and a strong pacifist movement among intellectuals in America and western Europe, military history fell into even greater disfavor on college campuses in the 1960s. The very popular new social history, in which the lowest, most powerless levels of society were regarded as the most worthy subjects of study, had no place for military history. However, the changing mood of Western society and the recognition that ignoring the military was producing a highly inaccurate account of the past has led to vast growth of interest in the subject. One real benefit of the historical trends of the previous twenty years is that the techniques of the new social history are being applied to the study of war and the military. Armies are now being studied as social institutions; the question of what has made men fight is being studied through the principles of modern psychology; and investigations into the past economic impact of the military and war are being undertaken. Military history is moving for the first time into the mainstream of the historical profession.

Far more colleges and universities are now offering courses in military history, but the production of textbooks for these courses has lagged far behind. This work is intended to be a textbook for a college-level course on military history up to the French Revolution, or for the first part of a general survey of military history. Most such courses are placed at the junior-senior level, and I have written this book with that in mind. In particular I expect that the reader will have had a basic course in Western civilization, although I believe that I have explain matters clearly enough that such a background, while certainly helpful, is not absolutely necessary to understand the text.

I have established the inclusive dates of the work for two main reasons. First, the dates encompass a broad enough span of time to make the work useable as a textbook for courses in preindustrial warfare or, more likely, general surveys of European military history. Yet the time frame allows for a considerable amount of detail and discussion. Second, both dates mark significant turning points in military history: the first, the dominance of the Greek heavy infantry, and the second, the change from the elite professional armies of the eighteenth century to the mass armies of modern nation-states, armed with the products of the Industrial Revolution.

This work is not a series of biographies of great commanders or a description of the tactics of great battles, although a number of battles will be studied in some detail to illustrate the tactics of a particular era, commander, or weapons system. The book makes use of the recent scholarship of historians such as Geoffrey Parker, John Keegan, John Guilmartin, J. R. Hale, and William McNeill as well as my own research in the sixteenth century. The book's goal is to demonstrate the close correlation between social and economic change and military change. It reflects the changing attitude toward military history, which now is seen as an essential component of society that must be integrated into history as a whole.

My concept of an integrated military history for the period under consideration also includes the need to discuss those peoples outside of western Europe who have had a major impact on European warfare. The Byzantine Empire, the central Asian nomads, the Arabs, and the Ottoman Turks are given greater coverage than is usual in military histories.

A project of this sort requires the assistance of a great number of people. I would like to thank specifically my colleagues at Virginia Polytechnic Institute and State University, Glenn Bugh and William Ochsenwald, for reading and commenting on a number of chapters. Graduate student Mark Danley provided important insights into eighteenth-century developments and led me to several of the primary source readings for that era. Special thanks go to Linda Harris, Jan Francis, and Rhonda McDaniel for typing the work into the word processor. The maps and illustrations were prepared by Carl Estes of the Learning Resources Center at Virginia Polytechnic Institute. Lastly I greatly appreciated the help and advice of my editors at Greenwood Publishing Group, Mildred Vasan and Lynn Flint, and staff there.

1

Introduction

War has been a permanent part of human history. Whether it is natural to the human race is a debate better left to the anthropologists and philosophers, but certainly it has rarely been absent from Europe since the continent's recorded history began with the Greeks. War can be defined as the state of organized, socially approved, and regulated violence by one clearly defined group of people against another. This definition covers both primitive and civilized societies; it includes civil wars but excludes the opening phases of revolutions (which often become civil wars) and modern terrorism. A society gives a war its approval by defining it as a just war and by continuing to follow the leaders who direct the war effort, although there is often a substantial minority opposed to the war. When a large enough portion of a people become opposed to a war, it will probably end either through a unilateral withdrawal of troops or an overthrow of the leaders responsible.

The violence of war has always been carefully regulated either by codes of conduct or by law. Some armies and eras have been more rigorous than others in limiting what has and has not been permitted in war, but there have always been limits of some sort. Codes of chivalry, religious tenets, and international law have at different times dictated the controls on wartime violence. Those who transgress the limits of their societies have usually been quickly and severely punished, often by summary execution.

Army is the common term for the organized group of men who engage in war. Historically women rarely have participated directly in war, except when their states or societies were in dire emergency. The participants must carry weapons of some sort, have the rudiments of a command system, and have enough of a sense of discipline to act more or less as a unit in battle. In regard to weapons, there have been in history only two types: shock and missile. Shock weapons are those held in the hand when contact with the enemy's body takes place; their use is known as hand-to-hand combat. Missile weapons involve shooting projectiles of some sort at the enemy. Artillery is simply a special category of missile weaponry that depends on machines or large-caliber guns to launch projectiles heavier than those individual men can propel. Some weapons have functioned as both shock and missile; for example a spear can be used for both thrusting and throwing. Men equipped with missile weapons have preferred to keep their distance from the foe and avoid shock combat. They tend to wear little or no armor and depend on their ability to move quickly to escape an assault by the enemy. Accordingly men using missile weaponry are referred to as light infantry or light cavalry. Those using shock weaponry usually have had armor and are called heavy infantry or heavy cavalry, even if some shock troops actually have fought without armor, as did a number of barbarian peoples. In modern armies the use of firearms equipped with bayonets has confused the distinction between light and heavy troops.

The command structures of armies in history have varied enormously, from the chief of a primitive tribe who leads his men into battle to the complicated command structures of more recent armies in which the upper levels of the officer corps send their men into battle instead of leading them. The more sophisticated the society and the larger its army, the more likely the latter type of command structure has been used. But two of the best armies in history, Alexander the Great's in antiquity and the Swiss army of the early modern period, had commanders who led by example.

The key to every successful army is discipline. That term as it will be used in this book does not mean that, for example, the men correctly salute their officers or conduct themselves properly in the camps and barracks. Such correct behavior is at best an indication of proper discipline. One of the best armies, the Swiss, had no officers in the usual sense and was quite unruly off the battlefield. On it, however, the Swiss had real discipline—the ability of a group of men to function as a unit. This sort of discipline turns individuals fighting their own private battles into an army fighting with common purpose and effort so that the collective force and strength of the group is directed against the foe.

Discipline distinguishes an army from a war party, which is a band of men fighting as individuals and not as a unit. It also creates the distinction between soldiers and warriors. A soldier fights as part of an organized unit that is capable of creating formations more complicated than a massed mob of men. Warriors fight as individuals, not as part of a tactical unit. It is often difficult, however, to determine whether an armed force is made up of soldiers or warriors. In societies making the transition to real armies, the same body of men can display the characteristics of both types.

The most crucial element of discipline is the ability of a unit of men to hold fast in the face of the enemy without giving way to fear of death or injury and running from the field. That is difficult enough to achieve when an army is attacking a foe's lines; it is far more so when an army has to stand and take an assault, especially when a force of cavalry is bearing down on foot soldiers. Yet an infantry force capable of standing fast has generally been able to defeat heavy cavalry, despite the terrifying sight of armored men and horses bearing down upon it.

This form of discipline has been created in three ways, with a fourth, patriotism, appearing in the modern world. The earliest is through kinship ties. A sense of fighting to protect one's family and home is a potent incentive for men to stand and fight despite the terror of battle; even more compelling is the fear of being disgraced in front of one's kin, friends, and neighbors and perhaps even causing their deaths by a loss of nerve. The value systems of cultures that depend upon this sort of discipline brand cowardice as the most heinous vice. Anyone who breaks ranks and runs before the army as a whole does loses his honor, which is valued "more than life by the majority of men."[1] Armies that have depended on discipline created through kinship ties have demonstrated limited ability to execute offensive tactics and displayed limited staying power in the battle.

With the appearance of civilizations based on cities and a more complicated social structure came a decline in the power of kinship groupings. In such societies, especially those just becoming civilized, religion has occasionally provided the principal incentive for military discipline. It is not completely absent from the current world, as the Iran-Iraq war of the 1980s amply demonstrated. A fervent belief that one is fighting in defense of the true religion and will receive a proper reward in an afterlife can be an effective substitute for kinship in creating discipline. It is true that religious fanaticism can cause badly trained and poorly armed men to go into battle against a superior force and thus lead them to the slaughter, but there have been several instances where religious zeal has provided the edge for an army otherwise overmatched.

More often, in civilized societies the loss of kinship-induced discipline has been made good by drill and long-term service. These two features generally have been effective only if employed together. They were the secret of the success of the Roman legions and reappeared in Europe after 1600. William McNeill has suggested that the constant group repetition of large-muscle activities such as marching in step, triggers a primeval response that perhaps dates to mankind's days as a primitive hunter of large mammals. It leads to the creation of artificial kinship groups, specifically the cohort, the company, or the platoon, with small-group cohesion.[2]

Regardless of the anthropological explanation of what makes drill so effective in creating discipline, a well-drilled army has usually been a victorious one. Repeated motions on the drillfield seem to create an imperative to perform the same motions on the battlefield. Modern armies continue to use drill as a means of instilling discipline in their recruits and an automatic willingness to follow orders, although modern combat no longer makes much use of the motions learned on the drillfield. One great advantage of drill-imposed discipline is that it can be combined with that produced by the other forms, as kinship was in early Rome, or patriotism is in the modern world, to produce soldiers both disciplined and eager to fight.

Besides producing soldiers who have the discipline to fight despite bad odds, drill also allows the use of tactics beyond the simple mass charge at the enemy. Drill permits the creation of tactical units within an army that are capable of executing somewhat different movements on the battle field from one another. The term articulated (jointed) is used for armies in which tactical units are capable of different maneuvers. It tends to be applied to large heavy infantry forces, which in their more primitive form are massed without articulation. The nature of light infantry and light and heavy cavalry makes it less important that they form tactical bodies. Armies that include two or more of the basic types or military arms are referred to as "mixed" or "combined" arms. Most armies covered in this book were mixed in that there were usually units of infantry and cavalry present. How well the military arms were integrated and used effectively together has always been a key measure of a good commander.

Tactical bodies have been deployed in three basic types of formations. First, the line, which has greater breadth than depth; that is, it has more files (men in a row behind one another) than ranks (men shoulder to shoulder). Second, the column, which has greater depth than breadth and more ranks than files. A column can immediately become a line, and vice versa, by having the men face right or left. In battle, a line provides the opportunity to outflank the enemy formation or at least to reduce the threat of being outflanked; the column can concentrate greater weight on one part of the enemy formation, increasing the potential for a breakthrough. When used by infantrymen, the column requires less drill and discipline of its men than the line to be successful, and is more likely to be used by less advanced societies. Cavalry units usually use the line as their basic formation. Every column or line formation has right and left flanks. A wing, however, is a body of men on the flanks of the main force that is distinctly separate from the main body, can maneuver apart from it, and often is made up of a different arm. The third type of formation is the circle, which is strictly defensive. A force facing a much superior enemy, or already hard-pressed by one, has often formed the circle as a defensive formation. A circle formation can be effective against shock forces, but against light forces it is very vulnerable.

The term tactical bodies assumes that an army uses battle tactics more sophisticated than a massed frontal assault on the enemy lines. Tactics means the methods by which the army's objectives in battle are won. They involve decisions about how to deploy manpower and maneuver the elements of the army prior to and during battle, what weapons to use, and how to take advantage of the terrain. Strategy refers to the decisions that determine where, when, and why a battle will be fought or, for that matter, not fought. It establishes the objectives for the military in the battle or campaign. The term grand strategy is sometimes used to refer to the establishing of objectives for the war as a whole. These terms are not as clear-cut as the above definitions would suggest; there is a great deal of overlap among them. The same type of maneuver can be tactical or strategic depending upon whether it is used in the context of a battle or an entire campaign. For a long time the terms were used interchangeably; it was only after 1800 that the present distinctions began to be made.

The key to the successful implementation of both strategy and tactics is logistics. Defined simply, logistics is the provisioning of everything necessary for an army to fight—recruits, weapons, shelter, food and water, clothing, transportation, and a system of communications. Before the seventeenth century, armies rarely had a separate unit or quartermaster corps for logistics; the commanders usually attended to it as part of their overall duties. Too frequently, they were either inattentive to it or incapable of handling it well. The armies of such commanders usually were defeated because of their failure to give proper attention to logistics.

Although I have been speaking about warfare on land, most of the above discussion also applies to war at sea. The major difference is that when naval war first appeared, the societies employing it were already at a high level of civilization. The more primitive manifestations of discipline, command, and logistics are not found in navies, even the earliest ones.

These principles and definitions apply to modern warfare in most respects, but I have consciously tailored them to fit preindustrial warfare. This book ends with the War of American Independence, because two momentous changes occur in warfare after that conflict. In fact, the nineteenth century saw far greater change in warfare than had occurred in the 2,400 years after the Battle of Marathon. The first of the changes was the adoption of the nation-in-arms concept by the French after 1789. While this was not an entirely new concept, since many peoples had in the past employed every able-bodied male in their armies, revolutionary France was the first modern state to exploit its great population for mass armies. They have remained standard since then. Warfare changed even more when the spread of the Industrial Revolution in the nineteenth century enabled European states to equip their mass armies with assembly-line-produced weaponry such as rapid-fire rifled firearms.

The era after the French Revolution also saw the abandonment of the age-old principle that fighting men provide their own weapons. This principle was observed in the Roman Empire and in the two centuries before 1789 by deducting the cost of weapons provided by the state from the soldiers' pay. (Warriors never received pay, but did take booty.) For much of the history of warfare a fighting man needed to have enough wealth to afford to equip himself with the standard weaponry for his society. The expense of horses thus restricted cavalry service to a small elite, except in nomadic societies, where every man had several horses. The requirement that a fighting man provide his own weapons was one factor that kept preindustrial armies small, since a large portion of a society's males often could not afford the weaponry needed. Other factors contributing to the small size of armies included the difficulties of supplying them and of communication. Again there were dramatic improvements after 1800 that profoundly improved the capacity of states to feed and equip their armies and the ability of commanders to communicate on the battlefield.

It is probable that Alexander the Great or Hannibal, given some time to become familiar with gunpowder weapons, would have been able to command armies of the late eighteenth century successfully, since warfare from the Greeks to the French Revolution had a great deal of continuity. Warfare was vastly different after 1800.

NOTES

1. General S.L.A. Marshall, quoted by John Keegan and Richard Holmes, *Soldiers A History of Men in Battle* (New York, 1986), p. 52.

2. William McNeill, *The Pursuit of Power: Technology, Armed Force and Society since A.D. 1000* (Chicago, 1982), pp. 218-33.

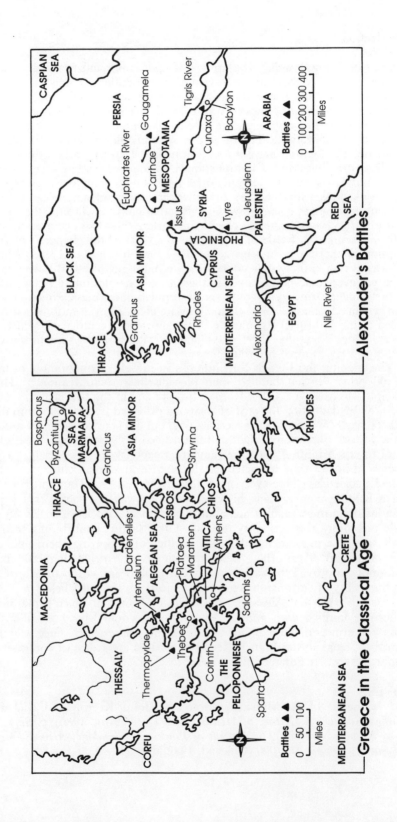

Greece in the Classical Age

Alexander's Battles

2

The Greek Phalanx

Do not fear the great number of men; do not flee before them,
But straight to the frontline ranks let every man bear his shield.
For those who, staying beside one another, have the courage
To engage at close quarters with the frontline ranks,
These men die in fewer numbers, and they save the army behind them.
But if they flee out of fear, all excellence is lost.
No one could ever recount all of the evils
That befall a man when he suffers disgrace.
But drawing close, hand to hand, let every man strike home
With long spear or sword, and kill his enemy.
With foot placed next to foot and shield resting on shield,
And having drawn near, plume to plume, helmet to helmet,
and chest to chest, let him fight his man,
Grasping the hilt of his sword or his long spear.

> By Tyrtaéus, a Spartan poet of the seventh century B.C., translated
> by Professor Glenn R. Bugh.

The famed Battle of Marathon, 491 B.C., is a fitting point at which to begin a military history of Europe. It was the first great battle fought on European soil; the first for which there is a reliable source, the "father of history" himself, Herodotus; and the first in a long series of battles between Europeans and Asians. The Greeks fought with shock weapons, the weaponry of choice for most Europeans in the preindustrial era, while the Persians used mostly missile weapons, the usual weaponry for the Asian foes whom the Europeans faced.

Europeans, at least those regarded as coming from Indo-European stock, have had a strong preference for shock weaponry. They considered hand-to-hand fighting, especially by individual heroes on a one-to-one basis, as the ideal. The *Iliad*, dating from a half-millenium before Marathon, clearly revealed the heroic tradition of shock combat. Homer expressed the belief that the use of missile weapons was cowardly, and that to die in battle from being hit by a missile was a humiliating death for a true warrior. After being largely suppressed among the Romans, that tradition would reappear virtually unchanged among the German tribes and the medieval knights, and was still present among European nobles well into the gunpowder era. Like the Middle Ages, early Greece emphasized cavalry, although it was chariot-drawn rather than mounted, and had a small noble class that dominated society. Because of the cost of mounted service, only the nobles could afford to serve in the cavalry. With a near monopoly on military service, they also held a near monopoly on political power.

THE GREEK PHALANX

In the seventh century B.C. improvements in metalworking brought down the cost of armor and weapons so that the middle classes of the Greek city-states could now afford to serve as shock infantry. The mountainous terrain of Greece provided few places where a cavalry force could operate freely. The rough terrain also created a vast number of political divisions, mostly city-states, with small populations and limited wealth. Heavy infantrymen, who had fewer expenses for equipment than did cavalrymen, could be more easily recruited from a small population base. Since their numbers were much greater than those of the nobility and they had enough discipline to stand up to cavalry, heavy infantry became the dominant arm of the Greek military. With the changeover to heavy infantry came an expansion of political rights to those classes serving in the infantry. Generally, political rights have been given to those in a society who provide military service, although there are so many exceptions to this point that it can hardly be called an axiom of history. In those states where only a small elite has served, political power has been very restricted. The expansion of military service to a broader part of the population was a major factor in the development of Greek democracy. It is noteworthy that in some parts of Greece, such as Thessaly, where cavalry remained dominant, democracy never gained a foothold.

With their preference for shock combat, the Greeks became dependent on heavy infantrymen known as hoplites, from the word for their shields. As was true in nearly all armies of the preindustrial world, the Greeks, with the exception of the Spartans, were expected to purchase their own equipment. Since most were militiamen, they received no pay or at best a very small amount for their service, and had to purchase their weapons from their own wealth. The light infantry, with equipment that cost less, was regarded as using men who were not only less courageous than hoplites but also came from the dregs of society.

A Greek hoplite carried a thrusting spear, six to eight feet in length with a spike at the butt end, as his principal weapon, plus a short sword for use in very close combat, and when his spear was broken. What made Greek

Two Greek hoplites in battle, from a sixth-century B.C. vase

heavy infantry so formidable was the unprecedented quality and quantity of its armor. The bronze armor of a typical hoplite consisted of a helmet that covered as much of the face as possible without impairing vision, a breastplate that reached the knees, and greaves (leggings). The typical Greek shield was circular, about a yard in diameter, made of wood covered with bronze, and weighed about sixteen pounds. The shield covered the holder's left side and the right side of his neighbor to his left. The extension of the shield to the hoplite's neighbor had two important consequences: it was a major reason why the Greek infantry maintained a tight formation in battle, a crucial factor in a successful infantry; and it created a tendency for hoplite forces to drift to the right as the men sought the protection of their neighbors' shields. The combined weight of shield and armor was exceeded only by the plate armor of the late medieval knight, who of course was usually on horseback. It greatly limited the mobility of the hoplites.

The tightly formed, deep formation of hoplites was known as the phalanx. Eight ranks were the norm, but there often would be more than that; in a few cases, there were more than sixteen. The first rank did the fighting. The next two ranks took the place of those in the first rank who had fallen. Those farther back served largely to push the men in front into the enemy line. Battles between phalanxes usually became shoving matches of shields against shields. The mass of men prevented those in the front from breaking ranks and running from the enemy. However, discipline in a phalanx was created largely by the knowledge that the individual hoplite's life depended on his neighbor to his right fighting as a bravely as he did.

Also, the awareness that cowardice in battle would be obvious to one's relatives and neighbors and might well cause their deaths meant that virtually all hoplite forces fought stubbornly so long as their formation remained largely intact. According to Tyrtaéus, those in the first rank who held their ground and closed ranks lost the fewest men and protected those beind them.

Tactics of a hoplite force were very elementary. A phalanx in the classical era (from Marathon to the time of Alexander) was not articulated: that is, it had no wings or divisions. The phalanx charged the enemy as a solid block, running for the last 100 yards—perhaps more if the enemy had archers—to to make its impact greater. Once the hoplites reached the enemy, they thrust their spears at their foes and tried to push them down with their shields. They made little effort to strike at the flanks of the enemy, and none to envelop his rear. A level field was usually chosen for the battle by mutual consent of the phalanx commanders. A hillside position would be a decided advantage for the side that had it, and the other phalanx would usually decline combat under such conditions.

The commander of a Greek phalanx, often elected by the people, had a limited role in a battle. He decided whether to form a deep formation or a broad one, chose the field through the tacit agreement with the foe's commander, and exhorted his men before the battle to fight well. Once the battle was joined, he placed himself in the right flank and had little or no influence on the outcome, except through his example of courage and prowess. A large proportion of Greek commanders were killed in battle. There appears to have been no real command structure in a phalanx; the veterans taught the new men how to stay in formation and use their weapons, but there was little drill.

All male citizens between the ages of eighteen and sixty who could afford the equipment of a hoplite, except those truly disabled, were compelled to serve. A Greek army thus had a large number of grizzled veterans who had seen many campaigns. Nonetheless, because the city-states were quite small, Greek armies usually were small, several thousand men at most, and campaigns were brief. Logistics consisted of having servants carry enough food to last several days. The substantial armor that hoplites wore kept the number of casualties low. It also limited their ability to pursue a defeated foe, which is when the majority of casualties are usually taken. Enough casualty rolls have survived to suggest that typically about 20 percent of the men in a phalanx battle were killed, in a ratio of three of the vanquished to one of the victors. A second battle in a campaign was rare, for a defeated city-state generally made peace without heavy concessions—although another campaign might well occur between the same foes the next year.

The Spartan phalanx was a significant exception among Greek armies. The Spartans were professional soldiers who were drilled from childhood. With the confidence born of long training and a tradition of victory, the Spartan hoplites marched into battle to the music of flutes and recorders. Their steady approach was more unnerving than the rush of other Greek armies. As well-drilled soldiers, the Spartans were capable of some articulation in their phalanx. In particular, they were able to take advantage of the tendency of other phalanxes to drift to the right in battle by forming a right wing and using it to strike at the left flank of their foes, often with devastating results. However, the Spartans developed their army to control their peasants; they rarely tried to project their power far from home.

THE PERSIAN INVASION

Altogether the Greek states, not including semi-Greek Macedonia and Thessaly to the north, could muster some 70,000 hoplites were they to act in concert. The threat that forced them to cooperate came from the Persian Empire. The largest state to have existed up to that time, Persia extended from present-day Afghanistan to the Aegean Sea. Although its army certainly was the largest in existence as well, the total amount of manpower Persia was able to muster has been strongly debated by historians ever since Herodotus. Given the estimated population of the empire, but considering that a large portion of the army was cavalry, a figure of 300,000 men is plausible. But a large part of that could not have been used against Greece because of the need for internal control and frontier defense.

The Persian army consisted mostly of light cavalry and light infantry, using the bow as their main weapon. The Persian bow was a "self-bow" (made up of one piece) with an effective range of 130 to 160 yards. The stirrup was not yet invented, but the Persians and other peoples in their empire had learned how to control their horses and draw a bow or throw a spear from horseback. They had largely abandoned the chariot, since the horse archer had greater mobility and firepower.

The Persian army included vast numbers of foot archers. Although they lacked the mobility of the cavalry, they partially compensated through greater firepower. Light forces generally spent little time in training beyond a great deal of shooting practice. They usually were an unarticulated mass of individuals firing almost at random at the enemy. If heavy forces were able to charge through the rain of arrows, and their armor usually made it possible to do so, the archers, whether on horse or foot, would be easily overrun or, more likely, would break ranks and run at first contact. Their light equipment enabled them to escape from the pursuing heavy forces with few casualties, unless they were trapped against a natural obstacle or another enemy force. Then the slaughter could be terrible.

Light forces almost always carried some sort of shock weapon, such as a short sword or club for use in the later stages of a battle. If they perceived that their missile fire had demoralized the enemy, they switched to their shock weapons to finish the job of defeating him. It is equally true that heavy forces usually carried some sort of missile weapons or had missile shooters present, to do some injury to the enemy before charging with their shock weapons. The best armies in history have combined effective use of a sceondary weapon with devastating use of their main weapon.

THE BATTLE OF MARATHON

The Greeks of the time of the first Persian invasion in 491 B.C. were not entirely lacking in either cavalry or light forces, but the circumstances of the Battle of Marathon set up a situation where only the heavy infantry of Athens was present to fight the Persians. Several cities were allied with Emperor Darius, and Sparta was delayed by an important religious festival at the time of the Persian landing at the Plain of Marathon. Darius had decided to invade Greece to secure his western frontier, because the Greeks had aided the Greek cities on the west coast of Asia Minor in their revolt against him of 499-93 B.C.. Herodotus related that the Persians numbered 100,000, but the fact that they crossed the Aegean by ship suggests a much smaller number. They included some cavalrymen, but not in the numbers to which the Persians were accustomed.

The command of the 9,000 Athenian hoplites who rushed to Marathon was given to their most experienced leader, Miltiades. The Athenians spent three days holding the passes that led to Athens from the Plain of Marathon. When Miltiades discovered that some of the Persians had reembarked to sail to Athens, he decided to attack. The Persian battle plan called for light infantry, which had no armor but carried wicker shields, to deploy in a loose array in the center with the cavalry on the wings. The bowmen in the center were to rain arrows on the Greeks, while the cavalry was to strike at their flanks and bring them to a halt, making the archers more effective. Miltiades' countertactics involved lengthening the usual line of the phalanx to fill the space of the plain between two creeks. Placing his flanks on the creeks served to reduce the impact of the cavalry charge. He also strengthened the flanks to twelve ranks while reducing the depth of the center.

Having advanced within the maximum range of the Persian archers, perhaps 130 yards, the Athenians charged into the enemy line. The weakened Greek center was pushed back, but the strengthened flanks beat back the Persian cavalry and achieved a classic double envelopment. The Persians, not willing to fight hand-to-hand against the better-armored Greeks, ran for their ships two miles away. Their lighter equipment and Miltiades' decision to regroup his forces before pursuing allowed many Persians to get away, but the Athenians caught the stragglers and captured seven galleys. Herodotus gave the Persian dead as 6,400 and the Greek as 192. The first number was probably exaggerated and reflected the usual tendency of chroniclers to overestimate the number of enemy casualties. Chroniclers have been more accurate in giving the casualties for their own side; the small number for the Greeks at Marathon reflected the armor they wore. Herodotus' figure for the Greeks probably did not include those who died of their wounds later, which is true of most casualty figures found in battle chronicles.

XERXES' INVASION

Marathon demonstrated the ability of a disciplined, well-led heavy infantry force to defeat combined arms of the sort the Persians deployed, but their defeat did not convince them that Greece was unconquerable. Darius' death delayed another attempt, but by 480 Emperor Xerxes had raised a huge army, perhaps approaching 200,000 men, to try again. Whatever its real size, there is little question that it was the largest army assembled up to that time. Led by the emperor, it crossed the Dardanelles (also known as the Hellespont) on two pontoon bridges. Supported by a powerful fleet, the Persian army pushed into northern Greece.

Faced with the approach of that enormous force the Spartans wanted to retreat to the Peloponnesus and defend the four-mile-wide Isthmus of Corinth, but the Athenians refused to abandon their city, as that plan required. Themistocles, the Athenian leader, pointed out that the Persian fleet could land anywhere in the Peloponnesus. Thus it was agreed that Sparta and several allies (many Greek cities had already come to terms with Xerxes) would send forces to central Greece to defend the passes there, while the Athenian fleet would take on the Persians in the Aegean.

The Spartans posted 6,000 men at the Pass of Thermopylae near the east coast of central Greece. Holding the narrow pass, they held off three days of assaults. Then the major problem of defending a mountain pass came into play: there is always another way through the mountains. A local Greek showed the Persians a path around the Greek position. Realizing what had happened, the Spartan commander kept 300 men at Thermopylae to cover the retreat of the rest of his army. They fought to the last man and are forever immortalized by one of the most famous epitaphs of history: "Traveler, if you come to Sparta, tell them that you have seen us lying here, as the law has commanded."

THE WAR AT SEA

The way to Athens now open, the Athenian fleet became the only defense of the city. Naval warfare in the Mediterranean Sea and the adjoining seas such as the Aegean was from the earliest times a matter for galleys. A galley can be defined as a sea-going vessel designed for fighting while being rowed. Sailing ships were not uncommon in that era, but they were used almost exclusively as cargo carriers. The weather conditions of the Mediterranean provide the principal explanation for the continued reliance on galleys until the early seventeenth century. For much of the year, the sea is quite calm, and the winds are light and undependable. War at sea required greater and more regular speed than a sailing vessel could provide under those conditions. Galleys did take care to be off the sea during the winter, when ferocious storms are common. The general serenity of the Mediterranean during the campaigning season meant that galleys could be lightly built and thus inexpensive. The numerous islands and peninsulas in the region also meant that the problem of provisioning the proportionately very large crew aboard a galley was not a great drawback, since numerous stops could be made on a voyage.

Boats with oars appeared very early in the eastern Mediterranean, but the first clear use for war dates to about 1000 B.C. in Egypt. Hand-to-hand combat after boarding an enemy ship was the tactical style. By 800 the Phoenicians were using galleys equipped with rams, which were driven into the sides of the enemy vessels below the waterline. The bursts of speed possible with a galley and its great agility—oars could be used on only one side for very short turns—made ramming an effective tactic. By 600 Greek *pentekonters* were operating in the Aegean. They had a single deck with fifty rowers, a helmsman to steer, and a time-beater to set the pace for the rowers. It is not clear how many fighting men, "marines," they carried for boarding enemy ships. Greek rowers generally were free men who could not afford the equipment of a hoplite. As free men they were more amenable to training than slaves, had higher morale, and could be trusted with weapons for hand-to-hand combat when needed.

By 500 B.C., triremes with three decks were well established. Their expense and the large number of rowers required (170) limited their use to the larger and wealthier city-states, especially Athens. A standard trireme was 120 feet long, 18 feet wide, and carried two square sails for use in the open sea with a fair wind and no threat of battle. Its strengths were speed and maneuverability, and it carried fourteen marines for boarding. An Athenian trireme once was recorded as maintaining a pace of 7 1/2 knots (nautical miles per hour) for a twenty-four-hour voyage. "Battle speed," a short sprint, was probably over nine knots. By shipping oars on one side, a trireme could turn around in about 1 1/4 boat lengths. Ramming was the usual tactic; but by training the rowers to pull in their oars at the last second, a trireme could slide alongside an enemy galley and break off its oars, leaving it a sitting duck for ramming.

In 483 Athens discovered a vast silver lode in the mines of Attica. Themistocles persuaded the city to use the windfall to increase its fleet to 200 triremes, which was accomplished by the time of Xerxes' invasion. The emperor had access to the vast shipbuilding capacity of the Phoenicians and the Greek cities of Asia Minor, and his fleet numbered about 200 galleys and hundreds of other ships. But only a small portion of them were triremes, and it seems accurate to say the Athenian fleet was of superior quality. The quality of the Persian fleet also was lowered by being a mixed fleet; a fleet is only as good as its worst vessel.

Greek strategy in 480 called for a double blocking action—one on land at Thermopylae and the other at sea to prevent the Persian fleet from moving into the strait between the island of Euboea and the mainland, since the Persian army at Thermopylae was heavily dependent on the fleet for its rations. Despite losing a large number of ships to a gale several days earlier, the Persians broke the Athenian blockade by winning the Battle of Artemisium (naval battles are usually named after the nearest point of land). The Greek galleys performed well in the battle but were driven off by the weight of the Persian fleet.

Both attempts at blocking Xerxes from Attica had failed, and Athens was open to Persian assault. As the Persians ponderously moved toward the city in September 480, it was hastily evacuated. Every fighting man was taken aboard the galleys. Themistocles persuaded the admirals to make a stand in the narrow strait between the island of Salamis and the mainland, to the west of Athens. He was convinced that fighting in the narrow waterway favored the more maneuverable Greek galleys, while the open seas favored the greater size of the Persian fleet. Part of the Persian fleet was sent to block the western exit from the strait, while the main body, numbering perhaps as high as 300 ships, moved into the strait from the east. With the addition of ships from several other cities, the Greek fleet numbered about 300.

As the Persians approached the Greek position halfway through the strait, the waterway narrowed considerably before opening up again where the Greek galleys were arrayed. The Persians were forced to go from a line-abreast formation, with the boats along side one another, the usual attack formation for galleys, to a line-astern, with the boats behind one another. As the Persians emerged from the bottleneck, the Greeks struck, using their speed to ram the enemy line from the flanks. The battle soon turned into a mêlée of hand-to-hand combat aboard the ships. With so many hoplites aboard, the Athenians had a clear advantage in that aspect of the battle as well. The narrow waterway fed the Persian ships piecemeal into the fighting, and they were not able to take advantage of their superior numbers. After seven hours of fighting, the Persians fled. Xerxes had watched the battle from a hilltop on the mainland. If Herodotus is accurate, the emperor saw the Greeks sink or capture 200 of his ships while losing forty of theirs.

Xerxes returned to Asia Minor with most of what was left of his fleet and half of his army, but he left a powerful army behind to continue the campaign. In July 479, it clashed with the Greeks in the Battle of Plataea near Thebes. Again the Greeks were victorious, this time largely because of the quality of the Spartan forces, which bore the brunt of the fighting. Thus the Greeks, drawing on far fewer resources and a much smaller population than the Persian Empire, had defeated the greatest army up to that time. Herodotus explained the Greek victory as one of free men over slaves, but this was hardly true since most Persians involved were professional fighters. The Greeks had the incentive of fighting to defend their homes and had the usual advantage of defenders against invaders of having more direct access to supplies and rations. The rough terrain of Greece also was a factor, in that the Persians never had a chance to fight on a field broad enough for their major strength, the light cavalry, to operate at its best. Ultimately, however, the Greek victory can be attributed to the fact that a disciplined heavy infantry force, capable of fighting as a unit against great odds, has generally been successful against the other types of military arms.

THE PELOPONNESIAN WAR

The next major conflict in Greek history saw powerful hoplite armies taking on each other in the Peloponnesian War between leagues controlled by Sparta and Athens. In the decades after the victory over Persia, serious tension had built up over Athens' successful efforts to control the Greek economy by means of its control of the sea and Sparta's attempts to maintain the status-quo. When in 433 B.C. Athens joined in a war against Sparta's ally Corinth, the Spartan-controlled Peloponnesian League declared war on Athens. Historians studying the war have as a source one of the best accounts of warfare ever written, Thucydides' *History of the Peloponnesian War*. Although he was an Athenian, his impartiality in describing the war is legendary. He participated in the war as a *strategos* (general) for Athens for a time, and thus provided a professional appraisal of strategy and tactics. He criticized the pursuit of the war by both sides, including his own part. Thucydides wanted to show the devastating impact of war on a society and how decisions made by Athenian leaders brought the city to ruin.

The war was fought largely by phalanxes of hoplites, whose tactics had changed little since 600 B.C. However, light infantry now made up a larger part of Greek armies than in the past. They had begun to incorporate archers and slingers and in particular lightly armored spear throwers, called *peltasts*. The light troops were able to harass a phalanx from a distance, cause a few casualties, and disrupt its order without much risk of being forced to fight hand-to-hand. Tactics using the new light infantry units called for their use at the front and flanks of the phalanx to open a battle. Then they retired to the rear, where the hoplites protected them when the enemy phalanx charged.

Most of the land battles of the Peloponnesian War were small events, as both sides deployed their forces across the whole of Greece trying to gain some small advantage. Athenian strategy was largely set by the great Pericles, despite his death in 429, shortly after the war began. He was convinced that Athens could win with its fleet, which he had built up to 300 triremes. With the fleet, Athens could strike freely at Sparta's allies, although not at Sparta itself, and bring in grain by sea for its people. Thus there was little need to try to defend the agricultural land of Attica, which the Spartans annually ravaged. Stout walls protected Athens itself as well as access to the sea. The four miles of wall from Athens to the sea were called the Long Walls, and had been completed in 437 B.C.

Greek fortification building in the era was quite unsophisticated. Mud brick was still the principal building material, although stone was becoming more common, as cities realized that stone, while more expensive, was far more durable. Two types of stone construction have been in use throughout history: rubble stone, in which uncut stone is put in no set pattern in mortar, and cut stone, in which stone was cut to fit closely together, with or without mortar. Since the mortar of this era dried out and crumbled quickly, large blocks of stone cut to fit tightly without mortar were the materials of choice, if the city had the time and the wealth to use that method. The absence of siege machines before 400 in Greece meant that walls were designed to prevent the besiegers from scaling them. Themistocles was reported as saying that he wanted to build a wall for Athens so high and thick that a handful of second-rate troops could defend it.

The Long Walls of Athens were in fact a little more sophisticated. They had two-story square towers every 300 feet, which served as watch towers, places for flanking fire against an assault force, and shelters for the garrison. Close to each tower was a small opening, called a postern. Concealed as much as possible, a postern was used for sorties against the besiegers. There were no gates in the Long Walls, probably because gates were highly vulnerable to assault.

Defense of the Greek fortifications was simple. The defenders used both shock and missile weapons to keep the assault force from reaching the top of the wall. Since the besiegers had little in the way of siege weapons, they usually resorted to a simple blockade of a city in hope of starving it into submission. After the Persian War the Greeks did begin to imitate the Persians by raising up large mounds of dirt to serve as ramps to the top of the walls and using rams, which had long been used in the Middle East.

The Spartans, who were extremely conservative, made little use of new ideas in their sieges; they simply blockaded Athens and ravaged Attica. By forcing the inhabitants of Attica to take refuge in the city, the sieges made Athens vulnerable to epidemics, which killed a large part of the population. That, along with a Spartan attack on a major source of grain for Athens in northern Greece, led to a fifty-year truce in 424. The ease with which Sparta had threatened their sources of grain frightened many Athenians, and they decided to send a great expedition to conquer the wealthy island of Sicily, colonized earlier by other Greeks and already the granary of the Mediterranean. In 413, a fleet of 136 triremes and many transports carried 6,000 troops to Sicily, but a delay in mounting an attack on Syracuse, the island's major city, prevented the quick conquest of Sicily. The Athenian force settled into a siege of the city.

Sparta responded by sending a force to aid Syracuse while resuming its siege of Athens. Fully committed to the conquest of Sicily, Athens sent reinforcements to Sicily, but they did not produce a successful assault on Syracuse. Sensing defeat and aware that Athens was having a difficult time maintaining its grain supply because of the use of so much of the fleet in Sicily, the Athenian commanders decided to reload their ships and pull out. Before they got away, Syracusan and Spartan ships attacked. The overloaded Greek galleys, many of which had sat idle for two years, lacked the speed to escape. They were driven back into the harbor. The Athenian commanders decided to make a overland dash to an allied city, but before they had gone very far, the pursuing enemy caught and destroyed the Athenian army. The disaster at Syracuse is a good example of the difficulties of large-scale amphibious operations and how, if victory does not come quickly, such operations usually end disastrously.

Despite the loss of half of its fleet and a great amount of manpower, Athens hung on behind its great walls and rebuilt the navy. Sparta sought to become more competitive at sea by making an alliance with Persia. From 411 B.C. on, the war was fought largely at sea. Knowing how vital grain from the Black Sea was to Athens, Sparta felt bold enough to challenge Athenian control of the Bosphorus in 403. Athens responded by sending all of its triremes to the region. While moored on the beach for the night, the Athenian fleet allowed itself to be caught by surprise. Only seven triremes escaped. Sparta now blockaded Athens by land and sea, but Athens, stubborn as ever, held out for six months before surrendering. Sparta required that Athens join its alliance and destroy the Long Walls.

The Spartan victory in the Peloponnesian War seemed to confirm the wisdom of relying on hoplites, as Sparta had made far less use of light infantry than had Athens. The hoplites' reputation persuaded Cyrus, the rebellious brother of the Persian Emperor, to recruit 13,000 of them for his campaign to topple his brother. Among them was Xenophon, a young Athenian, who later wrote a valuable account of his adventures, the *Anabasis*. In 401 Cyrus led his army of Greeks and some 40,000 Persians to a point 100 miles north of Babylon, where he clashed with his brother's forces. At the Battle of Cuxaxa the hoplites, forming one wing of Cyrus' army, were easily victorious, but the rest of his force was crushed and he himself killed. The Greeks found themselves isolated deep in hostile territory, but with superb discipline and courage they marched north to the Black Sea. For a while they were pursued by the Persians and then were attacked by mountain tribes of eastern Asia Minor. Both foes threw light cavalry and infantry at their rear and flanks while avoiding a head-on confrontation. Continually taking light casualties, the Greeks had been reduced to 6,000 men when they finally reached safety.

In the *Anabasis* and other works on military matters, Xenophon argued that the Greeks needed to make greater use of light troops. He also described the Persian logistics system, in which the state provided food and forage for the army though a system of quartermasters and transport carts. The Greeks still depended on what rations the individual hoplite and his servants could carry. He also remarked: "Persia belongs to the man who has the courage to attack it."

THE MACEDONIANS

The victories of Philip of Macedonia (359-36 B.C.) and the far greater ones of his son Alexander (336-320) were won in large part by their creation of a well-integrated mixed army of the sort Xenophon had advocated. However, Xenophon's influence should not be exaggerated, since both the terrain and the culture of Macedonia dictated a different type army from those of the Greek city-states. Macedonia was more open and flat than Greece proper, and cavalry had always been more important there. Its nobility, a larger part of the population than in Greece, produced excellent horsemen; they formed a heavy cavalry force that used a ten-foot spear weighing four pounds. It could be thrown as well as used for shock. Riding without stirrups, a heavy cavalryman of this era had to have long training to be effective in thrusting his spear or using his sword without knocking himself off his horse by the force of impact. Philip organized his heavy cavalry into fifteen companies of 200 men, called the King's Companions. In battle they used a wedge formation that was especially effective in exploiting gaps in the enemy line. The horsemen of Macedonia also provided their king with quality light cavalry, who used a throwing spear as their main weapon.

The Macedonian infantry combined the best characteristics of the Greek phalanx with greater articulation. The standard infantry weapon was a two-handed pike, twelve to fourteen feet in length. The heavy infantry wore heavier armor and carried a large shield but wore the shield slung over a shoulder in order to be free to use the two-handed pike. The shield was used largely for protection against missiles. Without the need to stand shoulder to shoulder, the files could be two or three feet apart.

The Macedonian phalanx was sixteen ranks deep, compared to the usual twelve or less for the Greeks. With far more drill required of it, it could pivot and maneuver in a way impossible for the Greeks. Philip also developed a medium-weight infantry, with less armor and a shorter pike, for position on the flanks of the phalanx. It served as a hinge between the slow heavy infantry and the faster cavalry. He further incorporated true light infantry—archers, slingers, and spear throwers—into his army to protect the rear and flanks and to serve as skirmishers in the front.

Philip's Macedonian army was the first to have a clearly defined organization, almost modern in its structure. The heavy infantry was divided into platoons, to use the modern term, of 64 men, companies of 128, battalions of 236, regiments of 1,024, and divisions (called simple phalanxes) of 4,096, each supported by the same number of cavalry and light infantry. The simple phalanx was capable of fighting alone, since it was composed of fighting men of all types of arms, or as a quarter of the great phalanx. In theory, if not always in practice, Philip's army had about 32,000 men. The precise nature of the command structure is not clear, but certainly he had to have had the full range of NCOs and officers to command these units. Philip added a corps of engineers for bridge building and sieges and even had something of a medical corps, although there was little his physicians and surgeons could do for wounded men.

Philip was determined to improve the logistics of his army. He severely restricted his men in the number of servants who carried their rations, for the servants also had to have food, and they slowed down the pace of the army. His soldiers were expected to carry much of their own rations. More importantly, he ordered the extensive use of mules. Mules had several advantages over servants and carts. One was that a single driver could run a long string of mules, reducing the number of people requiring rations. Another was that mules could cross rough ground and use muddy tracks not passable by carts, while carts had to be drawn by very slow-moving oxen, since the horse collar had not yet been invented. Without carts the Macedonians moved much more quickly than other armies of the era, particularly through mountains, as they did not have the long baggage train to slow them down while crossing the rough terrain.

The Macedonian army was the first, and one of the few in history, to have all four types of arms, and to have them as well integrated as possible. In its sophistication the Macedonian army was not matched for 2,000 years. King Philip was an excellent tactician and strategist. His typical battlefield tactic has been described as anvil and hammer. Deployed if possible on a level field, his heavy infantry was the anvil against which the enemy force was brought to a halt; while his heavy cavalry was the hammer that beat the foe into submission against the heavy infantry, striking at the flanks or rear or exploiting gaps in the line. The Macedonian army, moreover, was capable of fighting with different tactics and in rough terrain, as Alexander would show.

Philip spent the first ten years of his reign securing control of Macedonia itself and the lands to the north and northeast. Having established a secure base he began to seek allies among the Greeks in order to conquer

their major powers, which by then included Thebes as well as Athens and
Sparta. In 338 B.C., the rise of Macedonian power persuaded Athens and
Thebes to join forces against Philip. The two armies, about equal at 30,000
men, clashed at Chaeronea near Thebes. The battle of the two hoplite
phalanxes was bitterly fought. Some accounts suggest that the Greeks were
gaining the upper hand when young Prince Alexander led the Macedonian
cavalry into the rear of the Greek phalanx. The Greeks quickly collapsed
in disorder, and Philip won an overwhelming victory. The result was that
all the Greeks except Sparta allied with him, but Sparta was hardly a threat.
Having won domination over Greece, Philip turned his attention to Persia.
It is clear that he intended to free the Greek cities of Asia Minor from
Persian rule; but before he could do it, he was assassinated in 336.

ALEXANDER THE GREAT

It took Philip's son Alexander two years to restore royal authority in
Macedonia and Greece, but by 334 he was ready to strike against Persia.
He proclaimed a Greek crusade against the Persian Emperor in order to
gain Greek cooperation, but assured control of his home base by leaving
12,000 men under his best general in Greece. Historians disagree over
whether Alexander decided to conquer the Persian Empire only after his
initial successes or planned it from the first. It has been the nature of
young rulers to dream of grand conquests, but Alexander was one of only
a few in history to have had real success in fulfilling his dream.

In the spring of 334, Alexander crossed into Asia Minor with about
30,000 infantrymen and 3,000 cavalry. Almost immediately the Persian
forces in the region confronted him with similar or slightly larger numbers
along the Granicus River. The Persian army was supposed to have included 20,000 Greek hoplites, but that number is suspect. The Persian
army formed on the bank of the river to wait for Alexander, with its cavalry
in front of its hoplites. As soon as he arrived at the Granicus, Alexander
charged his army across, using his heavy cavalry as a spearhead to break
the Persian center. The Persian cavalry broke and ran, exposing the Greeks
behind to slaughter.

By the victory of Granicus, Alexander won control of western Asia
Minor. He probably now conceived his strategy for conquering the entire
Persian Empire. The Persian navy was substantially larger than his, and
its presence in the Aegean was a threat to his supply lines from his homeland, since Alexander depended heavily on sea transport for logistical
support. Not daring to give battle to the enemy fleet, Alexander decided
to capture its bases, of which the most important were the cities of Phoe-
nicia. He moved his army along the coast of Asia Minor, storming several
cities that resisted. As Alexander neared Antioch in October 333, word
came that Emperor Darius, leading an army of 100,000 men, had reached
the coast behind him at the Plain of Issus. Alexander marched back to
confront Darius, hoping for a decisive battle against the emperor himself.
The Persian army had some Greek mercenaries, but was as always strongest in light cavalry. Darius placed most of his light cavalry on his right

flank, which extended to the beach. Archers were set ahead of a double line of cavalry anchored in the center by Greek hoplites.

Alexander's formation was nearly the same, except that his strength was on the inland flank. Personally leading the Macedonian heavy cavalry, he crossed the river before the archers could slow his cavalry down, and broke the Persian line to the left of its center. Supported by his heavy infantry Alexander then rolled up the Persian center. Seeing his center collapse, Darius fled, quickly followed by most of his men, negating the advantage that the Persian light cavalry had been gaining on the right. The Macedonians pursued vigorously and inflicted very heavy casualties, although surely not the 30,000 they claimed. Alexander captured Darius' family as well. The Battle of Issus is an excellent example of the devastating effect of breaking through an enemy line.

Alexander did not pursue the fleeing Darius but pushed on to take the Phoenician seaports. Tyre, the main base for the Persian fleet, resisted, and he put it under siege. Tyre was situated on an island a half mile off the coast. It had high walls built at water's edge, leaving no place for a landing. Furthermore, the city's fleet could easily bring in supplies and relief forces. Despite those problems Alexander pushed on with the siege. He ordered a causeway constructed from the mainland to the island. Meanwhile he added ships from the conquered Phoenician cities to his fleet to take on Tyre's. After several inconclusive battles he was able to bottle up Tyre's fleet in its harbor.

As the causeway came within reach of Tyre's walls, both sides began to make extensive use of siege machines. This was probably the first large-scale use of mechanical artillery in history, although catapults were in use in the Middle East before then. The catapult and the ballista were the two basic machines in use at that time. Both were developed after the discovery of the power of torsion in twisted animal hair. The catapult used a free-swinging arm with a cup or sling at the end, into which a projectile was placed. The arm was attached to a rotating cross arm that was wound with animal fiber. When the arm was pulled down to a horizontal position by a gear system, the hair was twisted, creating great torsion. The catapult could throw stones up to fifty pounds to a distance of 300 yards. The ballista was a giant crossbow in which the arms of the bow were attached to rotating rods wrapped in animal hair. A windlass was used to draw the bow, and a stone, or, in the later Roman models, a heavy bolt, was placed in a trough on the stock. When a trigger system released the arms, the projectile was shot out at considerable force. In the hands of an experienced engineer, the ballista was far more accurate than the catapult, but it used smaller projectiles. The catapult was used to batter the walls of fortifications in hope of opening a breach, while the ballista was more of an antipersonnel weapon.

At the siege of Tyre both sides used artillery. Alexander even loaded siege machines aboard ships to bombard Tyre from the water. He also made use of siege towers, which were high platforms from which archers and small siege machines could be directed against the defenders. Placed on rollers, they could be pushed forward to the walls and, equipped with

drawbridges, be used to place men on the top of the walls. The Tyrians
hung leather bags filled with seaweed on the walls to absorb the impact of
the artillery projectiles and used grappling hooks to pull over siege towers
and grab attackers. The heroic defense of Tyre failed to discourage Alexander, who took the city after six months by combining an amphibious
attack from ships that had drawbridges in their bows with an assault from
the causeway. Alexander, usually a very magnanimous victor, decided to
make an example of the city that resisted him so well: Tyre was destroyed,
and its remaining inhabitants sold into slavery.

It still took a two-month siege of the city of Gaza in southern Palestine
to gain control of the entire coastline from Greece to Egypt, which Alexander occupied in 331. He was now ready for the strike into Persia proper.
After getting reinforcements from Greece and resupplying, he led 47,000
men north from Egypt through the Fertile Crescent into Mesopotamia.
Darius had assembled well over 100,000 men in the plains near Babylon.
Alexander was not willing to confront so large a force on a field where the
cavalry would be at an advantage. He stayed in northern Mesopotamia
until a frustrated Darius came north to confront him. Having reached the
vicinity of the Macedonian camp in October 331, he formed his army on
the Plain of Gaugamela northeast of present day Mosul. Darius had few
Greek mercenaries left, so most of his strength was in Persian cavalrymen.
He also had sixteen war elephants from India, which he placed in the center
front of his lines, in the expectation that they would terrify the enemy's
men and especially their horses. Reaching back to the past, Darius also
deployed 200 war chariots with scythes attached to their axles in front of
his main body of cavalry.

Alexander used much the same tactics as he had at Issus, but having a
larger army this time, he placed a large force of light cavalry behind each
flank to act as a reserve and to prevent a double envelopment. When the
battle began, the well-articulated and well-disciplined Macedonian infantry
opened gaps for the elephants and chariots to charge harmlessly through
and struck down their drivers from behind. After long, bitter fighting,
Alexander spotted a gap near the center of the Persian line and led the
Royal Companions and his heavy infantry into it. The Persian line buck-
led, and, as at Issus, Darius panicked and fled. His army quickly followed.
Alexander pushed a vigorous pursuit and inflicted very heavy casualties.
He himself at the head of 300 hand-picked men chased the fleeing emperor.
After eleven days he caught up to Darius, whom his own men killed as
Alexander approached.

Alexander was now the undisputed master of the Persian Empire.
Convinced that his destiny was to rule the world, he pushed on to the East.
In Afghanistan he defeated the superb light cavalry of central Asia, and in
western India in 326, he took on a formidable force that included 100 war
elephants. The resourceful Macedonian army again opened gaps for the
elephants and killed their drivers as they rushed past. The rest of the Indian
forces failed to exploit the gaps opened by the elephants. After this victory
at Hydaspes, the veteran Macedonian troops refused to follow Alexander
any farther east, having already gone 3,000 miles from home. He was

forced to return to the West. Reaching Babylon in 323, he became ill and died. His empire was far too vast to hold together for long anyway, but the succession of an infant son caused it to break up more quickly. Alexander's will divided his empire among three of his generals, who soon fell out among themselves and wrecked the unity of the empire.

During his fifteen-year reign, Alexander established himself as the ideal military commander of history. Only Genghis Khan can compete with him among history's great generals in terms of territory conquered and different military styles faced and defeated. No other commander has had as unerring a sense of strategy and tactics or has understood as well the value of a well-coordinated mixed army and well-disciplined professional troops. All of Alexander's traits and victories were carefully described in the Greek accounts of his campaigns, and they became a major part of classical literature and a source of inspiration to military men down to the present. Alexander's greatest influence on would-be conquerors after him was, however, not entirely beneficial. His example as commander of the Royal Companions, leading them on horseback into the midst of the conflict, became the ideal for young princes for 2,000 years. Yet very few had either the ability or the kind of forces with which such tactics could be successful. They often ended up destroying themselves and their forces trying to imitate the great Macedonian.

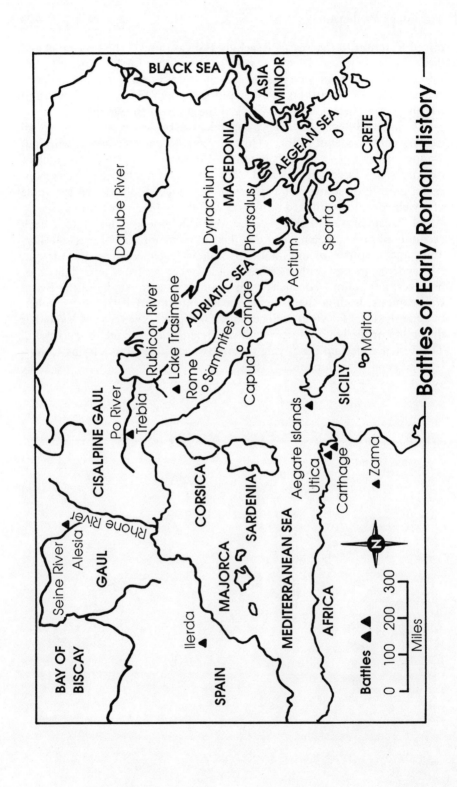

Battles of Early Roman History

3

The Roman Legion

Victory in war does not depend entirely upon numbers or mere courage; only skill and discipline will insure it. We find that the Romans owed the conquest of the world to no other cause than continual military training, exact observance of discipline in their camps and unwearied cultivation of the other arts of war. Without these, what chance would the Roman armies, with their inconsiderable numbers, have had against the multitudes of the Gauls or...the Germans? The Spaniards surpassed us not only in numbers but in physical strength....But to all these advantages the Romans opposed unusual care in the choice of their levies and in their military training. They well understood the importance of hardening them by continual practice, and of training them in every maneuver in line and in action. Nor were they less strict in punishing idleness. The courage of a soldier is heightened by his knowledge of his profession, and he only wants an opportunity to execute what he is convinced he has been perfectly taught. A handful of men, inured to war, proceeds to certain victory, while on the contrary numerous armies of raw and undisciplined troops are but masses of men dragged to slaughter.

Flavius Vegetius, *The Military Institutions of the Romans*, trans. John Clark (Harrisburg, Penn., 1960), p. 13. The author was a Roman of the fourth century A.D., who hoped to restore Roman military might by recalling ancient practice.

One reason for the enormous success of Rome during its nearly 900 years of victory in war was that it was not plagued with would-be Alexanders. Not until the nineteenth century did commanders again appear who were as free of the Alexander syndrome as were the Romans. Although Rome had its share of ambitious generals, their ambition was directed toward controlling the Roman state, not conquering the world. Rome's vast empire was built in large part because adding to it was for several centuries the essential way of gaining political power. The Roman Empire was put together piecemeal and the lands conquered were integrated one by one; this was a major factor in its long duration compared to Alexander's empire.

At its best, the Roman army was the infantry par excellence of the preindustrial world. Like the Greeks, the Romans early on abandoned an emphasis on cavalry and turned to the phalanx as their military style. The dense population of the region around Rome provided plenty of manpower for infantry, and Rome's location at the crossing of several trade routes brought enough wealth into the society to acquire iron for weapons and armor. By 400 B.C., the Roman military system was well established. It was a militia in that all able-bodied male citizens of the constantly expanding Roman state were obliged to serve while carrying on their non-military careers, mostly as small farmers. Unlike the Greeks, the Romans drilled extensively from early on in their history.

THE EARLY LEGION
Having settled on heavy infantry, Rome first used the phalanx. However, in the long war of 327-304 with the Samnites south of Rome, the Romans found that their enemies, unlike the Greeks, would not agree to fight on a level field but instead took advantage of the region's rough terrain. The solid block of men in a phalanx could not operate successfully on rough ground. The Romans made changes that created the legion, although the word itself predated this war. The solid phalanx was broken into smaller units called maniples, which were composed of two centuries. Originally a social unit, basically the clan, the century was reduced to sixty men, so that the maniple consisted of 120 men. The two centurions of a maniple each commanded a century and saw to it that it kept its place in line and closed gaps created while moving across rough terrain or by enemy action.

Command of the army was held by the two consuls, who were really co-mayors of Rome elected annually. A man was not elected consul unless he showed some military talent, but the system did mean that the best commanders in Rome might not be in charge during war. On the other hand, at least until 100 B.C., the system ensured that no one could use long-term command of the army to dominate Roman politics. The Roman constitution did provide for the appointment of a dictator for a six-month term in dire emergencies. It was expected that he would be the best commander available. In the early legion six tribunes served as staff officers, while the centurions combined the functions of junior officers and NCOs, drilling the maniples off the battlefield and commanding them on it. As Rome expanded and the number of legions increased, command of individual legions was taken by officers called legates. These officers came from the Roman aristocracy, while the centurions were plebeians who worked their way up from the ranks.

A legion of the early period had 3,000 heavy infantrymen divided into three lines. The first line had ten maniples made up of men in their early twenties with little battle experience. The second, also with ten maniples,

Modern drawing of a Roman ballista

included the men around thirty years old who had greater experience. Thus the men who in strength and experience were the best soldiers served in the second line. The third line consisted of older men of long experience to steady the entire legion; it had ten maniples of only one century apiece. The youngest men, under age twenty, served as light infantry, about 1,000 to a legion. They were placed in front of the legion and opened a battle by throwing darts and light javelins at the enemy and then retreated to the rear through gaps between maniples. The light infantry helped protect the rear of a legion in battle, as did the several hundred cavalrymen armed with spears posted on the flanks. The total strength of such a legion was about 4,500 men. By the time of the Second Punic War, 218-202 B.C., a second legion recruited from Rome's Italian allies always accompanied a Roman one.

In battle formation the maniples acted as small phalanxes, set about twenty yards apart with a depth of six ranks and a width of ten files. The maniples of the second line were set about 100 yards behind the gaps between those of the first, and the maniples of the third line behind the gaps of the second, creating a checkerboard appearance. This formation gave the legion a great deal more flexibility and articulation than the Greek phalanx, and it allowed the first line to retreat through the second if necessary without disrupting the maniples of the second, and so on through the third line.

The legionary's weapons included a *pilum* (a throwing javelin), a short thrusting sword, and a dagger. The Romans regarded thrusting weapons as more effective than slashing ones, because slashing weapons were too often deflected by armor, or the wounds they inflicted were too superficial to put an enemy out of action immediately. Also thrusting weapons exposed less of the body to the enemy than did slashing ones. Each legionary of the first two lines carried two *pila* of about seven feet in length. By 100 B.C. they had been differentiated into a light pilum that would be thrown from some distance as the legion advanced toward the enemy, and a heavy one that was thrown just before contact. Well before then, the Romans had devised pila that had iron heads attached to the shaft by a narrow neck. The shaft usually broke off as the head imbedded itself in a shield or a body. Thus they could not be reused against the Romans. It also made it more difficult to pull the pilum's head out of a victim's body.

During the Second Punic War the Romans replaced their short swords with the Spanish sword, two feet in length with a broad double-edged blade. It was one of the best weapons ever devised for close combat. The legionary's armor consisted of a cylindrical shield, a bronze vest, a helmet with variously colored crests, and greaves to protect the shins. The Romans preferred to be on the attack against most enemies, marching rapidly toward the foe, throwing their pila at close range, and then rushing in with the short sword. Thus the Roman soldier combined missile fire with shock combat in a manner not matched again until the advent of bayoneted muskets.

ROMAN DISCIPLINE AND LOGISTICS
The Romans were able to make their legion system work because of their high level of discipline. It appears to have been inborn, but was greatly amplified through constant training and exercises. The natural discipline created by fighting alongside relatives and neighbors was greatly enhanced by drill. As the Roman state expanded and the legionaries no longer were fighting with kin and neighbors, drill became far more important in creating discipline, even among recruits from peoples who were poorly disciplined in their native armies.

The Roman army was equally notorious for the other kind of discipline. Harsh punishments were meted out for the most minor offenses; death by crucifixtion was common for such violations as falling asleep on guard duty. Once, the son of a legion commander was executed for accepting a challenge to single combat, a serious breach in an army that had no place for individual heroics. If a unit of a legion or an entire legion was deemed guilty of a serious violation, every tenth man was executed; that is, the unit was decimated. The result of such ferocious discipline was that a Roman soldier was more afraid of his centurion than of the enemy—a state of affairs commanders have always been eager to achieve. But one consequence of this immense psychological pressure was that the Romans rarely showed the unexpected acts of mercy of which most fighting men, even the most barbarian, have been capable. Massacres of entire tribes were no rarity in Roman history, and Roman warfare became extremely bloody.

Because of the rigid discipline in the legions, the legionaries were willing to use the spade, something most fighting men of history have regarded as beneath them. A legionary carried a spade, an ax, and two long stakes on the march. Every day on campaign the army halted in mid-afternoon to build a camp. The men dug a ditch in a 2,100-foot-long square, throwing the dirt up against a palisade made from the stakes they carried. They then erected their eight-man tents that were carried by mules; the eight men of a tent formed the equivalent of the modern squad. Each maniple always kept exactly the same place within the fortified camp. When the legion was not on campaign, it would build practice camps to keep in shape and to train new recruits. Thus a reasonably well-fortified camp could be built and struck within several hours. Having fortified encampments meant the Romans had less to fear from a night surprise attack, and they had a fortified position to fall back to if defeated.

The close attention to detail found in the encampments was also true for logistics. One aspect of logistics at which Rome excelled and at which it was not matched until modern railroads, was the building of roads for the quick movement of troops and supplies. Already in the early fourth century B.C., Rome pushed the Appian Way through the marshes south of the city to facilitate the conquest of the Samnites. Slaves largely built that road, with its bridges, pilings across marshes, and paving stones; but the principal labor supply for the rest of the huge network of roads that crisscrossed the Empire by A.D.150 was the manpower of the army.

Roman roads were built first of all for military purposes. While the legions used whatever trails that existed when campaigning in enemy territory, they quickly pushed roads into newly conquered regions to make the conquest permanent and to facilitate the conquest of the areas beyond. The roads were used to move troops and supplies rapidly to where they were needed across the Roman domains. Ships were an even more efficient forn of military transportation, especially after Rome gained control of the Mediterranean after 200 B.C.

Once the supplies reached the staging area for a campaign, mules and the soldiers themselves became the means of transportation. A legion of the early Empire had 500 mules just to carry its siege machines. Roman sources state that the legionaries carried a half-month's supply of food along with his weapons, armor, tools for camp building, a sleeping mat, a spit, a cooking pot, and a cup. Modern scholars estimate the weight of it all at about 100 pounds. Little wonder that legionaries were called "Marius' mules" (after the great general of 100 B.C.). But it is unlikely that the soldiers carried much food except in rare cases; the Romans were too shrewd to wear out their men before the enemy was ever sighted. Wheat was the primary foodstuff; making a unit eat barley instead was a form of collective punishment. Almost all of what a legionary needed—food, weapons, armor, and clothing—was supplied after 300 by the army and paid for by deductions from his pay. The earliest Roman troops received no pay for their service, since service was expected of every citizen. According to legend the first pay was given in 396 B.C., when a siege lasted into winter, during which season service was not expected, and, therefore, pay had to be given.

THE FIRST PUNIC WAR

For the first three centuries of the Roman Republic, both officers and troops regarded themselves as a citizen militia. This concept was idealized by Cincinnatus in the mid-fifth century, who left his plow to lead the defense of Rome and then returned to it. The army asembled only when a campaign was needed. In the third century B.C., a series of long and bitter wars began to undermine that principle as well as the republican constitution. One of these was a six-year war against King Pyrrhus of Epirus in Greece. He arrived in southern Italy in 281 as the protector of the Greek colonies there. Although he won two major battles against the Romans, his losses were so heavy that the term "Pyrrhic victory" was coined for such a situation. Pyrrhus finally abandoned Italy in 275. The Greek cities of southern Italy were now added to the Roman system of alliances. From its first conquests, Rome had been ready to extend alliances to its defeated foes, if they were willing to give Rome control of foreign policy and provide Rome with troops. The Romans also granted citizenship to their allies after a period of service. Thus Rome built up a network of mutual interest and dependence and maintained peace and prosperity in Italy. The first obligation of the allies was to form allied legions that fought alongside Roman ones.

Shortly after Pyrrhus was defeated, the Roman Confederacy, as the system of alliances is often called, was given a far more difficult test in the Punic Wars with Carthage. The term Punic War came from the Latin word for Phoenicians, the builders of the city of Carthage. Carthage was founded about 800 B.C. near modern Tunis. Having an excellent location for trade and a populace of skillful merchants, it rapidly became a large, wealthy city. When the Phoenician homeland fell to the Persians, Carthage became the leader of the Phoenician colonies in the central and western Mediterranean, and began to colonize Spain and Sicily. In the struggle for control of Sicily, one of the Greek cities there called on Rome for aid in 264 B.C., and touched off the First Punic War.

In that war Rome fought against a naval power for the first time, and had to build a fleet virtually from scratch. With its own wealth and that of its Italian allies, Rome in a very short time built a large fleet based on a type of galley called the quinquireme, similar to Carthage's. Legend says the Romans copied a beached Carthaginian galley. Much is known about Roman history in most respects, but one mystery is the exact design of the quinquireme. Among several possible meanings of the word, what little evidence there is favors the view that it had two decks, with two rowers per oar on one deck and three on the other. To take advantage of the Roman talent in heavy infantry and reduce the impact of the lack of skilled seamen, Roman galleys were built for boarding the enemy, not for ramming, and carried up to 120 marines. A swinging bridge was added at the bow, some eighteen feet in length, which could be lowered anywhere along an arc of nearly 270 degrees. When the bridge was dropped on the deck of an enemy galley, it was held fast by a spike under the forward edge. Roman marines then rushed over to the deck of the enemy. The Romans lost several early battles at sea, but with their new swinging bridge they won a major victory in 260 off Sicily.

Further victories at sea enabled the Romans to occupy Sardinia and Corsica, but inexperience at sea resulted in the destruction of the fleet in a storm with losses put at 100,000 men. In 241 the rebuilt Roman fleet crushed the Carthaginians in the Battle of the Aegates Islands off western Sicily. Carthage then sued for peace, and Rome, weary of the long war, offered moderate terms. The peace recognized Roman domination of Sicily.

THE SECOND PUNIC WAR

While Roman attention was turned to battling the Celts in Cisalpine Gaul (northern Italy), Carthage turned to dominating Spain and, in 219, attacked a Greek city on the east coast that was a Roman ally. Rome demanded the freedom of the city and the punishment of the general who had led the attack, Hannibal Barca. When Carthage refused, the Second Punic War was on.

Hannibal was the son of a general who had fought Rome in the earlier war. His father had made him swear an oath of revenge on Rome when he was still a small boy. As the Carthaginian commander in Spain, Hannibal devised a bold strategy against Rome. He would carry the fight to Italy and Rome itself. He would take the best Carthaginian soldiers, along with mercenaries recruited from North Africa, Spain, and among the Celts through whose territory he would pass on his way to Italy. Hannibal's emphasis was on the heavy cavalry, but his was a true combined-arms army, with all four arms of cavalry and infantry. He also had an officer corps capable of coordinating the different arms.

Roman strategy called for attacks on North Africa and Spain with armies transported by sea. Both Roman forces were on the move when word came that Hannibal had crossed into Gaul with 40,000 men, including about 10,000 cavalry and eighty elephants. The Roman force headed to Spain landed at the mouth of the Rhône River in hope of preventing Hannibal from crossing it. Aware of their arrival he crossed the river well upstream. Although it was now autumn, Hannibal pushed his army across the Alps, hoping to catch the Romans by surprise. Snow had already fallen in the high passes, and the local tribes attacked his army. Despite the difficulties Hannibal reached the Po River in early November, although he had lost a large portion of his manpower and most of his elephants. The Roman army in northern Italy offered battle on the Trebia River near its junction with the Po. Hannibal placed his Celtic allies in the center, and his Carthaginians, both infantry and cavalry, on the flanks. When the Romans attacked, they pushed the center of his line back, but his flanks closed in, pulling off a double envelopment. A small Carthaginian force then struck at the Roman rear, and the Romans were routed, with losses placed at 30,000 men.

After spending the winter on the Po, Hannibal crossed the Appennines and headed south toward Rome. Hearing that a large Roman force was pursuing him, he set an ambush in a narrow gorge along Lake Trasimeno

due north of Rome. Hiding his cavalry and light infantry on the moun-
tainside, he used his heavy infantry to block the road. When the entire
Roman army had been brought to a halt, Hannibal deployed his light infantry against the stalled column while he sent his cavalry to block off a
retreat. Three-fourths of the 40,000 Romans were killed or captured. It
remains the classic ambush in European history. What makes it so amazing is that Hannibal pulled it off in Rome's own backyard, a consequence
of his excellent use of cavalry to destroy Roman reconnaissance parties.

As was true throughout his long campaign in Italy, Hannibal lacked the
manpower and the siege train to besiege Rome, so he pushed on to
southern Italy. He expected the cities there to hail him as a liberator, but
he was badly disappointed. Rome responded by appointing a dictator,
Quintus Fabius, to direct the war. Fabius was determined to avoid pitched
battles with Hannibal and instead wage a war of attrition. His tactics gave
rise to the term "Fabian tactics" for such a strategy. However, two years
of Fabian tactics failed to produce any clear results, and the Romans, becoming restless, returned to the system of two consuls alternating in command on a daily rotation.

Hannibal, whose sources of intelligence were exceptional for the ancient
world, was well aware of that change and what it meant. He set about to
bring the Romans to battle at a place of his choice. In July 216 he captured
the Roman supply depot at Cannae on the southern Adriatic coast, and
waited for the Romans to arrive. He chose for the battlefield a broad plain
flanked by a river, where his superiority in cavalry would offset the Roman
strength in numbers. Hannibal had about 32,000 heavy infantry, 8,000
light infantry, and 10,000 cavalry. The Romans arrived with 55,000 legionaries, 8,000 light infantry, and 6,000 cavalry.

On a morning that he knew the more impetuous consul, Caius Varro,
would be in command, Hannibal formed battle lines. He placed his Celts
and Spaniards in the center and the Carthaginians on the wings. The right
flank rested on the river. He recognized that his center was not likely to
hold up against the powerful Roman heavy infantry, and would be driven
back; this would set up, as at the Battle of the Trebia, the opportunity for
a double envelopment. Varro made Hannibal's task easier by deciding to
assemble his vast manpower in depth rather than in breadth. Hannibal
opened the battle by moving the center of his line forward to form a V.
As expected, the Romans pushed it back, but Hannibal's center did not
break. Then the Carthagenian heavy infantry on the wings, which had
done almost no fighting, pressed in on the Roman flanks. Soon after that,
Hannibal's cavalry, which had driven the Roman horse off the field,
smashed into the Roman rear. The Romans found themselves crushed
together by pressure from all directions. Their formation disappeared and
they became a crowded mob. Many, it was said, were unable to use their
weapons because of the crush of men around them. Roman casualties
were awful—48,000 dead and 12,000 POWs—while Hannibal's losses were
6,000 dead.

The Battle of Cannae has served ever since as the model of perfect
battle tactics and the classic example of double envelopment. It is even

more outstanding because of the Roman superiority in manpower and their deserved reputation as among the best soldiers in history. However, for all its brilliance, Hannibal gained rather little from Cannae. With barely 40,000 men, he could not besiege Rome, while the Romans still had twelve legions in Italy. Most of Rome's allies remained steadfast, although a number of cities, including Capua, the second largest city in Italy, joined Hannibal. Carthage could do little to reinforce Hannibal because of Roman control of the seas, which was so complete that after a defeat in 217 off Sicily, the Carthaginians did not even try to contest Rome at sea. Hence Hannibal was doomed to continue the campaign in Italy.

After Cannae the Romans returned to Fabian tactics. By 212 B.C., they felt strong enough to lay siege to Capua with over 100,000 men. While some manned the siege lines, others faced Hannibal in four major battles. Despite being victorious in all four, Hannibal could not break the siege. It was a unique situation in military history—a victorious relief force unable to relieve a besieged position. Hannibal hoped to distract the Romans from Capua by marching on Rome, but with only 30,000 men he could not invest it adequately. The strategem failed to draw many Romans away from Capua, and the city surrendered in late 211.

Despite a casualty rate that was approaching 200,000 dead after eight years of war, Rome had increased its forces to that same number. It was a war effort unequaled in Europe until World War I. The dedication of Rome to total war extended to using boys under seventeen years old in the army. It allowed the Romans not only to keep Hannibal in check in Italy but to carry the war to Carthaginian Spain. A small Roman army had been operating in Spain since 217, and it had kept Hannibal's brother Hasdrubal from going to Italy to reinforce him. In 210 Roman reinforcements arrived under the command of Publius Scipio, who took command of the Spanish campaign. He showed that he had learned tactics well from Hannibal, defeating Hasdrubal in several battles over the next three years.

Hasdrubal, realizing that there was little he could do in Spain, led his 50,000 men across Gaul and the Alps to reinforce his brother. Hannibal, informed of his march, moved his army to central Italy to wait for him. Rome sent two armies of 40,000 men each to deal with the two brothers. Once Hasdrubal came out of the Alps, he sent messengers to Hannibal, but the Romans captured them. Hannibal failed to learn of his brother's arrival and had to remain in camp. The Roman consul Nero, shadowing Hannibal, took 10,000 of his best men and rushed north to join the army confronting Hasdrubal. The combined Roman army caught Hasdrubal trying to withdraw, destroyed his army, and killed him. The story goes that Hannibal first knew of his brother's arrival in Italy when the Romans catapulted his head into Hannibal's camp.

THE ROMAN VICTORY

Despite his brother's defeat, Hannibal hung on in Italy, continuing to demonstrate his brilliance while being outnumbered four and five to one. In Spain, however, Scipio, who had fought at Cannae, destroyed the remaining Carthaginian forces with his own classic double envelopement in

206. Scipio then spent a year preparing a picked force of 30,000 men to attack North Africa. Roman sea power allowed him to transport his army without challenge. In 204 he destroyed the Carthaginian home army in the Battle of Utica.

The only recourse left to Carthage was to recall Hannibal, still undefeated in Italy. He returned to Africa with 18,000 men; very few were veterans of the campaign of 218. Pulling together the last scraps of Carthaginian manpower, he drew on allies in Africa to raise 9,000 cavalry to complement 34,000 infantry. Hannibal marched his army southward away from Carthage, probably to draw the Romans from their supply bases on the coast. Near a place called Zama he turned on the pursuing Romans. The battle opened with the Roman cavalry driving off the enemy horse, but as often happened, the victorious cavalry dashed off in pursuit of the fleeing enemy. It has been suggested that Hannibal expected that to happen. The Roman legionaries cut their way through the first two lines of Carthaginians but were halted by the third, where most of Hannibal's veterans were waiting. The hard-fought battle came to a sudden end when the Roman cavalry returned to the scene and charged into the Carthaginian rear. Hannibal escaped, but three-fourths of his men were killed or captured.

The Battle of Zama ended the Second Punic War. Carthage accepted peace terms that reduced the city to a puppet of Rome and forced it to pay a huge sum of gold that was expected to keep it near bankruptcy for a long time. However, the quick revival of its prosperity excited Roman fear and anger, and in 149 B.C., on the pretext of a Carthaginian quarrel with a Roman ally in North Africa, Rome declared war again. The main feature of the Third Punic War was a three-year siege of Carthage and its complete destruction when it finally fell in 146.

THE TRANSFORMATION OF THE LEGION

As of 202 Rome was in position to build a vast empire in the Mediterranean basin. Eastern Spain and part of northern Africa were already in its control, and there was no power capable of contesting Roman domination. The Second Punic War had broadly transformed the Roman military, largely for the better, at least as far fighting power was concerned. Citizen soldiers and officers largely had given place to professionals with long terms of service. Scipio's commands in Spain and Africa had been granted for the duration of the campaign, not for a year at a time. Professional soldiers usually have been more loyal to their commander, if he leads them for any length of time, than to the state that pays them—unless the commander and the head of state are identical, as in a monarchy. The close relationship between the command of armies and the development of the office of emperor is revealed by the term *imperium*, originally used to describe a consul's authority over the army, as the root word for emperor. The development of the emperorship was a long-term process; the most important step in it was the appearance of a military dictatorship under Marius after 107 B.C.

The long Punic Wars had also undermined the class of small farmers, which had provided most of the soldiers for the Roman army. Long absences from their farms had ruined many; the Roman aristocrats, grown wealthy from war profits and plunder, bought up the farms and worked their great estates with slaves, available in huge numbers after the wars. Long-term military service was the answer for many dispossessed Romans, while others moved into the city of Rome, forming the Roman mob that was so easily manipulated by demagogues, mostly military leaders, after 100 B.C. The use of the legions as garrisons in Spain and Africa and soon many other places also promoted long-term service.

The divorce between landholding and military service upset many Romans after 130 B.C. Their solution was to use land as payment for military service, but they attempted to push the proposal through a senate dominated by large estate holders. Twenty years later Marius, wielding vast power in Rome, instituted the practice for his veterans of sixteen years' service or more, and it became a permanent part of military compensation. But it was the generals who were responsible for their veterans' land grants, which tied the men even tighter to them. Neither marriage nor land was available to a Roman soldier before retirement, since the Roman ideal now was the soldier wedded to the army. Many soldiers did take unofficial wives from among the women of the region where they were posted. As the practice of land grants at retirement became standard, the retirees were usually settled in colonies near the frontier. This practice had several advantages. It provided a militia of experienced troops for frontier defense; it developed the agriculture of those areas and provided food and supplies for the frontier forces; and it helped to spread Roman culture among the peoples of the frontier regions. As Rome began to recruit manpower from conquered peoples outside of Italy, Roman citizenship was another reward granted for long-term service.

The first century B.C. saw Rome almost constantly at war outside Italy. Most of the rest of the Iberian peninsula was subjugated as were the Celts of northern Italy and southern Gaul. The major war was with Macedonia, largely caused by its alliance with Hannibal. In a series of four wars from 198 to 146, the Roman legion proved to be superior to the Macedonian phalanx. Macedonia was at the end occupied as a Roman province. In the next seven years a Greek league led by Corinth was defeated, and Greece became a Roman province. In turn, most of Asia Minor was conquered. At the end of the century, the Roman military faced two massive slave revolts and the invasion of northern Italy by two large Germanic tribes.

By then the changes the Roman legion begun by Scipio in the last years of the Second Punic War had been largely completed. The most important was the adoption of the cohort as its main tactical unit. The maniple continued to exist, but as an administrative unit, not a tactical one. Ten cohorts formed a legion. A cohort consisted of 360 to 400 heavy infantrymen in ranks eight deep and files fifty wide. A cohort had two formations: close order, with men three feet apart for marching and maneuvering; and open order for combat, with the men six feet apart, which gave the men room to use their weapons. Battle formation for a legion usually called for a front line of four cohorts, and three apiece in the second and the third lines. While maneuvering prior to battle, the cohorts were in close order with a cohort-wide space among themselves. Just before contact, they would shift to open order. That filled the spaces between cohorts, so that the legion presented a solid phalanx to the foe. This system allowed the legion to keep most of the articulation of the maniple formation while giving it the solid front to deal with foes who charged in mass with no articulation. Previously the Iberians, Celts, and Germans attacking with a massed front had had some success in exploiting the gaps between the maniples.

The old distinctions by age among the men of the three lines disappeared, because the legions now consisted almost entirely of experienced men. The teenaged light foot was replaced by archers and slingers from recently conquered lands that had reputations for such skills. The same was true of the cavalry, as few Romans continued to serve on horseback. The actual battle tactics changed little, however. The legionaries still made a dash of 100 yards or so at the enemy, throwing light pila from some distance and then heavy ones from close in before weighing in with their swords. The third line now carried two light pila, which were thrown over the heads of the first ranks, often after hand-to-hand combat had begun. A new twist was the use of field artillery. Each legion had thirty small ballistas and catapults for use during battle. These often terrified barbarian warriors when first seen in action, usually to open a battle. The legions also had engineers to build bridges and heavy machines for siege work. The skill of Roman military engineers was one of several aspects of Roman life that were not matched in Europe until the modern era.

JULIUS CAESAR

As soon as Marius had demonstrated that control of the professional legions led to political power, other generals pursued the same course. None did it as well as Julius Caesar, who perhaps better than anyone else in history combined successful military command with equally successful political intrigue. He was already forty-two years old, quite old for his first major command, when he was named proconsul for Cisalpine and Transalpine Gaul in 58 B.C. His *Commentaries on the Gallic Wars* is regarded as the most detailed firsthand account of war from the ancient world.

Appreciating how a campaign of conquest endeared a commander to his men and to the Roman mob, Caesar invaded Gaul in 58 in one of the most famous campaigns of history. Well-populated and wealthy, Gaul had vast numbers of tough Celtic warriors, many of whom were able horsemen. The Celtic tribes, however, found it very difficult to cooperate with each other against the Romans. Caesar successfully used the rivalries among the Celts to recruit auxiliaries within Gaul. The Celts also lacked the discipline and training of the six legions Caesar led against them. Like most Indo-European barbarians who used shock weapons, the Celts depended largely on the weight of massed manpower in a furious charge to break their enemy's lines. Once that failed, they had no talent or taste for prolonged fighting.

Caesar proved to be a most able tactician against the Celts, but the superb Roman logistic system and his intelligent use of it were major factors in his victories. Operating deep in enemy territory on long campaigns, he was able to outlast the local tribes fighting on their own lands. Roman logistics, along with their talent for fortification, meant that Caesar on several occasions was able to wait in secured positions until the tribesmen began to drift off, as they were completely unprepared for siege warfare. Caesar would then lead his more evenly matched legions against what remained of the Celtic armies. Caesar often demonstrated a new trait of Roman armies: the complete massacre of defeated tribes. He showed no compunction in wiping out an entire tribe to give an example to others. The opponents he allowed to live crowded the slave markets of Rome.

Only after it was too late did the Celts find a national leader, Vercingetorix, to unite a number of tribes in central Gaul to oppose Caesar. The Romans thought their conquest of Gaul was secure when in 53 B.C. Vercingetorix gathered some 100,000 men and gave them the training and discipline they had lacked. He had enough control over the tribes he led to impose a scorched-earth policy: everything useful to the Romans that the Celts could not carry was destroyed, regardless of how much it harmed the local people. When Roman foraging parties went seeking food, the Celts cut them down. This strategy forced the Romans out of central Gaul. In July 52, Vercingetorix overtook the retreating legions in eastern Gaul and gave battle. The battle was inconclusive, but he grew pessimistic of his chances of beating the Romans in a field battle, and retreated to the fortified town of Alesia on a mountaintop northwest of Dijon.

Caesar was one of the great siegemasters of history. The Roman ability to build fortifications enabled him to erect a double line of siegeworks around Alesia. The inner one, facing the besieged town to protect against sorties, was known as a wall of contravallation, and the outer one, protecting against a relief force, was a wall of circumvallation. The length of the outer wall was over fourteen miles. Both walls proved their worth, as Vercingetorix made several powerful sorties, while a large Celtic army attacked the wall of circumvallation. None of the attacks broke through the walls.

Meanwhile the full range of Roman siege machines went to work on Alesia. Giant catapults capable of throwing 300 pound stones and ballistas worked on the walls and the defenders. Rams (which were not very effective against the earth-and-timber walls) and bores worked at the base of the walls. The Romans also used mining by this time. The miners cut a tunnel or a deep ditch, protected by a roof of wet hides, which were fairly fireproof. When the cut reached under the wall, its roof was propped up by timbers and it was filled with combustibles, which were set on fire. When the support timbers burned away, the roof collapsed, bringing part of the wall down and opening a breach. Then came an assault through the breach. The legionaries attacked with a formation called the "tortoise"; ten to twenty men put their shields over their heads and overlapped them, so that from above they looked like a turtle shell.

The siege of Alesia never came to the point of a large-scale assault. With a large number of women and children, the Celts' food ran out fairly quickly, and after three months Vercingetorix surrendered rather than subjecting them to starvation. He was hauled off to Rome, displayed for Caesar's triumph, and executed. With Vercingetorix dead, the Celts resigned themselves to Roman rule. Soon they made up a large part of Rome's military, especially the cavalry.

At the same time as the Celts had risen in rebellion, Crassus, the proconsul of Syria and one of Caesar's allies in Roman politics, was also involved in a major campaign. He too recognized how important military success was for political power in Rome. He led an army of 39,000 men against the Parthian Empire, which had been created about 175 B.C. out of the ruins of Alexander's empire in the area south of the Caspian Sea. Its army was entirely cavalry, including heavily armored horsemen, sometimes called the real ancestors of the knight, but its strength was its very mobile horse archers. The Parthians expanded their empire into Mesopotamia and eastern Asia Minor. In those areas they came up against the Romans, who were also seeking to control the same lands.

In 55 B.C. Rome declared war on the Parthian Empire, and two years later Crassus moved eastward out of Syria. In the open desert near Carrhae (modern Haran) in northern Mesopotamia, the Parthian light cavalry attacked the Romans. Caught in the open, the legions formed a large defensive square. The Parthian archers made no effort to close with them but fired arrows from a distance. As each unit of horse archers exhausted its arrows, it pulled back for another unit and resupplied from a train of 1,000 camels loaded with arrows. The constant rain of arrows soon took a large number of Roman casualties. Crassus, unable to close with his foes, started to retreat toward Syria, but the Parthian pursuit prevented an orderly withdrawal. He was killed, and only 5,000 Romans reached Syria alive. The Battle of Carrhae confirmed that light cavalry was the arm most capable of defeating or at least keeping at bay heavy infantry which was largely unsupported by other arms. Crassus did have some cavalry, but not enough to be a factor. The Parthian victory ensured that Mesopotamia would continue to be a war zone, as Rome did not give up its goal of conquest. The Romans did in fact control the region several times over the next four centuries.

CIVIL WAR IN ROME

The death of Crassus had a great impact on Roman politics. It unhinged the balance of power and led to the civil war between Caesar and Pompey, another ambitious general whose earlier conquest of Syria and Palestine had lifted him to power in Rome. The war between them was not the first time legions had faced each other over the political ambitions of their commanders, but it was the longest of Rome's civil wars. In 50 B.C. Pompey, recognizing the significance of Caesar's conquest of Gaul, persuaded the senate to order him to return to Rome without his legions.

Caesar defied the law that forbade the posting of provincial legions in Italy and brought a legion across the Rubicon River, which marked the northern border of Roman Italy. It was a declaration of war against the senate and Pompey.

Caesar had nine legions in Gaul, while Pompey had legal control over twenty-seven legions and the fleet. But his legions were scattered across the Roman domains and could not be consolidated. Furthermore many of his officers were sympathetic to Caesar, especially in the legions in Italy. Pompey, aware of this, left Italy for Greece where he collected the men he had commanded in the Middle East. Since Caesar lacked sea transportation, he planned to pursue Pompey by the land route around the Adriatic. He realized, however, that the seven legions in Spain loyal to Pompey were a threat to his control of Gaul, and by a rapid march could strike at his rear as he crossed northeastern Italy for Greece. So he decided to strike at Pompey's forces in Spain.

In June 49 B.C., Caesar crossed into Spain with 37,000 men. He confronted the main Pompeian force of 65,000 at Ilerda on the Ebro River. Neither side wanted a battle, not only because of Caesar's reputation and the Pompeian manpower advantage but also because many of the men knew each other. Caesar decided to force the surrender of his foes by maneuver rather than by pitched battle. They were well entrenched and prepared to try to outwait him, since they had had considerable time to prepare for his arrival. Nonethless, with his always careful attention to logistics, Caesar was able to keep his army supplied, while the Pompeians began to run out of food. After two months they decided to move to another camp held by their men with better access to supplies.

Although Caesar's legions were behind their foes at the start of the march, by using his cavalry to harass them, he slowed them down. Meanwhile, he doubled-timed his infantry to get to a pass ahead of the Pompeians. Faced with the prospect of fighting their way through, they returned to Ilerda. Now entirely without food they surrendered four days later when Caesar offered not to force them to join with him against Pompey. Caesar's tactical brilliance had defeated a superior force without a battle.

Caesar was now free to pursue Pompey to Greece, and arrived there in January 48. There Pompey had an even greater manpower advantage, of about two to one; he also controlled the seas, and so had better access to supplies. Pompey's defect as a general was his reluctance to engage in battle, while Caesar's audacity was perhaps his greatest strength. He decided to carry the fight to Pompey in his main camp at Dyrrhachium on the Adriatic (in modern Albania). He built a line of field fortifications around the camp some fourteen miles in length and pulled of the amazing feat off investing an army twice as large and nearly as good as ggod. As always Caesar found a way of supplying his army for the three months the armies faced each other across the fortifications. Finally in July, Pompey attacked Caesar's lines and easily broke through. Caesar rallied his forces and retreated into the interior. Pompey pursued and caught up near Pharsalus on the Eripeus River.

Both armies rested a flank on the river as they formed for battle. Despite his great manpower advantage; Pompey stood on the defensive, while Caesar advanced immediately to the attack. As he later commented, it was in the nature of men to want to charge the enemy instead waiting passively for an attack. But the spirit of attack might not have been enough if Caesar had not devised a brilliant tactical move. He placed six hand-picked cohorts behind his flank away from the river. When the stronger Pompeian cavalry charged that flank, Caesar led the six cohorts in an assault on it and scattered it. They then drove through the light infantry on the enemy wing and crashed into flank of the heavy infantry. The jolt of the charge was felt across Pompey's entire line just as it was most heavily engaged. His line shattered, and he fled to Egypt. There his associates assassinated him in hope of currying favor with Caesar.

Caesar still had two years of hard fighting before all of the Pompeian legions were defeated and he could return in triumph to Rome in July 45. Nine months later he was dead, assassinated by a group of Roman politicians fearful of his power and his disregard for traditional Roman government. His death did not end the civil wars. They entered another phase, with Caesar's assassins on one side and Mark Antony, regarded as his political and military heir, and Octavian, his nephew and legal heir, on the other. Antony commanded in the eastern Mediterranean and Octavian in the western. After five years of bloody campaigning, the two eliminated their foes, but then had their own falling out over domination of Rome in 33 B.C.

THE VICTORY OF OCTAVIAN AUGUSTUS

Antony had allied himself, both politically and personnally, with Cleopatra, the beautiful queen of Egypt. Her resources helped him gather a force of 80,000 men and 360 ships in western Greece. Taking his time to prepare, Octavian crossed the Adriatic in 31 with 100,000 soldiers and 400 ships. Suspicion of Cleopatra had spread to Antony's forces, and he, believing his fleet to be more loyal, decided to fight at sea. Antony's fleet was drawn almost entirely from the East, and this was reflected in the large ships in his fleet. Most were multi-decked. If several contemporary sources can be believed, several had ten decks. Octavian's ships were smaller. The Roman fleet had switched to smaller galleys as a result of action against pirates from the east coast of the Adriatic. In the switch to smaller boats, the Romans had not abandoned their reliance on boarding, but they had developed a new weapon, the *harpax*. It consisted of an iron hook at the end of a long pole to which a length of rope was attached. A small catapult shot the harpax to an enemy ship, and when hooked fast, a windlass reeled in the enemy ship until it could be boarded. The harpax had proven itself in several earlier battles.

Octavian's fleet drew up in three divisions at the mouth of the Gulf of Arta, near the Point of Actium; hence the battle of September 2, 31 is called the Battle of Actium. That day Antony personally led his fleet, also formed into three divisions. He commanded his right wing, and the bitter fighting was centered there. However, much of the rest of his fleet proved to be disloyal, and surrendered with little fighting. When Antony realized what had happened, he fled with Cleopatra to Egypt. In despair over his defeat, Antony could not rally his remaining forces and committed suicide when Octavian arrived in Egypt early the next year. Cleopatra followed her lover in suicide.

Octavian was now alone atop the Roman world. Not willing to take the title of king, which the Romans detested, nor to do away with the trappings of the republic, he revealed his power through a new name, Caesar Augustus, and two new titles. *Princeps*, first citizen, reflected his standing among the Roman people and his authority in the senate; the term had none of the connotations of royalty it gained in the Middle Ages. *Imperator* referred to the *imperium maius*, the ultimate command of the army; that term revealed the real source of Octavian's power, his control of the military. Octavian's taking the titles in 29 B.C. is regarded as the beginning of the Roman Empire; and until its fall, the title of emperor meant first of all control of the army, not a hereditary right to rule. Many times in the next four centuries those who commanded the legions would dispute the title among themselves. Like the first emperor, most Roman emperors were above all successful military commanders.

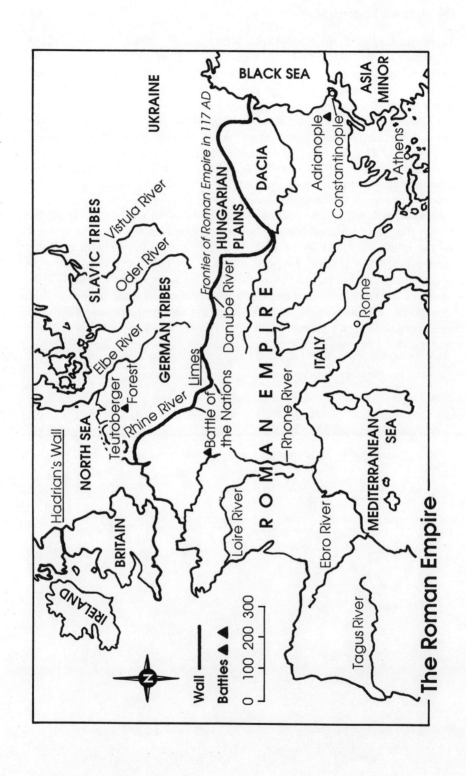

The Roman Empire

4

The Fall of the Roman Empire

On the field of battle it is a disgrace to the [German] chief to be surpassed in valour by his companions, to the companions not to come up to the valour of their chief. As for leaving a battle alive after your chief has fallen, that means a lifelong infamy and shame. To defend and protect him, to put down one's own acts of heroism to his credit—that is what they really mean by "allegiance." The chiefs fight for victory, the companions for their chief....The Germans have no taste for peace; renown is easier won among perils, and you cannot maintain a large body of companions except by violence and war....You will find it harder to persuade a German to plough the land and to await in its annual produce with patience than to challenge a foe and earn the prize of wounds. He thinks it spiritless and slack to gain by sweat what he can buy with blood.

> Cornelius Tacitus, *On Germany*, translated by Harold Mattingly (Baltimore, 1948), pp. 112-13. Tacitus was a Roman soldier and administrator of the late first century A.D.

With his domination of the Roman state established, Augustus set about reducing the size of the army and institutionalizing his control over it. The sixty legions he commanded in 30 B.C. were reduced to twenty-eight and in 13 B.C. to twenty-five, which number then rarely changed for the next 300 years. Some 100,000 veterans were pensioned off, mostly with land on the frontier. The number of heavy infantrymen in each legion was raised to 5,500. From 3,000 to 4,000 cavalry and light infantry served as auxiliaries in each legion as well. The legions were posted along the frontiers with the greatest number where the foreign threat was the greatest. In A.D. 23, for example, the Rhineland had eight legions and Syria four. The legions were posted in the same place for decades and even centuries and kept the same name and number; for example, *Legio III Augustus* was in North Africa for over 200 years.

Augustus was determined to make it impossible for a legion commander to challenge him, so he strengthened the laws keeping legions out of

Italy and the interior provinces. They were to have no military presence at all, except within Rome itself, where the Praetorian Guard was posted. The Guard had evolved from the bodyguard of the legion commanders. Augustus created a more powerful force of elite troops as his personal guard in Rome. Over the centuries its size varied, but most often it was ten cohorts strong. The presence of the Guard in the heart of the empire with no competition close by gave it power over Roman politics well beyond its size and quality. Until A.D. 200 the Guard played a major role in seating the emperors.

ROMAN FRONTIER DEFENSES

By 29 B.C. the Roman domains had nearly reached their limits, but Augustus felt the need to round off some frontiers to make them easier to defend. In particular the use of the Rhine and Danube rivers as the northern frontier created a very long defensive line that could have been shortened considerably by using the Elbe instead of the Rhine. After some initial successes, the three legions involved in the conquest of central Germany were ambushed and destroyed in the Teutoberger Forest in A.D. 9. Heartbroken by the loss of those legions (their names were permanently retired) Augustus pulled back to the Rhine, which became the permanent frontier. As a consequence, most of the German tribes were left out of the Roman Empire and its civilizing influence. Later emperors added England and Romania, largely because they wanted to celebrate a triumph in Rome.

The most unsettled frontier was in the Middle East, where the Parthians and the Romans continually battled for control of Mesopotamia, Armenia, and Syria. Rome did have its victories when the legions were well supported by cavalry, but the Parthians were the most dangerous foe Rome faced between 100 B.C. and A.D. 300. Fortunately for Rome, the Middle East was the only frontier where the legions faced a large and capable cavalry. When in the fourth century A.D. more and more of Rome's enemies were mounted, the decline of the Roman legions was made all the more obvious.

In the first century A.D., Rome still had an offensive mentality, but after the year 100 the Roman military began to shift to a more defensive posture. An obvious sign of that change was the building of the *limes*, a line of fortifications between the Rhine and the Danube where no natural obstacles formed a frontier. The best-preserved example of Roman frontier defenses is Hadrian's Wall in northern England, which was begun in 122. It was seventy-two miles long and had an average height of fourteen feet. Along the outside ran a ditch twenty-six feet wide and ten feet deep. Small square forts a mile apart housed small garrisons, and a road ran along the inside of the wall to aid the quick movement of troops to trouble spots. Using walls and natural defenses, Rome defended its frontiers with a total

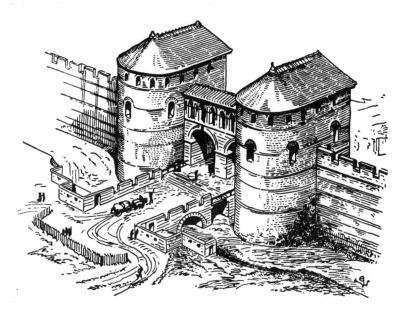

Modern drawing of the fortified gate of a city of the Late Empire

force very small in proportion to its population; thus the army was quite inexpensive in relation to the Empire's wealth. It has been estimated that the army cost the empire 450,000 sesterces a year in the second century A.D. Julius Caesar's fortune is thought to have been well over 200,000 sesterces, or nearly half of the army's budget.

The Roman navy after the Augustan period cost little, because there was no need for a large fleet. The pirate fleets that had appeared during the civil wars before Augustus' reign were wiped out, and none reappeared in the next three centuries because Rome controlled the entire Mediterranean coast. There was no place to locate a pirate base. There was no significant naval action in the Medditerranean from Augustus to A.D. 400. Small fleets were built for the occupation of Britain and the defense of the North Sea coast, and for the rivers that served as the frontier in the north, but their limited nature permitted no technical advances. If anything Roman shipbuilding in A.D. 400 was less advanced than it had been in 30 B.C.. Building a first-rate navy almost from scratch when it was needed after A.D. 400 was by then far too expensive for the Roman fiscal system and perhaps beyond Roman technological capacity as well.

The interior provinces had no military presence at all, except in periods of power struggles among the legions for control of the imperial throne. It may have been precisely the lack of high taxes and a large-scale military presence that contributed to the later Roman decline: the Romans had gotten out of the habit of military service and paying heavy taxes when both became necessary in the late Empire.

DIOCLETIAN'S REFORMS

After some 200 years with almost no change, the Roman military underwent an extensive transformation in the late third century. The coincidence of the legions abandoning their frontier camps to take part in the internal power struggles of the period and increasing pressure by Rome's enemies on the frontier allowed the barbarians to penetrate far into the empire. For example, they struck deep into the empire in 268, and sacked Athens. The open cities of the interior, which for centuries had been unfortified and undefended, were open to plunder. When Emperor Diocletian restored stability upon winning the throne in 285, he changed the nature of Roman defense, reflecting developments several decades in the making. He abandoned the concept of an active defense on the frontier, with its preemptive strikes into barbarian territory, for a defense in depth. Forts and fortified towns near the frontier were to serve as strong points to anchor the defense. Garrisoning these forts required a large number of men, but the training and discipline of these *limitanei* did not to have be of high quality because of their essentially static situation. The Romans thus used large numbers of recently recruited barbarians for the garrisons.

Fortification had always been important in the Roman military scheme. The frontier walls and the fortified legion camp, whether temporary or long-term, were essential elements in Roman success. But they were simple both in design and construction; the forts and walled towns of the late third century A.D. required a transformation in design. Rome itself was enclosed in the Aurelian Wall, built between 270-288. It was over eleven miles long, with 381 square towers every 150 feet projecting outward to provide cover fire along the wall. Similar designs were used for most of the city walls built in that era, but the frontier forts were far smaller and generally in the shape of a square. Numerous medieval castles were built on Roman foundations; but as small as the Roman forts often were, the medieval ones usually occupied only a part of the old works.

Complementing the static defense of forts and walled cities were the legions, which were to move rapidly on an expanded military road system between the fortified positions to drive away enemy forces. Rapid mobility was of far greater importance than before; so the infantry was made lighter, and cavalry now made up a larger proportion of the army. The number of legions was increased to fifty-three. Thus, while the size of a legion was decreased, the total amount of manpower required surpassed 400,000 men. At a time of dwindling population caused in part by epidemics and declining wealth, the increased size of the army required the empire to draw more and more on non-Romans, the *foederati* (allies). This term was used for large groups of barbarians, often whole tribes, which were recruited for military service and settled on land in the empire as their payment.

Diocletian's reforms brought the empire three or four generations of peace and relative stability before the full-scale barbarian invasions began in the late fourth century, but they also contributed to the eventual collapse of the Roman military, at least in the West. His division of the empire into two separate governments for East and West harmed the West in the long term because the heavy flow of tax revenues from the wealthier East was largely cut off. The army of the West began to show the effects of the revenue shortfall as payment in coin and rations for the soldiers was supplemented by payment in land. (Soldier comes from solidus, the coin used to pay the Roman army.) Previously soldiers had received land at retirement but never while in active service. A legionary tied to a specific place and tilling the soil there became essentially a militiaman with a subsequent decline in drill and discipline. This change compounded the problem created a century earlier when soldiers were given the right to marry and live with their wives while on active service. Both changes reduced the soldiers' previous total commitment to the army.

As the decline in the quality of the Roman military became obvious to more astute observers, some sought to reverse the decline. One such person was Flavius Vegetius, who shortly after 383 compiled a long handbook of traditional Roman military practices in hope that it would aid in restoring the strength of the army. His *Military Institutions of the Romans* is the most thorough description of the legions and their training and tactics, both as they had been at the time of Rome's greatness and as they were in the fourth century. While not a great captain himself, Vegetius was a good historian, and drew intelligently from the histories of Rome's wars to give a good picture of the old practices. Numerous histories of Roman wars and campaigns, such as Caesar's *Gallic Wars*, survived into the Middle Ages, but Vegetius' book was the only military manual that was available to medieval men. Manuscript copies circulated at the time of Charlemagne, and about 150 copies were made from the years 1000 to 1400. Vegetius was translated into French, German, English, and Italian during the late Middle Ages, and the first printed edition dates from 1473.

While it was the main textbook on military matters for 1,300 years after it was written, the *Military Institutions* had little impact in its own time and did little or nothing to halt the decline in the late Roman military. In particular the author failed to appreciate how the economic decline of the empire accelerated the trend toward hiring less costly barbarian mercenaries, which he denounced. As the quality of Roman soldiers declined, the barbarians, mostly Germanic, were viewed as having the martial spirit and skills now lacking in the Roman population. With the disappearance of Roman discipline, the legionary's style of fighting with the pila and short sword, the essence of Roman military success, began to disappear as well. Even Roman recruits began to fight in the German style. The foreign troops were loyal to the empire and with strikingly few exceptions fought well and bravely for it. But the Roman army of which they now constituted the core was no longer clearly superior to those barbarian tribes that sought to invade the empire rather than serve it.

THE GERMANS

Nonetheless, with Rome's vastly superior political structure and economy, there is every reason to suppose that the empire could have assimilated vast numbers of barbarians, most of whom were eager to enjoy Roman civilization, not destroy it. The empire could have continued for several more centuries along the lines of the Byzantine Empire, as the Eastern Roman Empire is known from the sixth century on. Developments outside of the empire were the immediate causes of the collapse of the western empire and the end of classical civilization, bringing against the empire forces that it was no longer capable of withstanding or assimilating.

As both divisions of the Roman Empire came under increasing pressure after 370 from the barbarians, Roman ability to cope with them was hindered by the presence of a revitalized Persian Empire on the eastern frontier. In the early third century, a restored Persian monarchy defeated the Parthians and reestablished its empire. By 237, the Persians were engaged in a full-scale war with Rome for control of Mesopotamia, Syria, and Armenia. The Persians used both light and heavy cavalry, but put greater emphasis on the mailed heavy trooper than had the Parthians. Persian successes in the long war, while not enough to drive the Romans out of the Middle East, diverted resources from the northern frontier and also hastened the Roman shift to cavalry.

The chief danger came from the Germans, if only because of the enormous length of the frontier that they threatened, from the North Sea to the Black Sea. The Romans had clashed with the Germans as soon as the Roman army had reached the Alps in the third century B.C.. The German style of warfare had changed rather little in the five centuries since then. The Germans were divided into tribes of perhaps 25,000 people with some 5,000 fighting men. Large tribes often split in two, while small tribes were absorbed into larger ones. There was almost no spirit of cooperation among the tribes despite the fact that they often spoke similar dialects. The warriors of the tribes were divided into clans or "hundreds," so called because the clan could put in the field some 100 fighting men. If a clan became much larger than that, it would become too unwieldy for the system of clan governance and would split up. Kinship ties created what discipline there was within the ranks of the Germanic warriors. Discipline, however, was less important than impetuous courage and rash enthusiasm for battle.

In the era before A.D. 370, the Germans relied largely on infantry. Although the wealthier had horses that they rode to battle, they rarely fought as cavalry. They used mainly short spears for throwing and thrusting, swords, and a round wicker shield with little or no body armor. If German fighting power had improved by 370, and the evidence for that is not clear cut, for their greatest victory over Rome occurred in A.D. 9, the principal reason was the greater amount of iron available to them. By the fourth century the Germans had enough iron to use a one-handed battle-ax and some body armor, thus enhancing their ability to engage in hand-to-hand combat with the Roman legions.

The short spear remained their main weapon, and the type of formation in which it was most successful was a tightly packed phalanx formed in depth, intended to overrun the enemy by the weight of its mass. The front of a German phalanx, however, was not usually a straight line but a wedge called the boar's head, consisting of the best and boldest warriors wearing what little armor was available. With their light equipment, the Germans moved rapidly to battle and required little time to form their ranks, since they made little use of tactics. They depended largely upon a headlong rush at their foe and their contempt for wounds and death to gain victory. Despite the sharp blow that such a force could inflict upon first impact, a disciplined legion could easily parry it and break the German phalanx into smaller parts that were far easier to defeat.

The Germans were led into battle by the heads of the tribes and the clans. The headship of the clan was not hereditary, but it was in the usual order of things that the new head would be chosen from the family of the previous one. The Roman authors referred to the head of the tribe, the *herzog*, as the prince or king. In wartime some tribes chose the best and most experienced warrior to serve as commander, whom the Romans called the duke. Certain families that were regarded as descending from the gods provided the king as chosen by the assembly of free warriors. In times of migration or war (the two were virtually synonymous) the need for a center of authority enhanced the authority of the tribal leaders; they emerged from the era of the Germanic invasion of the Roman Empire more worthy of the title of king in the medieval sense.

In war the German leaders marched at the head of their warriors and led the charge into the foe's ranks, commanding more by example than by verbal orders. Thus they had to be among the most experienced and toughest warriors available. Their deaths, especially early in a battle, could have proven disastrous to a German force, but another German institution, the personal retinue of the herzog called by the Romans the *comitatus*, reduced the impact of the leader's death. The comitatus was the herzog's retinue of young warriors, usually the best available, who served as his bodyguard and companions. In war its members surrounded the herzog, and if he was killed, they were expected to fight to the death to avenge him. The greatest humiliation possible for a member of a comitatus was to survive a defeat in which his leader was killed. Thus the example of the comitatus fighting on after the herzog had been cut down served to rally the rest of the warriors to continue to fight.

In exchange for their service, the members of the comitatus received the first share of the booty of victory—weapons, prisoners for slaves, women, cattle and horses. The herzog and the comitatus were bound together not only by mutual advantage but also by a powerful oath, regarded by the Germans as the most inviolable possible. This personal bond of loyalty and service was a major foundation of feudalism.

According to Tacitus, the Roman writer of the early second century A.D., the German free men did virtually everything armed. Arguments quickly became bloody fights. The penalty for a causing death in such a situation was a fine; its amount depended upon the rank of the person killed. Such behavior did reduce the warriors available to the tribe, but also provided it with a corps of hardened fighters. A tribe needed such men because of the constant warfare it faced, either in search of new lands or when confronted with other tribes seeking new territory.

Migration was a constant state of affairs for the Germans long before the movement into the Roman Empire began. The most significant Germanic migration before the fourth century was the move of the Goths from southern Sweden to the Ukraine. It took several centuries, but by 275 they were settled along the Dnieper River in the Ukraine. The plains they now occupied were far different from the forests and swamps of northern Europe, and the people with whom they competed for the land were accomplished horsemen. When the Goths changed to cavalry, they still used the spear as a lance from horseback and not the bow as did the Eurasian nomads. Like most Germans they used the bow very little in war.

THE HUNS

It was the misfortune of the Goths to be the eastern most of the German tribes when the Huns struck into the Ukraine in A.D. 373. No word, not even Vandal, conjures up as terrible an image as Hun—savage, hideous, destructive for the sheer love of destruction. The image has a certain basis in fact, but it reflects as well the terrified exaggerations of the European peoples with whom the Huns came into contact. The Huns struck terror into the Europeans both because they were extraordinary warriors and because they were so different. They were the first of a long series of Asian nomads to have a major impact on European history, all of whom had a great deal in common in culture, fighting style, and historical impact.

The Huns were a nomadic people from central Asia north of the Himalayas. They were similar to but not identical with the Hsiung-Nu nomads of the Gobi Desert who invaded China in much the same era and are often referred to as Huns. The harshness of life in the cold, dry plains of central Asia (steppes, to use the Russian word) bred a very tough, ruthless warrior with extraordinary stamina and courage, while the fierce and constant competition for control of grazing lands for the tribe's herds produced seasoned and ferocious fighters. These nomads spent so much time on horseback that some in the civilized world thought of them as half-human, half-horse. The Huns were said to be able to sleep on horseback and in extremity to drink their horses' blood. While much of the description of the Huns by European contemporaries was exaggerated, there is little question that they were tougher and more ferocious than any of the peoples with whom they came into contact in Europe.

The nomadic tribes were lured constantly westward by the steppe gradient: coming westward from central Asia, the grassland steadily improves because of increasing precipitation until the Hungarian Plains are reached. As a Central Asian tribe, pushed out of its original homelands by overpopulation, changes in climate, or defeat in war, followed its herds westward along the steppe gradient, it made contact with peoples increasingly less capable of standing up to them. The toughest and most dangerous of the Asian nomads were the most likely to reach eastern Europe. Although the nomads had to engage in constant fighting as they pushed westward, they could maintain or perhaps even increase their population during their migrations despite losses in battle, because they found better grazing as they migrated and were used to living on the move.

The military advantage the Asian nomads gained by their extraordinary mobility was vastly enhanced by the use of the reflexed composite bow, a weapon perfectly matched to the horse. A relatively short bow, under five feet in length (infantry models were longer), the construction of its stave involved the use of several materials, specifically wood, cattle horn, sinew from the legs of horses and cattle, and glue. As a rule, a wooden core was backed by sinew and bellied by horn. When completed, the bow was strung by bending it against its curve. Such a bow required an expert to find the right materials and mold them into shape. It also took a very long time, up to five years, to manufacture, since the superb glue made from horse hooves and sinew was very slow drying, and numerous applications had to be made. The use of that kind of bow was limited, therefore, by the difficulty in making it and by the years required to master its use on horseback. Also, western Europe lacked cattle with long enough horns for its manufacture.

In the hands of an experienced archer, the composite bow, having a draw of up to 160 pounds, was accurate and deadly to 200 feet and had an effective range of 500 feet against lightly protected adversaries. A nomadic archer could release shafts at the rate of ten to twelve a minute for several minutes before tiring. Although many of the horse archers used the Parthian rump shot, firing over the rump of their horse as they wheeled away from the foe, the Huns fired off the shoulder or side of the horses. One advantage of the Parthian method was that the horse would not be disturbed by the snap of the string and the whistle of the arrow. Composite bows could be used by light infantry, but matched with the horse it was an awesome weapons system, probably the best in the preindustrial world when in the hands of a steppe nomad.

The Huns depended largely on the speed of their attack and their ability to inflict casualties by bow from a distance, but they did not hesitate to close with their foes, fighting hand to hand with spears, swords and daggers, and lariats. They used a small amount of iron armor, but their common protection consisted of leather strips of with bone and horn attached and heavy quilted cloth that afforded some protection against blade slashes and arrows shot from a distance. Like all nomadic cavalry, the Huns used the feigned flight to try to disrupt the formation of a steadfast adversary.

THE BATTLE OF ADRIANOPLE

Set into motion before 300 by the drying up of central Asia, the Huns had reached the Gothic lands by 373, easily overwhelming the defenders. By then the Goths had split into two groups, the Ostrogoths (East Goths) and the Visigoths (West Goths). The Huns quickly subjugated the Ostrogoths and stampeded the Visigoths westward. In 376, the Visigoths reached the lower Danube and requested permission to enter the Roman Empire as allies. Since the eastern Emperor Valens was fighting the Persians with most of his forces, there was little he could do to keep them out. Furthermore, he badly needed more manpower to defend the Balkans. Once the Goths crossed the frontier, bitter quarreling soon broke out between them and Roman officials over the provisions the government had promised to give them. The Goths turned to plundering the countryside, forcing Valens quickly to make peace with the Persians and return to Constantinople.

The great battle took place in 378 near the city of Adrianople, northwest of Constantinople. Told by scouts that the Goths numbered only 10,000 men and convinced that he was clearly superior in numbers, Valens decided to give battle. While there is no accurate count of the Roman army, it must be presumed that it was considerably larger than 10,000 men. The Goths proved to be more numerous than reported but certainly were no more than 10 percent of the 200,000 men that Roman sources attributed to them. The limited contemporary accounts suggest that the Roman infantry was carrying the field against the Goths when a large force of Germanic horsemen that had been foraging some distance away crashed into the side of the Roman army. They easily broke through the Roman cavalry—mostly Arabian—and drove into the left wing of the Roman infantry. The men of the left wing were driven into the Roman center, disrupting the ranks there and throwing the entire army into confusion. The Roman situation was made impossible by the tight packing of men in the center, which prevented them from re-forming their lines and even, so the sources declare, from lifting their swords.

Roman losses were extremely high, including Valens himself, but certainly nowhere near the 40,000 men claimed by contemporary sources. The immediate consequences of the battle were limited. The Goths marched on to Constantinople but lacked the means of assaulting its walls, so they accepted a new offer to settle in the eastern Balkans. There they soon grew restless and pushed on to Italy, where they sacked Rome in 410. By 430, the main body had moved on to the west and had established the Visigothic Kingdom of Spain and southern France that endured to 711. Their king, like most of the rulers of the Germans who established themselves in the Roman Empire, acknowledged the authority of the Roman emperor, however slight it may have been in fact, and accepted the position of foederati.

The Gothic victory at Adrianople, contrary to an often repeated assertion, did not convince the German tribes to adopt cavalry as their main arm. In fact the Visigoths made greater use of infantry as they moved westward. The most important consequence of the battle was its impact on the Eastern Empire's military. A devastating defeat of the sort the Romans suffered in 378 can often be salutary as long as the state itself is not destroyed. New commanders and innovations are called for, and fundamental changes can take place. For the eastern Romans, already long engaged against Persian cavalry, the success of the Gothic horsemen at Adrianople persuaded them to give far greater emphasis to building a cavalry force. Valens' successor, Theodosius, began to hire Gothic horsemen. Within six years, Theodosius had 40,000 German cavalrymen, who were the chief factor in his victory over a Roman rival for the throne. The eastern emperor was able to integrate the Germanic horsemen into his army as individuals or small units, so that Roman control over them was maintained. Thus he did not have the problem of German generals controlling German armies paid by the empire, which plagued the West as the government began to lose control over its German mercenaries. The Eastern Empire began to develop its own native cavalry and thus abandoned the emphasis on the infantry legion that had served Rome so well for 700 years.

Another difference between the divisions of the empire was in the nature of the command systems. Constantine had created the positions of field marshal of the infantry and of the cavalry. In the East, not only did the two positions remain separate, but the number of each increased. Thus the eastern emperor dealt with several commanders, none of whom became overly powerful. In the West the two postions merged into one field marshal of the army, who after 370 were usually German. The emperors of the West became little more than figureheads contolled by the marshals, who could not hope to take the throne themselves because of their barbarian origins.

THE HUNS IN THE WEST

Meanwhile the Huns had moved on westward. Shortly after 380, the main body settled on the Hungarian Plains, and in the following years raided far and wide across Europe, reaching the Rhine on several occasions. Their raids jostled the German tribes along the Roman frontier into flight, usually into the empire. Some Huns, however, served as mercenaries for the Romans. It has recently been argued that in the more cramped confines of the Hungarian Plains, the Huns, like all the nomads who settled there, found it difficult to raise enough horses to run the string of eight to ten that was the norm for steppe nomads. Thus it would appear that they began to make greater use of infantry by the mid-fifth century.

The Huns originally were a loose confederation of tribes; but once they had established themselves in Hungary, their political structure became tighter. By 420 Roman authors were referring to the king of the Huns. By the time the infamous Attila appeared as king about 441, the Huns had become a well-organized state ready to try to conquer a large empire in Europe. In the first years of his reign, Attila struck at the Eastern Empire in the northern Balkans, winning little territory but gaining a tribute of 2,100 pounds of gold annually. He then turned his attention to the West. Passing through southern Germany and impressing into his army those Germans who had not fled before him, he crossed the Rhine in 451 and pushed on into France as far as Orléans. Aetius, the field marshal of the army in the West, had his forces greatly augmented when the Visigoths to the south decided that the Huns were a threat to them and joined the Romans. Attila retreated to the northeast, seeking a large open field on which to deploy his cavalry.

In July 451, the two armies clashed near Châlons in northeastern France, in what is known as the Battle of the Nations because of great number of different peoples involved. Little is known of the battle's tactics or of the size and composition of the armies, but certainly the 700,000 men attributed to Attila is a gross exaggeration. There is little question, however, that the size of both armies was huge compared to the norm of the era. It is not impossible that Attila's army approached 100,000 men, and Aetius' could not have been much smaller. Aetius deployed his forces with his own Gallo-Romans on his left, the Visigoths on the right and a rather small division of Alans and several other peoples in the center. Attila placed his Huns in the center, with his German allies on the flanks. The fierce attack of the Huns against the center forced the Alans to retreat; but Aetius may have intended it, since he was now in position to threaten a double envelopment of the Huns. Attila recognized the danger and withdrew in time to save most of his forces. Thus the battle was a stalemate, but the Huns could not afford their losses since they were fighting far from their home base. Accordingly they retreated to Hungary.

The following summer, Attila led his forces into northern Italy. Using siege machines presumably built by Roman deserters, he plundered the cities of the north. But while the Huns were laying siege to cities, they were struck by a devastating epidemic. Under attack by Aetius as well, Attila agreed to meet Pope Leo I to negotiate a withdrawal, giving rise to the pious legend of how the pope single-handedly persuaded the Scourge of Europe to withdraw from Italy. Back to Hungary Attila went, where he died the next year, during a drunken orgy according to another legend. With his death the Huns began to break up, not only because of the heavy losses they had suffered in the previous two years but also because living in central Europe was rapidly changing their lifestyle. As late as 490, however, Hun cavalry units were serving as mercenaries in the Eastern Empire and were regarded as the best archers in its army.

The brief but dramatic appearance of the Huns in the history of Europe had two major consequences. First the Huns did much to enhance the reputation of cavalry and helped to bring about the most momentous military development in the late Roman Empire—the emergence of cavalry as the dominant arm. Second, by driving German tribes across the frontier and by their own deeds, they did enormous damage to the frontier defenses and provinces of the Roman Empire. Although they actually put greater pressure on the East, it was the West that suffered more permanent damage. After 452 there was little left of the western defenses to prevent the German tribes from invading. If in places a decent Roman force still stood guard, the barbarians simply outflanked it. Without the Huns the gradual assimilation of Germans into the Roman military as foederati and into Roman culture as well might have continued for centuries. In essence the Huns served as a catalyst that sped up the rate of change in the military and political systems of the late Roman Empire and, in fact, accelerated it out of control, bringing about the early Middle Ages.

5

The Byzantine
and the Arab Empires

Then the Romans [Byzantines] also formed up and raised their standards. And so the barbarians [Persians] extended the length of their line, intending to create thereby an impression of a countless multitude on the forces contending in opposition. But the Romans made a deep formation whose density gave it weight, so that the array appeared to be virtually solid and to stand steel-resistant....The barbarians were dismayed at the sight. And so they fired arrows against the Roman companies, so that the sun's rays were hidden by the discharge of missiles, and on account of the furious outpouring of shafts a winged roof appeared to be spread in the air above their heads. The Romans engaged in hand-to-hand combat, resisting the barbarians with spears and swords, cutting short the assault of the missiles' onslaught; hence they rendered the opponents devoid of stratagems. Accordingly a most memorable battle between Romans and Parthians occurred, the Persian host was broken because their ranks were not organized in depth, the rearguard of their armament was at a loss...next, when the opposing force pressed heavily, the barbarians faced destruction and veered away in flight.
    Theophylact Simocatta, *History*, edited by Mary and Michael Whitby (Oxford, 1986), pp. 94-95. Theophylact, a Byzantine historian of the late sixth century, gave a highly rhetorical description of this unnamed battle of 576 in Armenia.

At the same time as the Western Roman Empire was collapsing, the military forces of the Eastern or Byzantine Empire were recovering, as they were being transformed. The Byzantine military built a record of duration, if not one of brilliant victories, rivaling that of Rome.
    The heart of the Byzantine defenses was the city of Constantinople. When Emperor Constantine decided to build a new capital for the Eastern Empire in 330, he placed it on the superb site of the ancient Greek city of Byzantium on the straits between the Black Sea and the Aegean. Situated between the two seas and on the crossroads of Europe and Asia Minor, the city had an excellent position for both military and commercial advantage.

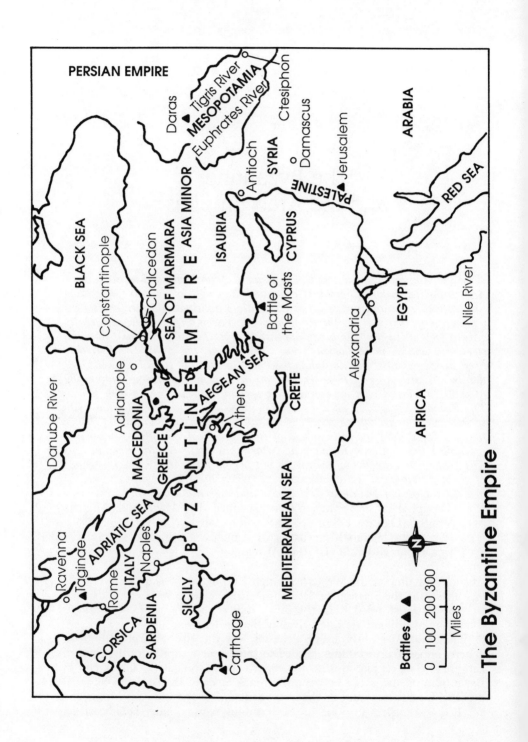

The Byzantine Empire

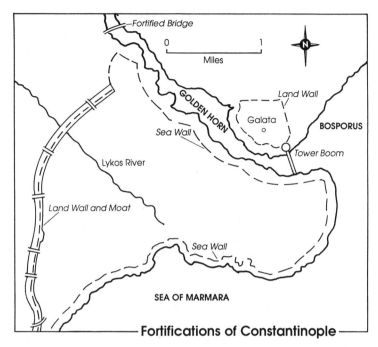

Fortifications of Constantinople

The great wealth of the city, usually judiciously taxed, was a significant
factor in the long duration of the Byzantine Empire.

THE DEFENSES OF CONSTANTINOPLE

Constantinople's site ,on the nub of a peninsula formed by the Sea of
Marmara and a deep inlet called the Golden Horn gave it an unexcelled
potential for defense, matched by no other major city in Europe. One
obvious advantage was that the city could be supplied by sea if besieged
from land and vice versa. A foe had to have both a powerful fleet and a
great army to take the city. Only thrice in 1,100 years did an enemy bring
both against it: the Arabs in 717 but without success, the Fourth Crusade
and the Venetian fleet in 1204, and the victorious Turks in 1453.
Constantinople's peninsular location also reduced enormously the length
of the main walls needed to defend its landward side, which in turn limited
the size of the garrison. The traditional number of men used to defend the
city was 24,000. This meant that Constantinople could be defended at
small expense and with little manpower relative to its wealth and population. Since the Byzantine Empire needed a large fleet to control its possessions in the Mediterranean, in times of acute danger the fleet could be
recalled to defend the capital or resupply it.

The city quickly outgrew the wall built by Constantine. Thus when
Rome fell in 410, Emperor Theodoric II quickly threw up a more formidable wall well outside the old one. In 447 an earthquake destroyed much
of the wall. After repairing the damage, the government built a new wall

just outside Theodoric's. For the rest of the Middle Ages Constantinople was protected by what was referred to as the Theodorian Wall. Nearly five miles in length, it began with a moat sixty feet wide and twenty to thirty feet deep with a hydraulic system to flood it at a moment's notice. Next to the moat was a breastwork about eight feet high followed by an open space of fifty feet. Then came the wall of 447, twenty-five feet high with square towers every 150 to 300 feet. After another open space of similar distance came the great wall of 410, which was forty feet high with ninety-six towers that were sixty feet in height. Even when manned by about a third of the usual garrison in 1453, the walls proved to be a most difficult obstacle for the enormous Ottoman army. Along the water's edge a single wall protected the waterfront. The entrance to the waterway called the Golden Horn was protected by a chain and boom of logs attached to strong towers on both shores. Permanently in place under water they could be quickly raised to the surface in times of danger. The tower on the opposite shore was itself defended by a wall and defensive works that protected a suburb. Within the Golden Horn were the naval yards, the great arsenal, and the anchorage of the fleet.

Numerous enemies—Goths, Huns, Avars, Arabs, Bulgars, Russians, and Turks among the more dangerous—spent their armies against these formidable defenses. In 1453, with only 8,000 men to man the walls, the residents of Constantinople were still optimistic about their chances of withstanding the Ottoman Turks.

THE BYZANTINE ARMY

While Constantinople stood as a last line of defense for the Empire, the Byzantine army and navy were also essential to the Empire's long existence. As of 400 the eastern military may well have been in worse shape than the western, since it had been involved in three extremely bloody battles in the previous forty years: Emperor Julian's defeat by the Persians in 363, Adrianople in 378, and a battle in 394 between two rivals for the throne. The Byzantine army's recovery after 400 was in part a result of having a secure base, Constantinople, from which to rebuild and in part a product of better commanders facing fewer problems. Certainly in the fifth century the Eastern Empire was as dependent on foederati as the West, but it never lost control of its German forces, as happened in the West. Emperor Leo I (457-474) took care of the problem of overly powerful German generals by arranging the assassination of the German Aspar, who had in fact been largely responsible for Leo's accession to the throne. He also worked to increase the proportion of natives (mostly Greek speakers) in the army. His successor Zeno (474-491) was the first to exploit the military potential of the Isaurians from the mountains of south Asia Minor. They formed the core of the Byzantine army until the eleventh century. Zeno also persuaded the Ostrogoths to leave the Balkans and migrate to Italy.

After 490, with the Persian Wars in hiatus and little barbarian pressure on the Balkan frontier, the Eastern Empire had the time to recover its strength economically and militarily. When Justinian came to the throne in 527, the Eastern Empire was ready to go back on the offensive. The army was about half native troops and half foederati, the latter still largely German but less so than in the past. There always were vast numbers of men of fortune on the frontiers of the empire, especially in the north, ready to serve as mercenaries. As time passed, the empire went further afield, so that in the course of its history representatives of every nation in Europe and western Asia appeared in the ranks of its army. Well paid and highly regarded, the mercenaries were used especially in units close to Constantinople, for the emperors regarded them as more likely to be loyal to them personally than native soldiers.

Justinian's army was largely a cavalry force. Since the Battle of Adrianople the Eastern Empire had increasingly made use of the heavily armored mounted archers called *cataphracti*. Similar to and perhaps based on Persian and Parthian models, the Byzantine version also carried a lance, a sword, and often an ax for hand-to-hand combat. They depended heavily on the bow, however, and this gave them a real advantage when confronting the nomadic horse archers. They did not have to engage in close combat with the nomads to do them injury, while their armor gave them greater protection against the nomads' arrows than the nomads had against theirs. The cataphracti were recruited mostly from the landholders of Asia Minor. By Justinian's time the Byzantine infantry was well on its way to serving largely as garrison troops on the frontiers.

Almost as soon as Justinian came to the throne, he put his military into action across the breadth of the Mediterranean and against Persia. Justinian was able to carry off his campaigns in the sea because he had a fairly large fleet to transport the army and give it support. The wealth of the Byzantine Empire had enabled it to rebuild the fleet, so that it was large enough to transport 16,000 men during one expedition under Justinian. The navy was strong enough to control the sea, although the Vandals in North Africa did give it a severe test.

BELISARIUS

Justinian also had the good fortune of having Belisarius, one of the great captains of history, in his service. Belisarius and the other generals of the Byzantine army in this era had their own personal retinue of soldiers in imitation of the Germanic comitatus; many of the retainers were Germans. Belisarius reportedly had 7,000 such retainers at one point in his career. Despite such a potent independent force, he always remained loyal to Justinian, although the emperor badly mistreated him out of jealousy of his success.

In view of the fact that Belisarius' army had 25,000 men at its greatest and usually had less, his accomplishments are even more impressive. His first great battle was against the Persians in 533 near the Tigris River. The Byzantine Empire had built a fort at Daras a decade earlier as a forward position in Mesopotamia. The Persians put the fort under siege, and Belisarius, as commander of the Byzantine forces in Mesopotamia, arrived with a force of 25,000 to relieve it. He confronted some 40,000 Persians. Although he had a large proportion of infantry, he chose to have his cavalry carry the brunt of the fighting. The infantry was deployed in the center but behind a deep trench, while the cavalry on both wings was placed well forward. The Persian commander chose to concentrate his forces against the Byzantine wings, so that the infantry in the center on both sides hardly came to blows. Belisarius won the battle by judicious use of his cavalry reserves on his right wing. The Persian cavalry fled, exposing their infantry to destruction. With their defeat at Daras, the Persians agreed to a peace that allowed Justinian to turn his attention to the West.

Having proven himself at Daras in 533, Belisarius was sent with an army of 15,000 men to regain control of North Africa, ruled for the previous century by the Vandals. In close contact with the Byzantine fleet, Belisarius' army moved out of Egypt along the coast of North Africa to Carthage. There the Vandal fleet, still a potent force, was destroyed, and Belisarius crushed the Vandal army in two battles. In the second battle he demonstrated his high regard for cavalry by deciding not to wait for his infantry, which was a full day's march behind. In an hour's fighting, the Vandal force, also largely cavalry, was destroyed.

After a Roman-style triumph through Constantinople with the Vandal king in tow, Belisarius was sent to reconquer Italy, then under the rule of the Ostrogoths. In 535 he landed in Sicily with few more men than the 7,000 of his personal retinue. According to a contemporary source, he intended only to ascertain the tactics of his new enemy and then bring in a larger force. He soon found, however, that he could defeat the Ostrogoths with the small force he had. Belisarius found that the Ostrogoths were about equally divided between cavalry and infantry. The former were lancers who closed with an enemy for hand-to-hand combat, while the latter were bowmen who preferred to stand off and shoot their arrows. With infantry always deployed behind the cavalry, the mounted troops would rush at the Byzantine forces without supporting fire from the infantry. The Byzantine cataphracti, using their bows, would halt the charge of the Ostrogoth horse and drive it off with their own charge. The exposed infantry would then quickly flee.

Aided by the support of the native population, Belisarius occupied Sicily and seized Naples. Rome then welcomed him as a liberator. The permanent conquest of Italy was slow work, however, because the small size of the Byzantine army prevented Belisarius from inflicting a crushing defeat on the Ostrogoths, who were fighting on their home ground.

The greatest battle of the twenty-year war was fought in 552. Here the Byzantine commander was not Belisarius but his second-in-command, Narses. Belisarius had been called back to Constantinople in 549 because of Justinian's growing fear of his popularity and power. The Battle of Taginae was fought high in the Appennine Mountains of central Italy. The Byzantine forces had been reinforced since 535 and numbered perhaps 25,000 men. Instead of facing a horde of hundreds of thousands as related by the contemporary accounts, Narses fought a foe that probably numbered fewer than his men. The battle is interesting in how it foreshadowed Crécy in the Hundred Years War. Narses dismounted his cataphracti and deployed them in the center with a mounted reserve behind them. On higher ground on each flank he positioned his foot archers. The rain of arrows from the foot archers slowed the charge of the Gothic lancers and allowed the dismounted cataphracti to withstand their much-diminished assault. Narses then sent in his mounted reserve to drive the Gothic cavalry off and slaughter the infantry, which had hardly participated in the battle.

THE PERSIAN WAR

Taginae secured Byzantine rule over most of Italy, but this did not endure for long. The arrival of a new German tribe, the Lombards, across the Alps after 570 deprived the Byzantine Empire of control of north Italy. Justinian's advantage over the Persians also was short-lived. By 540 the war was on again, with its usual pattern of short truce followed by war on a grand scale. The same locations in Mesopotamia, Syria, and Armenia served as sites for battle after battle, generation after generation; but neither side could conquer the other. Their resources were too evenly matched, and the zone of conflict was too far from the centers of power for both empires.

It was largely in the context of the Persian War that Emperor Maurice (582-602) developed his military theory, as laid down in his *Strategikon.* Maurice adopted Belisarius' idea that a beaten enemy should be allowed to flee unmolested, lest in extremity he turn on the pursuing force and turn defeat into victory. Both commanders believed that creating "golden bridges." or clear escape routes, would tempt the enemy forces to take them before being truly beaten. Maurice also emphasized the need to avoid battle whenever possible and depend on the threat of overwhelming force to persuade an enemy to retreat.

Maurice's strategy and tactics certainly reflected the changed nature of the Byzantine army. Its core clearly had become the well-trained, veteran cataphracti, who came from the native landed classes. Their importance in society, as well as the difficulty of replacing them, explains Maurice's reluctance to expend them in battle. The number of foederati, especially the Germanic element, had declined considerably since Justinian's era. But mercenaries remained the dominant element in the garrison troops for Constantinople and the royal body guard, on the grounds that well-paid foreign troops were less likely to engage in revolts and plots. On much the same grounds, Maurice emphasized the need to reduce the size of the generals' private retinues and gain more control over the officers. Maurice's effort to create an officer corps loyal to the emperor was far from successful, since it appears that objections to such a policy led to his assassination in 602. Revolt by ambitious generals was always a real threat to the stability of the Byzantine Empire, and it made little difference whether the men they led in revolt were native or foreign.

After Maurice's murder, the army erected as emperor a general who proved to be incompetent. The Persians under King Khusru took advantage by launching their greatest offensive in the long war with the Byzantine Empire. Their successes were astounding: Antioch captured in 611, Damascus in 614, Jerusalem in 615, Alexandria in 616, Chalcedon in western Asia Minor in 617. Virtually the entire Asian portion of the empire had fallen to the Persians. The new emperor, Heraclius, a successful general given the purple by the army, was so desperate that he was ready to flee to Carthage. Word leaked to the people of Constantinople, who rioted to prevent it. Unable to escape, Heraclius rallied himself and his army and took the offensive in one of the great reversals in military history.

In 623, taking advantage of his fleet, his sole remaining military asset besides the defenses of Constantinople, Heraclius transported an army along the coast of the Black Sea to northeast Asia Minor and struck into Armenia. His successes there prompted King Khusru to make a supreme effort to take Constantinople before the Persians were forced back from the straits. He made an alliance with the Avars, an Asiatic nomadic people present in strength in the Balkans, to attack Constantinople. Byzantine naval power prevented the Persians from crossing the straits and joining the Avars in the attack. They were forced to watch helplessly from several miles across the water as the defenders of Constantinople repulsed the Avars.

After the failed assault on the city, Heraclius went on the offensive across all of western Asia. By 627 he had driven the Persians out of Mesopotamia and had sacked Khusru's capital. The Persian generals soon assassinated Khusru. In 628 Heraclius and the new Persian king signed a treaty that called for the return of all conquered territory and prisoners. The bloodiest and the last in the long series of Rome's Persian/Parthian wars ended with no significant results except the exhaustion of both realms.

THE RISE OF ISLAM

At the moment of Heraclius' greatest triumph, the return in 629 of the "True Cross," which the Persians had taken from Jerusalem, there occurred an ominous portent. An Arab war party proclaiming a new religion struck at a Byzantine fort east of the Jordan. It was a minor irritant at the time, but it demonstrates how closely the Arab invasion followed the end of the Persian war. By battling to a stalemate, the Persians and the Byzantines set the stage for the remarkable conquests of the Arabs.

The great and at times almost impossibly easy Arab victories over the two vast empires are all the more difficult to explain because the Arabs, although nomads, did not use the composite reflexed bow until some time after their initial victories. They used stave bows, which were not very effective from horseback, plus swords, spears, and daggers and wore some body armor. Combat was hand-to-hand, as often on foot as mounted. Kinship ties were the most important factor in creating what discipline existed in pre-Islamic Arabian forces. It was usually enough to allow them to form a tightly packed body of men for a charge at the enemy.

The initial conversion of a small group of Arabs to Islam changed the situation rapidly. Muhammad indicated that God would grant warriors who fell in battle against infidels immediate entrance into paradise—a place where all the pleasures denied the Bedouin because of the harsh land in which he lived, and now because of the dietary laws of Islam, would be fulfilled. Muslim warriors were prepared to fight to the death and take as many infidels with them as possible. In close association with these points was the concept of "holy war," *jihad*, which imposed a sacred duty on Muslims to struggle against unbelievers. Muhammad's leadership rapidly united the Arabs, and he directed them on their first raids against Christian Arab allies of the Byzantine Empire in northern Arabia. Muhammad's direct involvement in military activities is unique among founders of major world religions, and it may help explain the strong streak of militarism in Islam.

By the time of Muhammad's death in 632, he had successfully harnessed the martial energies of the Arabs and directed it outward. Their first raids into the two neighboring empires were originally intended for plunder, not conquest. Raiding turned into conquest in large part because the peoples they attacked submitted so quickly. The quick submission of Palestine, Syria, and Persia was a consequence of the heavy tax burden imposed by both empires because of the recent war and, in the Byzantine Empire's provinces, serious religious conflict. A Christian heresy called Monophysitism, the belief that Christ's nature was entirely divine and not human, had won over many of the Christians of the Byzantine Middle East. Harsh repression had seriously undermined loyalty to the empire. When the Arabs struck, the majority of the Christians in those provinces not only were hardly prepared to fight for the empire, they also found Islam's strict monotheism appealing. Many converted, since the Muslims offered easy terms to those who agreed to join them.

The Arabs were immensely successful also because of their great mobility and their ability to survive in the desert that made up much of the region. Using camels as well as horses, they used the desert as the Vikings did the sea: as a highway for themselves and an insurmountable obstacle for their enemies. Morale of Arab warriors was very high compared to their enemies because fighting was the most respected activity in Arab society. It was also the most profitable, since the individual warrior received a clearly defined share of the always plentiful booty and tribute exacted from conquered lands. Already by 632, Arabs showed a sense of battle tactics by dividing their forces into three divisions and a reserve. Within the divisions, tribal units were preserved; the warriors fought under their tribal banners held aloft by one of the bravest members.

Once a region had been conquered, the Arabs little bothered their new subjects except to demand tribute; subject peoples were excluded from service in the Muslim military unless they converted. The Arabs themselves settled in huge camps in the conquered territories partly to ensure control and payment of tribute, but also to keep themselves separate from other peoples. A key element of Arab thought in the first century of conquest was to maintain the purity and distinctiveness of the Arabian people. Conversions and the taking of concubines from the local population soon began to undermine that goal.

The Arab conquest of the Middle East was also aided by the fact that the defenses of Byzantium and Persia were still disorganized and damaged because of the recent war. This was especially true in the Byzantine prov-

inces of the Middle East because the Persians had been slow to withdraw
from their conquests as pledged in the treaty of 628. Aided by moderate
demands for tribute and a willingness to tolerate Christianity, the Arabs
won the allegiance of much of the population. Thus Damascus surrendered without a fight in 635; Ctesiphon, the Persian capital, in 637; and
Jerusalem in 638, but only after a siege. By 641 the Arabs had conquered
both Egypt and Persia.

THE ARAB SIEGES OF CONSTANTINOPLE

As the Arabs pushed into eastern Asia Minor, they ran into far stiffer
resistance. The inhabitants were largely Greek speakers, Eastern Orthodox
in religion, and far more loyal to the Byzantine Empire. During the wars
with the Persians, the empire had built a large number of forts manned by
local militia to defend the routes into Asia Minor. In coming up against
them, the Arab advance was drastically slowed. But by then they had begun to pick up more advanced military tactics and engineering skills from
the peoples they had conquered. They continued to push on, but at a
much slower pace and greater cost.

Two new factors aided the Arab drive across Asia Minor. One was
Emperor Constantine II's decision to try to reverse Lombard advances in
Italy. He personally went to Italy to lead the Byzantine army in combat,
visiting Rome in 663. The other factor was the creation of an Arab fleet,
which quickly challenged the Byzantine navy for control of the eastern
Mediterranean. Mu'awiya, governor of Syria and then Caliph from 661 to
685, the greatest of the Arab commanders, was largely responsible for the
building of the fleet as well as the strategy of using it to transport an army
to besiege Constantinople. In 655, the Arabs had scored a devastating
victory over the Byzantine fleet off southwest Asia Minor, which the Arabs
called the Battle of the Masts, apparently because of the great numbers of
ships involved. With control of the seas temporarily in Arab hands, they
were free to raid Byzantine-held islands such as Cyprus and Sicily, and attack Constantinople.

Delayed by internal factionalism over the succession to the caliphate,
the Arab attack on Constantinople began in 669 with a short siege supported entirely from the sea. The Arabs lacked the manpower to storm the
walls, and soon withdrew. Five years later the Arabs returned with a much
larger force and established a permanent camp on the Asian side of the Sea
of Marmara. The siege lasted for four years but was lifted each year in late
fall and resumed in spring; the naval blockade, however, was in place
throughout.

It is noteworthy that the Arabs were able to maintain a siege for four
years dependent entirely on sea transportation, a convincing demonstration
of Arab sea power. The eventual Byzantine victory depended on regaining
control of the sea, and more specifically on the mysterious "Greek fire."
The most feared weapon of the Middle Ages, it first reported use was in
671. The precise recipe was a very tightly kept secret. Probably because
few men knew it, it was lost in the thirteenth century, perhaps during the
attack on Constantinople in 1204 by the Fourth Crusade. From the vague

descriptions in Byzantine sources, it appears that Greek fire was composed of petroleum, sulphur, saltpeter, and unburnt quicklime. It burned on water and could not be extinguished by water, but required sand or vinegar. The most controversial characteristic attributed to it was self-ignition, which many modern scholars reject as chemically impossible and a figment of the imaginations of ill-informed chroniclers. Both the smoke and the stench that Greek fire gave off terrified foes, but its great advantage was that it could be propelled through a copper siphon against enemy ships. While its best known use was as a naval weapon, it was also dropped on foes from walls or shot in jars from catapults.

At first Greek fire was used aboard fast, light boats, which devastated the Arab fleet in the Sea of Marmara. Without their naval support the Arabs were forced to lift the siege of 678. The Arabs themselves, however, soon developed something very similar to Greek fire. Both fleets were forced to put heavy lead plates on their ships to protect them against the fire. The much heavier ships, called *dromons*, carrying siphons for Greek fire and a ram, required about 100 men to row and had a seventy-man battle force. With the necessary sailors and officers, a dromon carried a total of about 200 men. The severe reduction in speed and range made the Byzantine navy primarily a force to defend the straits around Constantinople, and it helps to explain their loss of control after 680 over the outlying provinces in the central Mediterranean. The enormous increase in expense put tremendous strains on the Byzantine treasury, but the fact that the empire depended upon a weapon that destroyed enemy ships rather than effecting their capture and reuse suggests that the burden was not intolerable.

Despite their defeat in 678, the Arabs were far from through. They remained on the offensive in Asia Minor, slowly driving westward. They were aided by the appearance of a new factor in the Balkan Peninsula, the Bulgars. The Bulgars were still another nomadic people from the Asian steppes. Some had been serving as foederati in the empire's army since 474. Pushed into the Balkans by the arrival of the Avars, the Bulgars had crossed the Danube shortly after 600. By 679, a unified Bulgar kingdom on the south bank of the Danube had combined with several Slavic tribes in the region to form a potent threat to the Byzantine Empire's northern frontier.

With Byzantine resources drained by fighting the Bulgars, the Arabs were able to force their way to the straits. In 717 they launched their greatest attack against Constantinople. Contemporary sources placed the size of the Arab army at 180,000 men and the navy at 1,800 ships. While these numbers were probably exaggerated, there is no question that the Muslim forces were enormous for the era. However, the emperors had been expecting an attack for forty years, and the city's defenses and supplies were well prepared. Under Leo III, a most capable commander, Byzantine forces demonstrated excellent resourcefulness in combating the threat. Using Greek fire effectively, the Byzantine fleet prevented supplies from reaching the Arab army that besieged Constantinople over the winter of 717-18. Adding to the Arab supply problem were widespread epidemics and an attack by the Bulgars, whom Leo III had drawn into a temporary alliance. After a siege of a year, the Arabs withdrew. What was left of their fleet was caught in a terrible storm and all but destroyed. Arab sources put the total manpower lost in the campaign at 150,000 men. The defeat ended Arab hopes of taking Constantinople. Thus it was a most important victory for Christendom, since the city continued to stand as a barrier against Muslim penetration into eastern Europe for another 700 years.

THE ARABS IN NORTH AFRICA AND IBERIA

Even as the Arabs were being defeated before Constantinople and subsequently were driven out of most of Asia Minor, they were having great success in the western Mediterranean. Having occupied Egypt in 641, they moved westward along the coast of North Africa. The Berber tribes of western North Africa put up a stiffer resistance than had the local Byzantine subjects, although the Berbers had little more affection for their nominal ruler, the Byzantine emperor, than had the peoples of the Middle East. In the three-cornered struggle for North Africa, the Arabs gained the upper hand through their naval power. In 698 they destroyed the Byzantine fleet of the central Mediterranean off Tunisia and quickly captured Carthage, the imperial capital of North Africa. With Byzantine forces eliminated, the Arabs concentrated their strength on the Berbers and decisively defeated them in 700. Like so many other defeated peoples, the Berbers became Muslims and joined forces with the Arabs.

In 711, the Muslims crossed the straits of Gibraltar to the Iberian peninsula. The Visigothic kingdom still in power there was badly torn by factionalism in the ruling dynasty; one faction had in fact asked for Muslim aid. Easily disposing of the Gothic army that tried to stem the invasion, the Muslims, largely Berbers, pushed on to Toledo, the capital, and captured it with little effort. They settled themselves as land-holders over the local population, but as was usually true, the conquerors retained their restless and warlike character for several generations before truly settling down to enjoy their new properties. Thus the Muslims pushed across the Pyrenees in 718 and occupied southwest Gaul. The defeat of an exploratory force at Tours in 732 (see Chapter 6) convinced the Muslim leaders that Gaul was not worth conquering, being cold, poor, and inhabited by warlike barbarians.

The year 732 marked the high-tide mark of the Arab Empire, although certainly not of the Islamic religion. It stretched from the Indus River in India to the Atlantic Ocean. Already by that date, however, the unity of the Arab state was collapsing, as the Umayyad dynasty that had occupied the Caliphate since 661 was being undermined by its rival, the Abbasids. By 750 the Abbasids had won control of Arabia and the Middle East, but Iberia remained under Umayyad rulers. By 950 Egypt and Persia had also broken free of the Abbasid empire. The Arabs also began to lose their warrior culture and became increasingly content to enjoy the fruits of their enormous conquests. The military advantage began to edge toward two barbarian peoples on the northeastern and northwestern fringes of the Muslim world—the Turks and the western Christians.

6

The Early Middle Ages
in Western Europe

When the army is on the march, [we order] that it should be the business of the count to proclaim by edict in his county that each man in lieu of 60 solidi should do military service, and that they should come to the assembly at the place where it is commanded. The count himself should have an eye to how they have been equipped, that is, lance, shield, a bow with two strings, and twelve arrows. Each of them should have these....and they should come on the day of the announced assembly and there they should show how they have been equipped. They should have breastplates, helmets and be armed for the season, that is in the summer time.

> The Capitulary of Aachen, quoted in Hans Delbrück, *The History of the Art of War*, Trans. Walter Renfroe (Westport, Conn., 1982), 3, p. 59. Charlemagne issued this decree in 806.

With the frontier defenses of the Western Roman Empire all but gone by 455, the German tribes were free to move into Roman territory almost at will. Any resistance more often came from Germans already settled there than from the remnants of the Roman military. The Germans were few in number compared to the Romanized population in place. They did not displace the Romans but rather mingled with them, except in Britain where the Angles and Saxons drove out a large part of the Romanized Britons. The Germans took over a large share of the cultivated land in the regions they occupied, but the Roman patricians maintained a significant portion of their property. Accordingly there were two types of wealthy landholders—German, still largely barbarian, and Roman, still sophisticated and cultured. In both populations the differences between the wealthy landholders and the ordinary freemen became greater. Since only some of the German freemen were granted landholdings, the remainder was forced to become their tenants. The widening social distinctions were crucial for the creation of feudalism.

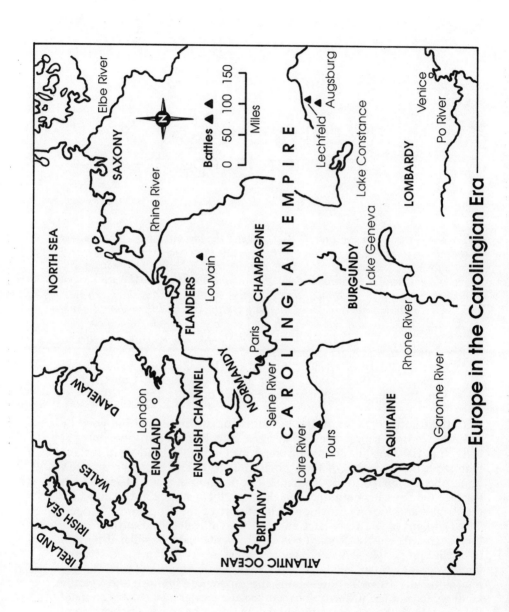

Europe in the Carolingian Era

There was little left of the Roman military to influence the Germans in the West after 455, and those tribes that settled in the Empire after that date showed no significant change in fighting styles. There were few professional fighting men of the Roman type, because the Roman administrative system, which the barbarian kings hoped to use to collect taxes to support their armies, rapidly withered away. Thus the German warriors were forced to concentrate on the cultivation of their lands for their livelihood, although booty and gifts from the kings were always an important supplement. The Roman population was prohibited from serving in the military both for reasons of security and as a reflection of the law of the late empire that restricted military service to a hereditary warrior caste. By the year 600, however, as the distinctions between Germans and Romans dwindled, Romans began to fight for the German kings as well.

The armies of these Germanic kingdoms existing within the old Roman Empire increasingly were of dubious quality. They found it very difficult and at times failed to defend their lands against other Germans, the Byzantine Empire, and, after 700, the Arabs. A major problem was their heterogeneous nature. Often made up of a mixture of peoples and fighting styles and an increasing number of mounted men, the German armies largely lost the essential characteristics of each tribe that had previously accounted for their successes.

Most serious was the loss of discipline. Spread out among the Roman population, the German clans or hundreds began to lose their cohesion; the number of men bound together by kinship ties, so crucial to the original discipline of the tribes, was reduced to small and ineffective units. This development was especially true of the Franks, since they had occupied a vast territory with a relatively small number of people. The loss of discipline was compounded by the incompetence of the Merovingians, the successors of Clovis (481-511), who was the first king of a united Frankish realm, and by the deteriorating economic situation. The latter problem prevented the regular payment of an army, and without regular pay, it was impossible to use Roman-style drill to instill discipline. Thus the infantry declined rapidly in effectiveness, since infantry's success has always depended more on the cohesion of the units of fighting men than on the courage and strength of the individuals in them. The use of foot archers might have been an alternative to shock infantry, but neither Germans nor Romans had a tradition of using the bow.

THE CREATION OF THE KNIGHT

Cavalry was the answer to the breakdown of discipline in the European infantry. The use of the horse not only allowed the mounted man to be more effective than infantrymen in a unit lacking discipline, it actually dictated a less controlled style of fighting. The weaving and rearing of even the best trained horses made it impossible for mounted men to fight as a closely knit, highly cohesive unit in which the men relied on the shields of their neighbors for part of their protection. Mounted warriors also have had a clear advantage of height, leverage, and intimidation over a mob of individual footmen, which is what infantry becomes when it loses discipline. Only a well-disciplined infantry could hope to stand in the face of a thundering cavalry charge. Among the Franks and other early medieval peoples, the need to travel long distances to reach a mustering point or battle site also encouraged the use of horses.

As discipline failed in the Frankish infantry, the advantage of the cavalry increased. That attracted more and more of the best warriors to fight mounted, further extending the gap between the two styles. Lacking in training, motivation, and leadership, the infantry continued to atrophy. Above all it lacked that cadre of born warriors whose headlong dashes into battle have been so crucial in inspiring the rest of the army to fight. It must be emphasized, however, that foot soldiers never disappeared entirely from the battlefields of the medieval West. They continued to be present, often in great numbers, but were rarely effective.

Two technical innovations, stirrups and horseshoes, added substantially to the advantage of the cavalry. The stirrup first appeared in central Asia perhaps a century after Christ, but the peoples to the West were slow to see the advantage it offered. It reached France about 600, but was adopted slowly. Drawings of horsemen from as late as 850 in northern France depict some without stirrups. Only by 900 was the device clearly in general use. The slow spread of the stirrup forces a reappraisal of the theory that its appearance created the medieval heavy lancer, the knight. If it had made such a great impact, presumably it would have been adopted much more quickly. Mounted warriors without stirrups had long used the lance as a shock weapon.

Nonetheless there is little question that the use of the stirrup did enhance the impact of the mounted lancer. The vastly improved balance the device afforded the horseman permitted the use of what became the identifying weapon of the knight—the couched lance. The lance was held under the armpit and the point directed with the hand. This technique gave the lancer far greater accuracy in striking the enemy, and it combined the force of the weight of the man, his armor, and his horse into the lance's impact. Only in the eleventh century does conclusive evidence of the use of the technique appear; even in the Bayeux Tapestry, celebrating the Norman conquest of England, some Normans were pictured as holding their lances overhead, in the older style. Stirrups also made it possible for a mounted man to stand in them and swing his sword downward with great force. That encouraged the use of heavier swords and led to the development of the broad sword. The mounted warrior had now vastly increased his advantage over the infantry.

The horseshoe, appearing about the same time from central Asia, also improved the capabilities of the cavalry. The lack of shoes in the Roman era had greatly reduced the effectiveness of the horses in rough terrain and had required that they be put in soft pasture for a time to allow their hooves to grow back after a rough campaign. Shod horses could be used on longer campaigns and in rough or stony terrain and could carry heavier loads such as an armored man without splitting their hooves. The appearance of the horse collar from China in much the same era also enabled horses to pull heavy wagons and carts. Although the logistical systems of medieval armies were far from the level of the Romans, the use of horse-drawn carts was an improvement. Generally, however, medieval forces relied mostly on foraging.

There is little reason to doubt that the defensive response to the increased effectiveness of the mounted warrior was greater use of armor, since the dating of the evidence corresponds to the increased use of the stirrup. That device made it possible to step up onto horseback while in heavy armor, in contrast to the need to jump up onto a horse without the stirrup. Chain mail armor was known in the ancient world, but the early Germans had had very little. Perhaps the increase in the amount of iron available to them once they had settled in the Roman Empire was a factor in the greater use of armor. There were at least two types of mail in use in the early Middle Ages: a covering of metal studs hammered flat and sewn onto an undercoat, and a type more accurately called chain mail, iron rings linked together to form a vest. The latter was the more common and provided a flexible armor that was effective against both slashing and thrusting weapons, but less so against clubs and arrows at close range. For protection against clubs, a heavy garment was worn underneath the mail. The chain mail of the era before 1250 gave reasonable protection against the weapons of the time, but it did have one serious defect: a blow that in itself was far from fatal often broke the links of iron and forced pieces under the skin, causing blood poisoning.

There is no real reason why mounted men needed armor more than infantrymen; but since it was the wealthy who fought on horseback, it was the cavalry that had most of the armor as well. In order to be effective against other armored cavalry, a nobleman had to have as much armor as he could afford. This was one more element in the complex chain of events that led to the eventual identification of noble status with military service as an armored cavalryman.

THE CAROLINGIAN EMPIRE

Serving as a mounted warrior in an agricultural society was very expensive, far more so than service as an infantryman. Horse, lance, sword, and the usual armor in use about the year 800 cost the equivalent of fifteen cows. Our understanding of the era from 600 to 900, however, remains too unclear to provide an answer to the problem of whether wealthy Frankish landholders became cavalrymen because of their wealth or whether a small portion of the Frankish warriors was given land to enable them to serve the monarchy as cavalry. Those historians who argue the first position find their best support in that some Franks were using horses well before 700 and that the process of converting the Frankish army to heavy cavalry was long and drawn out, beginning well before the era of Charles Martel and extending well beyond him. The historians who maintain the second point of view find support in contemporary accounts of how the first Carolingians, especially Charles Martel, created feudalism in order to have their own cavalry force.

This view is centered specifically around the Battle of Tours (732), where Martel's Franks defeated an Arab expeditionary force sent to explore

the feasibility of conquering Gaul. There is no good evidence on the size
of the forces involved, although the Arab army seems to have been relatively small. There is a strong suggestion that some of the Franks arrived
at the battle site on horse, but Martel, having earlier faced the Arabs in
southern France, apparently decided that a mixed force of horse and foot
would only dissipate their respective strengths. He ordered all to fight on
foot. This decision anchored the Frankish lines with well-armored and
experienced warriors whose presence served to stiffen the ordinary footmen.
Thus the Franks could be described by a chronicle as "standing as mo-
tionless as a wall; they were like a belt of ice frozen together, and not to
be dissolved as they slew the Arabs with the sword."[1] The fighting continued into the night as charge after charge of Arab horsemen splintered
on the resolute Franks.

Apparently fearing a feigned retreat by the Arabs, Martel refused to allow his men to break their lines to pursue them once it appeared that the
enemy had broken off. When the next morning it became clear that the
Arabs had indeed fled, Martel reportedly was very angry over his lack of a
strong cavalry to pursue and destroy the fleeing enemy. According to legend, he decided then to build a strong Frankish cavalry by providing lands
seized from the Church to a number of chosen warriors so that they would
have the resources to equip themselves as mounted warriors. Whether or
not the story is true, it reveals the essence of feudalism—a grant of land to
warriors in exchange for military service as cavalry.

A full description of the feudal system must wait until the next chapter,
but a quick overview of the system of the eighth and ninth centuries is in
order here. Both the Roman world and the German tribes had a practice,
known as commendation, by which a weaker freeman would attach himself
to a more powerful protector. Many such retainers simply did menial labor
and eventually merged with the gangs of slave field laborers, all of whom
became the serfs of the early Middle Ages. Some of the commended men,
however, were called on to fight for their benefactors, as in the German
comitatus. Although numerous terms were used early on for such men,
by the eighth century the term vassal (from a Celtic word for retainer) was
in common use for a military retainer. To provide support for these warriors, their benefactors usually provided grants of land, known at first as
benefices, later as fiefs, in Latin *foedum*, hence the term feudal.

There was in this early period no clear identification between holding
a benefice and providing military service, since many of the officials of the
early Frankish monarchs were given such grants. Another practice of the
Merovingian era that became associated with landholding was that of immunity. Many landholders were given exemptions from the exercise of
royal authority on their lands. The practice placed the administration of
justice, tax collection, the maintenance of roads and bridges, and in some
cases troop raising, all powers of the state, into private hands.

The reign of Charlemagne (768-814) was a major period of transition
in the Frankish military. The great Charles gained his name largely
through his military prowess and conquests. In conquering the Lombards
in northern Italy he added a potent cavalry force to his army. It was largely

the Lombard horse that enabled him to defeat the Avars, central Asian horse archers, who had settled in the Hungarian Plains. Wars against the Lombards, the Avars, and the Arabs in northern Spain, all cavalry-based societies, served to emphasize the value of a strong cavalry for the Franks. Yet the long and bitter war against the Saxons in northern Germany, still largely footmen, was carried on mostly by infantry forces.

Besides the expansion of his empire, which carried Frankish customs and military styles to central Europe and northern Italy, Charlemagne's most significant contribution to feudalism was his success in forcing those wealthy landholders, mostly descendants of Roman aristocrats, who had held their property free of any obligation to the king, to regard their lands as benefices from the monarch. Thus military service could be demanded of them as well. By the end of his reign most of the land in the empire was regarded as within the feudal system.

In the last decade of his life, Charlemagne issued several edicts on the military that reveal much about his forces. The distinction between the wealthy landholder who served mounted and the poorer freeman who fought on foot was made clear. The much harsher penalties imposed on the former for seeking to avoid military service point to an effort to increase the number of mounted men in service while showing little concern about the number of footmen. Those men who held twelve or more *mansi* (a unit of land) were ordered to serve in a coat of mail, which appears by that time to mean serving as cavalry.

Also very informative is a summons to duty sent to an abbot in 806. It ordered him to arrive at the assembly point with his men by May 20 of that year. Every horseman was to have shield, lance, several daggers, and bow and quiver. The inclusion of the bow is the best evidence that Charlemagne hoped to introduce its use to the Franks, probably a result of his war against the Avars. The effort, however, failed. The men were ordered to be prepared to serve in any part of the realm, and to bring enough food for three months and clothing for six. The provision carts were also to carry spades, axes, and picks. The summons also included a strict ban on foraging while en route except for water, wood, and grass. Charlemagne's attention to these sorts of logistical details helps to explain his successes; he was able to exploit to the fullest the potential of the Frankish military. None of the other Frankish kings were able to reach anywhere near that level of efficiency.

That accomplishment was, however, very much the personal achievement of Charlemagne, building on the work of his ancestors. In the hands of far less capable successors, beginning with his son, Louis the Pious, the Frankish military declined rapidly. The loyalty of the great nobles was splintered among Louis' sons, in bitter competition with each other and their father for power and influence. Charlemagne's efforts to keep the great nobles from forcing the lesser nobles into subjugation and the latter from reducing the free peasants into serfdom were halted. Thus the monarchy began to lose control over the armed men of the realm.

The division of the Carolingian Empire among Louis' three surviving sons at his death in 840 did not solve these problems. Even the three

smaller successor kingdoms, especially eldest son Lothair's middle kingdom, which stretched from the North Sea across the Alps to northern Italy,
proved impossible to govern. The economic and political structures of the
era were far too primitive to support large powerful states with effective
standing armies, a problem compounded by the total inadequacy of communications. What government existed had to be administered on a very
local level in territorial units far smaller than the largely chimerical kingdoms of the era. That in itself fostered the development of feudalism.

NEW INVADERS

As happened in the late Roman Empire, the appearance of new invaders greatly accelerated trends already in progress. The Saracens in the
Mediterranean, the Magyars from the Asian steppes, and the Vikings from
Scandinavia all took advantage of the decline of the Carolingian Empire to
make deep incursions into Europe. The Saracens, a term used for Muslim
sea raiders, were the first to strike into Europe, raiding the Mediterranean
coasts from the mid-eighth century. In 846, they sacked Rome, the most
notable feat of a full two centuries of attacks. Like most such raiders in
history, the Saracens eventually began to occupy the lands they first raided,
conquering Sicily and for several decades maintaining a foothold in southern Italy.

The Magyars were more significant in the development of feudalism
because they struck into regions where an early form of feudalism was already present. They were a nomadic people from central Asia who used
the composite reflexed bow as their main weapon. They probably were
every bit as terrifying as the Huns, but the earlier presence of the Huns and
the Avars had reduced the shock of their appearance. The Magyars apparently were set in motion westward in the eighth century, and, taking
advantage of the power vacuum in the Hungarian Plains caused by the
crushing of the Avars, had occupied Hungary by 860. They then proceeded
to raid their new neighbors, striking into eastern Germany for the first time
in 862. By 899 their leaders felt bold enough to raid northern Italy.

In 910, Louis the Child, the last of the Carolingian kings of the east
Franks (Germany), called a general levy of his nobles to drive the Magyars
out. In a major confrontation near Augsburg, the Magyars used the
feigned retreat, a tactic typical of Asian horse archers. Part of their forces
engaged the Germans and after brief contact retreated. The rest of the army
lay hidden in ambush, and struck at the rear of the German army as it
dashed by in disorderly pursuit. The other Magyars then wheeled about
and attacked the Germans again, resulting in an overwhelming victory for
the Magyars.

As raiders the Magyars preferred not to fight such battles, and for nearly
a half century they avoided them, striking instead at unprotected villages
with small bands that had exceptional mobility and range, even for Asian
horsemen. On several occasions larger bands crossed the Rhine into
France, and the Alps into Italy. In 954 the greatest of their expeditions
went as far west as central France, then turned south through Burgundy,
and crossed the Alps into Italy before returning to Hungary.

This long raid into France and Italy probably took place, however, because the Germans by then had begun to devise defenses for their homeland: well-garrisoned forts (*burgs*) along every possible invasion route, and a heavily armored cavalry force. Created by King Henry I king of Germany (919-936), and his son Otto I (936-973) who took the title of Holy Roman Emperor in 962, this defensive system compelled the Magyars to call on their full manpower for an attack into Germany in 955. Otto I collected a force of 8,000 mounted men and met the Magyars on the Lech River near Augsburg.

The most reliable of the several conflicting accounts of the Battle of Lechfeld reports that Otto struck at the rear of the Magyar forces drawn up for a siege of Augsburg. The battle itself was brief, as the Magyars quickly broke off when they saw the size of the forces arrayed against them. But the vigorous pursuit of the Germans cut down many Magyars, whose horses had tired, since they lacked enough horses to have the usual string of six or eight per man found in the steppes. More drowned in the deep pools of the Lech River as they fled across it. Having suffered heavy losses, the Magyars retreated to Hungary, where they henceforth remained, converting to Christianity and establishing the kingdom of Hungary.

THE VIKINGS

Whereas the Magyars inflicted heavy damage in central Europe for less than a full century, the Vikings were on the attack for twice as long and over a much wider range of lands. Some of their targets, however, had little or no role in the development of feudalism. Scandinavian society, from whence the Norse came, had changed little from the Germanic tribes of five hundred years earlier. Still pagan and barbarian, the Vikings differed little in their fighting style and warrior ethic from the early Germans. Their main weapon, however, was a heavy two-handed ax that was capable of cleaving any armor of the era. The Vikings also used the bow. In 800 they had little body armor, but by 900, through plunder and trade, they had become well armored. For most of the Viking era, the usual expedition was a war band of several hundred men under the banner of a noted chieftain.

The key to Viking success was, of course, the Viking boat or long ship. Light yet sturdy, long and narrow, it was built to be rowed, with a single square sail on a mast amidship for use in a fair wind. Later larger versions were called dragon ships. With about twenty rowers on a side, a typical boat of the ninth century carried about 80-100 men, all of whom were both rowers and warriors. Thus when a boat reached a target, most of the men could grab their weapons and go plundering, leaving a small squad behind to watch the boat without worrying about guarding a mob of slave rowers.

The Vikings were capable of crossing vast expanses of the cold and very rough seas off northern Europe in their light boats using natural navigational methods. The long voyages to Iceland and beyond were made in a somewhat larger and broader boat called the *knarr* that made use of a sail for propulsion. Sighting the stars and sun was their preferred navigational method; but in their absence, a common situation in the northern waters, they navigated by the swell of the ocean, the flight of birds, or the direction of driftwood. The Vikings' greatest asset was their ability to strike hard and fast with their boats, plundering a district and escaping long before a relief force could be mustered. The shallow draft of their boats and the use of two steering oars in the stern, which could be lifted up, enabled them to beach their crafts freely or strike far up the rivers of continental Europe as well, although in the West such feats awaited the collapse of the Carolingian Empire.

The Norse were not exclusively raiders; they were equally willing to be traders should they reach a region that was well defended. Often they traded the plunder that they had taken a short distance away. The enormous hoards of precious metal found in their homelands demonstrates the success they had in both activities. The three national divisions of the Norse—Norwegian, Swedish, and Danish—were already present in the Viking age, at least in respect to the different regions they attacked. The Swedes stayed mainly in the Baltic, moving up the vast network of rivers of Russia to exploit the Slavic peoples there, and reaching the Black Sea. The great city of Kiev and even the name Rus are generally regarded as Swedish in origin. The Norwegians, while active in raiding the British Isles early on, concentrated on the north Atlantic. They were largely responsible for the Viking colonies in Iceland, Greenland, and, for a short time, North America. The Vikings who terrorized western Europe were mostly Danes.

The first targets of opportunity for the Vikings in the West were the British Isles. Three ships raided the north coast of England in 789. Their favorite targets were the wealthy but ill-defended Celtic monasteries on the coasts of Ireland and Scotland. Their ability to push their small ships through the rough seas and dangerous rocks off the coasts of Scotland and Ireland is clear evidence of the quality of both their ships and seamanship at the very beginning of the Viking era. Viking raids did much to destroy the flourishing Celtic Christian culture of the Gaelic lands. None of the British Isles had the political unity needed to confound the Norse. By 830 their raids were striking deep into the interior of the islands, and they were establishing long-term camps on the coasts.

The few Viking raids on the coasts of the Frankish Empire late in Charlemagne's reign had led him to take vigorous action to defend the coasts. He even ordered a navy built. But after his death, the capacity of the Franks to defend themselves declined rapidly. In 834 the city of Utrecht in the Netherlands was sacked, and in 843 the first Viking winter camp in western Europe appeared on an island off the mouth of the Loire River. With success came more Vikings, attracted by the rich plunder taken by their fellows. By 850, it must have seemed that all of Scandinavia was abroad in the summer months. The small raiding parties had grown into armies with permanent bases, usually on islands in the mouths of the major rivers of western Europe. These island bases were impregnable to the local forces, which usually lacked a fleet of any sort. The river basins consequently were wide open to raids. By 866 the Norse had gone beyond relying only on their boats, and had taken to stealing the horses of a region where they landed and raiding far into the interior. They did, however, always fight on foot.

One of the best-known attacks of the Norse was the siege of Paris in 885-86. By that date the kings of the West Franks had undertaken the construction of a number of fortified bridges at key points on the major rivers, especially the Seine, in hope of stopping the Viking forays into the interior of France. In 885 a Viking force fought its way up the Seine, overpowering several such fortified bridges on the way. The strongest defensive works were at Paris. The manpower available at Paris made the site a far more formidable obstacle than the isolated forts downriver.

By November 885, the Vikings had reached Paris, but failing to take the defenses by assault, they settled into a siege. Although the number of Vikings most certainly was not the 40,000 men related by the chronicles, the force present at Paris must have been very large for a Norse army. In August 886, Charles III of the West Franks reached Paris with a relief force, but he did not attack the Vikings. Four months later, with his provisions depleted, he agreed to pay the Vikings a large bribe to withdraw. This event demonstrated the weakness of the later Carolingian kings in dealing with a resolute enemy, but it also pointed to the future—the importance of fortified positions for defending the realm.

Five years later, King Arnaulf of Germany personally led an assault by dismounted warriors across a wide marsh against the Viking camp near Louvain in Belgium. Arnaulf's courageous assault broke through the palisade around the camp and forced the Norse back into the river that surrounded much of the camp, inflicting heavy losses. It is true that the Vikings returned to the site several months later, but the battle showed how a forceful leader could make a formidable army out of the Frankish warriors of the time.

It is usually said that Arnaulf's victory prevented the permanent Norse occupation of the north German coast of the sort that occurred in England and Normandy. In England the creation of the Danelaw was a gradual process by which the Danes spread inland from their bases on the northeast coast. By 878 they had occupied about half of England. But in conquering land instead of raiding it, the Danes made themselves vulnerable to attack, and they proved to be no more capable of defending towns and farms than the Anglo-Saxons had been. Under Alfred the Great (871-899) the Anglo-Saxons went on the offensive, pushing a line of *burhs* (forts) into the Danelaw and building a fleet. By the end of the reign of Alfred's grandson (939), the Danes had submitted to Anglo-Saxon rule.

In northeastern France, the permanent conquest of a large territory by the Vikings came about much more rapidly. They began the process of occupying lands inland from their bases on the coast only after 900. Unable to dislodge them, Charles the Simple, king of the West Franks, in 911 persuaded their chief, Rolf, to accept the title of duke and control of a large region in exchange for his submission to the king as his overlord. Charles also could call on Rolf's services for defending the Seine basin against further Norse incursions, and Rolf's Norse, or Normans, agreed to become Christians. Promised plenty of good land, Viking bands that were encamped up and down the French coast came to join Rolf. Duke Rolf's Normans kept their word, providing valuable service against Viking raids from Scandinavia in the next decades. Shortly, they had become thoroughly French in language and culture, but for several centuries they kept the martial spirit of their Viking ancestors as well as their love of adventure. Norman knights seeking land and adventure made up a disproportionate part of the great military expeditions of the High Middle Ages.

By 950, the consolidation of royal power in the Scandinavian realms had reduced the opportunities for free-lance war bands to strike out on their own into western Europe. And western Europe was by then far better prepared to deal with the raiders, who continued to strike until around the year 1000. The transformation of the forces of western Europe into cavalry-based armies (except for England) and the building of an enormous number of fortifications gave the Europeans the means to repulse highly mobile invaders, whether Saracens and Vikings in their boats or Magyars on their ponies. These two developments also gave final form to the medieval military system.

NOTE
    1. Quoted by Charles Quigley, *Weapon Systems and Political Stability: A History* (Washington, D.C., 1983), p. 830.

7

Feudalism

I love to see a lord when he is the first to advance on horseback, armed and fearless, thus encouraging his men to valiant service; then when the fray has begun, each must be ready to follow him willingly, because no one is held in esteem until he has given and received blows. We shall see clubs and swords, gaily colored helmets and shields shattered and spoiled, at the beginning of the battle, and many vassals all together receiving great blows. Once he has started fighting, no noble knight thinks of anything but breaking heads and arms—better a dead man than a live one who is useless. I tell you, neither in eating, drinking nor sleeping do I find what I feel when I hear the shout "At them" from both sides.

> Bertran de Born, quoted in John Keegan and Richard Holmes, *Soldiers: A History of Men in Battle* (New York, 1986), pp. 25-26. De Born was a twelfth-century troubadour.

By the time the raids of Saracen, Magyar, and Viking had ended, the feudal system had achieved maturity, at least in its heartland, which extended from Normandy across northern France to the Rhine. In most of west and central Europe, protofeudal structures were eventually transformed into complete feudalism, but fringe areas such as Switzerland, Scotland, and Scandinavia remained largely nonfeudal.

Despite all the connotations of the term feudalism—a social system, a form of landholding, a means of allotment of labor—it was first of all a military system. Its purpose was to provide local military protection at a time when states could not support standing armies. It was the means by which a small force of mounted warriors could provide local defense, or a vast host be assembled to defend the kingdom, without drawing on the minute revenues of the central government. Land was the only form of wealth available in the quantity needed to support such a force, especially since by the mid-tenth century those obliged to serve did so as cavalry, which was the vastly more expensive military style. In short, feudalism was a system in which payment for military service was made in land.

In the theory of feudalism, the king was the lord or suzerain of the entire kingdom, the proprietor of all the land, even the large amount held by the Church. Feudal theory proclaimed that in order to provide for the defense of his realm, the king had given huge grants of land (strictly speaking, only its use) to his chief warriors—essentially the dukes and counts—who served as the high officers of his army. The grant of land, regardless of its size, was called the fief; the man who granted it was the lord; the warrior who received it was a vassal. In order to meet their obligations for military service, the counts and dukes, vassals of the king, in turn had to give out smaller fiefs to more fighting men, their vassals. At the bottom of the system were the petty knights who held one or two manors, the basic unit of the system.

A manor can be defined as the amount of land, commonly 600 to 700 acres, along with the peasant labor permanently attached to it, which could support one mounted warrior. One must be certain not to identify the fief with the manor; a fief could vary in size from the single manor of a petty knight to the thousands of manors in a duchy or county. Because the church lands were also held as fiefs, abbots and bishops were responsible for providing military service. They often provided it themselves, until the Church in the twelfth century forbade the clergy from direct involvement in combat. After that, the higher clergy had to hire knights to perform their service.

VASSALAGE

All fiefholders were vassals, and all vassals, except for the petty knights, were also lords over their own vassals. Most feudal nobles, therefore, both owed military service to a lord and received it from their vassals. In terms of a system of military command such nobles were officers who received orders from above and gave them to the men below. In that respect the feudal system corresponded to a modern army, but there were several major differences. One was that the command system was not uniform throughout a realm. The number of levels between king and a petty knight varied enormously from one district to another, ranging from as few as three or four subdivisions below the king to as many as twenty.

Even more significant a difference between feudalism and a modern army was that a vassal owed obedience and service only to his immediate lord and not to the levels above. When a vassal refused to obey his lord and called on the service of his own kin, vassals, and subvassals to fight his lord, only the recalcitrant vassal was liable to punishment; his vassals and subvassals were free from penalty. This encouraged the revolt of men higher in the system—barons, counts, dukes—against the king, because they could draw on their vassals, who were obliged to serve their lord and not the king. It was as if in a modern army, a colonel could defy the general and oblige the officers below him to obey him and not the general; yet only the colonel could be punished if the general forced him to submit. In France in particular, most of the great vassals of the king had enough vassals and subvassals to defy him if they wanted to, with little fear of penalty.

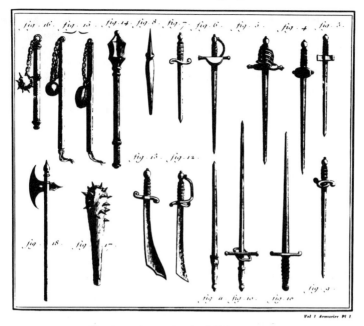

Weapons in use in the Middle Ages

This aspect of feudalism was a major cause of the enormous amount of petty warfare that permeated feudal Europe from around 950 to 1100.

Assuming that vassals did obey their lord's summons to military service, a distinction was made between defensive and offensive service. A vassal had an obligation to defend his lord's lands against an invader until the threat was over. If the lord undertook an offensive against an opponent, however, the vassals were committed only to a specified number of days of service per year per manor held. The number varied from fief to fief, but the most common was forty days. A vassal was free to return home after the required time of service, even if the fighting continued. Yet the love of fighting endemic among knights, and the promise of plunder—the only way most petty knights had to increase their wealth—ensured that most vassals stayed on for the duration of the campaign. Another duty vassals had was garrison duty in a lord's castle, since from the year 1100 on, every noble in the middle and upper levels of the feudal system had a castle to defend his lands. Garrison duty also varied in length of time but was calculated in addition to field service.

The feudal system was based on military service, but a vassal had other important obligations to his lord. "Suit to court" referred to the vassal's obligation to attend the lord's court when called upon to give advice on matters of interest to the fief as a whole, such as going to war, the lord's plans to go on a crusade, or his choice of a wife for himself or his eldest son and heir. Suit to court also meant sitting in judgment of a fellow vassal accused of violating his oath to the lord, and settling disputes between the lord and a vassal or between two vassals. Fellow vassals under the same lord were one's peers, and feudal justice thus was trial by peers. The lord also had the right to aid: his vassals had to help pay his ransom if he was captured in battle and to give him gifts at the knighting of his eldest son and the marriage of his eldest daughter. Aid for going to war or building a castle was also expected. Lastly, the vassals had the obligation of hospitality: to shelter, feed, and entertain the lord and his entourage for a specified number of days a year.

Along with these obligations, a vassal was prohibited from causing physical injury to his lord or seducing his wife and daughters. The lord was equally enjoined against such acts in regard to his vassals. Beyond that, the key obligation of the lord was to protect his vassals from invaders. He also was bound to give a vassal justice in his court, which extended to allowing a vassal to levy charges against him to be judged by his fellow vassals. Examples of a vassal's peers actually finding against the lord appear to have been very few.

FEUDAL LAW

This set of mutual obligations and duties was known as feudal law. Since it was established entirely by custom, it varied slightly from fief to fief and more widely from kingdom to kingdom. The penalty for a vassal found in violation of feudal law was to be stripped of his fief. Except perhaps for the petty knight at the bottom of the feudal pyramid, any vassal facing that penalty would certainly fight to prevent its execution, calling on his own vassals and relatives and seeking allies among his lord's enemies. Fighting was the common response to a judgment against a vassal; this was the principal reason for the petty warfare endemic to Europe in the tenth and eleventh centuries. In some cases, however, when the lord was weak and could not count on the loyalty of many vassals, he was forced to ignore violations from some vassals lest he be defeated and lose all credibility. In particular the kings of France prior to Louis VI the Bruiser (1106-1137) had to accept defiance by their great vassals to avoid the worse consequences of defeat at their hands.

In theory, incidents of vassals defying their lords were not supposed to occur in the feudal system because of the power of the oath that a vassal took in the ceremony of homage. In homage, a new vassal placed his hands in the lord's hands and swore fealty, which was defined as loyalty and service. The feudal oath was regarded as being as binding as the marriage vows of the era. Yet such an attitude did not prevent numerous violations of fealty. A new vassal doing homage was either the eldest surviving son of a deceased vassal or a knight whose service the lord was ready to reward with a vacant fief. Early feudalism was not strictly hereditary, but by around the year 1000 it had become so. The concept of primogeniture was by then well entrenched: in order to prevent the diminution of the family's status, the eldest son inherited the father's entire fief. In the case of the petty knight, the division of his small holdings among several sons would render each incapable of providing service as a knight. Among the great nobles, however, it was not unusual for the younger sons to receive some part of the patrimony.

Since the purpose of granting a fief was to provide fighting men, a daughter could not hold a fief, although warrior women were not all that rare, especially in the early Middle Ages. In the early period a family that had only daughters might well have dropped from noble status, but by about 1100 it had become possible for a daughter to pass on a fief to her husband or, more rarely, a son. The search for a wealthy heiress to wed became an important part of the activities of young nobles. The lord, however, had the right to reject the choice of a spouse for his vassals or their heirs and heiresses in order to prevent an enemy from gaining control of part of his lands. Unfortunately for France, Louis VII was not strong enough to enforce his right when in 1152 Henry Plantagenet, future duke of Normandy and king of England, married the greatest of the medieval heiresses, Eleanor of Aquitaine.

If a dead vassal left as heir a son who was too young to provide military service, or an unmarried daughter, the lord provided a guardian who could serve. Usually it was the child's mother's brother, since he had no possible claim to the fief and thus was likely to protect his nephew's or niece's interest. A paternal uncle did have a claim to such an inheritance, and it was expected that he would try to defraud the child. If a vassal died with no direct heirs or if he was stripped of the fief for breaking his oath, the fief reverted back to the lord in escheat. The lord had the obligation to give it out again, but could grant it to any knight he wished, often his own younger son.

TRAINING AND EQUIPPING A KNIGHT

The predominant consideration in granting a fief was gaining a warrior who could provide military service. Consequently all the sons of a nobleman (with the exception of those few who entered monasteries as boys) had to be trained to fight; the younger sons had to be prepared to take over the family fief if the first son died before or soon after the father. The younger sons, despite being trained as knights, often were placed in high offices of the Church, for which their training gave them little preparation. Small wonder that many wound up in combat providing their own service for the Church's lands.

At about the age of six a noble's son was sent to the court of a great noble to begin training. He learned about weapons and horses and engaged in rough play with fellow pages to toughen his body. As was said about the sons of Henry II of England:

They strove to outdo the others in handling weapons. They realized that without practice the art of war did not come naturally when it was needed. No athlete can fight tenaciously who has never received any blows: he must see his blood flow and hear his teeth crack under the fist of his adversary, and when he is thrown to the ground he must fight on with all his might and not lose courage. The oftener he falls, the more determinedly he must spring to his feet again. Anyone who can do that can engage in battle confidently.[1]

At about age fifteen, the page became a squire and was assigned to a specific knight to help him with his equipment and horses. He accompanied the knight to the battlefield as an aide, bringing him fresh horses and new weapons and helping him off the battlefield if severely wounded. The squires were not obliged to fight, but they often did, especially as they approached their twenty-first year, the age of manhood. A squire who fought well was knighted after the battle by the ranking noble. In the later Middle Ages, especially in England, the ceremony of knighting became much more elaborate and took place in church, but the practice of dubbing after a battle never disappeared completely.

Dubbing sanctioned the young man to fight as a knight. The term knight is used in English to identify a mounted, armored warrior of the Middle Ages, who was expected to fight according to a well-defined code of conduct.   Both the German equivalent, *ritter*, and the French, *chevalier*, came from terms for rider and demonstrate clearly the essence of the concept. Knight, however, came from a Germanic word for youth, and the German cognitive *knecht* was used for low-born sergeants. The English use of the word may well have reflected the social divisions in England after the Norman Conquest: Anglo-Saxons served as knechts to the Norman nobles; and as the Normans were assimilated into English society, the Anglo-Saxon word became used for the mounted warrior.

The right to fight as a knight was the essential feature of nobility. To be noble was to have the right to fight as a knight, and to fight as a knight conferred nobility. It was a blood right conferred on a small portion of the population. The social theory of feudal Europe declared that accession by lower-class men to knighthood was impossible. One had to be born noble to fight as a knight. Nonetheless, because of the high mortality rate from war, accident, and disease, the number of nobles in a region sometimes fell below what was regarded as necessary to defend it, and commoners were promoted into the nobility to fill the ranks.

To fight as a knight meant to fight in armor and on horseback, although it was not a breach of status for a knight to dismount and fight on foot. For a knight to appear without his armor was described as being naked. When reading the chronicles and epics one must not immediately assume that a knight who is said to have fought naked had no clothes on, but that he more probably had been caught without his armor. The type of armor in use from around 950 to 1300 was still chain mail. The knee-length mail shirt was called the hauberk. Mail leggings and arm coverings were in common use, and by 1200 a new type of helm known as the *bascinet* had replaced the simple metal cap with a nose guard. The bascinet added a moveable visor and mouth guard that was often sharply pointed outward. It usually included a long collar of mail to protect the neck.

By the twelfth century the knights wore wool hoods under their helmets and a heavy cloth tunic or surcoat over their armor. The latter may have been a result of the Crusades, intended to keep the desert sun off of the armor, which must have come close to broiling the man inside, or perhaps to keep the armor dry in the wet climate of western Europe. Regardless of its original purpose, the surcoat quickly became a place to display heraldic devices. They were used for identification, especially after the practice of ransom became common, since the rank of a captured knight was the major consideration in deciding whether to hold him for ransom. Heralds, noncombatant observers of a battle, also depended upon heraldry to determine who had done what great deeds in the battle.

The typical shield carried by a knight had to do double duty against lance and sword—strong enough to withstand the shock of all but the best-placed lance blow, while light enough to be moved freely to parry sword blades. Arrows were not much of a worry in western Europe until the improvement of the crossbow after 1200, although the crusaders certainly had to be concerned with them. The variety of shields was vast, but the most common type was somewhat cylindrical, with a straight top and a pointed bottom to protect the knees. When fighting on foot some knights would drive their shields into the ground so as to have both hands free for their weapons. A typical lance as determined largely from contemporary illustrations, was about nine feet long; the dearth of authenticated models from before 1200 makes determination of its weight impossible. The illustrations do make it clear that a lance driven into a foe by the combined weight of man, horse, and armor could pierce shield, armor, and man.

The sword, however, was the favorite weapon of the knight. He lavished his pride and affection on it, probably because a sword was both more personal and more permanent than a lance. Swords frequently had names and were handed down from generation to generation. The broad sword of the twelfth century was about thirty-five inches in length with a one-handed hilt, used for slashing or hacking, not thrusting. Swords were gradually lengthened in the course of the Middle Ages, so that by 1500 they had reached fifty inches and were two-handed.

As expensive as all of a knight's accoutrements were, his horses put the greatest burden on his finances. Chargers were very expensive, and a knight usually had three. For example, the best chargers of the count of Flanders in 1101 cost 300 French pounds, about the annual income of an average manor. Less well-off nobles obviously had to settle for less expensive horses; and as horses began to carry armor after 1200, another expense was added. It was true, however, that a king or great noble often paid his vassals for horses killed in a campaign. Plunder and the ransom collected from wealthy captives were a knight's best hope of making a profit from his military service, but some kings paid a small sum for service beyond or outside of the feudal obligation, usually about enough to cover a man's ordinary daily expenses while on campaign.

FIGHTING STYLE OF THE KNIGHT

Trained from childhood to fight, sitting astride his great charger, and encased in his armor, a knight was a formidable warrior. His mettle was well demonstrated in the Crusades, when small forces took on and often defeated vastly larger forces of Turkish horse archers, excellent fighters in their own right. The knight has a reputation—well cultivated by his contemporaries as well as modern writers—for a love of fighting and bloodshed, a disdain for personal injury, and a fear of being branded a coward. These led him to extraordinary feats of courage on the battlefield or, in the minds of more prudent men, acts of stupidity. War was both the occupation and the pastime of the knights, and they calculated their worth largely by how much and how well they fought. The epics and romances supported that view with their descriptions of the ideal knight as one who "thinks of nothing but breaking heads and arms."

The view of history one gets from the medieval epics is about the same as that of the American West garnered from novels and movies—a kernel of truth but little more. It is clear from other sources that fear of death or maiming was very much present among the knights. A chronicler who was present at a battle during the Sixth Crusade wrote that the knights herded together like sheep in a sheepfold. A solution to this apparent paradox requires recognizing the fact that because of their long training, code of honor, and glorification of fighting, an army of knights had a higher proportion than most forces in history of what are sometimes called "berserkers": men whose headlong dashes into battle force their companions also to fight, lest they be accused of cowardice. In addition the bravado of the knights was vastly increased by the coats of steel in which they were encased. The armor made them all but invincible against any foe man for man except other knights.

Such considerations help to explain the general absence of discipline in medieval armies. Muslim and Byzantine observers were astonished at the lack of discipline in the crusader forces; yet the crusaders were usually more under control than knights fighting in their homelands. Perhaps the Germanic tradition of having the most respected warrior lead the army into battle was reflected in the competition among knights to be the first into the fray, and their frequent refusal to wait for the army to execute its elementary tactics before clashing with the foe.

These characteristics have led some historians to assert that medieval armies made no use of tactics beyond the simple frontal assault. Certainly the descriptions of many battles seem to bear this out. Nonetheless recent research has shown that medieval commanders often did have at least a rudimentary grasp of tactics, even if the impetuous nature of their troops often made it difficult to execute any tactical maneuvers. Compounding the problem was the nature of the feudal system, which brought together forces that spent no time in drilling together. Yet there were a number of military manuals during this era. The legacy of Greek and Roman warfare was known largely through Vegetius' *Military Institutions*, which was read by such eminent captains as Richard the Lionheart and Philip Augustus. The fourteenth-century poetess Christine de Pisan recommended that the wives of barons read Vegetius in order to be prepared to defend their properties in the absence of their husbands. After 1200 there were numerous vernacular translations of the work, and an even larger number of commentaries on it. A number of more original texts on the art of war also appeared in this era. Their influence, however, is hard to assess. Certainly the chroniclers' descriptions of battles seem to reveal little evidence of their impact.

When the call for war went out from the king or great noble, the petty knight gathered his equipment, his horses, foodstuffs to last several weeks, and one or two strong young peasants of his manor to drive the cart and serve as footsoldiers and sergeants; all assembled at a place chosen by the lord. Typically some twelve to twenty knights assembled under a lord's banner, creating a unit called the *conroi* or banner, commanded by the lord. Several conrois or about 100 knights assembled under the banner of a greater lord, who usually was a baron. This larger unit was called a battle. A battle with its some 100 knights, a number of mounted squires, and accompanying footsoldiers was a formidable force duing much of the Middle Ages. Consequently barons were men of considerable power and independence, especially since they usually could afford to build stone castles once they came into vogue after 1050. Depending on the nature of the war, whether it was a local or a national conflict, anywhere from about 100 to 3,000 knights assembled under the banner of the highest ranking lord who had declared war.

KNIGHTLY TACTICS

On the battlefield the knights generally formed up in their conrois, packed together around the banner of their lord. Other conrois formed up alongside, creating a long line. If the army was large enough, the line would be two or three ranks deep. The more formidable the foe, the more closely packed the knights were, leading to statements that a glove or an apple thrown among them would not have fallen to the ground, or that the wind could not blow through the lances. The usual tactic was a charge at the enemy. If the army was large, rarely would the whole line charge at once, but rather section by section, usually beginning from the right. The horsemen would begin moving slowly forward and pick up speed until they struck the enemy line at full gallop. The goal of the charge was to achieve a breakthrough—to splinter the enemy's line and expose his units to piecemeal destruction. Unless the two armies were badly disproportionate in size or fighting quality, a breakthrough was not likely to be achieved. Instead the battle would develop into a mêlée, the "mixing-up" where hand-to-hand combat prevailed. It was common for a commander to pull his men back after a failed charge or even out of the mêlée to rest and reform for a new charge.

Feigned retreat was a tactic used fairly often, according to the chronicles. It is easy to see how it would be effective when used by knights against resolute but slow-moving infantry, but it is less clear why it should have worked against other cavalry. The pursuing horsemen presumably would have been close behind the lines of the army attempting a feigned retreat, making it very difficult for it to turn, re-form, and charge again. Perhaps what the chronicles relate was in fact the flight of a beaten army that was given the opportunity to reform and return to the fight by the failure of the enemy to pursue vigorously or in good order. The chroniclers would be inclined to credit the move to a planned tactic rather than admit that noble knights had lost their courage even briefly.

Before the Crusades there is little evidence of efforts to use a reserve or attempt to outflank an enemy, perhaps because the small size of most forces made such tactics unfeasible. After fighting the Turkish light cavalry in the Crusades, whose principal tactic was to try to outflank an opponent, western commanders showed greater appreciation of the importance of flanks and a reserve.

Effective use of tactics requires discipline among the troops. The major reason why both tactics and discipline were largely absent from medieval armies was that the knights did not drill or train together, except for occasional tournaments once they became popular after 1100. Further complicating the task of the commander to get his men to fight as a unit were the bitter rivalries that often raged between men who were expected to fight together. Acutely suspicious of each other and perhaps more eager to fight one another than the designated foe, rivals often refused to cooperate. This was truly a problem if they were major vassals of the commander and lords of a large proportion of the army. A further reason for the absence of tactics was that the detachment of a group of knights to strike at the flanks or rear of an enemy sometimes was taken as flight by their comrades in the main body, who proceeded to flee themselves.

The absence of drill, the inability to use more than the most rudimentary tactics, and the lack of effective battlefield communications combined to make the banner of the commander the key to the fate of a medieval army. The banner was attached to a lance and held high overhead. As long as it was flying, the knights were expected to continue to fight. Once it had fallen, they were free to flee on the grounds that the battle was lost. The knight who held the banner was forbidden from using the lance to which it was tied, lest his comrades take the dropping of the banner as a sign of defeat and flee. Commanders often carried a second standard to replace one taken by the enemy so as to keep their men fighting.

In the era from around 900 to 1100 most knights were early on introduced to battle and gained vast experience in the many petty wars that permeated the early feudal period. Many of those wars are referred to as private warfare, because they were not sanctioned by royal or ducal authority. The ability of minor lords to raise bands of a few dozen knights from among their vassals and families ensured that quarrels would turn to bloodshed. Long-term feuds between families, or sometimes within families, committed generation after generation to constant war, albeit on a small scale. Both churchmen and rulers opposed private war as a waste of good manpower that could be put to better use, protecting the realm or fighting the infidel, but it did provide western rulers with a cadre of battle-hardened veterans.

The atmosphere of assassination, ambush, and general thuggery that pervaded private warfare produced warriors who were tough, bloodthirsty, and slow to show mercy. Captured and wounded foes were quickly slaughtered after a battle, but the concept of ransom provided some opportunity, at least for the wealthier knights, to save their lives in defeat. The use of ransom, never entirely absent from early medieval society, grew largely as a consequence of the permeation of Christian values into European society, and a growing sense of brotherhood among the knights, fostered by eleventh-century epics, the chansons de geste. It was also encouraged by a growing appreciation of the wealth that could be gained by capturing a great noble and holding him for ransom. As the wealthier nobles came to appreciate how ransom reduced their chances of being killed, they also encouraged the practice. By around 1100 the code of conduct for knights recognized the right of ransom and called for the sparing of the lives of captured knights. The same code came to dictate that a knight only engaged in fair fights against other knights capable of defending themselves. To kill a fallen enemy who could not defend himself was a violation of the code, although the principle did not extend to a dismounted knight still capable of fighting on foot.

MEDIEVAL INFANTRY

The task of killing fallen knights not worth ransoming or badly wounded fell to the sergeants and valets, knifewielders whose low-born status allowed them to do the dirty work not permitted to the nobles. When they found themselves caught up in a mêlée, they were free to flee to safety, but they could expect no quarter from the foe if caught. The presence of sergeants, some mounted, some on foot, at virtually every military encounter of the Middle Ages reveals that commoners were a part of the military system, albeit usually not a very important part. Not only sergeants but true infantry units were a regular part of medieval armies. For example, the majority of the army that Louis VI of France raised in 1124 was infantry.

Although mercenary infantrymen were found throughout the Middle Ages, often the infantry was a mass of hastily conscripted peasants with no training or military bearing. Their weapons frequently were sharpened agricultural implements like hoes and sickles. Peasant archers would have had some effect against the mailed cavalrymen of the early Middle Ages, but continental nobles were inherently opposed to placing a weapon like that in the hands of their serfs. Peasant archers would have also been effective competitors in hunting large game, which the nobles reserved for themselves as their favorite pastime besides fighting.

When infantry units appeared on the medieval battlefield, the commanders of the era had little idea of how to use them, and, of course, the infantrymen had even less an idea of tactics and discipline. The infantry was usually used to open a battle, to do what they could to inflict injury on the enemy or at least disorder his lines. The knights despised the foot, and many could not bear the affront to their honor to see the low-born soldiers open the battle. It was not unusual for knights to ride over their own infantry in their haste to rush the foe. Even when such knightly behavior did not disrupt the efforts of the footmen, they had little value, since foot soldiers, by the fact of their low birth, were expected to flee as soon as the fighting began. This was frequently a self-fulfilling prophecy. After 1100, however, with the growth of towns and cities, urban militias, often using crossbows or pikes, began to provide a more reliable infantry. The experience of the Crusades also showed the value of an effective infantry.

THE BATTLE OF HASTINGS

It is necessary to note that some areas of western Europe always remained strongholds of infantry forces—in particular Scotland, Wales, and Switzerland. The last large region to make the transition to cavalry was England. The Anglo-Saxons had retained many of the practices of the Germanic tribes. All free men of the nation—the *fyrd*— were expected to take arms in defense of their region, fighting on foot with spears and battle-axes. The heavy ax in common use was too heavy to be wielded effectively from horseback; that may be the principal reason why the Anglo-Saxons did not make the transition to cavalry. Yet it is clear that many rode to the battles, especially the thanes, the warriors par excellence of Anglo-Saxon society, who were rewarded with landholdings. A smaller group of elite warriors, the housecarls, were directly associated with the ruler, essentially the Germanic comitatus. As of 1066 thanes and housecarls had steel caps and mail hauberks similar to those of the continental cavalrymen but somewhat old-fashioned in style.

The Anglo-Saxon military record prior to 1066 was mixed. In the ninth century the Danes had conquered northeastern England, but by 950 the Anglo-Saxons had reasserted their control. In the early eleventh century Canute, king of Denmark and Norway, conquered the entire kingdom, but again the Anglo-Saxons threw the Danes out (1042) and reestablished their monarchy. The occupant of the restored Anglo-Saxon throne after 1042 was Edward the Confessor, whose title derived from his pious devotion. It apparently extended to refusing to have intercourse with his wife; at any rate he died childless in early 1066. Three men claimed the throne: the leading Anglo-Saxon nobleman, Harold Godwin; Canute's successor in Norway, King Harald; and Duke William of Normandy, whose great-aunt was Edward's mother. When the assembly of Anglo-Saxon nobles chose Harold Godwin as king, the other two claimants both declared their intentions of taking the kingdom by force. The Viking tradition was still largely intact in Norway, and Harald had little difficulty raising an army and a fleet to invade England. Hearing that Harald had landed on the northeast coast, Harold rushed northward and defeated and killed him.

Three days after that battle, William's army landed on the south coast. It consisted largely of adventurers, since most of his Norman vassals refused to serve on the grounds that their feudal obligation did not extend to fighting overseas. Younger sons of Norman nobles and footloose knights from across western and northern France, eager for their own fiefs, formed the core of the army of about 7,000 men. It included a large contingent of archers and some heavy infantry, as Viking traditions had not yet completely disappeared from Normandy. But it had been about a century since Normans in any number had been to sea; William's achievement in assembling a large enough fleet must be recognized. Also it must be noted that the king of France at the time was a minor and in no position to lead an attack on Normandy while William was abroad. In different circumstances William probably would not have dared to leave his duchy.

Having been informed of the Norman landing, Harold rushed south-ward with his thanes and housecarls. Although his men were tired, he de-cided to confront William immediately instead of drawing the Normans into the interior, where the Anglo-Saxons presumably would have had a greater advantage. Perhaps the medieval attitude that a challenge de-manded an immediate response is as good an explanation for Harold's de-cision as is possible. It has also been suggested that the devastation of the land around Hastings forced Harold to respond immmediately or lose the loyalty of his followers. His army was about the same size as William's or slightly larger. He established his forces in a broad formation on top of a hill barely a mile from the beach. The town of Hastings was actually nine miles away. The hill had fairly steep slopes on the flanks and woods to the rear, well chosen for an infantry force confronting cavalry. The Anglo-Saxon army was not divided into divisions, nor did it have a reserve. Everyone had essentially the same weapons and fought in the same man-ner. It has been called the last truly homogeneous army to be involved in a major battle in Europe.

The Norman army had three divisions—Norman in the center, French on the left, and Breton on the right. William attacked with a broad front and revealed a grasp of tactics unusual for his era: he used the threefold battle sequence of missile (arrow) barrage, infantry shock assault, and ca-valry shock assault, with the cavalry expected to complete the victory. The Bayeux Tapestry, a contemporary Norman depiction of the battle, shows that the archers were quite effective, but the shock infantry, perhaps lacking sufficient manpower, made little impact. The cavalry then charged, but as was usually true in history, it failed to break the resolute infantry lines. The horsemen retreated to rest and re-form, while the archers again stepped forward. This pattern was repeated several times from late morning to early evening. The Anglo-Saxons stood on the defensive the entire battle. Harold made no effort to attack the Normans and drive them off. Only once did any Anglo-Saxons move forward: part of the left wing pursued William's right after one of its charges, only to be cut off by Normans coming over from the center and destroyed.

As twilight fell, the Normans executed what contemporary sources de-scribed as a feigned retreat, which drew many of the Anglo-Saxons out of their lines. They turned on the now disordered Anglo-Saxon infantry and crushed it, killing Harold in the process, probably after he had been shot in the eye. Some military historians reject the possibility of a feigned re-treat on William's part, preferring to see it as the last of several Norman charges followed by withdrawals. This time, they say, many Anglo-Saxons, probably badly drained by the ordeal of taking charge after charge for nearly eight hours, lost their discipline and dashed down the hill after the enemy. There is no hint that Harold had ordered an attack; in fact there is no evidence that he gave any orders at all after the battle began. It has been suggested that the Anglo-Saxon host at Hastings was too large for a commander on foot, as Harold was, to be effective.

Anglo-Saxon losses, as heavy as they were, should not have prevented them from waging an ultimately successful war of attrition against William.

It was the loss of their leaders—Harold and his two brothers—that explains the lack of continued resistance. William moved on to London, where he had himself crowned king by right of inheritance. Those who had fought against him at Hastings were deprived of their lands for violation of feudal obedience, and the lands were distributed as fiefs to William's knights. Several Anglo-Saxon revolts over the next ten years gave William a pretext to seize the lands of most of the remaining Anglo-Saxon nobles. England was turned into a thoroughly feudal society with a largely Norman nobility. Heavy cavalry became the principal arm of the English military, although the tradition of a strong peasant infantry did not die out as completely as it had in France.

After the Battle of Hastings the armored knight dominated the battlefields of western Europe for 250 years. The arrogance that such domination bred in the knights would eventually lead to humiliating defeats at the hands of infantrymen; but in the decades after Hastings, the élan, pride, and sense of invincibility bred in the knights enabled them to accomplish a great deal, especially the great victories of the First crusade.

NOTE

1. Roger of Hoveden, *Chronica*; quoted by J. F. Verbruggen *The Art of Warfare in Western Europe during the Middle Ages* (Amsterdam, 1977), p. 29.

8

Holy War in the Middle East

"Let those," [Pope Urban II] said, " who are accustomed to wage private war wastefully even against Believers, go forth against the Infidels in a battle worthy to be undertaken now and to be finished in victory. Now, let those, who until recently existed as plunderers, be soldiers of Christ; now, let those, who formerly contended against brothers and relations, rightly fight barbarians; now, let those, who recently were hired for a few pieces of silver, win their eternal reward. Let those, who wearied themselves to the detriment of body and soul, labor for a twofold honor. Nay, the sorrowful here will be glad there, the poor here will be rich there, and the enemies of the Lord here will be His friends there....When winter has ended and spring has come, let them enter the crossroads courageously with the Lord going on before."

Fulcher of Chartres, quoted in Edward Peters, *The First Crusade* (Philadelphia, 1971), p. 31. Urban II called for the crusade at Clermont, France in 1095. Fulcher was a chaplain for one of the leaders of the First Crusade.

While western Europe was coping with the last barbarian invasions and petty feudal wars, the states of the Middle East were engaged in protracted warfare at a much higher level in respect to the size of the armies involved and the tactics employed. The Byzantine Empire continued to stand at the center of affairs, as it had to deal with periodic attacks from the Arabs, the Bulgars, the Slavs, and, after the year 1000, the Seljuk Turks.

After the failure of the Arab attack on Constantinople in 718, the Byzantine army drove the Muslims out of most of Asia Minor in the course of several campaigns and established a fairly stable frontier in the east. Yet there remained a state of permanent war, since Islamic belief demanded that the Byzantine Empire submit to Islam; but the attacks were sporadic and only occasionally pushed much beyond the frontier provinces. The attacks did not prevent a significant economic relationship between Arabs and Byzantines from developing, and truces of varying duration were signed. A permanent peace, however, was impossible. The heart of the

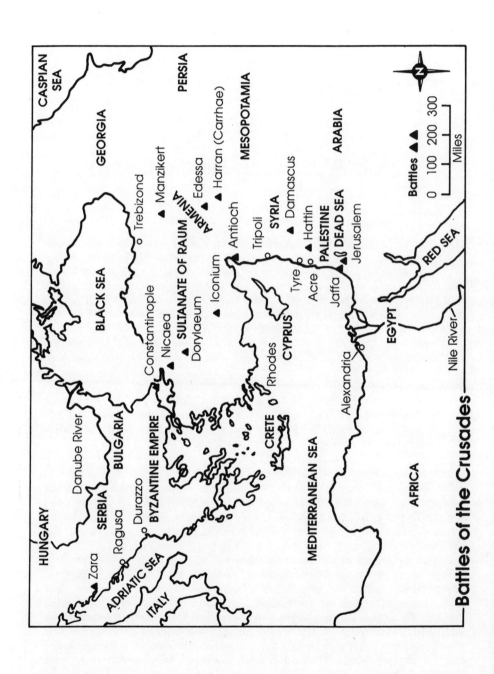

Battles of the Crusades

Empire was little affected during the attacks; the last Arab attack that reached western Asia Minor occurred in 838. Thus the Byzantine economy remained prosperous and the military strong.

The high level of Byzantine military theory was demonstrated in the *Tactica* of Emperor Leo VI. It was heavily dependent on Maurice's *Strategikon* of 400 years earlier, it is true; but the *Tactica* reveals a keen sense of the importance of using cavalry and infantry in support of each other, and shock and missile weapons in combination. The work further shows that the Byzantine tactics had not changed a great deal in the three centuries since Maurice.

In the wars with the Arabs, the Byzantine emperors had recognized early on the need for a permanent force in the frontier provinces. They created a military-political division that became known as a *theme*, from a Greek word for a detachment of troops. Land was given to soldiers, many of whom had been withdrawn from provinces lost to the Arabs, so that they could support themselves yet be ready to defend their region. The structure of the original six frontier themes was expanded to all of Asia Minor and, because of Bulgar attacks, to the Balkans. By the year 900, there were thirty-one themes, including three naval themes along the southwest coast of Asia Minor to raise men for the navy.

CHANGES IN THE BYZANTINE ARMY

With the creation of a force permanently located in one place, almost a militia, the nature of the Byzantine military changed. Except for the 20,000-man force at Constantinople and the imperial guard, which were largely foreign in origins, the troops were natives, mostly small landholders commanded by the great landowners of the theme. The first purpose of these forces was to man the numerous forts that protected the invasion routes, which in eastern Asia Minor were obvious. Their second function was to come to the relief of besieged forts, and the third was to prevent an enemy army from foraging on Byzantine territory. They were not very adept at preventing large armies from striking into the interior of Asia Minor. Thus on several occasions prior to 840 large Arab forces drove into western Asia Minor before being forced to withdraw. On those occasions the emperor struck back at the Muslims with a large army gathered from the themes one by one as the army moved eastward.

The commander of a theme was the *strategos*; appointed by the emperor, he was provincial governor as well as military commander. A frontier theme had greater manpower than the others. Determining the manpower available to a strategos, however, is made almost impossible by the Byzantine practice of having varying numbers of men in the units so that an enemy could not easily determine the size of the force he faced. The split between cavalry and infantry among the 6,000 to 12,000 men in a theme was about half and half. Because of the speed with which they could be assembled and their mobility, the horsemen were the usual force called upon when an invader breached the frontier. The infantry usually served as garrison forces. Since most cataphracti still carried the bow as well as the lance, they had less need for supporting infantry. The infantrymen were of two types: archers, who were the majority, and heavy infantrymen with lances, swords, and axes. Men of the same regiments wore the same color surcoats for easy identification in battle.

Byzantine generals were usually willing to force invaders to withdraw across the frontier rather than destroy them. They were not as eager for battle as most commanders in history have been. They relied on a wide network of spies and agents to inform on impending attacks and to spread dissension in the enemy's ranks. When an unexpected attack did occur, a system of beacons at the top of mountains spread the news quickly. The men of one or two themes would be assembled in the hope that a show of force would convince the invaders to withdraw. A strategos prided himself if he succeeded in avoiding a battle, for conservation of men and resources was his primary goal.

If a strategos was forced to give battle, he took the attitude that a series of coordinated blows against the enemy would yield victory, and that the last blow should be decisive, rather than having the maximum shock occur at first contact. Many battles were fought entirely without infantry, in which case the cataphracti used their bows to soften up the enemy before charging with shock weapons. A full-fledged Byzantine army of equal cavalry and infantry placed the infantry in two lines in the center, with cavalry at the flanks and in the reserve. When the infantry was pushed back, as often happened, the cavalry was in good position to execute an envelopment. Byzantine generals also liked to hold a large force in reserve to send in when a battle was in the balance. A sharp blow during the battle, especially from an unexpected direction, was often enough to bring victory to the Byzantines.

This emphasis on sophisticated tactics, unique to the time, required professional officers and soldiers. The officers, mostly from the nobility, worked their way up the chain of command, unlike the the situation in the West, where family status often placed a youth in command of a large force. The soldiers were drilled and trained in a manner unknown elsewhere. A view of warfare as a science was also emphasized by the military manuals of several emperors.

By the year 900 the Arab threat had subsided somewhat, and the Byzantine Empire could go on the offensive against them occasionally. The Byzantine military was distracted, however, by the rise of the Bulgar empire as a major power in the Balkans. In 912 the Bulgars even put Constantinople under siege, but like so many other attacks on the city, that effort was futile. The Byzantine Empire then reached its highest point since Justinian under Basil II the "Bulgar-Slayer" (985-1025). In 1011 he routed the Bulgar army and, according to legend, blinded the 10,000 captives except for one out of every ten, who were left one eye to guide the rest home. The Bulgar emperor was said to have died of shock at the sight. All of the Balkans returned to Byzantine control, and Armenia, Crete, and Cyprus were recovered. Basil also reinforced his control over southern Italy, where Muslim, Lombard, Norman, and French adventurers were seeking a foothold.

In domestic politics, Basil turned his attention to a long-term trend that was threatening the Byzantine military. Over the centuries, the high military-political officers had steadily increased their landholdings and influence. Their power had reached the point that they could make and unmake emperors. Faced by revolts by strategoi early in his reign, Basil tried to reverse the trend, which was impoverishing the lesser land holders and peasants and undermining both the tax base and military recruiting. He declared most of the more recent acquisitions illegal and forced the high aristocracy to disgorge their gains. Basil was secure enough to ignore the resulting complaints, but his successors were not. The process resumed and accelerated after his death, cutting deeply into the domestic sources of manpower. The Empire had to return to its extensive use of mercenaries.

The most famous mercenaries of this era were the Varangians—Swedes and other Norsemen who had settled in Russia. Basil II himself owed his throne to the 6,000 Varangians that his new ally Prince Vladimir of Kiev sent him during his struggle with a rival general. The Byzantines regarded them so highly that they were organized into the Varangian Guard of the emperor. Eventually other Europeans were recruited, including hundreds of Anglo-Saxons after 1066. In 1081 the Anglo-Saxons of the Guard would face the Normans another time in southern Italy. Despite the same courageous and resolute fighting as at Hastings, they were again defeated, and southern Italy slipped out of Byzantine control.

THE SELJUK TURKS

More ominously, a new threat appeared in the Middle East. The Seljuk Turks were another nomadic people out of the vast reservoir of tribes in central Asia. The word Turk is used for a member of the large linguistic family that dominated central Asia after 600. The Turks increasingly came under Arab-Muslim influence. In 751 the Arabs had defeated the Chinese in the great Battle of Talas east of the Aral Sea—the westernmost point the Chinese have ever engaged in war. With Muslim influence now dominant in the region between the Aral Sea and the Hindu Kush Mountains, the Turks were drawn into the Muslim world.

The response of the Turks to Muslim civilization was similar to that of the Germans to Rome. First the Turks began to give up their primitive religion for the more sophisticated Islam. Then they began to enter the military service of the caliphs, settling their families in Muslim lands much like the German foederati. The Turks were horse archers with a barbarian warrior ethic, and they found the Islamic concept of the Jihad attractive. Soon they began to replace the Arabs in the Muslim military, who had largely settled down by 900 and had lost much of their earlier enthusiasm for war. As a larger proportion of the Abbasid Empire's army became Turkish, Turks emerged as generals and caliphmakers. In particular a group of Turks known as the Seljuks gained power and influence. In 1055 at Baghdad their leader was proclaimed sultan ("one who has authority") of the Arab Empire, although the office of caliph remained for several more centuries. From Mesopotamia the Turks pushed on to Palestine and Syria, and up against the Byzantine Empire.

The great Seljuk sultan Alp Arslan encouraged the holy war against the infidel Christians as much to divert his warriors from despoiling their new homelands as to expand his empire. After 1060 the Turks began to raid the Byzantine frontier, which had been largely free of Muslim raids since Basil II. War bands of Turks roamed quite freely through eastern Asia Minor, in large part because the reduction in the Byzantine recruiting base had left the frontier posts undermanned. In 1071 a new emperor, Romanus IV, who had just won a power struggle for the throne but whose enemies were still strong, decided to lead a full-scale expedition against the Turks. His immediate goal was to recover the fortress of Manzikert in Armenia, but perhaps more important to him was the need to establish himself in the eyes of the people as the rightful ruler by a great victory.

The best account of the battle places the size of Romanus' army at 60,000 men. The number of Turks they faced is unknown, but all the Byzantine sources were certain that the Turks badly outnumbered the Byzantine army. Leo VI had given explicit and very intelligent advice on how to deal with armies of horse archers: be aware of ambushes, do not fight with uncovered flanks or rear, and do not allow the units of the army to become separated. Only partly through his own fault, Romanus failed in all three areas.

Romanus' forces appear to have been entirely cavalry, probably because he felt he needed mobility to deal with the Turkish horse archers. The Battle of Manzikert began in a fashion typical for nomad warriors: swarms of Turks hovered along the front of their foe, probing for a weak point and seeking an opportunity to turn the flanks. Romanus ordered his army to move forward to drive the Turks away, but in the absence of a natural obstacle to force them to stand and fight, they simply moved out of range with the Byzantines in pursuit. At sunset after spending nearly the entire day in pursuit, the emperor ordered a return to camp. The disorder caused by the army turning around gave the Turks the opportunity to attack again. Romanus ordered his men to turn again and face them. The reserve, whose task it was to protect the rear, failed to stop, either because of the treachery of its commander, a supporter of Romanus' rival, or simply because he failed to receive the order. The main body was caught in an open field without protection, either natural or human, for the flanks and rear. The Turks immediately recognized their opportunity and turned the flanks. In growing darkness the Byzantine army was destroyed, and the emperor himself captured.

The loss of most of the army at Manzikert was compounded by the conflict over a successor to Romanus, who was deposed because of his captivity. When Alp Arslan allowed Romanus to be ransomed four years later, his return home increased the civil strife. Thus little effort was made to prevent the Turks from overrunning Asia Minor. By 1080 they had reached the Sea of Marmara. The Empire had lost its best recruiting grounds, especially the frontier provinces of Isauria and Armenia, which had been on the front line of the war with Islam. The empire's problems were compounded by a revolt of the Bulgars and the Norman attack on southern Italy. With little left of the empire except Constantinople itself, it was forced to recruit foreign mercenaries in large numbers, even hiring some Turks. A battle that a general named Alexius Comnenus fought against a rival in 1079 involved entirely mercenaries on both sides, including a body of French knights. Impressed by the fighting caliber of these men and the Normans in Italy, Alexius decided to recruit westerners once he had won the throne. Determined to recover Asia Minor, he sent a request in 1094 to Pope Urban II for 8,000 to 10,000 mercenary lancers to augment his forces.

THE CHRISTIAN RESPONSE

Frightened by the Muslim victories over the Byzantine Empire and enraged by the barriers the Turks had placed against pilgrimages to the Holy Land (the Arabs had rarely interfered with Christian pilgrims), western leaders were ready to respond. Even before 1094 western Christians were on the offensive against Islam. In Spain the petty Christian kingdoms on the south slope of the Pyrenees took advantage of the collapse of the Umayyad caliphate there to push southward, capturing the great city of Toledo in 1085. In Muslim-ruled Sicily Norman adventurers began to arrive in 1040 and succeeded in conquering the island by 1091. Not only were the Muslims driven out of Sicily and Sardenia, but also the new Italian fleets of Genoa and Pisa were raiding North Africa. The entry of the Italians into the struggle for control of the Mediterranean was a significant factor in the Crusades. Another element was the chanson de geste, in which the Germanic warrior ethic was given a Christian gloss in its ideal of fighting for the Holy Faith. The *Song of Roland*, with its tale of Charlemagne's war against the Moors, was popular well before 1094.

Pope Urban's motives in turning the Byzantine request for mercenaries into a holy war against Islam seem obvious enough. He wanted to direct the martial energies of the western nobles away from killing each other in petty feudal quarrels and against the infidels. The request was also seen as an opportunity for the pope to assert his leadership in Christendom. Accordingly Urban traveled to central France in 1095 and preached the call for a great military expedition against the Muslims to end the disgrace of their occupation of the Holy Lands. The pope proclaimed it a holy war. Although his promise that those who died in it would go to heaven was theologically more hedged than that of Islam, most who heard it took it literally. They shouted "God wills it!" and put a red cross on their surcoats, becoming crusaders, from the Latin word for cross.

THE FIRST CRUSADE

Urban was aware that winning his goal required plenty of good fighting men, and that the Turks would not be vanquished simply with faith and enthusiasm. He labored to pull together a powerful army of the best troops of western Europe. His careful planning did much to overcome the inherent weaknesses of armies of that era, especially the knights' unwillingness to obey commanders. No king was involved in the First Crusade, but there was a large number of great nobles including Robert, duke of Normandy;

Godfrey de Bouillon, duke of Lower Lorraine; and Bohemond de Hauteville, a leader of the Normans in south Italy.

In 1096 the crusaders began to move eastward. The recent conversion
of the Magyars to Christianity opened the Danube to the crusaders. Other
routes were down Italy across the Adriatic to Durazzo (in modern Albania), or down the east coast of the Adriatic to Durazzo, and then on to
Constantinople. All met there in early 1097. Emperor Alexius was
shocked at what had arrived: a rowdy mass of perhaps as many as 10,000
knights and 20,000 support troops, as well as a large number of servants
and, surprisingly, women and children. His daughter Anna Comnena
provided in her memoirs a long description of the powerful bodies and
uncouth manners of the barbarian Franks (as all westerners were called by
the peoples of the Middle East) and the awe they inspired in the people of
Constantinople.

Alexius was eager to get the Franks out of his territory because of their
atrocious behavior— they plundered their hosts and even burned a suburb
of Constantinople. He and the crusader leaders agreed to combine forces
to attack Nicaea, which the Turks had established as the capital of the
sultanate of Raum (Rome). After the assassination of Alp Arslan in 1072,
the unity of the Turkish state had disappeared. The sultanate of Raum and
several other splinter states contended for control of the Middle East along
with an Arab dynasty in Egypt.

Thus the situation was favorable for the Franco-Byzantine assault on
Nicaea in May 1097. The fact that the first battle of the crusaders against
the Turks was for a position the Turks had to defend was a great advantage
for the Europeans. It forced the Turks to stand and fight rather than using
their usual tactics. The crusaders were given a taste of the Turkish style
of fighting without facing them at their best advantage in the open plains.
Fighting alongside the Byzantines also enabled the crusaders to pick up
information about the Turks. Nicaea fell after a month's siege. Complaining that they had not been allowed to plunder the city, the Franks
then left for Palestine. The emperor was upset that they did not remain
with his forces to drive the Turks out of Asia Minor, but the impetus from
the taking of Nicaea, along with the damage the crusaders did to the Turks
as they moved eastward, enabled the Byzantines to reclaim western Asia
Minor.

The Franks marched southeast from Nicaea in two columns on two
routes. According to one source it was because of distrust among the
leaders; according to another, because of the lack of enough forage for the
full army on either route. Regardless of which was correct, both explana-
tions point up major problems for the crusaders. As they moved eastward,
the two columns did not keep in contact with each other. Thus when the
division led by Bohemond de Hauteville was attacked by a large Turkish
force near Dorylaeum about 100 miles southeast of Nicaea, its leaders had
no idea where the other column was. Leaving his infantry to defend the
baggage train, Bohemond used his knights to face the foe. The Turks
fought in their usual manner, since the battle took place on an open field.
Recognizing that charging the horse archers would accomplish nothing,

Bohemond tried to keep his line intact; but groups of frustrated knights charged on their own. The Turks easily avoided such charges, and, as the knights returned to their lines, cut down many of them. After five hours of such action, the crusaders, losing manpower and morale, were herded into a tight mass, while the Turks, growing bolder, drew in close to engage in hand-to-hand combat.

When all seemed lost, the lead elements of the other column appeared over a hill. Although few in number, they charged into the rear of the Turks, who had massed for a final assault. The Turks were taken completely by surprise; apparently they had not known of the second column. When Bohemond's knights rallied and charged, the Turks were routed. Although crusader losses were reported as larger than the Turkish, the Battle of Dorylaeum was the only major effort of the Turks to impede the crusaders' march to Antioch. The battle demonstrated that the knights' armor was effective protection against Turkish arrows at medium range, but they also found that their horses were highly vulnerable to the arrows and fatigue.

THE CRUSADERS IN THE MIDDLE EAST

After suffering greatly on the march because of the heat, the desolate countryside, and poisoned wells, the crusaders reached Antioch in late October 1097. Contact with Christian Armenians in the mountains north of Antioch allowed them to resupply, and they settled into a siege of the well-defended city. A Turkish relief army, variously reported to be 12,000 to 24,000 men, arrived in February 1098. The Europeans showed that they had learned something from their previous battles. They prepared to meet the larger Turkish army in a narrow defile with a lake along one side. The Turks could form only a narrow front in that terrain. The crusaders reportedly had only 700 knights for the battle because of a lack of horses, but their charge was enough to throw the forward ranks of the Turks back into the main body. In the cramped space, the knights had the clear advantage in the mêlée that followed. By the time the Turks could break free to escape, they had suffered some 2,000 casualties versus almost none for the Franks.

With this defeat, morale in the garrison in Antioch dropped disastrously. In June, Bohemond bribed the captain of a tower to surrender it to him. As the first leader to enter the city, he claimed the right to rule it, a claim accepted by the crusaders but one that ignored the rights of the Byzantine Empire over the city. Bohemond's high-handed act did much to poison relations between the emperor and the crusaders. They had hardly secured the city when a huge Turkish army appeared from Mesopotamia. Since the city had already been stripped of supplies, the Franks had no choice but to give battle. Their morale was given an enormous lift when a commoner in the army declared that a dream had revealed to him the location of the lance that had pierced Christ's side at the Crucifixion. A rusty spear point was discovered under the altar of an ancient church, and the crusaders proclaimed that this was God's sign of their ultimate victory. They made ready to take on the Turks with enthusiasm. This event demonstrates much about medieval armies, where signs and portents had more to do with inspiring men to fight than did their commanders. The Sacred Lance would serve as the rallying point of the crusaders until the end of the Crusades.

The Franks had captured enough horses that they could put over 1,000 knights into the field. Many still were left unhorsed, so it was decided to make use of them as infantry, integrating them into the common foot soldiers to stiffen their resolve. Since it was decided to put the infantry in the front, special care was taken to organize it and make it into an effective force. A large part of the foot were archers; the Frank captains must have already noticed their effectiveness against the horse archers. The Franks were numerous enough to fill the entire space between a mountain and a river. So again the usual Turkish tactics were not effective. Opening the battle, the Christian foot archers were reported to have done a great deal of injury to the Turks. A charge by the knights drove the Turks back to their camp; a second charge cleared them off the field.

By that time the crusaders had developed the tactics that would serve them well in combat with the Islamic peoples: fight on a narrow field with natural obstacles on both flanks; use footsoldiers, especially archers, to keep the enemy off the heavy cavalry until the moment was right for a charge by the knights; and do not extend the pursuit of the fleeing horse archers very far, for they could easily turn and destroy disordered pursuers. The Turks, it must be said, did not make good use in these early battles of their most effective tactic, the feigned retreat, which was well suited to take advantage of the rashness of the Europeans. When Turkish commanders used the feigned retreat later in the crusader era, the Franks seem to have forgotten the hard-earned lessons of their predecessors. Ironically, had the Muslims chosen to fight as heavy cavalry in hand-to-hand combat against the western knights, they would have had the advantage of better weapons and armor. The Arabs had picked up from India a technique of making higher quality steel than that available in the West, called Damascus steel.

After the victories at Antioch, the crusaders pushed on to Jerusalem against little resistance, while a group under Baldwin of Lorraine continued eastward to take the key city of Edessa in northern Mesopotamia. They were aided by a sense of invincibility created by their victories and by the divisions among the Muslims, some of whom hoped to use the invaders to their advantage in their political struggles. In early June 1099, they reached the Holy City and put it under siege. Aided by the "miraculous" discovery of a cache of lumber that enabled them to build siege machines, the Franks successfully assaulted the walls on July 15. There immediately followed the infamous massacre of the city's Muslim and Jewish inhabitants. Carried out, it seems, largely by the commoner soldiers, the number of victims may have reached 40,000. As the massacre was going on, the leaders of the Crusade marched to the Church of the Holy Sepulcher, where they were reported as weeping in joy at their victory over the forces of evil.

THE CRUSADER KINGDOM OF JERUSALEM

With Jerusalem in Christian hands, many crusaders returned home to the accolades of all. The knights who remained elected Godfrey de Bouillon as their monarch. He modestly took the title of Defender of the Holy Sepulcher. Palestine and crusader-controlled regions of Syria and Lebanon were divided into fiefs, although much of Palestine had yet to be conquered. Historians studying feudalism look to the Latin Kingdom of Jerusalem, as the crusader state is termed, for the ideal feudal system as it was perceived to be in 1100, since feudalism was imposed entirely from above onto virgin territory.

Within a month after the capture of Jerusalem, the Franks had to defend it against the Arab caliph of Egypt, but his army, mostly lightly armored lancers, was no match for the knights. The victory gave them southern Palestine, and for a short time the westerners were secure in their possessions. About 1,000 knights and perhaps 5,000 foot soldiers held the several crusader states against their far more numerous enemies. They did have the support of the local Christians, especially the Armenians, in the northern regions controlled by the Franks.

Control of the ports of Acre and Tyre gave the crusaders easy access to the sea, where they were able to receive supplies and reinforcements carried mostly by Italian ships. Italians, Byzantines, and Muslims vied for control of the eastern Mediterranean in this era. Despite the fear of the sea felt by most medieval people, it was the safest way to go to the Middle East. The dangers of the land route were made manifest in trials of a large group of reinforcements who left from Constantinople in 1101. Caught by a large Turkish force in north-central Asia Minor, they were all but wiped out in what may have been the greatest battle of the Crusades. Certainly it was the longest, as it lasted three days. The major result of the affair was that the few survivors blamed Emperor Alexius and the guides he provided for the disaster, embittering further the bad feelings between Byzantines and Franks.

Despite the failure of the "Crusade of 1101," enough reinforcements made it to the crusader states to replace earlier losses. As the Franks settled into their new lands, some brought their European wives to their fiefs; others married local women, often Armenian. A large proportion, however, never married, which made it difficult to build a self-sustaining force of occupation. Many of the crusaders were men with a strong streak of asceticism who saw themselves as Christ's warriors, and were little concerned with personal pleasures except for fighting the infidel.

The presence of a large number of such men explains the creation of two great military orders—the Knights of the Hospital of St. John (Hospitalers) and the Knights of the Holy Temple (Templars). Both were created originally for the purpose of protecting Christian pilgrims in the Holy Land, but quickly they became bands of military elites, true "knights of God" who were to fight only for the purest of motives. What is unique about them is that they were monks as well as knights, men who combined in their persons knightly valor and monastic vows of poverty, chastity and obedience. The rules of the two military orders were strict, and the members pledged absolute obedience to their grand masters. The discipline thus created is certainly a major reason why they gained such a brilliant reputation as military men.

Both orders were divided into three classes: the knights, who were entirely noble by birth, the sergeants, who could be commoners, and the clerks, who were priests and did not fight. The military code of the Templars is in particular very revealing in what it permitted and prohibited to the knights and the sergeants. Among the rules was a prohibition against ransoming any member who fell into enemy hands; a Templer grand master died in Muslim captivity. Each order also had its own uniform, which was unique in the era: the Templars wore a white tunic with a red cross, and the Hospitalers had a black tunic with a white cross.

Consisting, at least early on, of those crusaders who were most fierce in their hatred of the infidel, full of contempt for death, and with least concern for personal gain or comfort, the military orders quickly became the shock troops of the Latin Kingdom of Jerusalem. Small units were dispatched to trouble spots on the frontiers, but their major function eventually was service as garrison troops for the many castles that the crusaders built to secure their lands. Since the orders soon became very wealthy through large and numerous donations, the property that each new member signed over upon entering, and the large proportion of plunder they received for their services, they built many castles from their own substantial treasuries. The Hospitalers, for example, built and manned the famous Krak des Chevaliers in Syria.

At their largest the Hospitalers numbered few more than 500 knights and the Templars 300. The formidable nature of the knights, however, made that number a powerful force for the defense of the Holy Land, and their presence had much to do with the long duration of crusader strongholds against great odds. The Hospitalers remained more loyal to their original ideals and so escaped the storm of controversy that destroyed the Templars in 1314. Later known as the Knights of Rhodes and then the Knights of Malta, the Hospitalers carried the crusading spirit well into the modern period.

The story of the military orders and the crusader states is one of never-ending war. The career of King Baldwin II of Jerusalem (1118-1131) has been described as being one grand chanson de geste: constant fighting against enormous odds, and great deeds of personal courage. As long as the Franks paid attention to the lessons of 1097-99, the weight of their cavalry charge usually would carry the day. But as early as 1104 a Frankish force ignored those lessons and was routed. Count Baldwin of Edessa attacked the city of Haran to the east. In the course of the siege, a Turkish relief army attacked Baldwin's force and then retreated into an open plain. The crusaders pursued it until their horses were exhausted. The Muslims turned and caught the Franks in the open. No more than half of the Franks escaped. Ironically, the site of the battle was virtually the same as for the Battle of Carrhae, where a Roman army was destroyed in much the same way in 53 B.C.

THE TURKISH RESURGENCE

The crusader state of Edessa survived this disaster, but it was the most isolated Frankish position. When the Turks finally began to unite against the invaders, Edessa could not be held; it fell in 1144. The loss of any land held by the crusaders was regarded as an insult to the Holy Faith, and so a new crusade was launched. In 1147 the Holy Roman Emperor Conrad III and Louis VII of France led two large forces to the East in what is known as the Second Crusade. Both divisions suffered severe losses in the trek through Asia Minor. When they reached Frankish territory with greatly diminished forces, they were persuaded to attack Damascus, the major Muslim city of Syria, rather than retake Edessa. Damascus was far too large to be invested by the small crusader army. After several weeks camped outside the walls on one side of the city and several more on the other side, both monarchs gave up and went home.

The failure of the Second Crusade allowed the Muslims to hasten the pace of their chipping away at the crusader states. Even more significant, however, was the emergence of the great Saladin as the commander of the Muslim forces. Chivalrous and brilliant, Saladin came closer to being the ideal knight than any of his European foes, including the famous Richard the Lionheart. By 1186 he had become ruler of both Egypt and Syria, and was ready to wage full-scale war on the Franks in Palestine.

In early 1187, Saladin led a large army across the northeastern frontier of the Latin Kingdom, and laid siege to Tiberius, a crusader stronghold on the Sea of Galilee. King Guy of Jerusalem gathered every available fighting man from his kingdom and the county of Tripoli, leaving his garrisons badly undermanned. He collected a force of about 1,200 knights, an equal number of light cavalry that had learned how to fight in the manner of the Turks, and a vast number of foot soldiers — one source says 18,000. The army, which included most of the Templars and Hospitalers, gathered in a well-watered, narrow valley eighteen miles west of Tiberius. Ignoring the excellent advice that he wait for Saladin there, King Guy decided that knightly honor required that he go to the relief of Tiberius. The crusaders marched toward Tiberius through terrain always difficult, but now made worse by the destruction of forage and water supplies by the Turks.

About halfway there, the Franks were confronted with the forward units of the enemy, which cost them time and casualties. Only three miles from the Sea of Galilee, they halted for the night, as Guy did not want to risk a late evening battle with the main Muslim force between him and the sea. They spent a miserable night, without water, harassed by Turkish archers, and with eyes burning from the grass fires lit by the enemy. At daybreak the Franks were hardly in condition to fight; yet they had to, in order to reach water. Their infantry, however, refused to leave the momentary security of a high hill; so the cavalry alone moved onto the open plain that bordered the sea. There it was easy game for Saladin's forces.

After this Battle of the Horns of Hattin, the Muslims were surprised to find few of the Christian knights had been killed or seriously injured; their armor had protected them well. They were simply exhausted; more seriously, their horses were too. The infantry, however, was slaughtered where it stood. Saladin treated most of the knights generously, allowing them to be ransomed, including King Guy; but he ordered the execution of all captured Templars and Hospitalers, the uncompromising enemies of his religion. With nearly all manpower of the Latin Kingdom dead or captured, Saladin easily overran Palestine. Jerusalem surrendered after a twelve-day siege. Because the count of Tripoli and his men who had formed the vanguard had been able to fight their way through the Turkish lines, Tripoli and Tyre remained in Frankish hands, as did Antioch, whose leaders had not been involved.

THE THIRD CRUSADE

The loss of Jerusalem revived the sagging enthusiasm for crusading in Europe. The three great rulers of western Christendom of the time — Emperor Frederick I Barbarossa, King Philip II Augustus of France, and the Anglo-Norman monarch, Richard I the Lionheart — agreed to take the cross. Barbarossa's large German army marched first, in early 1189. It took the overland route to Constantinople and through Asia Minor. The sultanate of Raum, still in control of central and eastern Asia Minor, was a formidable foe, but the emperor demonstrated his capacity as a commander by beating off attack after attack and storming the sultan's capital, Iconium. The enormity of the loss the crusaders suffered when Frederick drowned in a stream in southeast Asia Minor can hardly be calculated. His army pushed on to Antioch, but many returned home from there without any further fighting.

The other two crusading monarçhs were slower to get organized. They sailed from Sicily in early 1191. Richard stopped en route in Cyprus and responded to a slight to his honor on the part of the Byzantine governor by conquering the island. In the next several decades Cyprus passed through several hands until it was taken over by the Venetians. In mid 1191, Philip and Richard reached Acre, a Muslim stronghold, which had been under siege already for two years. King Guy, whom Saladin had allowed to be ransomed, had gathered the scattered crusaders from across the Middle East and had attacked Acre. Since it was on the coast, the crusaders were easily supplied and reinforced from the sea. They dug themselves in around the city, and several attempts by Saladin to relieve Acre failed. The arrival of the two kings convinced its garrison to surrender. King Philip, ill and eager to make trouble back home for his rival Richard, returned to France, although much of his army stayed in Palestine.

Richard was now supreme commander. His march to Jerusalem was clearly the greatest feat of his career. The best route was south along the coastline to Jaffa, and then due east. Following the coast allowed the crusaders to be supplied from the sea, and the shoreline covered one flank of the marching army, which was harassed all the way by Saladin's army. Moving very slowly to prevent his forces from tiring or getting strung out, Richard put the knights of the military orders in the rear. They kept up an incessant running battle with the Turks, who hoped to catch the crusaders from the rear. On the landward side of the main body, Richard placed half of his infantry to repulse attacks. The other half served as porters, since the army lacked pack animals, walked along the water's edge. Several times a day the two divisions exchanged tasks and positions.

Richard knew that he had to confront Saladin before he turned inland, when his army would be much more vulnerable. Whether by design, as most of the sources imply, or not, Richard loosened the tight formation that he had kept for 100 miles while under constant harassment. Saladin sent his forces rushing in. The infantry on the landward flank, which included a large number of Italian crossbowmen, brought down many Turkish horsemen. When the Muslims had closed in, the knights suddenly charged, catching them by surprise. Knowing that they were at a deadly disadvantage in close combat with the armored Christians, they broke and fled. Richard's control over his forces enabled him to keep them from pursuing the Turks too far. This Battle of Arsuf broke the morale of Saladin's army, and Richard easily took Jaffa and marched on to Jerusalem.

However, Richard's army was constantly being reduced by casualties, desertion, and the need to garrison captured forts. By the time he reached Jerusalem, he lacked the manpower to assault it. So he arranged a truce with Saladin that gave the crusaders control of a coastal strip from Tyre to Jaffa and allowed Christians free access to the holy places. In October 1192, Richard left Palestine, returning through the Balkans. In Austria he was captured and held for ransom by agents of the Holy Roman Emperor, his enemy. Although he was ransomed two years later, his captivity, which was contrary to the guarantees provided to crusaders, badly damaged the image of the Crusades.

THE FOURTH CRUSADE

The Fourth Crusade dealt further damage to the Crusading ideal. The election of Pope Innocent III in 1198 put a man on the papal throne who was determined to recover the Holy Land. The rulers of Europe were distracted by their own affairs, so the new crusade was led by French nobles. The unsettled conditions in the Balkans convinced the crusaders to meet at Venice to take ship for Egypt, from whence they would march to Palestine. At Venice they found that they did not have enough money to pay for their transportation. The Venetians had always regarded the Crusades as a business enterprise, not a religious undertaking; and they demanded enormous sums from the crusaders. They told the crusade leaders that they could finance their voyage by capturing the city of Zara, midway down the east coast of the Adriatic, for Venice. Zara had been under Venetian rule until 1186, when it revolted.

In October 1202, the crusaders sailed on Venetian ships to Zara and took it after a two-week siege. Pope Innocent, informed of the project as the ships sailed from Venice, excommunicated the crusaders for attacking a Christian city. Their leaders were little concerned, however, since they now had a new project. In 1195, a palace revolt in the Byzantine Empire had overthrown Isaac II and put his brother Alexius III on the throne. In 1202, just before the crusaders sailed for Zara, Isaac's son Alexius arrived at Venice with an intriguing proposition: if they restored Isaac to his throne, he would provide money to pay off their debt to Venice, 10,000 troops for one year in Palestine, and 500 men to garrison Jerusalem. He also pledged that the Eastern Church would accept the supremacy of the pope. The offer was too attractive to pass up. In April 1203, the crusaders sailed from Zara to Constantinople in Venetian ships. Alexius III had done little to prepare the city for an assault; he expected the great walls to hold off the small crusader force. There seems to have been considerable popular support for Isaac in the city, or at least an uneasy feeling among the defenders that they were fighting for a usurper. That is the only explanation for the ease with which the few westerners captured the city.

In early July the Venetian fleet landed the crusaders on the opposite bank of the Golden Horn, where they captured the tower that anchored one side of the great boom across the waterway. They then moved inland to assault the city's great landward walls, while the Venetians fought their way into the Horn and assaulted the wall on its shore. Led by their ninety-one-year-old doge (duke), and using long ladders that swung from the ships to the tops of the walls, the Venetians captured twenty-five towers on the seaward wall. Alexius III lost his nerve and fled the city. Isaac was restored to the throne, and his son declared co-emperor. However, they could not raise the money pledged to the crusaders, who refused to leave without it. Thus the crusaders spent the winter in a suburb of Constantinople, while friction between Latins and Greeks grew apace.

The Byzantines took out their anger on Isaac and Alexius, deposing them for a new emperor who repudiated all of the pledges to the crusaders. In reply, the Franks attacked the city again in early April 1204. Using the Venetian fleet they assaulted the wall along the Golden Horn, still damaged from the previous year's attack. The defenders fought with greater zeal than the year before, but after three days of assaults they lost control of a gate to the westerners. A day's fighting inside the wall put Constantinople in the crusaders' control. They proceeded to plunder and rape mercilessly. Later Byzantine writers would contrast the generosity of Saladin upon his capture of Jerusalem in 1187 with the rapacious behavior of the Franks.

The new political dispensation in the Byzantine Empire most favored Venice. Venice got the lion's share of the plunder, complete control of Byzantine commerce, and numerous islands and seaports across the Empire, Crete being the most significant. Venetian gains in 1204 turned what was already a major political and economic power into a great one. Six of the twelve electors of the new Byzantine emperor were Venetian, as the victors set about turning the Empire into a feudal state, known as the Latin Empire of Constantinople. Baldwin of Flanders was chosen emperor. The Franks, however, could not move fast enough to win control of all of the empire. Large areas in Asia Minor remained in Greek hands under local rulers. In particular, the Comnenus family ruled the city of Nicaea. It served as a base from which the Byzantines retook Constantinople in 1261, during the absence of the Venetian fleet.

By 1261 the crusading spirit was all but extinguished. Two more expeditions large enough to be called Crusades had failed to achieve anything, while the Seventh Crsuade, led by Louis IX (St. Louis) of France, in 1270 had yet to run its futile course. The Crusades were ultimately failures. The Muslims eventually recovered all of the Middle East, while the damage done to the Byzantine Empire by the Fourth surely made its eventual fall in 1453 a great deal more certain. But the Crsuades did have some noteworthy consequences, although the long span of time over which they occurred makes definitive statements impossible, since many of the changes might have taken place anyway.

Although thousands of knights and sergeants had fought in the Middle East and returned home, they did little to change European military techniques, despite their contact with the far more sophisticated military systems there. A greater appreciation of battle maneuvers, especially outflanking an enemy, developed; but it is also true that many of the battles of the later Middle Ages showed no evidence of such tactics. The infantry, especially bowmen, appear to have gained some respect from commanders at least. Improvements in armor and weapon making have been traced from the East. The most obvious military impact of the Crusades, however, was in fortification building. As will be examined in the next chapter, the westerners learned a great deal both in design and in construction techniques in the Middle East and used the information back home.

Lastly, the Crusades had a major impact strategically. They blunted the power of the Seljuk Turks at a time when the Byzantine Empire appears to have been very vulnerable. While the Fourth Crusade did enormous damage to the empire, the First Crusade may well have been the reason why it survived to 1204 and beyond. The Crusades were a key factor in keeping the Turks out of eastern Europe for another three centuries.

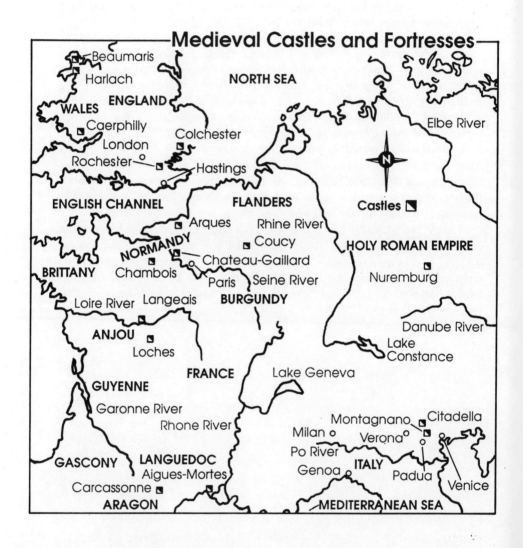

Medieval Castles and Fortresses

Beaumaris
Harlach
NORTH SEA
ENGLAND
Elbe River
WALES
Caerphilly
Colchester
London
Rochester
Hastings
ENGLISH CHANNEL
FLANDERS
Castles
Arques
Rhine River
Coucy
NORMANDY
HOLY ROMAN EMPIRE
Chateau-Gaillard
BRITTANY
Chambois
Paris
Seine River
Nuremburg
Langeais
BURGUNDY
Danube River
ANJOU
Lake
Constance
Loches
FRANCE
Lake Geneva
GUYENNE
Garonne River
Montagnano
Citadella
Rhone River
Milan
Verona
Po River
ITALY
GASCONY
LANGUEDOC
Genoa
Padua
Aigues-Mortes
Venice
Carcassonne
ARAGON
MEDITERRANEAN SEA

9

Castles and Siegecraft

The king of France [Philip II] turned his attention to the construction of machines and rockthrowers, suitable for attacks and which he determined to ply night and day, and he had one of superior quality, to which they gave the name of "Bad Neighbor." The Turks also had one they called "Bad Kinsman," which by its violent casts, often broke "Bad Neighbor" in pieces; but the king rebuilt it, until by constant blows, he broke down part of the principal city wall. There was one rockthrower, erected at common expense, which they called the "petraria of God." Near it, there constantly preached a priest, who collected money to restore it and to hire persons to bring stones for casting. By means of this engine, a part of the tower Maledictum was at length shaken down. In addition to these two, King Richard had constructed two others of choice workmanship, which would strike a place at an incalculable distance. These engines were plied day and night, and it is well known that a stone sent from one of them killed twelve men with its blow. Such stones and flinty pieces of rock, nothing could withstand; but they either shattered into pieces the object they struck or ground it to powder.

    Geoffrey de Vinsauf, "Chronicle of Richard the First's Crusade," in *Chronicles of the Crusades* (London, 1848; reprint New York, 1969), pp. 205-06. Vinsauf was describing the siege of Acre in 1191 during the Third Crusade.

By the fourth century A.D., the level of Roman expertise in fort building had declined significantly. The technical skills required for building quality forts had essentially disappeared from western Europe by 500. The highly durable character of numerous Roman fortifications did permit many of them to be used well into the Middle Ages, and to serve as models long after.

    The disappearance of ancient skills in masonry and fort design meant that timber and earth piled in simple structures were the materials for most fortifications of the early Middle Ages, although old Roman walls were occasionally kept in good repair or quarried for stone and brick. For the most part, early medieval fortifications regressed in technical skill to the era prior to the Greeks.

In the Carolingian era, towns and the buildings of large estates were usually encircled by a ditch. Dirt from the ditch was thrown up on the inside bank, and a palisade of timbers erected on top of that bank. Called burg in Germany and burh in England, these works afforded some protection against small bands of invaders, although they rarely were capable of withstanding a siege of any sort. Siege machines were very rare, because of the loss of knowledge of how to build them and the lack of sufficient iron. As the only places of any refuge in a region, these towns became bases for wandering merchants, and the small garrisons created something of a local market. The burg or burh's role as the foundations of numerous cities is made abundantly clear in the number of German cities that end in "burg," and the use of "borough" (boro) in England.

MOTTE-AND-BAILEY CASTLES

During the barbarian invasions of the ninth century, more effective defenses had to be found, and the motte-and-bailey castle began to appear in the tenth century. The word castle came from the Latin *castellum*, "fortress"; in the Middle Ages it took on the meaning of a well-defended residence of a powerful man. The motte was an earthen mound built as high as forty feet from dirt thrown out of the ditch that had been dug around it. Generally cone-shaped, with a flat space at the crown as wide as sixty feet in diameter, the motte was often placed on a natural high point to give it even more command of the area. The bailey was a space enclosed by a wooden palisade that encircled the crown of the motte; the word also became used for a second palisade often constructed around the base of the motte. A wooden tower (called a keep or donjon) was erected at the crown of the motte. Access to the top of the motte was limited to a bridge that could be easily pulled up in case of an attack.

Relatively easy and inexpensive to build, motte-and-bailey castles were built in vast numbers in western Europe after 950. Their builders ranged from kings and dukes, who used them to protect the frontiers of their domains, to lesser nobles, who built them not only to provide protection for their families and serfs but also to gain freedom of action in regard to their feudal lords. Control over the building of private castles became a crucial factor in the extent to which feudal lords dominated their vassals. In Normandy, for example, Duke William prohibited anyone from digging a ditch deeper than the depth from which a man could throw a shovel of dirt by hand. In the county of Anjou, Count Fulk Nerra (987-1040), the "Great Builder" to his contemporaries, appears to have had a conscious strategy of building castles to control his vassals, protect his frontiers, and use as bases from which to invade his neighbors. His castle of Langeais, begun about 994, may have been the first fortress to have a stone donjon.

The absence of castles in the area of Hastings or on the road to London made the Norman task of occupying England a great deal easier. Immediately upon landing, William erected a prefabricated wooden castle that he had ordered shipped across the Channel. After his victorious march to

Left: The Norman Keep at Rochester with its circular tower rebuilt a century later. Right: A medieval siege. Note the cat at the bottom, the trebuchet above it, and the belfry above that.

London, he ordered the Norman nobles to build castles in the fiefs he gave them. The purpose was to dominate the Anglo-Saxons, whose sullen defiance of their conquerors erupted into several small revolts. The new king himself built castles at a number of key places in his kingdom. It is clear from the Domesday Book of 1086 that all but a very few of the Norman castles of that time were timber and earth structures.

NORMAN KEEPS IN ENGLAND

A wooden motte-and-bailey castle was very vulnerable to fire, and by the mid-eleventh century, pots of Greek fire (or something similar to it) were being hurled against the wooden structures. The problem was more serious on the continent, since England was quite peaceful for several decades after the last Anglo-Saxon revolts had been crushed. Stone castles thus appeared first in France, where Duke William built the prototype Norman stone castle at Arques about 1040. The Norman castles, however, are better preserved in England, largely because the island setting exposed them to less war and destruction, and thus there was less need to rebuild them according to new designs.

With vast amounts of cheap Anglo-Saxon labor available, the Norman lords of England found it inexpensive to use stone as a primary building material. The building of romanesque churches had created a corps of skilled stonemasons capable of constructing large stone structures. The masons easily moved back and forth between military and church projects. The heavy weight of a stone keep erected on an artificial motte usually caused the ground to settle unevenly, which cracked the structure. Consequently, stone castles were typically built on stone outcroppings, or at least on level ground.

The earliest known examples of the Norman stone keep in England are the Tower of London and the Castle of Colchester in Essex. In 1078 William decided that the wooden castle in London did not provide him sufficient protection against "the vast and fierce populace." The site chosen for a new structure was in one corner of the old Roman wall that had defended London. The new keep, called the White Tower because it was kept whitewashed, included all of the buildings that would have been enclosed within the bailey in a motte-and-bailey castle. In the basement was a great storeroom and the all-important well. The only windows were a few narrow slits, to prevent an enemy from crawling in. On the first floor were the quarters for the garrison, with more but equally narrow windows. The second floor was the king's quarters, containing a great hall, royal chamber, and a chapel that extended up two stories and had large windows at the top. The keep was ninety feet high, and its interior area was sixty by eighty feet. Because of the width of the building, a thick wall bisected it and served as a spine for the floor joists. This created a further defensive position within the keep. The base of the exterior walls was fifteen feet thick, tapering to ten feet at the top. The building material was coarse stone mixed generously with mortar. The stones were kept quite small, so that chipping or boring would not dislodge a large part of the wall at one time.

The castle at Colchester, of which only the first floor remains, was built largely of brick quarried from the local Roman fort. Its foundations are larger than those of the Tower of London, and medieval descriptions suggest that it was higher as well. Both keeps were surrounded by a wall and a ditch that enclosed considerable space, which probably filled quickly with wooden buildings.

The great keep at Rochester was erected somewhat later, about 1127. Built to control the road between London and the sea, it stood about 114 feet high and was 70 feet square. It withstood several sieges, including one during the Puritan Revolution of the seventeenth century, when cannon were unsuccessfully directed against it. In 1215, however, when King John attacked it while it was held by rebels, he undermined one corner and opened a breach. A round tower at the corner was built to restore the keep.

The entrances to these square keeps were at the second floor level; access was gained over a wooden bridge or ramp, which was easily removed at the threat of attack. The arrangement, however, meant that the garrison was capable only of passive defense; a sortie outside the keep was all but impossible. The narrow windows and tapering walls made it very difficult for defenders to direct missiles directly to the base of the wall. Thus the best method of assault was to destroy or undermine the base of a wall, especially at a corner. This was done under the shelter of a portable roofed structure, generally referred to as the "cat," which gave protection to the men working at the wall. The thick walls were essentially invulnerable to the siege engines of the time. Long passive sieges were usually futile, because the small garrisons required to defend these keeps used up their vast stores very slowly and used little water from their wells..

The square keeps were, however, very expensive, and often could not be built at many strategic locations because of the nature of the ground at the sites. Norman barons then turned to another design —the shell keep. This was a high, circular or polygonal structure that enclosed a considerable space, often the crown of a motte. Within the open space of the shell keep were wooden buildings. The shell keep rarely had the massive walls of a square keep. It appeared after 1100, when the wooden castles thrown up immediately after 1066 had begun to fall into disrepair. The shell keep's lighter construction made it possible to place one on an old motte with less fear of destructive settling. The shell keeps were circular not only because they crowned the motte but also because the corners of square keeps left dangerous blind spots where enemy sappers could work virtually unchecked. Because the wall of a shell keep was not very thick, a stone wall was thrown up around it to increase the cost of assaulting it. The early shell-keep castles were essentially motte-and-bailey castles wrought in stone. Already by 1150 bailey and city walls were being built with projecting towers, usually round, which provided some positions for flanking fire.

INNOVATIONS IN CASTLE BUILDING

While England had little fear of an invasion in the twelfth century, rebellious barons and royal sons generated plenty of military activity, especially sieges; new castles with innovations in design were continually being built. The returning crusaders brought back new ideas also. One of the earliest innovations to appear was crenellation on the parapet. A crenel was a gap in the masonry through which a defender could discharge a weapon at the enemy below and then step behind a merlon, a raised portion of the wall, for protection. Rochester was perhaps the earliest English castle to have crenellation. It also has holes in the masonry near the top of the walls for the heavy beams used to construct hoarding, although the holes could have been punched through after it had been built. Hoarding (French *hourdis*) was a wooden gallery that was hung outside of the parapet. With its slitted floor, it allowed defenders to shoot arrows, drop stones, or pour boiling liquids directly down on the enemy at the base of the wall, without exposing themselves the way they did leaning over the parapet. But the wooden hoarding was vulnerable to fire or rotting away over time. It was soon replaced by a permanent stone gallery called machicolation, which was built into the walls. The idea probably came from the Middle East, where the lack of timber required more extensive use of stone. The decorative appearance of machicolation, which has become an identifying feature of medieval castles, belies its deadly purpose.

An enemy attacking a shell keep, to say nothing of the more massive walls of a square keep, often directed his attention to the gate, usually the weakest part of the structure. Recognition of this problem led to the creation of the barbicon. Defined as a projecting defensive work in front of a gate, the most common sort of barbicon was made up of two towers set in front of the gate on either side. In castles built after 1200, the gate itself would be flanked by two towers as part of the wall, creating a square of four towers surrounding the gate. A structure was built over the space enclosed by the four towers, and holes were left in the ceiling over the entranceway, appropriately called murder holes, to allow the defenders to rain deadly objects down on anyone in the entranceway.

The entrance was also protected by a drawbridge over the ditch that was dug around most fortresses. A counterweight allowed the drawbridge to be swung up quickly. Massive wooden doors sealed off the gateway, and a portcullis, usually made of iron, was always suspended over the gateway, ready to be dropped at a moment's notice while the doors were being closed. The use of barbicons transformed the gatehouse of a castle into its most secure place, and in the smaller castles, the castellan, the castle's commander, had his apartments there.

Historians tend to concentrate on the Anglo-Norman castles, because their survival allows better analysis of changes in castle design. Castles on the continent that date from before 1200 are far fewer and usually badly damaged. The most spectacular early French keep is the donjon of Loches, begun before 1000 by Fulk Nerra of Anjou. It reached 122 feet in height, but equally unique was that it was entirely faced with cut stone. Thus it looks newer than castles built 200 years later. There was considerable exchange between England and Normandy, but the lack of accurate dating and the destruction of so many castles from that era in Normandy prevents an accurate assessment of the lines of influence.

In Germany, castle building lagged behind; simple motte-and-bailey castles, mostly wooden, were the rule. The independent and wealthy German cities showed greater inspiration in building their walls, particularly in the use of flanking towers. In Italy, old Roman walls were kept in reasonably good repair across much of the peninsula in the early Middle Ages. In the regions controlled by the Byzantine Empire, some improvements along Byzantine lines can be noted.

CRUSADER CASTLES

Byzantine influence is clear in the fortresses built by the crusaders. Most crusaders passed through Constantinople, and the great impression that its fabulous walls made on them was well recorded. Their education was furthered by their sieges of such well-fortified places as Nicaea and Antioch, whose fortifications were entirely Byzantine. The Byzantine method involved building double and triple lines of defense around a central stronghold, with towers at close intervals along the walls for flanking fire.

Poorly supplied with manpower, but well-endowed with financial resources, the Franks set to work building castles to hold their new domains
upon their victory in 1099. From the first their fortresses were closer in
design to Byzantine examples than western ones. Flanking towers were
placed in the curtain walls, and two and three concentric walls, each one
higher than the one outside it, allowed archers to launch a rain of arrows
on the enemy. Machicolation probably was invented in Frankish Palestine. Posterns allowed men to sally out to harass the besiegers and destroy
their equipment. Thus the idea of an active defense was combined with the
most effective passive defense.

The long duration of Frankish rule in the Middle East was largely a
result of the quality of their fortresses, given the very limited manpower
available. The inability of the crusaders to maintain adequate garrisons
even in their key strongholds was a major reason why the Muslims slowly
reduced them one by one over the course of nearly two centuries. A lack
of manpower also prevented the formation of relief armies. A skeleton
force of Knights Hospitaler was sufficient to hold Krak des Chevaliers, the
greatest crusader fortress, for five months in 1271. Only a Turkish ruse
involving a forged letter supposedly from the order's grand master calling
on the knights to surrender gave the Turks the castle.

The Krak remains today a truly impressive fortress, even after heavy
Israeli bombing in recent wars. Located about thirty miles northeast of
Tripoli, it sits on a long narrow spur of a mountain ridge. The site gives
it formidable natural defenses on three sides. At the point commanding the
most accessible approach stood a huge tower, rectangular in shape but
presenting a rounded face to attackers so as to allow projectiles to glance
off. Two massive concentric walls, specially thickened at their bases, with
projecting towers, comprised the main defensive works. Twelve Muslim
assaults on the fortress failed prior to 1271.

The influence of crusader forts began to appear in western Europe in
the mid twelfth century. A clear example is Richard I's great castle,
Château-Gaillard. He was intimately involved in its construction, and he
can be called its chief architect. It was begun in 1196 and was completed
just before his death three years later. Built on a high ridge commanding
the Seine, it was intended to dominate eastern Normandy and protect it
from any French force pushing westward down the river. Its plan con-
centrates the defensive works toward the narrow ridge from which the only
strong assault could come. A great tower formed the apex of a triangular
wall, which an enemy first confronted. Separated from the main structure
by a wide ditch, this outwork can be called the first bastion. Two great
towers at the corners of a somewhat irregularly shaped quadrangle protected the curtain wall facing that ditch, should an enemy take control of
the bastion. At the far end of the bailey or enceinte formed by the main
wall stood a nearly circular wall that was made up of a continuous series
of near-semicircles. Within that wall was the final stronghold, a massive
donjon with masonry machicolation, which was among the first examples
of machicolation to appear in the West. Château-Gaillard was a superior
fortress for its era, and it is intriguing in its anticipation of some key con-

cepts of Renaissance fortification. Yet, as shall be seen, it was taken only five years after it was built.

Even more impressive, although less innovative in design, is the fortified city of Carcassonne in southern France. Sited along a major invasion route across the Pyrenees, the city was attacked by a rebel force based in Spain in 1240. King Louis IX decided to rebuild and strengthen its defenses. Carcassonne has a natural location for a stronghold, high on a hill above a river. The site had been fortified since prehistory. Much of the ancient Roman foundation was used for the reconstruction of the inner wall. Louis' contribution was building a concentric outer wall. At regular intervals both walls had projecting towers; at key points the towers were broader and higher. If an enemy broke through the outer wall, itself a formidable undertaking, he found himself in a cramped space exposed to fire from the inner wall and towers as well as from any towers on the outer wall he had not yet taken. Posterns in the inner wall also threatened attackers with the possibility of a mounted sortie. A covered pathway to the river was guarded by a great barbicon at water's edge, and another where its walls met the outer wall. The defenders would thus still have had access to river water for some time after being invested. Finally, placed at the point of the steepest slope down to the river but within the inner wall, lay the count's castle, itself a first-rate fortress. Unlike Château-Gaillard, Carcassonne was never tested once it was completed, in large part because it was regarded as impregnable.

The single most impressive military structure of the Middle Ages was the great donjon of Coucy, about seventy-five miles northeast of Paris. Built of course on a high hill, the tower rose 180 feet above a small town and the surrounding countryside. It was ninety feet in interior diameter and had walls twenty-four feet thick at the base. The donjon was said to have been able to hold over 1,000 men during a siege. Begun in 1223 and completed in seven years, the tower and the castle it defended were not the property of a king or duke but a family of simple barons, who took advantage of the immunity the donjon offered to defy royal commands for two centuries. The tower, in bad repair but still standing, was blown up in 1918 by retreating German forces because of the excellent artillery observation post it offered the advancing French.

In England the later twelfth century saw a turn away from massive keeps and the introduction of new ideas from the Middle East. Most of the castle building of the thirteenth century took place in Wales, as the English kings Henry III and Edward I struggled to secure control of the region. The narrow, crisscrossing ridges and valleys of Wales required a large number of castles for secure control, yet they could be small because there was little fear that they would be attacked by a large force.

Castles such as Caerphilly, Harlech, and Beaumarais show a number of features in common. The principal one is their concentric design; all have two or three lines of defense. Because they are quite small, there was not room for a keep to serve as the castellan's quarters, which were in the barbicon. That put the commander in the strongest part of the castle and placed him in a forward position to stay aware of the progress of a siege.

These castles, while small, were expensive. Harlech cost 9,000 pounds or nearly a year's income for the monarchy. But a garrison of thirty-seven soldiers defended it against an attack in 1294, making it well worth its cost.

CONTINENTAL CASTLES

Elsewhere in Europe the thirteenth century was one of extensive castle building, which dropped off sharply in the next century. Castle building in Italy reached its peak under Holy Roman Emperor Frederick II (1215-1250); he filled his realms in southern Italy with royal castles after pulling down all those in private hands. His castles are all symmetrical in design. A fine example is Castel del Monte in Apulia, built about 1240. Its plan is that of an octagonal wall; at each of the eight corners of the wall, an octagonal tower the same height as the wall projected outward. Castello Ursino in Sicily, on the other hand, was square with a round tower at each corner and a round tower at the midpoint of each wall.

More typical of Italian fortifications were the urban walls, of which an enormous number were built and many still stand. The town of Montagnano near Verona had to build new walls about 1360 because of the growth of the town. Montagnano has remained within the confines of these walls—it did not face the problem of some cities such as Florence, which outgrew its walls three times. Like most Italian works, brick was the primary building material used at Montagnano. The wall, still in excellent condition, is one and a half miles long, with polygonal towers, about twice the height of the wall, every 250 feet. A space along the interior side of the wall the width of a street was kept clear of obstructions and buildings for the easy movement of men and equipment from tower to tower. The town's two gates were strongly fortified with the tallest towers on the wall. The two most powerful families of the town controlled the gate towers, from which they could monitor all traffic in and out of the town.

Montagnano's walls and towers had "Guelf" merlons, that is, flat topped. Many other towns and castles demonstrated their loyalty to the other great political faction of late medieval Italy by their "Ghibelline" merlons, V-notched, which give so many Italian fortifications their distinctive look. In general Italian works of this era are marked by their deep crenels, elaborate machicolation, and square towers that rise well above the walls.

Late medieval Italy also saw the creation of entirely new towns for military purposes. The urban powers thought in terms of using walled towns rather than castles to extend their control over a region. For example, Padua built the town of Cittadella in 1220 to secure a disputed area. It was laid out in a checkerboard design and was surrounded by a high wall. This plan was common to such new towns, not only in northern Italy but also in eastern Germany, where colonization of Slavic lands was occurring. A fine example in France is Aigue-Mortes, built on the delta of the Rhône by Louis IX as a fortified seaport. Erected in a desolate region with no natural reason to exist, the town has remained virtually unchanged since the thirteenth century.

EARLY SIEGECRAFT

Until the advent of gunpowder weapons, defensive works held the advantage, one so obvious to military leaders that many of the best fortresses went untested. While siege techniques improved from 1000 to 1300, fortification did even more. By 1300 the odds of a strong force successfully forcing a well-built and well-defended fortress were less than they had been three centuries earlier.

As of the year 1000 there were five methods of assaulting a stronghold: setting it afire, scaling the walls (escalade), battering them, undermining them, and starving out the defenders. Once stone had become the common building material, fire lost its capacity to destroy a fortress by itself, although it always remained a useful means of harassing the defenders. The height of stone keeps also reduced the attraction of scaling the walls. A Norman square keep was all but impervious to battering. Thus undermining the walls or starving out the garrison were the usual options left to a besieger after the Norman keep came into vogue.

The best example of the successful mining of a castle was King John's taking of Rochester Castle, held by rebellious barons, in 1215. He ordered his miners to drive a shaft under the southeast corner of the great keep. The shaft was propped up with timbers, filled with straw and the fat from forty pigs, and set afire. After the timbers had burned through and the great heat had cracked the masonry above, the corner of the keep collapsed into the mine. John's troops rushed through the breach, but were halted by the great cross wall present in that kind of keep. The defenders were temporarily safe, and the well was on their side; but they had lost most of their food. Several weeks later the garrison surrendered.

The rebels at Rochester apparently made no effort to sink countermines, the usual way to oppose mining. A common tactic was to tunnel under the enemy's mine and fill the countermine with combustibles. A hole or two would be poked through the floor of the mine above, a fire lit, and the enemy smoked or burned out. Often, however, one of the two opposing groups of miners would cut into the enemy shaft, and a violent battle for control of their underground world would occur, often in darkness.

A passive or nearly passive siege, in which the goal was to starve out the enemy, was commonly used when there was little possibility of a relief army appearing. Such was usually the case in the long war of King Stephen (1135-1154) in England against his rebellious barons. The rebels held numerous castles across the realm, but made no effort to organize an army in the field. Thus Stephen was able to take castle after castle, most of which surrendered after using up their stores. He did make use of siege castles, which were high earthen mounds or wooden towers thrown up a short distance from the walls. The besiegers used them to see what the defenders were up to and to harass them with arrows and other projectiles. But the progress Stephen made in reducing the rebel castles was slow, and much of the realm was still in rebel hands at his death.

The great siege of the Middle Ages in western Europe was the capture of Château-Gaillard by Philip II of France in 1204. In September 1203 the

French army arrived in strength to besiege the castle. King John had reduced its garrison considerably to save money, and he made no effort to relieve it during the six-month siege. Thus it was not really a true test of the fortress. After spending several months clearing the space in front of the castle and filling in ditches, Philip brought up his siege engines in February 1204. They were used to crush the top layer of stone on the great tower and the two adjoining curtain walls. That made it easier for sappers, men who worked to undermine the foundation of a castle, to pull stone away from the walls.

With the tower thus weakened, mining brought it down. The design of the castle was well prepared for such an event, and the garrison pulled back to the middle ward. A small body of French troops succeeded in scaling the wall of the middle ward and crawled through a small window left undefended because of the small size of the garrison. Not realizing how few men had made it inside, the English retreated back to the third line of defense with its great donjon. Philip moved up "the greatest machine ever seen" to smash the facing. Mines then brought down part of the wall of the third ward. With the wall breached, the small English garrison, down to 140 men, could not hold the breach or retreat fast enough to the donjon. The active assault on the fortress itself took five weeks to reach successful completion.

SIEGE MACHINES

The great machine that Philip used in 1204 was called a *perrier* (rock thrower). It is not clear what it was exactly, since the term was used loosely, but it probably was a type recently developed known as a trebuchet. The use of twisted animal hair for artillery seems to have disappeared with the Roman military. The medieval ballista was a simple, giant crossbow that usually shot huge bolts; and the mangonel was a simple catapult. The poorly built versions used in the early Middle Ages were useful in keeping defenders from standing in the open on fortress walls, and for throwing burning objects into the castle, but they lacked the power to do much damage to the structure itself. Nor were they accurate enough to cause damage by striking the same spot repeatedly.

The place and time of the development of the trebuchet (the word perhaps comes from Latin word for wooden beam) are unknown. But since it appeared in western Europe at about the same time as the influence of the crusader castles, it perhaps was developed in the Muslim Middle East. It was constructed from a long beam that pivoted a quarter of the way from one end on two uprights. At the shorter end there was attached a box filled with heavy weights, the number of which could be varied to adjust the distance of the projectile. At the long end a sling was attached in which a heavy stone, fire pot, or other type of projectile was placed. The long end was pulled down and held in place, lifting the short end with the weights high in the air. When the arm was released, the weights pulled the sling upward at great speed, throwing the projectile in a parabola toward the target. A large trebuchet, requiring fifty men to work, could throw a stone of up to 300 pounds as much as 500 feet, a clear improvement over the Roman catapults. Such a monster appears to be what Philip II used against Château-Gaillard. It could do tremendous damage to the masonry of a castle. A trebuchet used during a siege of Toulouse in 1211 was reputed to have knocked down a tower with one stone. Thus the move toward round towers, which allowed most projectiles to deflect off without doing extensive damage. An experienced engine master, after several shots with a machine, could become quite accurate with it.

A problem, however, was finding large stones that did not shatter upon impact, which reduced their destructive work on castle masonry, although the flying pieces of a shattered stone often did considerable injury to the defenders. During the reign of Edward I, the English were reported to have used carved round stone, the precursors to the stone cannon balls of a century later. In 1304 Edward had thirteen trebuchets at a siege, which threw 600 stones against his objective. The trebuchet also was used to throw other objects, such as the corpses of captured enemies, animals, or according to one famous drawing, even horses into the besieged stronghold in hope of spreading disease among the defenders. These machines were very expensive, and generally only monarchs could afford them. Their effectiveness in taking castles thus enhanced royal authority in a way that prefigured the role of cannon.

The new siege engines reduced the importance of the battering ram, but rams continued to be used. A ram, usually made of a single huge tree trunk with an iron cap that was often pointed, was sometimes swung directly by a gang of men; but far more effective was hanging it from a frame and allowing it to swing back and forth freely. Such a ram was protected by a wooden roof covered with raw hides to reduce the threat from burning materials dropped by the defenders. These protective structures for working at the base of a wall, whether they held rams or not, were known by a variety of names, but "cat" was the most common. Rams were most effective against gates and doors, and the development of barbicons and sophisticated gatehouses made them less useful.

Another siege device was the siege tower or belfry. It was built as high as the walls of the stronghold and often made with an iron framework. It also was covered with raw hides to reduce the danger from fire. As it was pushed toward the walls on wheels, or more probably log rollers, bowmen at the top shot at the defenders. When it had been moved close enough, a drawbridge was dropped onto the top of the wall, and dozens of knights and soldiers rushed onto it. A siege tower used at a siege of 1218 was said to have held 400 knights and 150 bowmen. The bow in use was probably the crossbow, which was better as a siege weapon than a field weapon.

SIEGES IN PRACTICE
When a stronghold was put under siege, the attacking army would first try to persuade the defenders to surrender by promising to respect life and property. It was accepted practice that resistance to an attack placed the lives of everyone within, including noncombatants, at the mercy of the enemy commander. He could, and often did, order a massacre of everyone captured after a successful assault. It was universal practice that a captured

town that had resisted was subject to sacking by the victors. If the demand for surrender was refused, the siege began in earnest. It was necessary to fill in the moats before the cats and belfreys could be moved up. The labor required for all of the work to prepare for the assault on the walls was enormous, and archers and engine masters were present in great numbers as well. The goal, however, was to put fighting men inside the walls, and a good number of knights were present to engage in hand-to-hand fighting on the walls or in the breaches.

The besiegers usually outnumbered the defenders by ten to one or more; yet in a well-built castle, a small force could effect a successful resistance under the right circumstances. The first responsibility of a commander of a stronghold, besides making sure his defensive works were in good repair, was to lay in an ample supply of food and water. When an enemy force appeared, unnecessary persons had to be forced to leave and gateways blocked. Around 1200 a typical defense force would include crossbowmen set on the walls and towers and in the arrow loops cut in them. Small siege machines were set on platforms atop towers and walls. When the attackers came in range, they would be met with a rain of arrows and stones. Nonetheless, a determined force using cats for protection had little difficulty in working its way to the base of the walls. Then the defenders, standing on hoarding or machicolation, dropped flaming substances and heavy stones and swung grappling hooks to catch hold of both men and devices. Should mining commence, the defenders had to begin countermining.

By 1200 most strongholds had postern gates through which men, often mounted knights, could sally forth in hope of catching the enemy by surprise and destroy his machines and structures and in general disrupt the siege. Despite the best efforts of the defenders, however, the time often came when the enemy was atop the walls or in breaches. Then desperate, hard fighting was all that could save the castle. On occasion, the attackers were thrown back from their footholds atop the defenses.

No historian has ever calculated the percentage of sieges that resulted in success for the attackers, largely because of the problem of establishing what should be considered a true siege and what should be regarded as success. But there is no question that numerous sieges failed because the resolute defenders wore out the enemy's resources and patience, or a relief army arrived in time. The disproportionate resources needed to take a castle in comparison to defending it, once it had been built of course, was one of the key reasons for the constant rebellions of the nobility that characterized medieval politics. The nobles often could defy their lords with impunity, at least in the short term, behind the walls of their castles. The edge that fortification provided also helps to explain why small states, especially cities, could be major players in European politics and why kings often appear not to have looked beyond their immediate domains, since there was always a nearby castle of a rebellious baron to be reduced. It can be argued that no other era of history saw fortification play as major a role in war and politics as the period from around 1000 to 1300.

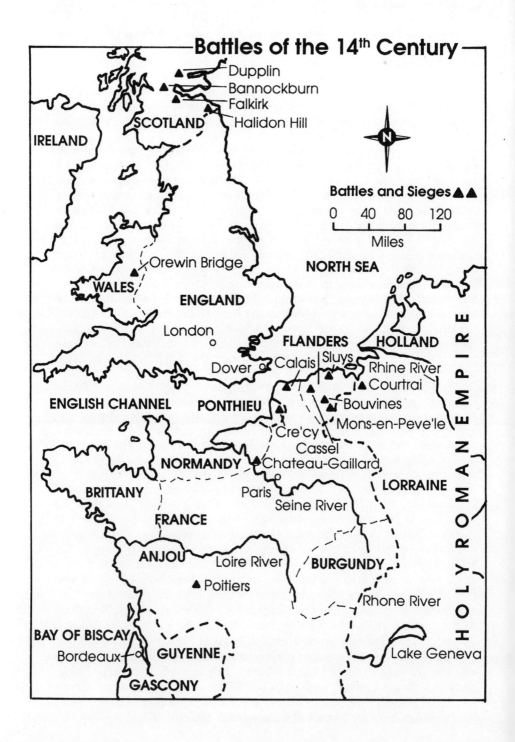

Battles of the 14ᵗʰ Century

Dupplin
Bannockburn
Falkirk
Halidon Hill

SCOTLAND

IRELAND

N

Battles and Sieges ▲▲

0   40   80   120

Miles

Orewin Bridge

NORTH SEA

WALES

ENGLAND

London
○

FLANDERS   HOLLAND

Dover ○   Calais | Sluys   Rhine River

Courtrai

ENGLISH CHANNEL   PONTHIEU   Bouvines

Mons-en-Peve'le

Cre'cy

Cassel

NORMANDY   Chateau-Gaillard

BRITTANY   Paris   LORRAINE

Seine River

FRANCE

ANJOU   Loire River   BURGUNDY

▲ Poitiers   Rhone River

BAY OF BISCAY   Lake Geneva

Bordeaux ○   GUYENNE

GASCONY

H O L Y   R O M A N   E M P I R E

10

War in the High Middle Ages

This crossbow is a bow of the barbarians [westerners] quite unknown to the Greeks; and it is not stretched by the right hand pulling the string whilst the left pulls the bow in a contrary direction, but he who stretches this warlike and very far-shooting weapon must lie, one might say, almost on his back and apply both feet strongly against the semi-circle of the bow and with his two hands pull the string with all his might. In the middle of the string is a socket, a cylindrical kind of cup fitted to the string itself...and through this arrows of many sorts are shot out. The arrows used with this bow are very short in length, but very thick, fitted in front with a very heavy iron tip. And in discharging them the string shoots them out with enormous violence and force...they pierce though a shield, then cut through a heavy iron corselet and wing their way through and out the other side....Such then is this monster of a cross-bow, and verily a devilish invention.

> Anna Comnena, *The Alexiad*, trans. Elizabeth Drew (New York, 1967), pp. 255-56. The author was the daughter of the Byzantine emperor at the time of the First Crusade.

The twelfth century was the prime era of the knight. He dominated the battlefields of western Europe, where the lessons of the Crusades went largely unlearned. Twelfth-century commanders, facing forces almost identical to their own with little chance of being surprised by different tactics and weapons, had little reason to be innovative or try to develop effective infantry.

THE BATTLE OF BOUVINES

The most interesting battle fought while medieval cavalry was in its prime was the Battle of Bouvines (July 1214). Despite the fact that it was fought between French forces and those of the Holy Roman Emperor Otto IV, it was largely a consequence of the long effort of the French monarchy to drive the Anglo-Norman rulers from their French fiefs. Henry II and Richard I had defended their fiefs with skill and tenacity, but Richard's death in 1199 passed the Anglo-Norman titles to John Lackland, a far less capable commander. As has been seen, John failed to come to the relief of Château-Gaillard, allowing the key to Normandy to fall into French hands. Even worse for John, he provided a legal pretext for Philip II to strip him of his French fiefs by marrying the fiancée of one of his French vassals, which was considered adultery in medieval law. The injured vassal called on the French king for justice. John refused to answer the summons to go to Philip's court for judgment, and so was declared stripped of his fiefs. By 1205 Philip had occupied all of John's fiefs north of the Loire.

King John belatedly responded to his losses, but his feuds with the English barons, which would soon lead to the drawing-up of the Magna Carta, prevented him from calling on his English vassals. Accordingly he made an alliance with his nephew, Otto IV, who also hated Philip II. In early summer of 1214, the allies were ready to move. An Anglo-Gascon force was to strike at Paris from the south, while Otto's army of Germans and Flemings was to strike from the north.

The presence of the Flemings in Otto's army reflects a crucial development in medieval politics. The county of Flanders was nominally a fief of the French monarchy, but by 1200 its relationship with its feudal lord had become extremely contentious. Flanders had become the commercial center of northern Europe, having a very favorable location for trade across to the British Isles, to Scandinavia and into the Baltic, and into the center of Europe on the Rhine and several other rivers. A thriving woolen cloth industry had created large and wealthy cities. Flanders was the wealthiest and most urbanized region of northern Europe. Its counts chafed under French interference, and the wealthy merchants who controlled the cities felt little in common with the French king and his nobility. Eager to free themselves from French rule, the Flemings put themselves at the service of John and Otto. They invited foreign forces into Flanders and set the stage for the first of many great battles fought there, which have given the region the title "The Cockpit of Europe."

Because of poor communications and irresolution on Otto's part, his army failed to move quickly enough to join up with John's. Philip II decided to leave a small force in the Loire valley to shadow the English army, and moved most of his men north to Flanders. His army consisted of about 1,400 knights, 3,000 squires and mounted sergeants, and 6,000 to 7,000 footmen. The Imperial army, made up of Germans, Flemings, Italian mercenaries, and a few Englishmen, was very similar but probably a little larger.

The two armies marched around in Flanders for several weeks, passing each other without being aware of it, a good example of the lack of reconnaissance that was typical of medieval armies. Upon hearing that Otto's army was now to his west, Philip turned his forces southward back to France. Otto moved in pursuit. Near the village of Bouvines, the French were stopped by a deep river over which only a narrow bridge provided passage. Part of the French army had already crossed when word came that Otto's army was approaching. Philip ordered his men back across the bridge to prepare for battle, despite the fact that it was Sunday.

St. Anthony's Gate at Rhodes. Note the machicolation at the top of the towers of the barbicon.

Otto, hearing that a part of the French forces was across the river, rushed toward the spot in hope of catching the French with their army split.

Philip divided his men into three divisions spread out across a large open field. The French king strengthened his right with extra knights, since the imperial army would approach toward that flank. The imperial vanguard, made up largely of horsemen, came up and attacked before the French foot had moved out to the right wing. Thus the fighting on the French right was almost entirely between knights; it was probably the largest pure cavalry engagement of the Middle Ages. It was a series of cavalry charges and mêlées in which the better armed and more experienced French slowly proved their superiority. After three hours of bitter fighting, the imperial commander on that wing, the count of Flanders, was unhorsed and captured, and his remaining knights fled.

By then the fighting in the center, where both rulers commanded, had also reached its climax. The bulk of both forces was in the center. The fighting there was opened by a charge of imperial knights that easily broke through the mass of French foot in front and engaged the French cavalry in a bitter mêlée. Meanwhile the imperial foot fought its way to Philip's position in the rear and unhorsed him. His armor and the quick response of his household knights saved him. The French then counterattacked and succeeded in unhorsing Otto. His bodyguard also rescued him; but he fled, and imperial resistance in the center collapsed.

The battle on the French left was slow to develop, and it was hardly underway when the French forces were reinforced by men coming over from the center and right. The count of Boulogne, a French subject fighting for the emperor, fought on well after the battle was lost, surely because of his status as a traitor. He formed several hundred Flemish pikemen into a circle (or perhaps a semi-circle). The count and a small number of knights moved in and out of the circle to rest and re-form for another charge. The French were hesitant about attacking the bristling circle of pikes, but after some time, additional French manpower from the other divisions wore down the remaining enemy forces.

The French victory at Bouvines appears to have been a result of having the greater amount of manpower directly committed to the battle. A large part of the imperial forces, strung out on the road, never reached the battlefield. Both monarchs fought in the battle as knights rather than commanding as generals, and neither showed much of sense of tactics or gave evidence of holding a reserve. The battle is interesting because there were three distinct styles of fighting: a rare purely cavalry encounter on the French right, a typical medieval battle with both infantry and cavalry in the center, and the effective use of pikemen on the left as a harbinger of the future.

The fruits of victory for Philip included retaining Normandy, Anjou, and Flanders for the French crown. After the battle Philip moved his army to the Loire but was unable to drive the English from their positions south of the river or to persuade the nobles of the southwest to break with their more distant English lord. But the loss of Normandy broke the close ties between the duchy and England, which had allowed the Anglo-Norman nobles to remain French in language and culture. With these ties broken the Anglo-Norman nobles slowly became Englishmen.

Bouvines also demonstrated how good the odds of surviving a battle were for the knights of that era. Despite swearing to die fighting, the count of Boulogne was captured and delivered to his fate of a life in chains. At most 170 imperial knights were killed, and French losses definitely were fewer. Infantry losses, however, were much higher. One thousand imperial footmen were reported killed, but again French losses were smaller.

NEW WEAPONS: THE CROSSBOW

The near immunity from battlefield fatalities that medieval knights had enjoyed began to decline after 1250. The reason was the development of two weapons, the crossbow and the longbow, which were capable of being used effectively by footmen and were deadly against armored knights. The crossbow was the first to appear. The ballista of the Romans was a giant crossbow, and the Chinese had crossbows well before the time of Christ. Despite several hints at the presence of crossbows in the early Middle Ages, the earliest definitive reference dates to the mid-tenth century. In the next century they are frequently mentioned. Despite their simple construction, being little more than staves to which a cross piece had been affixed, they became increasingly lethal. Anna Comnena described them at the time of the First Crusade as weapons unknown to the Byzantines.

In 1139 the Catholic Church issued the first of the prohibitions against their use on Christian foes, under the threat of excommunication. The decision was clearly influenced by the threat the crossbow posed to knights, who could be killed from a distance and by commoners, a doubly dishonorable death, and reflected the Church's commitment to the feudal system. Whether the Church's decree influenced the captains of western Christendom is hard to determine, but the crossbow is little mentioned, at least in France and England, for the next half-century. Richard I, for all his reputation as a truly chivalrous knight, seems to have been the first leader to make extensive use of crossbowmen in Europe. Perhaps it was appropriate that he was killed by a crossbow bolt in 1199.

By then the crossbow had been vastly improved. A typical model had a stirrup at the bow end of the stock, in which the bowman placed his foot while bent over. He then straightened up, pulling the cord up to engage a nut that was attached to a trigger. A short but thick bolt, usually with a quadrangular iron head, was placed in the trough on the stock of the bow. When the trigger was pulled, it turned the nut, releasing the string and propelling the bolt. The bolt had a tremendous impact at short range but rapidly lost force because it wobbled as it was shot out of the bow trough. The need to use only very small fletchings, usually made of thin strips of wood rather than feathers, also affected the stability of the arrow at longer distances. Thus a crossbow of this type had a range of about 200 yards but was highly inaccurate at that distance.

As improvements continued to be made in the crossbow, the range increased. By 1300 mechanical devices such as screws and windlasses were used to span (draw) the cord. They permitted the use of much more powerful crosspieces, which by 1370 were being made of steel. The word arbalest was used for those powerful bows with ranges up to 400 yards. One problem with such powerful bows was that the force of the cord would sometimes shatter the bolt when released.

The advantages of the crossbow included the fact that its manufacture, while complicated, did not require the special skill or materials of the sort required to make a composite or long bow. Using it was a skill rather easy to acquire, requiring little training or strength, at least after the devices for spanning it were invented. The crossbow became a weapon favored by urban militiamen because someone with little training could be effective with it. Urban troops also took to it because it was a weapon well suited for defending fortifications. It required a smaller opening to use from a wall, exposing a man less than a long bow did. The crossbow's great impact at close range reduced the protection given attackers by cats, and it could be cocked and held in ready until a target presented itself, a feature more useful on a wall than in the field. These characteristics also made the crossbow a valuable weapon for besiegers and for use on ships. In 1294 Philip IV of France ordered that his galleys in the Mediterranean each carry sixty crossbowmen and 6,000 bolts.

The development of the crossbow required a corresponding improvement in armor, since a bolt from a crossbow easily penetrated chain mail at close range. Plate vests were in use by 1300, and the continuing improvement of the crossbow led to the use of more and more plate armor for both rider and horse. Helmets also began to change; they became more pointed to deflect missiles and were extended to cover parts of the head less vulnerable to sword slashes, such as the back of the neck and the throat. By 1400 the amount of armor a knight wore had increased to fifty pounds or more, and its cost had increased enormously as well.

Perhaps because it was the most highly urbanized part of Europe, northern Italy gained a reputation for providing quality crossbowmen. Those from the city of Genoa in particular were in demand as mercenaries. The crossbow, not the longbow, was in use in England during the twelfth century. There is no mention of longbow archers in the English military census of 1181. It is generally agreed that the longbow was Welsh in origin and that the English came to appreciate it during their campaigns to conquer Wales in the early thirteenth century.

THE LONGBOW

The wood of choice for a longbow was yew, although ash and elm were also common. Making a good bow was an art that required long training and experience. Over five feet long, it had a draw of up to 150 pounds and an effective range of 250 yards. The string was drawn to the shoulder rather than to the chest, as was usual for other self (one-piece) bows. In battle the arrow was not aimed but was pointed in the proper direction and released; the archer depended on his experience to be able to place arrows in the close vicinity of his target and on his rapid rate of fire to hit it within a short time. Longbow archers could release ten shafts a minute in short bursts, and a corps of longbowmen could literally rain arrows on their foes.

It was Edward I (1272-1307) who first recognized the military value of the longbow. It was being used by commoners called yeomen, who had a fairly comfortable living for that era. They received a small wage for their services. The process of creating permanent units of archers and integrating them into his army began during Edward's campaigns in north Wales, the subjugation of which had stymied the English for nearly two centuries. Its rugged terrain permitted the small bands of Welsh warriors to conduct a very effective guerrilla war against the English. Edward solved the Welsh problem by building a large number of small but well-designed castles to control key points, by pushing roads through previously untracked terrain, and by using small, permanent armies of knights and archers, which remained in the field through the winter. All these required money and a source of fighting men apart from Edward's vassals, who provided only short-term service. The English monarchy had created the practice of scutage, by which the feudal nobles were excused from their military obligation for a fee. With that money, Edward could expect to keep an army of 1,000 to 1,200 knights and 2,000 to 3,000 archers in the field through the winter if necessary.

In December 1282, the most important battle of Edward's Welsh campaigns took place at Orewin Bridge. His army included pikemen and crossbowmen, who were still being paid better than the archers. Archers were not yet a majority of the infantry. The Welsh forces, almost entirely unarmored pikemen, were assembled at the top of a hill. The English knights had learned from experience how foolhardy it was to attack a resolute body of Welsh pikemen, so the bowmen were sent forward to do what damage they could. The longbow archers proved to be far more effective than the crossbowmen because of their greater range and rate of fire against the unarmored Welsh. The Welsh could not attack the bowmen because of the presence of the English knights, who would have ridden them down if they had tried to rush the bowmen. The great success of the longbowmen against the unarmored men, who were forced to stand and take their fire until they broke and ran, seems to have persuaded Edward to emphasize the longbow over the crossbow. The crossbow soon disappeared from the English army.

By 1295, after several more battles of that sort, the Welsh were pacified. Edward had already turned his attention to Scotland, which he claimed as a fief. The Scots had been constantly raiding northern England. Wales and Scotland were similar in that both had rugged terrain where ambush could be effective, and military forces that were largely unarmored pikemen, although the Scots did have some knights. Scotland also had the advantage of offering a superb place of refuge in the Highlands.

Serious fighting began in 1297 when Edward I, stung by an earlier defeat, led an army of perhaps 2,500 knights, many of whom had been raised by the feudal levy, and 12,000 to 13,000 infantry north to the Forth of Firth. There he confronted a vast Scots army of possibly 3,000 mounted men and 30,000 infantrymen. These are the lowest numbers given in any of the sources, although in reality they were probably fewer. The Scots had taken positions on a hillside. The Battle of Falkirk began with an English cavalry charge that drove off the Scots knights, but the English were brought to a quick halt by the mass of resolute pikemen. The English king ordered his archers to the front to shoot into the great crowd of Scots. After a few minutes, huge gaps opened up in the Scots lines, but they dared not charge the archers because of the menacing presence of the English horse. Edward then ordered his knights to charge into the gaps, and they easily broke up and scattered the formation of the Scots. Although their casualties were great, the surviving Scots escaped into the Highlands; Edward's victory at Falkirk gave the English no permanent advantage.

Sixteen years later Edward II was in Scotland in force, fighting a man who had been present in the English forces at Falkirk—Robert the Bruce. The Bruce had learned well the lesson of Falkirk: a mass of infantrymen, no matter how courageous, could not stand up to the judicious use of archers and cavalry. He allowed the English army to move almost unhindered deep into Scotland in order to draw it into the rough terrain of the Highlands and permit the inevitable numerous desertions to occur. The Bruce assembled his forces on a rise above the Bannock, a small burn (stream). He kept 500 horsemen mounted while several hundred more were dismounted and spread among the 10,000 to 15,000 infantrymen to stiffen their resolve.

The English army was probably larger than at Falkirk, especially in infantry, but it was weary from an all-night crossing of the Bannock and the marshes along it. The English probably were not in good battle order when the Scots charged down the hill at them. The charge apparently took the English by surprise, who expected the Scots to wait on the defensive, as they had in all previous encounters. The English cavalry was in the best position to stop the charge and did so but with heavy casualties. The English archers formed their lines to fire into the Scots infantry, but they had just begun shooting when the Bruce charged his cavalry into their flanks. The archers immediately broke and ran. Without the support of their archers, the English knights took the brunt of the fighting, although some cavalry units and all of the English pikemen never reached the front line. When Edward II fled with the knights of his household, the battle was over.

As long as the Bruce was alive, the Scots held the upper hand, but with his death in 1329, the English regained their advantage. Three years later, a small English force led by several nobles who had fought before with the Scots encountered a much larger Scots army at Dupplin. The English captains took up a defensive position at the top of a hill, and ordered all but forty of their knights to dismount and form a solid line of armored infantrymen. They spread out their archers at an angle on both flanks of the dismounted knights. The Scots ignored the archers as they charged up the hill against the center. The weight of their charge drove the English center back some distance, but it remained intact. The result was to expose more of the flanks of the Scots army to devastating archer fire. After a short time facing both the hard fighting of the dismounted knights in the center and the fire of the archers, the Scots broke and ran, only to suffer further casualties from the pursuit of the English mounted reserve.

A year later, in 1333, young King Edward III entered Scotland with a large army. The English captains who had fought at Dupplin were with him, and obviously described their tactics there to him. At the battle of Halidon Hill, Edward improved on their tactics by dividing his cavalry into three divisions of dismounted knights, and placing archers between the divisions as well as on the flanks. The hail of arrows was so devastating to the Scots as they charged the English lines that few made their way to exchange blows with the men-at-arms in the center. Just in time for the beginning of the Hundred Years War, the English had learned the most effective way of combining armored men with archers. As for Scotland, despite the rout at Halidon Hill and several succeeding defeats, the English never were able to control that realm. Always, it seems, in their darkest hour, the Scots found a new leader who remembered Robert the Bruce's dictum that strategic retreat and ambush were the only way to deal with the enemy from the south.

CAUSES OF THE HUNDRED YEARS WAR

The Hundred Years War saw numerous English victories using exactly the same tactics as at Halidon Hill, and the English continued to use those tactics without significant change until after 1500. The causes of the war were disputes over the county of Flanders, the duchy of Aquitaine, and the succession to the French throne. Flanders had not submitted quietly to the

French monarchy after Bouvines in 1214. Flemish resistance peaked during the reign of King Philip IV, who infringed on numerous Flemish privileges. The Flemings put the castle of Courtrai, a French stronghold, under siege in 1302. Philip's brother, Robert, was sent into Flanders to relieve it. He called out the feudal levy of northern France, and raised a large force of infantry as well. Opposing him was an army composed largely of urban militiamen and peasants; only a few knights were present because most of the Flemish nobles no longer supported the rebellion. The Flemish army was made up mostly of pikemen with some crossbowmen, and numbered perhaps 10,000 men. Its commander, Guy of Namur, chose a large field that was itself high and dry but was backed by a large river and fronted by smaller stream edged by marsh. With their backs to the river, the Flemings were faced with victory or death.

Prince Robert, with about 5,000 horsemen and 3,000 footmen, sent his crossbowmen, largely Italian, forward to the edge of the marshes to shoot at the Flemings. They had been drawn up in a solid block of men with their own crossbowmen in front at the opposite edge of the wet ground. After exchanging bolts for several minutes, the French crossbowmen drove the entire Flemish army back some distance. When Robert saw this, he ordered his cavalry to charge, since it now had some dry ground on which to recover its formation and momentum after crossing the marsh and creek. Crossing the wet ground proved to be more difficult than the French had expected, and the Flemings had added to their problems by digging horse traps at their side of the creek. As the French knights struggled to get out of the mud and regain formation, the Flemish pikemen charged, catching them in serious disorder. Driving the French back into the marsh, the Flemings concentrated on killing all those who were wearing the spurs of nobility, including the prince. They claimed to have collected 700 sets of spurs from dead knights, hence the name Battle of the Golden Spurs.

Numerous French legends attempted to explain that devastating defeat at the hands of commoners, but none acknowledged the truth: a disciplined force of infantrymen had defeated the flower of French knighthood. The contempt of the French nobility for commoner fighting men is evident in both the conduct of the battle and the later legends. It would prove very costly in the Hundred Years War. Also the French failed to learn the lessons of Courtrai because they gained a measure of revenge in 1304 at Mons-en-Pévèle and, more completely, at Cassel in 1328; both battles were fought on open fields well fit for a cavalry charge.

The issue of the French succession erupted the same year as the Battle of Cassel, when Charles IV, the third of Philip IV's sons to rule after him, died without a son, as had his two older brothers. Edward III's mother was a daughter of Philip IV, and Edward claimed the French throne on the grounds that he was the closest male relation of the deceased Charles IV. French lawyers, acting on behalf of the French candidate Philip of Valois, a nephew of Philip IV's, declared that the Salic Law prohibited a woman not only from wearing the French crown but also from passing the title through her to a male descendant. In May 1328, Valois was crowned Philip VI.

Edward, still a teenager and unsure of himself, was pressed into going to France to give homage for his French fiefs—the duchies of Guyenne and Gascony in the southwest and the county of Ponthieu on the English Channel— in June 1329. This act clearly demonstrated his recognition of Philip's status as king. A year later, however, the French lawyers, determined to nail the point down and to resolve some ambiguity about the French king's authority in Gascony-Guyenne, demanded that Edward repeat his homage under a new formula much more explicit about the rights of the French king. Although Edward reluctantly did so in 1331, he was enraged by it and refused to fulfill the conditions Philip had set concerning the duchies. He was declared to be in violation of feudal law; the legal decision was given in May 1337 that he had forfeited his fiefs. Edward, now greatly matured and the victor in several battles with the Scots, whom the French were actively aiding, declared that Philip was a usurper. It was a declaration of war.

At first glance Edward's decision seems foolhardy, since his realm would be hopelessly outnumbered in the conflict. The best population estimates put England in that era at just over 3 million people, while France had about 16.5 million, although Edward could draw on the men and resources of Gascony-Guyenne. France was by far the wealthier kingdom, but the English administrative structure and tax system did allow Edward to draw on a strong fiscal base. On the other hand, the expeditions against Scotland had put Edward deeply in debt; it is hard to see how he expected to find resources for a much more expensive war. Finally, France possessed the most highly regarded military force in western Europe, its cavalry, whose reputation had been largely restored after being blemished at Courtrai. The French knights badly outnumbered the English and were regarded as superior in quality.

Given the disproportionate resources, so obvious to historians, why did Edward III go to war? In that era war was fought on such a small scale that the disparity of resources was neither obvious nor would it have been regarded as a problem. He could also expect to receive help from Flanders, where the remaining rebels had recognized him as king. Furthermore, what was at stake was Edward's honor; it outweighed all other considerations. Last, the type of war that he expected to fight was not intended to win control of France but to gain plunder and ransom money for himself and his nobility. By 1337 the economic decline and the adverse change in climatic conditions, which were setting the stage for the Black Death ten years later, had begun to affect both realms. The ruling classes responded to the economic downturn by resorting to violence to recoup. Neither king had difficulty recruiting for his army.

THE WAR BEGINS

The first encounter of the Hundred Years War, in the late summer of 1337, revealed the heavy dependence of the English on the longbow and the advantage it gave them. A small English force under the earl of Derby, trying to land on the coast of Flanders, was confronted at the beach by a body of crossbowmen. The longbowmen on the ships drove them back, inflicting heavy losses. After the English had secured a beachhead, a force of French cavalry attacked. Posting his archers on the flanks of his knights, the earl inflicted a sharp defeat on the enemy. The only result, however, was that the English freely plundered the immediate region before returning to England for the winter.

Archers also played a major part in the greatest sea battle of the war three years later. The typical ship in the northern waters after 1200 was the cog, a single-masted ship with a square sail. It had a removable sternpost rudder, which was a clear improvement over the steering oars of earlier ships. The cog could be sailed with a small crew and carry a large cargo. Its design also permitted the building of high structures fore and aft from which men could shoot down at an enemy ship. Because they were built with crenels, these structures were called castles. With the high incidence of piracy in that era, merchant ships had to be able to defend themselves. Thus they could be easily pressed into service for war. In the course of the thirteenth century crossbowmen and, on English ships, longbowmen began to be used for naval firepower.

Both Philip IV and Edward I had put great effort into building up their fleets for control of the extensive trade between Bordeaux and England in wine and between Flanders and England in wool. In 1297 Edward had a fleet of 305 ships, nearly all of which were merchant ships impressed into royal service. Using the fleet to carry on war in Wales, Scotland, Ireland, and southwestern France, the English had vast experience transporting a fleet by sea as of 1337. Philip IV recognized that Edward's ability to transport an army by sea was the key to the winning war. He contracted a large number of Italian ships and created a large fleet.

In June 1340, Edward assembled nearly 300 ships to transport some 8,000 men to Flanders. Heading for the harbor of Sluys (on the present Dutch-Belgian border) he encountered a French fleet of about the same size. The only contemporary source for the battle relates that both fleets were split into three divisions, which formed lines much like a battle on land. The bowmen on both sides opened the fray and played a major role throughout. The superior rate of fire of the longbowmen apparently determined the battle, although there was also bitter hand-to-hand fighting as the ships grappled with each other. The English captured some 200 ships, but there is no mention of any being sunk.

With the victory at Sluys, Edward had control of the Channel. The English never really lost it for the rest of the war, although the French did raid the southern English coast on several occasions. Edward routinely transported an army across to France for plundering expeditions or *chevauchées*, to use the French term, and returned to England in the fall. In 1346 a typical campaign began with the English landing on the Norman coast in late July. Control of the seas permitted the English to take a longer route across the Channel instead of the quick dash across from Dover. For a month Edward plundered Normandy without encountering serious resistance. Part of the English fleet had been sent home with wounded men, plunder, and prisoners held for ransom. The rest of the fleet went as well, leaving Edward without transportation and without any idea

of where or when his fleet would reappear. He decided to push on to
Flanders, where he could expect help.

THE BATTLE OF CRÉCY

After highly dangerous crossings of the Seine and the Somme rivers,
Edward decided to give battle to the pursuing French army if it approached
too closely, since he now had a clear route for a retreat to Flanders if defeated. On August 26, 1346, near the village of Crécy, he found a position
he regarded as highly suitable to his style of fighting: a high hill protected
on one flank by a thick forest and on the other, by a steep slope and the
village. English manpower for this battle has been estimated at 2,000
knights, 6,000 archers, and 2,000 pikemen. The dismounted knights were
formed into three divisions, two of which were placed in the front line and
the third placed behind to use as a reserve under the king's direct command. The archers were arranged on the flanks of both divisions of men-
at-arms, creating the outline of something like an M. The pikemen were
placed behind the archers, who dug holes in front of their positions to slow
any French cavalry charge against them.

The French army, perhaps twice the size of the English, was strung out
for miles in pursuit. Four knights sent out to find the English reported to
Philip their position near Crécy and recommended that his army halt for
the night, since it was late afternoon. The first French units, upon spotting
the enemy, refused to listen to the order to wait until the next day, as the
French knights chafed to be first in the field. As word of the enemy's
presence made its way back to the middle units, they too pushed forward.
When Philip arrived at the van of his army, he found a packed mass of
men nowhere near being in battle order and chafing to get at the foe. Either because he felt the same way or he believed that he could not control
his men if he did not give an order to attack, Philip ordered an advance
toward the English.

Several thousand Italian crossbowmen were sent into action first, halting a fair distance from the English lines and releasing their bolts. Most fell
short, because a sudden shower had wet the strings of the crossbows. The
longbowmen, who had removed their strings and covered them, then took
a pace forward and filled the air with arrows. After a few minutes of taking
the English volleys, the crossbowmen broke and ran. The forward units
of the French cavalry, thinking that the crossbowmen were fleeing out of
cowardice, refused to open any lanes for them but charged over the top of
them, slashing at them with their swords to get them out of their way. This
stupid act had the effect of nearly halting the charge in the teeth of the hail
of arrows. The French were thrown back; few if any reached the lines of
the English.

Seeing the vanguard driven back in disorder, the next French units
charged up the hill. They took the same route up the hill as the first units,
which permitted the English archers to hold their positions and eliminated
the problems that re-forming their lines would have caused. Furthermore,
the retreating French knights, many wounded or on wounded horses and
therefore thrashing about, crashed into the fresh units. This slowed their

charge, and they suffered the same fate. This pattern repeated itself perhaps as often as fifteen times as the trailing elements of the French army reached the scene. At no time was an effort made to organize a large number of knights into a strong line. The piecemeal attacks that did take place were directed entirely against the dismounted men-at-arms rather than the archers, who were free to shoot into the masses of French cavalrymen. The French charges continued well into the night—one account says until midnight—when finally Philip, who had had two horses killed under him, allowed himself to be led off the battlefield.

Early the next morning the English moved across the battlefield to assess their victory, count the dead, and take captive any wounded nobles worth ransoming. The latter were few, but the English put the French dead at 1,542 nobles. Casualties among the infantrymen was reported as moderate. At the cost of about fifty dead knights and a few bowmen, Edward had won a brilliant victory of a very rare sort, by an army standing entirely on the defensive.

Edward's army was too short of supplies and the end of the campaigning season too near to allow him to pursue the French. He pushed on to the coast where he put the city of Calais under siege. It was the best decision possible. The city's location, directly across from Dover, and its fine harbor made it the port of choice for crossing the Channel. English control of Calais would permit them to transport forces back and forth with near impunity.

Calais had superb natural defenses, being sited on a spit of land surrounded on three sides by water while the landward side was largely marsh. Its natural defenses were strongly augmented by man-made ones. Even a modest relief army probably could have broken an English siege of Calais, since the terrain around the city was illsuited to the English style of fighting. Only after a shattering victory such as Crécy could the English hope to take Calais, although it is hard to say whether Edward fully recognized that. Upon arriving at Calais in early September, Edward decided that it was too well defended to assault, so he settled his army into an eleven-month siege, one of the longest of the Middle Ages. In early spring of 1347 rumors reached Calais of the approach of a large French relief army, so the city refused to surrender despite the terrible misery of the long siege. It was only in July that Philip VI led a small force into the region, but he withdrew after the first skirmishes with the English; clearly both he and his forces were still shattered by Crécy. In August Calais surrendered. For the rest of the war, English forces in northern France always had a secure base from which to operate.

THE BATTLE OF POITIERS

The sudden appearance of the Black Death in western Europe in late 1347 put a halt to the war until 1355, as neither side dared to assemble a large group of men while the plague raged. In 1350 Philip VI died and was succeeded by John II, a chivalrous knight but a poor commander. In 1355 Edward III returned to the continent to lead a chevauchée into northern France. More ominously for the French, Edward's eldest son, called the

Black Prince from the burnished shine of his armor, led an expedition into Languedoc from Gascony. It was first large raid from English-held southwest France. In the summer of the next year the Black Prince moved north into the Loire valley, accumulating vast plunder in that wealthy region.

In early September 1356 the Black Prince learned of the arrival of a French army in the valley, so he retreated southward. A battle need not have occurred if he had been willing to abandon much of his plunder and speed back to Gascony. But since he would not, the French caught up with his force near the city of Poitiers. A day spent negotiating a possible truce gave the Black Prince's forces time to rest and establish a strong position at the top of a broad hill flanked on one side by a creek and marshland. The opposite flank was open, but the prince placed his wagons there to form a defensive line. His manpower was about 8,000 men, including 3,000 knights, although the majority of them were French vassals from Gascony. They established essentially the same formation as at Crécy.

The French army, commanded by King John himself, was about twice as large. He organized his knights into four divisions and ordered the men in three of them to dismount. John and his advisers had decided that the English had achieved victory at Crécy by fighting dismounted. The rough ground and hedges on the way up the hill to the English lines may also have been a factor in the decision, as it may have been feared that the horses would have trouble negotiating the terrain. It is also possible that the king or his advisers thought that without their horses, the men-at-arms would present a smaller target to the bowmen. The fourth division, much smaller than the others, was left mounted. In the hope that the some 500 mounted knights could force a gap between the two forward divisions of the Black Prince's men-at-arms, they were ordered to charge up the hill. The crossbowmen were placed behind them, another result of thinking about Crécy, and they never got into range. The small host of knights was riddled with arrows, and only a few reached the English lines.

The first division of dismounted knights was then ordered into action. Clanging up the hill in their heavy armor over hedges and ditches for 1,000 yards, they probably were close to exhaustion when they came into arrow range. Nonetheless they pushed on into the English men-at-arms with enough force that the prince had to use his reserves to hold his line. The French were thrown back, and the sight of the battered remains of the division fleeing down the hill caused the next division to lose its nerve. Its men proceeded to flee, giving the English a badly needed period of rest before the final, and largest, division under the king himself rushed up the hill.

The Black Prince ordered his men forward as well, perhaps to give them the psychological boost of going on the offensive. Having run out of arrows, the archers began to join in the hand-to-hand fighting. As fierce combat raged, the prince sent his last reserve, about 200 mounted men, to attack the French rear. This unexpected onslaught broke the resolve of many of the French, who turned and ran. King John fought on with great courage but diminished forces for a time before he was captured, along with his youngest son and numerous high nobles. French casualties were placed at 2,500 men, but unlike Crécy, the English dead were also numerous, over 1,000 men.

Having their king taken captive was a catastrophe for the French. The English demanded a huge ransom for King John, who was taken to London but treated as an honored guest. Edward's enormous demands were scaled down in negotiations between the Black Prince and John's eldest son, the Dauphin Charles, who agreed to the Peace of Brétigny. It recognized English sovereignty over Calais and Gascony-Guyenne, while Edward renounced his claims to Normandy and the French throne. The French king was to be ransomed for 3 million gold crowns.

Soon after the Battle of Poitiers, the dauphin, who now governed for his father, began to collect money for the expected ransom demand. The high taxes he demanded, combined with the disorientation caused by the king's captivity, led to revolts in Paris and the countryside of northern France. Peasant revolts were nothing new to France, but this was the largest by far. Striking out blindly at the upper classes during two years of carnage, the peasants did enormous damage to the property and persons of the nobility before the nobles crushed them. The most significant result of the peasants' revolt was that the French government and nobility were terrified at the prospect of putting weapons in the hands of their peasants. They had always been reluctant to do so, but after 1358 it became a hard and fast doctrine. This severely reduced the ability of France to compete with its neighbors who were beginning to make use of infantry. France would not have a quality native infantry until well after 1500.

In 1360 with the Peace of Brétigny, King John was released upon the down payment of 400,000 gold crowns, leaving two younger sons and several great nobles as hostages for the rest. One of those sons had recently been married, and, breaking his word of honor, he escaped from his English wardens to be with his bride. John felt obliged as a chivalrous knight to return to England until the full ransom was paid. It never was, as John died there in 1364 with over half of the 3 million crowns unpaid.

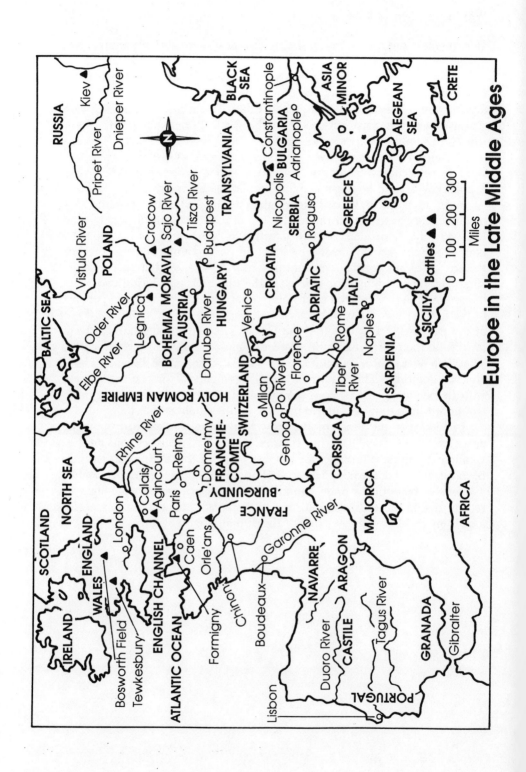

Europe in the Late Middle Ages

11

The End of the Medieval Military

The French threw themselves on the English archers, who had their sharp stakes fixed before them....And the French all retreated excepting three men; to whom it unluckily happened that by their horses falling on the stakes they were thrown to the ground, among the archers, and were immediately killed. The remainder, or the greater part of them, with all their horses, from fear of the arrows retreated into the French advanced-guard in which they caused great confusion, breaking and exposing it in many places, and caused them to retire to some new-sown ground for their horses were so wounded by arrows that they were unmanageable.   And thus the advanced-guard being thrown into disorder, the men-at-arms fell in great numbers and their horses took to flight, following which example numbers of the French fled.

    The lord of Saint-Remy quoted in Alfred Burne, *The Agincourt War* (London, 1956), p. 81. The lord of Saint-Remy was a Burgundian noble who fought for the English at Agincourt in 1415.

The meaning of the English victories at Crécy and Poitiers was clear enough to the more perceptive leaders in France, especially the new king, Charles V, and the constable, Bertrand Du Guesclin. Upon becoming king in 1364, Charles quickly revealed his style of rule: the use of cunning instead of direct confrontation, little commitment to the principles of chivalry, and a willingness to take small gains instead of waging all on one great battle. He was the first French king not to command in the field, leaving that duty to his lieutenants, especially Du Guesclin.

    The constable was from a petty noble family of Brittany, and his lowly origins were part of the reason why most French nobles hated him. More important, however, was his refusal to take on the English in pitched battles. Du Guesclin was determined to wage a war of attrition, striking at isolated forces, harassing armies on chevauchée, and raiding English-held castles. Illustrative of his tactics is the story that he used prostitutes to enter an English castle, who during the night opened the gates for his forces. The story goes that a prominent French noble refused to lead his men inside because the manner in which entrance had been gained was unchivalrous.

By 1380, the year of the deaths of both Charles V and Du Guesclin, they had recovered more territory than had been lost in 1356, restricting the English to Calais and an enclave around Bordeaux. By then both Edward III and the Black Prince were dead, and the English had largely lost interest in the war. Both governments consequently refused to pay the large number of troops in the field, who were left to shift for themselves. The English troops were far more a problem, since they were set adrift in a foreign land with little hope of getting home. They created the "free companies," gangs of several hundred to a thousand men who plundered and raped their way across France. In the last quarter of the fourteenth century, they were a greater menace than the English army. Expeditions against them by both the royal forces and local nobles suffered embarrassing defeats; Du Guesclin was killed battling a free company in 1380. Attrition and the lure of wars in Italy and Spain had largely removed them from French soil by 1400.

By then a far more serious problem had arisen for France. The new king, Charles VI, was racked by fits of madness. In 1392 he suffered his first incapacitating attack of what has been diagnosed as paranoid schizophrenia. While out hunting, he suddenly began to strike wildly at the courtiers about him. He killed three men before he was wrestled off his horse by courtiers who used a blanket because it was treasonous to lay a hand on the king, mad or not. The king's reoccurring fits of madness required that a regent govern for him. The competition for the office eventually came down to Philip, Duke of Burgundy, the king's uncle, and Louis, Duke of Orléans, the king's brother.

Philip had assembled an impressive collection of lands: the duchy of Burgundy itself, the duchy of Nevers to its west, and the county of Burgundy to the east. The latter, better known as the Franche-Comté (Free County), was actually a part of the Holy Roman Empire. Through his wife he controlled Flanders and much of the rest of the Low Countries. Able and ruthless, he left a powerful state upon his death in 1404 to his son John the Fearless, a still more ruthless man. In 1407 John arranged for the assassination of Louis of Orléans. Leadership of the Orléanist faction then passed to the count of Armagnac, hence the term Armagnacs for that party. In 1419 the Armagnacs, with the tacit support of Charles VI's last surviving son, the Dauphin Charles, assassinated John of Burgundy. The Burgundians blamed the dauphin for the murder, and the resulting blood feud became a major factor in the political history of the next 150 years.

THE BATTLE OF AGINCOURT

The immediate result of John's assassination was that his son made a firm alliance with Henry V of England (1413-1422). Upon becoming king, Henry had revived the war with France, largely to distract his realm from the questionable nature of his right to the English throne. His father Henry IV had seized the throne from Richard II in 1399. In 1415, encouraged by requests from both French parties, Henry V led an army of about 2,000

Joan of Arc, a near contemporary portrait

men-at-arms and 8,000 archers across the Channel. Landing at the mouth of the Seine he spent several months in Normandy, but with disease reducing his army to at most 7,000 men, he decided to go to Calais. In late October, a few miles short of Calais and very close to Crécy, a French army placed itself between Henry and Calais. The French by best estimate were 25,000 strong, including 10,000 men-at-arms. Although the duke of Burgundy had refused to serve, many of his vassals were present. The French were commanded by the Constable d'Albret, a veteran of Du Guesclin's time. He intended to force the English to attack, since he knew that they were short on food. Henry meanwhile had found a position suitable for the English style of fighting: a plowed field flanked by woods and the orchards and hedges of two villages, the larger being Agincourt. The 7,000 Englishmen asssembled in their typical formation to wait for the French attack.

Albret set his men up in the same formation as John II had at Poitiers—four divisions, with three of them dismounted. Despite the chafing of the men-at-arms to get into battle, Albret held them under control, waiting for the English to attack. Because of the lack of food, Henry realized that his army could not remain in place overnight, as it appeared the French were trying to make him do. He ordered his forces to advance 100 paces toward the French and then commanded the archers to fire. That act enticed the French into charging. Cavalry detachments at the wings of the French line went forward to clear the flanking archers, but apparently they were unaware of the sharpened stakes the archers had driven into the ground at an angle until they were nearly on top of them. Some horses were impaled on the stakes and their riders thrown, but most turned back or veered off. Those who turned back found themselves crashing into the two divisions of dismounted men-at-arms, one behind the other, charging at the English center. Their charge, already slowed by slugging across the muddy field in full armor, was further disrupted and their momentum lost.

Although they greatly outnumbered the English, the French *gens d'armes* (men-at-arms) formed a front no wider than the English front of armored infantrymen. When the two lines clashed, the numerical superiority of the French troops had only a negative result of pushing the front ranks of men, already tired and too closely packed to fight effectively, into the teeth of the enemy's weapons. A few moments after the men-at-arms clashed, the archers, now out of arrows, grabbed their swords and battle-axes and struck at the French flanks. The French dead and captured quickly mounted. Hundreds of noble captives were pushed to the rear of the English lines, having given up their weapons and their right gauntlets to their captors. The gauntlets would serve as proof of identity for those collecting their ransoms.

The third division of French armored infantry and much of the cavalry had remained in place while the first two divisions were being destroyed. They were still a powerful threat to the English and were probably equal in number. Thus when Henry V heard that his baggage train was being attacked—by the lord of Agincourt and some peasants, it turned out—he ordered the massacre of the French prisoners lest they pick up the numerous weapons lying about and resume fighting. The men-at-arms refused, probably because of a reluctance to give up their ransoms but perhaps also from a lingering sense of chivalry that forbade the killing of a defenseless man. The king then ordered 200 archers to do the bloody task. They set about it willingly, but after a short time Henry saw that the French were withdrawing, and he ended the executions. French casualties were estimated at 6,000 dead and 1,000 captured; the English, only about 600 dead.

The victory resulted in no immediate gains for Henry, who pushed on to Calais and back to England; but the Armagnac faction in French politics was badly weakened by its heavy losses at Agincourt, leaving the duke of Burgundy to dominate the realm. Resentment of that domination led to his assassination in 1419. His heir promptly made an alliance with Henry, giving Henry control of both Paris and the person of poor, mad Charles VI. In 1420 the Treaty of Troyes recognized the English king as Charles' successor and arranged for his marriage to Charles' daughter. The dauphin was declared illegitimate and was disinherited.

JOAN OF ARC

In 1422 both Henry and Charles died, leaving the infant Henry VI (1422-61) as king of England and France. He was crowned both at London and Reims. The duke of Bedford, his uncle, served as his regent in France and pursued the war against the dauphin, who retreated to Bourges from whence he governed most of central and southern France. The dauphin was a sickly young man who appears to have been deeply hurt by his mother's declaration that he was a bastard; it seems to have sapped him of whatever energy he might have had to resist the English. Bedford, seeking to extend his control south of the Loire River, decided in 1428 to take Orléans, the key to the Loire Valley and all of central France. His force was too small to take the city by assault, so he settled into a long siege.

At this desperate hour for France, the most famous heroine in history, Joan of Arc, made her dramatic appearance. Actually from the village of Domrémy in Champagne and not the nearby village of Arc, the young peasant girl was convinced that she had a divine mission to save France and see the dauphin crowned. She was also motivated by hatred of the Burgundians, who had raided her village several times. She convinced the local French captain of her mission, who took her to the dauphin at Chinon. Having convinced him as well, she was allowed to accompany a small relief force going to Orléans. Joan quickly gained the confidence of the troops and lifted their morale. Women warriors were not unheard of in the Middle Ages. A recent example was Julienne Du Guesclin, the sister of the constable, who although a nun had fought to defend her Breton town against an assault.

The relief force entered Orléans in May 1429 without any fighting; the English made no effort to block it. Joan persuaded the garrison to attack the besiegers; she was in the midst of a force that sallied out to assault an English siegework and, after hard fighting, took it. English resistance quickly collapsed, and they pulled out of the area. Orléans now secured, Joan led the dauphin and his army to Reims for his coronation as Charles VII. Then the French army pushed on to Paris, but it was too well defended to be taken. This check to Joan's string of successes heartened the English and the Burgundians; the latter laid siege to a small fort north of Paris held by a French captain. Joan rushed there with a small force. Fighting against very bad odds, she was captured, and the Burgundians sold her to the English. They put her on trial for heresy and witchcraft. Found guilty, she was burned at the stake in early 1431. In 1450 Charles VII arranged for a second trial that acquitted her.

THE FRENCH VICTORY

The momentum that Joan gave the French continued after her death, although at a slower pace. By 1435 the duke of Burgundy realized the tide had turned, and he made peace with Charles VII in exchange for territorial gains on the fringes of his domains. Steady French advances brought them back into control of most of northern France by 1450. The English had been driven out of eastern Normandy, and their garrison in Caen was under siege. The English commander in western Normandy pulled most of his garrisons out of their castles to form an army of about 5,000 men to relieve Caen. In April 1450, near the town of Formigny, it ran into a slightly larger French army. The English took their time-proven defensive position at the top of a hill. The French, however, had finally changed tactics. They brought up two small artillery pieces on each flank to enfilade the archers, firing from out of bow range. After some time of taking the cannon fire, the archers broke their ranks to charge the artillery positions. Although they did overrun the cannon, they had made themselves vulnerable to a charge by the French dismounted men-at-arms, and a fierce mêlée took place. The French victory was secured when a fresh force attacked the English flank. English casualties amounted to 80 percent of their manpower, in comparison to small loses for the French. Caen fell in July, driving the English out of Normandy entirely.

The English still maintained forces in Gascony, but a French army of 6,000 men moved into the region in 1452. Despite considerable support from the local population, which preferred the distant rule of the English monarchy, the English were thrown back on Bordeaux. In July 1453 the French had put Castillon, near Bordeaux, under siege. An English relief army under the earl of Shrewsbury arrived to find the French wellentrenched around it. The French refused to fight in the field, so Shrewsbury abandoned the standard English tactics and formed a powerful column out of his cavalry to attack the weakest point in the French lines. Artillery fire effectively blunted the English cavalry charge, and a French counter attack cleared the field, killing Shrewsbury. Except for the use of artillery instead of bows, the battle was a reversal of Crécy; it is fitting that it was the last battle of the Hundred Years War. In October the French entered Bordeaux against little opposition. There was no peace treaty. The English monarchy held onto Calais for another century and maintained its claim to the French throne for 200 years more, but the long war was over.

It was only at the very end of the war that any significant military changes occurred. For over a century both sides had fought with no real changes in tactics. Only the French use of field artillery was a noteworthy development. The French also produced the only innovations in military administration. One was actually a change in the tax system. In 1439 Charles VII was able to persuade the Estates General (roughly the equivalent of the English Parliament) to ratify a tax for the duration of the war. This differed from previous tax levies, which were established for specified short terms. The new tax, the *taille*, became permanent and the largest source of income for the French monarchy until 1789.

Using the money now available, Charles began to create a standing army. In 1445 he established the *compagnies d'ordonnance*. Each of the fifteen ordnance companies was to consist of 100 lances; a lance in turn included a heavy lancer in full plate armor, a sergeant, two archers, a *valet d'armes*, and a page. Only the first four were expected to fight, but all were to be mounted. Thus Charles intended to create a standing force of 6,000 combatants, whose core would be the 1,500 gens d'armes, all of whom received some pay from the king. The companies rarely if ever were at full strength. Charles also intended to create infantry companies of both crossbowmen and longbowmen to support the cavalry. Exemption from taxation was to be the major incentive for recruitment, but the absence of a military tradition among French commoners, and the enduring hostility of the nobles against arming their peasants, doomed the effort. France continued to rely on foreign mercenaries for another century.

THE WARS OF THE ROSES

In England the end of the Hundred Years War led directly into the Wars of the Roses. The return of the forces from France provided the two rival houses of York and Lancaster, which were competing for the English throne, with a core of veteran warriors. The coup of 1399 that had established Henry of Lancaster as king might have stood without serious challenge had not the third king of the line, Henry VI, the grandson of the mad Charles VI of France, gone mad himself in 1452. Leadership of the deposed royal dynasty had passed to Edward, duke of York, who used the Henry's incapacity to try to made good his claim to the throne. Both families used roses as their badges—Lancaster red, York white— hence Wars of the Roses.

Although the English had great difficulty in raising armies of more than 5,000 men in the last years of the Hundred Years War because of a decline in the prospects for plunder, the armies of the civil war often passed 10,000. Since the battles often took place in the next shire, it was easy to recruit men for short-term service. Both sides used the standard English tactics of the Hundred Years War; now one side, then the other stood on the defensive on a rise and waited for the enemy to attack. The presence of large archer corps on both sides ensured that the battles would be very bloody. Since, however, the archers largely neutralized each other, the deciding factor in battles was usually a bitter mêlée between the men-at-arms. One of the notable features of the war was the high casualty rate among the nobles in the battles, in large part a consequence of the massacre of noble captives after a battle. Both factions used artillery, but it does not appear to have been of much importance in deciding the battles.

Perhaps the most interesting battle was at Tewkesbury in May 1471, when a Lancastrian army under the duke of Somerset trying to reach the safety of Wales was forced to make a stand against an army under Edward of York. Posting his forces at the top of a small hill in the standard formation, Somerset waited for the enemy to attack. After a lengthy exchange of arrows, however, Somerset, presumably thinking that the Yorkists had been sufficiently softened up, ordered his men-at-arms to charge down the hill. Only the center obeyed the command, and Somerset found himself engaged in a mêlée with only a few of his men. The center was easily thrown back into the divisions that had remained in place. The entire Lancastrian line broke and ran. The fleeing men jammed up on the banks of the Severn River behind them and were slaughtered. This victory ensured Edward of York the throne, and he ruled successfully for twelve years.

Edward IV's death in 1483 reopened the civil war when his highly unpopular brother Richard usurped the throne from Edward's infant son. The extermination of the House of Lancaster had been so thorough that only a distant relative, Henry Tudor, was left to take up its cause. With aid from Louis XI of France, Tudor crossed the Channel from his French exile with 2,000 men in 1484. The next year he forced Richard III to fight at Bosworth Field. Richard's support had dropped so low that only about a third of the men with him were willing to fight for him. Richard, determined to die like a king, charged Tudor's lines with a few loyal supporters and died in fierce hand-to-hand combat. As Henry VII (1485-1509), Tudor established the Tudor dynasty and returned stability to England. But the stagnation in the English military continued under Henry, who was little interested in developments on the continent. Only with the accession of Henry VIII (1509-47) did some military change again occur. For well over 170 years the English military had remained largely as it had been in the early years of Edward III's reign.

GENGHIS KHAN AND THE MONGOLS

While the western Europeans were busy warring on one another, eastern Europe was bearing the brunt of attacks by two of the most powerful armies in history—the Mongols and the Ottoman Turks. The Mongols had probably the best of the preindustrial armies; certainly they conquered the greatest empire in history, although far from the longest lasting.

The Mongols were the most successful of the nomadic horse archers. Their weapons and style of warfare were little changed from those of the Huns. Although they did have more iron armor than the earlier nomads, they still relied largely on leather strips over heavy quilted cloth for protection against arrows. They generally depended upon kinship ties as the basis of their political and military systems. However, the lands of the Gobi desert were subject to erratic periods of rainfall. The population increase prompted by a period of more favorable weather would cause serious overpopulation when the climate changed for the worse.

The pressure created by overpopulation to find new pasturelands gave a tremendous impetus to territorial conquest, while the bitter competition among the nomads fostered by the hard times temporarily shattered kinship loyalties. Both circumstances permitted charismatic leaders to emerge who united the nomads through individual bonds of loyalty and promises of conquest. Genghis Khan (to use the most common spelling) was not the first chieftain to rise up in such a situation, but he was the most capable and by far the most successful. In 1206 he was strong enough to proclaim himself Genghis Khan (Supreme Ruler) of the Mongols. He declared that heaven had given him the empire of the world from east to west, and he set out to conquer it.

Genghis Khan's near success in conquering the entire Eurasian world depended in about equal parts on the nature of the men he led, their style of war, and his own talents as a commander. Like the Huns before them, the Mongols' speed, endurance, cunning, ferocity, and cruelty astounded all that beheld them. Mongol warriors received valuable training for war in their hunts. Columns of horsemen would enclose a vast territory of hundreds of square miles and drive the game to trapped be inside into a small space for slaughter. The coordination of thousands of men over a great distance was superb preparation for war almost anywhere, but especially in the vast spaces of central Asia. The tremendous speed and range of the Mongols provided them with numerous opportunities to catch their opponents completely by surprise. This combination of speed and surprise created some greatly exaggerated estimates of Mongol manpower. There can be little question that at the beginning of his conquests, Genghis Khan had no more than 100,000 men under arms, although the impressment of conquered peoples into his armies soon pushed the number well beyond that.

Genghis Khan harnessed the immense potential of the Mongol warriors for the conquest of a vast empire largely through his own great charisma and talents as a commander. He attended very carefully to auxiliary services such as intelligence, communications, and planning. Scouts and agents spent months before a campaign exploring the routes to a locale, viewing potential battle sites, assessing the enemy's defenses, and spreading disinformation. After all that, large columns of Mongol horsemen would ride to the target from as far as 1,000 miles away. The columns would usually follow widely separated routes yet would keep in close contact with each other and the central command so as to strike at the enemy at precisely the same time from different directions. The Mongols' small requirements for food and shelter, which reduced the size of their baggage trains, and their large strings of horses meant that they could cover vast distances in an amazingly short time.

The Mongol army was organized in multiples of ten, up to 10,000 men. Several of the latter units, called *tumens*, made up an army, which, if not commanded by the great khan himself, was always under a member of his family. A Mongol army was largely cavalry, both light and heavy, but it also included units of artillery men and engineers. Most Mongols were light cavalrymen, using the composite bow but also carrying swords and maces for hand-to-hand combat. An enemy wavering under the deadly fire of Mongol archers would often find itself suddenly assaulted by a charge of heavy cavalry. Wearing scale-mail armor these lancers struck with tremendous impact among an already disorganized enemy. A high-quality officer corps was ensured by the use of the khan's Imperial Guard as an officer training school. It is, however, impossible to speak of a standard Mongol battle tactic, since unpredictability, trickery, deception, and individual initiatives by the commanders were the norm.

After defeating the tribes on the fringes of the Gobi and incorporating them into his forces, Genghis crossed the Great Wall in 1213 to conquer northern China. He quickly demonstrated that he was a capable administrator. The government he established for his new lands included Chinese mandarins. As his empire spread westward, he developed the practice of appointing administrators chosen from one region to govern another region far away. Thus Europeans, for example Marco Polo, appeared in China, while Chinese were transferred to Persia and Russia.

In northern China, Genghis Khan came up against walled cities for the first time. He quickly learned the techniques of siegecraft, using captive engineers. Thereafter a highly mobile but powerful siege train was added to Mongol armies, and few cities proved to be more than temporary obstacles to their advance. The Mongols used catapults to throw pots of burning tar into cities, and on occasion, against enemy armies in the field. By the late 1200s they were also using gunpowder bombs and rockets. The latter caused little damage but did terrify the horses of the foe.

In 1218 Genghis Khan and his three sons led four armies in a massive campaign against the Muslim Turkish rulers of central Asia. The vast expanses of the region, the quality of its hardy horse archers, and the presence of a number of great cities such as Samarkind and Bokhara made the campaign a true test of the Mongol military and the Khan's leadership. The challenges were met brilliantly. It was the capture of the great cities of the region that was most impressive, since unlike the Chinese cities Genghis Khan had previously taken, these were massively fortified and experienced in withstanding sieges.

The Mongols sometimes captured a city with a sudden, unexpected dash to take one or more gates. If that failed and the city refused to surrender, the Mongols settled into a siege. Most of the army moved on to destroy any army that might come to the relief of the city, while the siege train was quickly brought up and set to work. Every technique of taking a city was employed—scaling, ramming, sapping, mining, and starvation. Gunpowder was used to undermine walls, and thus it was carried westward from China. Terror was another Mongol tactic. At times, when a besieged city was captured, its inhabitants were massacred and the city itself was razed. Yet another city similarly taken after long resistance might be spared. Genghis Khan and his captains were true masters at psychological warfare, using their record of terror and unpredictability as a way to sow confusion and dissension among defenders.

By 1221 the Mongols had taken all of central Asia, eastern Persia and Afghanistan as far as the Indus River. There the khan stopped to consolidate the lands already won. One army was sent westward across northern Persia to reconnoiter Russia. It crossed the Caucasus Mountains in winter and erupted into southern Russia in the spring of 1223. After mauling a Russian army, the force was ordered to rejoin the khan's army for a new assault on China. Late in 1226 Genghis crossed a frozen Yellow River and crushed the Chin Empire. He died the next year on his way back to Mongolia.

THE MONGOL EMPIRE AFTER GENGHIS KHAN

After a brief respite for the election of a new great khan from among Genghis' male descendants, the Mongol armies went back to the task of conquering the world on an even broader range of fronts. Korea was occupied in 1231, Kiev and most of Russia in 1240, Hungary in 1241, Asia Minor in 1243, Mesopotamia in 1258, and southern China in 1279. The extent of the Mongol Empire and the range of its armies are made evident by the fact that both Baghdad and Hanoi were sacked in 1258. this also shows that the Mongols were capable of fighting in both desert and jungle. They were equally successful in the heavily populated agricultural lands of China, the mountains of south central Asia, and the forests of Russia. In Russia not only did "General Winter" fail to stop them, as it did both the French and the Germans centuries later, they regarded it as their season of choice because the frozen rivers enhanced their mobility. Only the sea proved to be a barrier; the Mongols failed to conquer Japan despite attempts in 1274 and 1281. Yet in both cases it took storms of extraordinary ferocity (kamikaze, or divine wind) to stop them. And they did occupy the island of Java for several decades after 1292.

The Mongols were victorious against an equally wide range of military styles: fellow steppe horse archers, massed Chinese heavy infantry, Persian heavy cavalry, mixed units of Russian cavalry and infantry, Polish heavy lancers, a typical feudal army of knights and infantry, and even a Burmese army using war elephants. Of particular interest to us is the Mongol confrontation with the forces of eastern and central Europe. After defeating a Russian army of noble lancers in chain mail, supported by peasant infantry with spears and axes, in 1223, the Mongols returned in force in 1240 under Batu Khan, Genghis' grandson. The Russian princes failed to cooperate against the invaders and were defeated piecemeal, showing that the Mongols were capable of operating in forest lands. They established their domination over Russia for two centuries.

Pushing on westward in the winter of 1240-41, Batu divided his forces; part moved into Poland, while the bulk of them under Batu invaded Hungary. The Polish military of this era consisted entirely of noble mounted lancers, whose wealth determined how much mail they wore into battle. Poorly led by an inexperienced king, the Poles were routed near Cracow in March 1241. Some survivors fled westward and joined Moravian and German forces in making a stand at Legnica (Liegnitz) a month later. The Christian army, with its knights and peasant infantry, was essentially a feudal army. Its effectiveness was hampered not only by the usual problems of ill-disipline and poor communications but also by its mutli-national character. Nonetheless it fought hard and was defeated only by the stratagem of a feigned retreat, at which the Mongols were masters. Mongol progress further west was blocked by the castle of Liegnitz and the well-defended city of Breslau, and the Mongols lacked a siege train. Having accomplished their task of preventing support from being sent to Hungary, the Mongol forces swung south to rejoin Batu, about to engage in a major battle with the Hungarians.

Having used the winter of 1240-41 to move into northeastern Hungary, Batu Khan found himself facing the entire Hungarian, army assembled along the Sajo River. The Hungarians, under King Bela, were almost entirely cavalry, both lancers and archers. Bela had arranged his forces so as to defend the only bridge in the region over the fast-flowing river. Batu, seeing that the Hungarians, numbering perhaps as high as 60,000, occupied a relatively small zone around the bridgehead, sent a large detachment miles upriver to cross. In a splendid example of Mongol coordination of forces, Batu waited until that force was in position before assaulting the bridge held by the Hungarians. After some fighting around the bridge, which drew the Hungarians tightly around it, the Mongol detachment struck at their flank and rear. The Hungarians were good enough fighters that a sharp mêlée took place before they broke and ran. The Mongol pursuit slaughtered many, and there was nothing left of a Hungarian army to prevent the Mongols from ravaging the Hungarian Plains through the summer of 1241.

Detachments were sent on to the west, crossing the mountains of modern Yugoslavia and reaching as far as the Adriatic. A Mongol band, however, was trapped in a narrow mountain pass by the locals and badly cut up. By now much reduced in manpower, Batu decided to take his army with him when word came from Mongolia that the great khan had died and Batu was needed for the election of the next Khan. The Mongols never again operated west of the Vistula River, although they continued to control Russia for two centuries.

Even as the Mongols were gaining great conquests, the processes that would eventually undermine their hold on their new lands were underway. Rivalries among the descendants of Genghis Khan reduced the authority of the great khan. Those rivalries were exacerbated by the tremendous differences in the cultures of the lands the Mongols ruled, which had been parceled out to members of Genghis' family. As the Mongols began to adopt the advanced cultures of the regions in which they had settled, the cultural differences, for example between Persia and China, began to sap the unity of the Empire. And as the Mongols became assimilated in the advanced civilizations, they began to lose their original characteristics and became vulnerable to displacement. In China, Persia, and Mesopotamia, native rulers had replaced them by the end of the fourteenth century. In central Asia and Russia, where the cultures were not so superior to Mongol culture, the Mongols retained far more of their original lifestyle and, as a consequence, remained in control of those regions far longer.

THE RISE OF THE OTTOMAN EMPIRE

From a military point of view the Mongols merit the greatest admiration. It little detracts from their accomplishments to note that most of the major states they conquered were at the time of invasion badly divided or ruled by decaying dynasties. Nowhere was this more true than in the Middle East, where the Mongol incursion confronted a collapsing Seljuk Empire. The Mongols destroyed the remnants of the Seljuk state in Asia Minor in 1243 but soon withdrew. The power vacuum they left was soon filled by a new Turkish power, the Ottomans. The name came from their founder Osman (Othman), a successful warlord in western Asia Minor during the anarchy after the Mongol withdrawal. Osman was a devout Muslim dedicated to the jihad. He found abundant recruits for his holy war against the Byzantine Empire among the numerous Turks who had recently entered Asia Minor in advance of the Mongol army. In 1301 he defeated a Byzantine army, securing his control of the highlands to the south of the straits. By 1359 his son had extended his control to the Sea of Marmara across from Constantinople, and his grandson Muràd crossed the Dardanelles to begin occupying Europe, taking Adrianople in 1361.

The first Ottoman sultans were capable military commanders, building up a powerful army from among footloose warriors who had no reason to stay loyal to them except success. Their early forces were almost entirely light cavalry. As the sultans expanded their lands, they offered estates, or *timars*, to their warriors in exchange for military service. Despite the obvious resemblance to feudalism, there were two major differences: service was required for the entire campaigning season, and the timars were not hereditary. All the sons of a timar holder were obliged to find new lands for themselves, usually by taking part in the conquest of border lands. A newly occupied region quickly gained a corps of Ottoman warriors. The sultans were always willing to give timars to any Muslim cavalrymen who would fight for them, so they were able to recruit from across the Middle East.

The early sultans also created a bodyguard of mailed lancers, the *spahis*. As the Ottoman state grew, their number increased to several thousand, and they became a major element of its military. By the time of Sultan Muràd, another element had appeared, the famous Janissaries. They became so notorious that many writers think they formed the major part of the Ottoman army from the beginning, but this did not become true until the eighteenth century. The term came from the Turkish for "new troops," and they were raised from among the sultan's non-Muslim subjects. Legally the Janissaries were slaves of the sultan. The tradition of using slaves as warriors had appeared early in Islam, largely to avoid the prohibition in the Koran against Muslim fighting Muslim. They were called Mameluks, "owned"; Turkish slaves had constituted a major part of the military manpower of the Arab Empire.

Occasionally these Mameluks rose to high levels of government, and, most strangely, a group of them seized control of Egypt in the mid-thirteenth century. For two centuries they maintained a powerful state there, which was responsible for the final ousting of the crusaders from Palestine and Syria (the fall of Acre, 1291). More astounding, the Mameluk army, combining light and heavy cavalry, went undefeated in three major battles with the Mongols in Syria between 1260 and 1281.

Having inherited a tradition of using slave troops, Sultan Muràd began the systematic levy of Christian boys between ages seven and ten to serve as infantrymen. They were raised in the barracks to become both fanatical Muslims and disciplined soldiers. Not only did the Janissary system provide the Ottoman state with a corps of excellent soldiers, it also deprived its Christian subjects of a key part of their manpower for any potential rebellion. Since sons of converts to Islam were exempt, it prompted numerous conversions as well. The sultans ensured the loyalty of the Janissaries by selecting many of the experienced troops for high government office. The number of known defectors from their ranks is extraordinarily low. The Janissaries were primarily foot archers, but they also were capable of serving as shock infantry or as sappers at sieges. Until 1500 their number was no more than 4,000 men.

THE TURKS IN EUROPE

The superb army that Muràd built went on to success after success in Asia Minor and the Balkans. By 1395 the Turks had come up against the Hungarians. Their king, Sigismund, also duke of Luxembourg, used his contacts in the West to raise the call for a crusade against the Turks. Since the call came during a long lull in the Hundred Years War, there was little difficulty in recruiting a great number of knights, mostly French. Some 2,000 knights and double that number of infantrymen assembled in Budapest in the spring of 1396. They moved southward with 10,000 Hungarians, mostly cavalry. Sigismund was nominally in command, but the French rarely followed his orders. The arrogance and disrepute of the French contingent are well detailed in the chronicles of the crusade.

By September the army, following the Danube, had reached the well-fortified city of Nicopolis (Nikopal) in north central Bulgaria. The city was put under siege, but the crusaders, lacking a siege train, had to resort to a passive siege. They had no idea where the Ottoman army was until it appeared within a half-day's ride of Nicopolis. Sultan Bayezid had perhaps 20,000 men with him. Having fought in the area before, he chose a field flanked by ravines, where he hid a good number of his horsemen, and backed by a small hill, behind which he hid his spahis. Thus when the first French units arrived at the field, they had no idea that about half of the enemy was not in view. The French had rushed on ahead in order to have the honor of being the first in battle, disobeying Sigismund's orders that local infantry forces be used first to wear down the Turks.

The French easily scattered the front ranks of Turkish light cavalry, but then found themselves confronted by foot archers among rows of sharpened stakes. Despite taking heavy casualties, the French were driving the infantry off the field when the hidden light cavalry hit their flanks, shortly followed by the heavy horse from over the hill. Few French escaped the resulting carnage. The Hungarians came up soon after the first battle had ended. Sigismund, hoping that the earlier fighting had sapped the Turks, attacked, and a more evenly matched battle ensued. It was decided when a force of 5,000 Serbian horsemen in the sultan's service struck at the flank of the Hungarian army, and it broke up in disarray.

This devastating defeat created a highly dangerous situation for Hungary. But the sultan was forced to turn his attention to Asia Minor, where the infamous Timur (Tamerlane) a central Asian with Genghis Khan's genius if not his blood, had invaded with his vast army of horse archers. In 1402 Timur crushed the Ottomans in the Battle of Ankara and captured Sultan Bayezid, who died the next year in captivity. Christian Europe, however, failed to take advantage of the virtual destruction of Ottoman power. King Sigismund had been elected Holy Roman Emperor and was too deeply involved in the politics of Germany to respond. The decaying Byzantine Empire was incapable of taking the offensive.

THE FALL OF CONSTANTINOPLE

After Timur's death in 1405, Muhammed I, Bayezid's youngest son, ousted his older brothers to take control of what was left of the Ottoman state. By his death in 1422 he had restored its borders of 1402. His successor Muràd II (1422-1451) set to work to take the city-fortress of Constantinople, which was cut off from its hinterland. The Venetian and the Genovese fleets, both with a major stake in Constantinople's commerce, prevented it from being cut off from the sea. They and the poor remnants of the Byzantine fleet, along with the still formidable defenses of the city, foiled a Turkish siege in 1422.

The succession of Muhammed II (1451-81) brought to the throne a man with the drive to complete the task. In February 1453, he blockaded

Constantinople with a greatly enhanced fleet, and moved his army into place for a prolonged siege. The Venetian fleet tried to break the blockade but failed. Genoa provided 400 gens d'armes and 300 other troops. These two contributions reduce slightly the stigma on western Christendom for making no effort to relieve the city.

The total manpower available to the Byzantine Emperor Constantine XI (1449-1453) was about 8,000 men, well less than half of what had always been regarded as the proper-sized garrison for the city. The Turkish force has been estimated at 150,000 men, not an impossible number since the sultan put virtually all his resources into the siege. The key difference, apart from the small garrison, between this and earlier sieges of the city was the presence of huge cannon pieces in the Turkish lines, especially the super bombard called "Basilica," which hurled 800 pound balls. On April 21 they began to pound the walls. The quality of the walls, over 1,000 years old, was demonstrated by the fact that it took thirty-five days of constant firing before the outer wall was sufficiently breached to allow the Turks to enter the enceinte between the two walls. The inner wall, further from the guns, took even longer to breach.

Meanwhile the Turkish fleet attempted to gain entrance to the Golden Horn, but it was thwarted by the boom across the bay and a small Christian fleet. Muhammed ordered that a large part of his fleet be dragged overland to the Golden Horn, a distance of about a mile. On April 22 some seventy Turkish ships suddenly appeared in the Golden Horn, which made the low wall that ran along it highly vulnerable. Men had to be pulled from the main walls to defend it. Even with this major development, the attackers progressed slowly. Early assaults on the walls had resulted in very heavy casualties for the Turks, so Muhammed decided to put his faith in the artillery. Herculean efforts by the defenders to fill in breaches and repair the damage kept the attackers frustrated, but the defenders were running out of energy and supplies.

On May 29 the Turks made a general assault on the walls, including those along the Golden Horn. After several hours of vicious fighting, a body of Turks spotted a poorly defended postern gate in the inner wall and opened it. The presence of the enemy inside the wall compromised the defenses, and Turks began to enter in droves. Emperor Constantine was killed in the last Christian resistance, a fitting end to the Eastern Roman Empire. Constantinople's fall, after a full millennium of carrying on the legacy of Rome and protecting eastern Europe against the Muslims, to an enemy who made crucial use of gunpowder weapons, seems an appropriate point to end the military history of the Middle Ages.

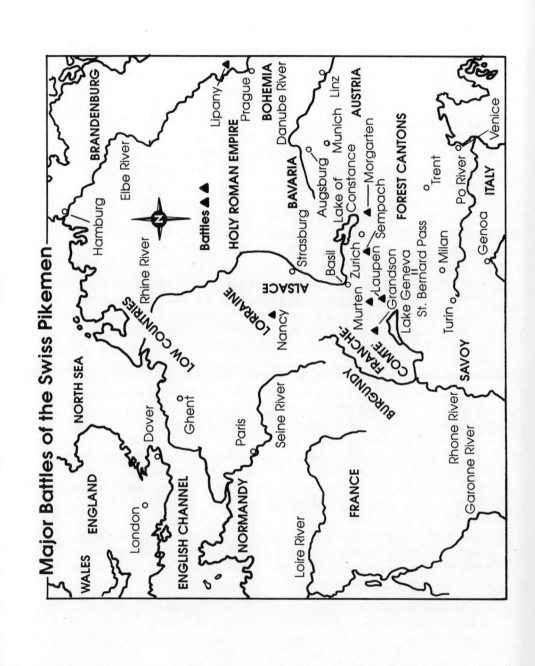

Major Battles of the Swiss Pikemen

12

The Fifteenth Century:
Pikes and Guns

When the Swiss start out to war, they swear a solemn oath that every man who sees one of his comrades desert, or act the coward in battle, will cut him down on the spot, for they believe that the courage and persistency of warriors is greater when they, out of fear of death, do not fear death. They begin a battle after they have formed their phalanx according to the old methods of war, and steadfast and fearless, they are almost indifferent to life and death. They threw away the shield which they had formerly been accustomed to use, like all other nations. They learned through experience that the shield could not in any way withstand the power of the phalanx and the lance.

Balcus, quoted in John Vincent, *Switzerland at the Beginning of the Sixteenth Century* (Baltimore, 1904; reprint New York, 1974), p. 16-17. Balcus was the ambassador of Milan to the Swiss Confederation from 1500 to 1504.

The fall of Constantinople is a convenient date to use as the end of the medieval era and its fixation on the superiority of cavalry, but the military key feature of the early modern period, the dominance of the infantry on the battlefield, was largely in place by 1453. By that date the Swiss infantry, using pikes as its major weapon, had already established its reputation as the preeminent army of the fifteenth century, and gunpowder weapons were on the verge of becoming the determining factor in war.

In the high mountain valleys of central Switzerland, where animal herding was more important than agriculture, feudalism and serfdom had never gained a foothold. The organization of society had changed little that of from the ancient German tribes. All free men of the clan fought together under the command of its head. Frequent clashes with neighboring clans and regions kept the men in fighting trim, as did mercenary service from 1100 on. Income as mercenaries along with the tolls on goods and persons crossing the Alpine passes enabled the Swiss to obtain a fair amount of iron. Much of it went into their weapon of choice, the halberd, a heavy ax with a long stout handle that eventually reached eight feet in length. It had an iron point for jabbing and a hook opposite the axhead for pulling knights off their horses. In the hands of a sturdy mountain man, the halberd could do fatal damage to even a well armored knight. The Swiss were not wealthy enough, however, to afford much armor until after they had established their reputation.

From 1100 to 1300, the population of the high valleys expanded considerably, and the canton, a somewhat larger political unit than the clan, developed. The authority of the canton was very limited, but its structure did provide a means for pulling together the armed men of several clans into a force of 1,000 to 2,000 men. Its command structure was very loose, being made up of the most experienced and respected warriors. The Alpine regions were part of a larger political entity, the Holy Roman Empire, but, as was true across the entire empire by 1300, the emperor's writ meant little. A greater threat to Swiss autonomy was the House of Habsburg, which originally controlled lands along the modern Swiss-German border and in 1290 had gained Austria. The Habsburg pretensions of sovereignty over much of Switzerland led to the creation in 1291 of a league of three cantons in west central Switzerland to resist the Habsburgs. It became known as the Swiss Confederation.

THE FIRST SWISS VICTORIES

By 1315 relations between the Swiss Confederation and Duke Leopold of Austria had deteriorated to the point of war. The duke led a force of about 3,000 men, mostly knights, into the high Alps. The confederation assembled close to the same number of men and waited in ambush between a mountain, the Morgarten, and a lake. A small body of crossbowmen (the story of William Tell predates this battle) was set behind a stone wall that blocked the narrow path the Austrians were on. The front of the Austrian column came to an abrupt halt at the wall, while the middle and rear continued to push forward. When they had become thoroughly jammed and confused, the Swiss halberdiers sprang from behind a ridge. Few knights were able to turn their horses to meet the Swiss before they were on top of them. Swinging their halberds with deadly effect, the Swiss tore into the Austrian ranks. The forward units could not retreat because of the crush of men behind, and they could not escape to the opposite flank because of the lake below them, so their casualties were very heavy. The Swiss victory was primarily one of choice of terrain, but it did secure the autonomy of the Swiss Confederation from the Habsburgs and persuade several more cantons to join.

Since the Battle of Morgarten was fought in circumstances badly to the disadvantage of cavalry, it is less noteworthy in military history than the Battle of Laupen in 1339. That battle occurred because of the expansion of the city of Bern. Bern's principal victim was the city of Fribourg, which organized a league of cities and minor princes to the west and north of Bern, a region known as Lesser Burgundy. Bern had taken the town of Laupen from Fribourg, and Fribourg's allies had put the town under siege with a large force of 4,000 infantrymen and 1,200 horsemen. Bern could put in the field a good-sized army of some 5,000 urban pikemen and a few

Top: An Ottoman Bombard of the mid-fifteenth century.   Bottom: A
French cannon and stone ball from about 1500.   The ball is over two feet
in diameter.

horsemen. The serious imbalance of cavalry persuaded the leaders of Bern
to contract with the federated cantons for 1,000 halberdiers.

Coming to the relief of its garrison in Laupen, the Bernese army
emerged from a thick forest atop a hill overlooking the Burgundian camp.
Since the Bernese were determined to fight a defensive battle, their captains
allowed the enemy, despite his surprise, to form ranks and attack. Because
the slope of the hill was less steep to their left, the Burgundians deployed
their cavalry on that flank. The 1,000 halberdiers formed the right of the
Bernese army, with a small number of crossbowmen in front and a few
knights in between. Once ready the Burgundians began to move up the
hill, but shortly before they reached the Bernese lines, the Bernese rushed
downhill at them. The cavalry brought the halberdiers to an abrupt halt,
but it could not break their ranks. Meanwhile the Bernese pike was easily
dispersing the enemy infantry. Victorious in the center and on the left, the
Bernese captains led their forces to the right; the combined units drove the
cavalry off the field. Since it was nearly dark, there was little pursuit, but
casualties among the Burgundians were heavy while the Bernese suffered
few. The Swiss had again defeated a force strong in cavalry, but this time
on a field far more suited to mounted warriors than Morgarten.

The results of the Battle of Laupen were twofold. Impressed by the
ease with which the Bernese pike drove off the cavalrymen, who admittedly

were already tired, the cantons began to adopt the pike as their main weapon. And Bern, Lucerne, Zurich, and several other cities entered into a loose alliance with the cantons. Over time they became full-fledged members of the Swiss Confederation, although relations among the members, especially between the cantons and the cities, often were very tense and occasionally bloody.

The growth of the confederation did not escape the attention of the Habsburgs, who had conceded nothing despite Morgarten. The Swiss for their part provided them with numerous provocations. The final straw was Lucerne's occupation of the town of Sempach in 1385, clearly a Habsburg fief. Duke Leopold II felt obliged to respond by leading a force of some 4,000 men, about one-third cavalry, into Switzerland in 1386. He decided to recover Sempach first before striking into Swiss territory. Leopold apparently left his infantry to invest Sempach, as there is no mention of Austrian infantry in the battle that followed. The Swiss assembled about 8,000 men with the speed that became their trademark, and rushed to Sempach.

The Austrian cavalry had left the immediate vicinity of Sempach, intending to cut the Swiss off before they could relieve the town. The vanguards of both forces were surprised to come upon each other about three miles from Sempach. Leopold, thinking that he had the entire Swiss army in front of him, decided to attack immediately. He ordered his first division to dismount and charge, leaving two divisions mounted in the rear. The armored infantry smashed into the Swiss with great force, capturing the standard of the city of Lucerne, home of most of the vanguard.

Much to the surprise of the Austrians, the main body of Swiss, arriving on the battlefield already in battle formation, then crashed into their flank. The Austrian line quickly collapsed. Duke Leopold ordered his second and third divisions forward. The second did so but with considerable hesitation, and it was in poor order when it collided with the Swiss and was routed. The third division, seeing what was happening to the second, broke and ran. According to the Swiss count, the Austrians left 676 men, including the duke, on the battlefield; the Swiss admitted to losing 120 men. When the duke's tomb was opened in 1898, it was discovered that he and nearly all the twenty-six important nobles buried with him had had their skulls split by halberds.

SWISS TACTICS

The Battle of Sempach confirmed Swiss independence, although the Habsburgs refused to recognize it for another three centuries. It also established the tactics that the Swiss used for the next 150 years. When an alert was sounded that an enemy had crossed the border, the several thousand armed men of each canton would assemble immediately under the command of the most respected fighter, chosen by an informal election. Generally Swiss armies were larger than the forces they faced. The forces of several cantons would join up and march to meet the enemy in three columns (it is not clear whether there were three columns at Sempach). Their lack of armor allowed them to move rapidly. The lead column was in the center flanked by a column on both sides. The flanking columns were some distance behind; thus the vanguard was often heavily engaged before the flanking columns, one after the other, smashed into the enemy's flanks. Should the lead column be forced back before the trailing columns arrived, a rare occurrence, they would not ruin the order and momentum of the trailing columns, as happened, for example, to the French at Crécy. The Swiss marched in essentially their battle order, so that once the enemy was spotted, they could rush at him with hardly a pause. Pikemen formed the head of a column, with halberdiers following behind to kill the enemy felled by the pike. Should the column be brought to a halt by contact with a powerful enemy, the halberdiers stepped forward to form a broad front.

Victorious in battle after battle, the Swiss had a tendency to overestimate their ability to take on a far larger enemy. This usually occurred when one or two cantons were engaged without the support of the entire confederation. On several occasions in the fifteenth century, a small Swiss force was put on the defensive against a strong enemy. In such a situation they formed the hedgehog, a circular formation bristling with pikes and halberds. An enemy strong in missile weapons could have made rather short work of such a formation, but the Swiss did not have to face one until after 1500. Shock forces, whether cavalry or infantry, would take very heavy casualties before destroying the hedgehog. The best example of the hedgehog occurred in 1444 at the Battle of Saint-Jacob, near Basel. A small Swiss force took on a French army, mostly cavalry. Convinced of their ability to defeat any army, even one said to be fifteen times larger, the Swiss attacked, but were quickly forced to form the hedgehog. Attack after attack was thrown back, but eventually the number of Swiss was reduced to nothing. According to the chronicles, 2,000 dead Frenchmen surrounded a heap of 1,500 Swiss in the center.

This and several similar battles helped to form an image of the Swiss as willing to accept death rather than surrender, while taking a very large number of the enemy with them. This image of indifference to death, whether their own or others', was compounded by their refusal to take captives for ransom. The absence of feudalism had prevented the practice from taking hold among the Swiss. In fact the Swiss took no prisoners at all, killing those few men who had fallen into their hands after a battle and executing the garrisons of forts that surrendered. The lethal reputation of the Swiss was a decided advantage for them in their battles of the fifteenth century, as many an enemy broke and ran before a battle had been settled.

THE WAR WITH CHARLES THE BOLD

That formidable reputation appears to have been a factor in the three great victories the Swiss won over Charles the Bold of Burgundy in 1476-77. Charles, who became duke of Burgundy in 1467, was determined to gain two major goals: the title of king to put him on an equal footing with his hated rival King Louis XI of France (1461-83), and the consolidation of his lands—Burgundy and the Low Countries—into a unified block of land from the Alps to the North Sea. In resurrecting the ancient claims of the kingdom of Burgundy and Emperor Lothair's Middle Kingdom, Charles was explicitly laying claim to a large portion of western Switzerland. Louis XI, known as King Spider because he "weaved webs of deceit around his enemies," used that threat and bribery to stir up the Swiss against Charles. Indeed it was a common contemporary opinion that the Swiss fought him as Louis' mercenaries.

The war began in 1474 when a Swiss force invaded and ravaged Burgundian territory and easily defeated a small unit of cavalry sent to expel it. Charles was determined to get revenge, but was able to free himself from other problems only in March 1476. He then led a large force of 3,000 heavy cavalrymen, 4,000 pikemen, 7,000 marksmen with crossbows and handguns, and a large artillery train into Switzerland. The wealthy lands that Charles ruled enabled him to hire some of the best fighters of several nations for his army: his own Burgundian knights, Flemish pikemen, Italian crossbowmen, German handgunners, and even a contingent of English archers. But the heterogeneous nature of his army would prove to be a problem in the battlefield.

Charles stopped to recapture the town of Grandson, which the Swiss had taken two years earlier and had executed its garrison. Having hanged the Swiss defenders of Grandson, Charles moved his army toward Bern. Several miles from Grandson his forces ran into the lead elements of the Swiss army. A surviving muster roll puts its strength at precisely 18,113 men. The Swiss were coming through a mountain pass, and so their three columns were spread out behind each other over a long distance. The Burgundians, on the other hand, were in a broad open space ideal for cavalry maneuvers. The lead Swiss column, about 8,000 men, seeing that their enemy was not quite in battle formation, rushed out of the pass to press their attack. Charles ordered his cavalry to strike from both flanks, while commanding several infantry units in the center to pull back to clear a field of fire for his artillery. The charge of the cavalry floundered on the sturdy Swiss pikemen. The failure of the cavalry coincided with the tactical retreat of the designated infantry units. Combined with the linguistic problems of the multi-national army, the two events led to panic in the rest of the army. The collapse of the Burgundian army was hastened by the appearance of the second Swiss column. The presence of the still dangerous cavalry force convinced the Swiss captains not to press their pursuit; and most of Charles' army escaped, although he lost all of his artillery.

Consequently Charles was able to re-form his army quickly, and in June 1476 was back on the attack. The contingents from the eastern cantons had returned home immediately after Grandson, and their absence reduced whatever apprehension Charles might have had about battling the Swiss so soon again. He struck at the town of Murten (Morat), fourteen miles from Bern. The duke settled his army of some 20,000 men into a siege of Murten, being careful to put his main camp in a place where his cavalry and new artillery would be most effective. A long palisade was built to protect both the camp and the siegeworks around Murten. The Swiss began to assemble, but several cantons were slow in arriving, and the captains put off any attack. Charles was well aware of the gathering of thousands of Swiss some ten miles away. He was also well acquainted with the

Swiss penchant for attacking as quickly as possible; when no attack came for over a week, he became convinced that they would not attack. So he relaxed his guard.

The Swiss were waiting for the Zurich forces to arrive. When they did, boosting Swiss manpower to about 26,000 men, including 1,000 knights from neighboring lands motivated by fear of Charles, they held a council of war. The account of the council is very revealing of the Swiss system of command. The captains from all the cantons and cities assembled to discuss when and where to attack and to elect a commander, in this case an Austrian knight. Once these decisions were made, the Swiss marched rapidly to the Burgundian positions. It was late afternoon when they arrived within sight of the Burgundians; a thick forest concealed their approach until they were within a half-mile of the Burgundian palisade.

Charles had already sent most of his force back to camp, leaving a few thousand men to guard the forward line. The Swiss immediately attacked the palisade, placing their cavalry on their flanks to protect against an attack by Charles' cavalry. Although the artillery took a heavy toll, firing into the massive blocks of Swiss infantry, the Swiss broke through the palisade before the guns could be reloaded. Panic seized the main units of the Burgundians when they heard the noise of battle, and only a few were able to form up before the Swiss were on top of them. Most of the Burgundians broke and ran. The direct line of retreat was blocked by Lake Murten, and the Swiss pursued vigorously. Burgundian casualties were very high—perhaps 8,000 men. Swiss losses also were heavy; one chronicle placed them at 3,000 dead.

The victory at Murten allowed the duke of Lorraine, who had sent some help to the Swiss, to recover much of his domain, including the city of Nancy. Despite the catastrophe at Murten, Charles rebuilt his army with his usual vigor and laid siege to Nancy. The duke of Lorraine called on the Swiss for help, but it was only after he agreed to pay them 4 1/2 guilders per man per month that they agreed to serve. In January 1477 he assembled an army of about 20,000 men and moved to relieve Nancy. Charles formed his infantry, perhaps 10,000 strong, into a solid block with his cavalry on both flanks, which in turn were flanked by a river on the right and a woods on the left. The Swiss formed two large columns, with only a small third column to serve as a rear guard. The vanguard moved to the right in order to strike at Charles' left flank from out of the woods, while the main column assaulted Charles' center. Simultaneously attacked from two directions by two powerful forces, the Burgundians broke and ran once again. Charles, trying to rally his men, was killed by a blow from a halberd, which split his helmet and skull. His frozen body was found on the battlefield two days later.

CONSEQUENCES OF THE BATTLE OF NANCY

These three great victories over Charles the Bold, while very different in details, are illustrative of the Swiss style of fighting. They outnumbered their enemy; they rushed quickly to the attack, catching the enemy in some disorder, even when he expected their attack; and their swift onslaught into the enemy's lines rendered his marksmen and artillery largely ineffective. Once they had broken the enemy, they gave him no quarter. The aftermath of the battles is also instructive: the Swiss were content to retire home quickly with their plunder and pay. Rivalries among the cantons and the cities made it impossible for them to remain together after the immediate danger had passed. For that reason the Swiss did not become a major political power, but remained simply a very potent military force. Had they wanted to, they could have easily carved out major conquests in Burgundy, Alsace, and Lorraine after 1477. That, however, would have benefited largely Bern. The mountain cantons, whose attention tended to focus on Italy and Austria, passed up the opportunity.

While the Battle of Nancy had little direct consequence for the victors, the death of Charles the Bold did have enormous repercussions. His heir was a twenty-year-old daughter, Mary. Louis XI tried to pressure her into agreeing to marry his seven-year-old son. (The wedding would have had to wait until the boy turned fourteen.) Mary refused with disdain; after all she was a Burgundian. She and her advisors sought a husband who would provide the help needed to protect her inheritance. Only nineteen-year-old Maximilian of Habsburg, son of the Holy Roman Emperor, was a plausible choice. The wedding took place in August 1477 at Ghent in Flanders, the new residence of the Burgundian court. Within a year a son, Philip, was born.

Maximilian, however, was not able to provide enough aid to keep Louis from making good his claim to the duchy of Burgundy, which was declared to be a vacant fief reverting to the king. Mary and Maximilian did hold on to the rest of Charles' lands — the Franche-Comté and the Low Countries. Upon Mary's death in 1482 after a fall from a horse, they passed to Philip, who eventually married Joanna of Spain, the heiress of Isabella of Castile and Ferdinand of Aragon. The fruit of that marriage was Charles of Habsburg, named after his great-grandfather. Upon the death of Ferdinand in 1516, he became Charles I of Spain, and when Maximilian died in 1519, he was elected Holy Roman Emperor as Charles V. Charles ruled four major realms—Austria, Burgundy, Aragon, and Castile. He was raised at the Burgundian court, and in a letter to his son he referred to Burgundy as his fatherland. Thus the bitter feud between the House of Burgundy and the French royal family was still very much alive in the sixteenth century, and it would have much to do with the constant warfare between the emperor and the French monarchs in that era.

There was nothing about the Swiss style of fighting that could not be learned by others, although certainly no one did it as well as the Swiss. In particular the southern Germans, long in conflict with the Swiss, began to adopt the Swiss system. These Germans became known as *landsknechts*, whcih originally meant trained soldiers but quickly took on the sense of mercenary infantrymen. When they and the Swiss clashed, the battles were very bloody and no quarter given. Generally the Swiss were superior, but the landsknechts had the advantage of being slightly cheaper to hire and serving longer without pay.

THE HUSSITES

The Habsburgs had some years earlier found themselves in the midst of another bloody struggle in which their enemy in this case, the Hussites, made good use of infantry. The Hussite were Czechs who were fiercely opposed to the German dynasties—the House of Luxembourg from 1346 to 1440 and then the Habsburg—that ruled their homeland, the kingdom of Bohemia. Nationalist opposition to the German rulers became identified with opposition to Roman Catholicism in the person of John Huss, a theologian at the University of Prague. His theological views were condemned as heresy, and he was executed as a heretic in 1415 with the cooperation of Sigismund of Luxembourg, both Holy Roman Emperor and king of Bohemia. The rage of many Czechs flared into open rebellion.

Few Bohemian nobles joined the rebellion, in part because many were German. The Hussites were left with a largely peasant army to face the masses of German knights whom emperor and pope summoned as crusaders. Religious zeal provided a basic foundation for the discipline the Hussites needed to stand up to armored cavalrymen, but it is unlikely that the untrained and poorly equipped Hussites would have endured for long had they not found a commander of the highest caliber in Jan Zizka. Zizka, who has been called the only real military genius of the Middle Ages, had gained vast experience in wars to the north and east of his homeland. During his time in Russia, Zizka had become familiar with using wagons as a means of defense against cavalry. The Russians used a train of wagons, which could be formed quickly into a circle, as an essential part of their tactics.

Zizka soon improved on the Russian system. In 1421 the Hussites won their first battle using the war wagons. Over the next year his tactics became well defined. Upon the news of a German invasion, the Hussite commander would find a position on the invasion route clearly favorable to his tactics and set up his forces well before the enemy appeared. The wagons were deployed in a line a few feet apart with chains and posts between them and, if there was time, a ditch dug in front. The dirt from the ditch was thrown under the wagons and a board hung down to prevent anyone from crawling under them.

Each wagon had a squad of ten men, twenty according to some sources. Half of the squad was armed with pike, spears, halberds and even sharpened farm tools; the Hussites did not have a uniform weapon. The task of these men was to defend the gaps between the wagons. The other half of the squad was armed with handguns; the Hussites were the first to use firearms extensively. The "hand cannons" of that era were clumsy and inaccurate, but the Hussites rested them on the sideboards of the wagons to provide greater control. The sideboards also provided protection for much of their bodies. Against the large target presented by mounted men, the handgun was reasonably effective, its impact compounded by its noise, fire, and smoke. What cavalry the Hussites had was drawn up behind the line of wagons, and sent out around it and through the gaps to charge the enemy at the right moment. By the time of Zizka's death in 1424 he had added artillery to his forces, which was mounted on special heavy wagons. It is not clear, however, how effective it was.

Zizka's death did not stop the Hussites, who went on to carry the war into Germany under his lieutenant. What did stop them was internal factionalism. From the first the Hussites were badly split over religious issues between moderates and radicals. The two factions were able to overcome their differences in order to carry on the war against the emperor, but by 1434 their successes had greatly reduced the external threat, and they began to fight among themselves. The final split came over a peace offer made by Sigismund, which the radicals, called Taborites, refused to consider. In the bloody Battle of Lipany, the moderate Hussites all but destroyed the Taborites, largely because the latter attempted to use the usual tactics against an enemy who knew them perfectly well. Accepting the peace with the emperor, the remaining Hussites let the war wagon system die out, and it appears to have had no influence elsewhere.

THE APPEARANCE OF GUNPOWDER

The Hussites are noteworthy as the first Europeans to make extensive use of gunpowder weapons. Such weapons were a century old by then. Despite strong objections from a number of historians, it is generally accepted that the Chinese invented gunpowder around A.D. 1000, and that the Mongols carried it westward. Whether the Chinese had gunpowder weapons beyond rockets is a matter of serious dispute among historians. There is no evidence for the diffusion of gunpowder to Europe, although it is known that Roger Bacon, the first European to record a recipe for it, did have contact with a European who had visited the Mongol capital. Bacon's recipe of 1249 called for saltpeter, sulphur, and charcoal in a proportion of 6-1-1. (The modern formula is 74-10-16.) His description of the powder as "fire for burning up the enemy" strongly suggests that there was then no thought of using it for propelling projectiles.

That step seems to have been taken by 1325. A Florentine document from that year strongly suggests the manufacturing of cannon. An English drawing dated to 1327 shows what seems to have been a primitive cannon. It is a potbellied vessel with a long neck, which is blocked by a piece of wood. Tied to the block is a large arrow. To the rear of the device a man stands holding a burning stick, and appears to be about to touch it to a burn hole. The weapon seems to be aimed at a castle gate, suggesting that early cannon were siege weapons. Whether the English had several small cannon at Crécy has been much debated; those who accept it as true say that they were useful for frightening the French horses. There is agreement that Edward III used cannon at the siege of Calais.

CANNON AND CULVERIN

While field artillery was used successfully by the Hussites in the 1420s, by the French in the 1450s, and by other armies in several battles in the same era, cannon developed largely as siege weapons. The earliest cannon were small pieces, but by 1370 great guns that were expected to smash walls were being manufactured. They became known as bombards, from the

Greek word for buzzing. Stone balls were used because their lower density required less pressure than iron balls of the same weight to be propelled at the same velocity. It reduced the strain on the cannon and thus the chances of bursting, although that remained a real problem in cannon of all sorts for several centuries. The irregular shape of the barrels meant that the less than circular shape of the stone balls was not a problem, since there was going to considerable windage regardless of the shape of the balls. Bombards were very short-barrelled, so the balls barely fit inside. That reduced their range and accuracy; but at the close distances involved in sieges, it was not a problem.

The enormous size that bombards achieved early on is shown by a piece made for Nuremburg in 1388 that fired a ball of 600 pounds. A bombard produced at Vienna about 1440 weighed 22,000 pounds and used 1,300 pound balls. Pieces of that size were moved on sleds pulled by teams of a dozen or more horses or oxen. The Turks at the siege of Constantinople manufactured their bombards at the site where they were to be used so they would not have to be moved. These huge cannon usually had individual names, which is suggestive of the near mystical character attributed to them.

Early pieces were cast from iron, but as their size increased and the quality of gunpowder improved, the quality of cast iron failed to keep pace. The most significant improvement in the making of gunpowder was the technique of forming it into grains or corns. Previously the components of the powder often separated as the powder was transported, making for burns of highly uncertain force—if the powder burned at all. Corned powder burned far more uniformly and reliably, and it also increased the force of the burn by increasing its speed. This had the desirable effect of increasing the muzzle velocity of the ball, but it also increased the strain on the piece. Metal fatigue, a consequence of the presence of impurities in the cast iron, set in after a few firings, resulting in the bursting of the guns. They were proofed at the foundry with an oversized charge of powder, and the recommended charge was scratched on the barrel, but that failed to take into account the problem of metal fatigue. Cannon bursting was a real problem, with often fatal consequences for gunners and bystanders.

There were two responses to the problem of bursting cannon. One was to develop wrought iron pieces. Wedges or bars of wrought iron were set together to form a circle, and hoops of red-hot iron were placed around them. As the hoops cooled, they contracted and sealed the barrel, although cracks along the seams were common. Guns of this sort tended to have short barrels and large muzzles, and were used largely as siege pieces. They were called cannon, from an Italian word for tube. They generally were breach loaders, having a removable pan in which the powder, wadding, and ball could be placed in advance, set in the cannon, secured in some fashion, and fired. Several pans could be prepared in advance to increase the rate of fire; however, if the next pan was put in too soon after the previous one had been fired, the heat could set it off. Improperly securing the pan also resulted frequently in accidents.

The second solution was to use bronze in guns. Long experience in making large bronze bells provided expertise in casting bronze, and the higher quality of bronze metal reduced the danger of metal fatigue. Bronze guns could be cast in one piece, with the molds designed to create thicker walls at the breach than for the barrel. A wooden cylinder was placed in the mold to create the barrel; the wood was later reamed out.

These pieces, called culverin from an Italian word for snake, were far more capable of using a large charge and throwing a ball with great force over a long distance. Because they were closer to being truly circular, the shape of the ball was important; and because they could take a larger charge, they could use iron balls. Consequently culverins had long barrels and narrow muzzles, and were muzzle loaders. They were more accurate and had a greater range than cannon and were used where such character-istics were deemed important, especially in the field and on ships. It was also discovered that an iron ball fired with a large charge from a culverin could do as much damage to a wall as a much larger stone ball. What kept culverins from completely replacing wrought iron cannon— until the mid-1500s, when improvements in iron casting were made—was the cost of bronze. The problem resulted in the practice that a conqueror had the "right of bells," the right to seize the bells of a captured town and melt them down for guns. While the terms culverin and cannon are used to identify the two general types of artillery of the era 1450-1600, there was an enormous variety in the size of the pieces and their names.

A major problem in using larger artillery was moving the pieces. Their weight and the primitive carriages made it a most difficult task in the mid-1400s. Rapid improvements occurred, especially in France from 1460 to 1490. Trunnions (loops) were added at the center of gravity of a piece to allow it to pivot freely up and down on the carriage. Carriages with large wheels, strong axles, and a long tail appeared, which could be quickly at-tached to a team of draft animals and moved. France gained a reputation for growing the large horses needed for pulling artillery. The task was made easier by using very large wheels. By 1494 the French had achieved rea-sonable solutions to the many problems of designing a gun carriage and had created the model that went essentially unchanged until the nineteenth century.

Determining the right elevation for a gun was one of two major tasks for gunners; the other was measuring out the gunpowder. A gunner's quadrant, an L with a plumb line attached at the angle, was intended to help with the first. Experienced gunners were more inclined to rely on their feel for the gun they were using, which was also true of the problem of determining the amount of powder. They used less powder than the amount scratched on the barrel at the foundry, but since metal fatigue could set in quite soon, bursting of the guns, killing the gunners, was a frequent event. In 1460 a piece of metal from a bursting cannon killed James II of Scotland. As late as 1553, the advisers of Henry II of France were furious with him for ignoring the danger when he personally touched off several guns at a siege. Gunners were regarded as civilian technicians, not soldiers. That allowed them freely to change sides after a defeat, but it also made them more liable to the revenge of the enemy's troops. The gens d'armes were especially quick to kill the gunners of the enemy, even as their commander was rushing to hire them for his army.

THE DEVELOPMENT OF FIREARMS

Handgunners faced the same thirst for revenge, because it was deemed unworthy for a commoner to kill a knight from a distance. Early "hand cannons" were smaller versions of the artillery. They were decidedly clumsy to use, unreliable, and inaccurate, and were used largely as siege weapons. After 1400, improvements came rapidly. One was the invention about 1420 of the match, a piece of string soaked in a saltpeter solution. It smoldered slowly but with a hot tip, and replaced the burning stick or heated iron rod used previously. This in turn led to the invention of the matchlock, a set of jaws into which the match was fixed. A spring-loaded trigger, of the sort already in use for the arbalest, thrusted the jaws and the smoldering string into the touchhole and the pan.

By 1460 the idea of using a finer powder in the pan to touch off coarser powder in the chamber had appeared. This early matchlock became known as the (h)arquebus, probably from the German words for hook and gun. The arquebus was fitted with a wooden stock that abutted the shoulder. This way of steadying the firearm replaced several earlier methods, ranging from hooking the gun onto walls or boards to bracing it against the chest. The latter method was so likely to break the breastbone of the gunner that only a small charge could be used. The new method enabled the trooper to use more powder and increase the range and impact of the ball. By 1500 the standard arquebus as it would last for over a century had appeared. A heavier weapon called the Spanish musket was developed shortly after 1500; it used a two ounce ball instead of the arquebus's one-ounce ball. It was far more effective in penetrating plate armor, but was so heavy that a forked rest was needed to steady it for firing. The fork became used for the arquebus as well, so the distinction between the two weapons is often difficult to make.

In the late fifteenth century, the handgun began to replace the crossbow. The two weapons had several similar characteristics: manufacturing costs were equivalent, although shot was cheaper than crossbow bolts; little training was needed for effective use; and similar time was required to reload. The arquebus gained its advantage on several minor points: slightly greater penetrating power and range; the psychological impact of the fire, noise, and smoke of the guns; and the fact that it could always be used as a club in hand-to-hand fighting. In 1507 the Holy Roman Emperor Maximilian ordered his forces to adopt the arquebus entirely. The crossbow, however, did not disappear that quickly; during the siege of Malta of 1565, for example, bows were brought out of storage when the rainy season began. The longbow's far superior rate of fire meant that the arquebus replaced the bow in England only at the end of the sixteenth century, after a vigorous debate on the relative merits of the two weapons. Because of firearms' slow rate of fire and the difficulty of using them on horseback, the Asiatic nomads continued to use composite bows long after 1600.

Early gunpowder weapons had little impact on war and tactics because Europeans had long been accustomed to the use of missile weapons and even the occasional presence of mechanical artillery in battle. Had the English appeared at Crécy with firearms instead of bows, it would have had little effect on how the battle was fought. Although the Hussites employed unusual tactics in combination with firearms, a strong corps of bowmen would have been as effective using Zizka's tactics. Only when commanders learned to combine firearms and pikes in coordinated units was there a significant change in tactics, although it is true that the same tactics probably could have employed bowmen effectively. It was in Italy that the new tactics were developed, during the long series of wars on the peninsula between 1494 and 1527.

13

War in the Renaissance

Of all the soldiers, the battle was especially deadly and very unequal for the French cavalry, for lead balls were sprayed by the Spanish surrounding them and ready on every side for their deadly volleys. These were shot no longer with the lighter firearms (as had been customary a little before) but with the heavier ones, which they call arquebuses, and they penetrated not only an armored horseman, but also often two soldiers and two horses. Thus the fields were covered with the pitiful slaughter of noble horsemen and by heaps of dying horses.

Paolo Giovio, quoted in Hans Delbrück, *History of the Art of War*, trans. Walter Renfroe, (Westport, Conn., 1985), 4, p. 43. Giovio, a sixteenth-century biographer, was describing the Battle of Pavia of 1525.

In the preceding chapters there has been little occasion to mention Italy, for Italy in military matters, as in so many other aspects of life, followed a different drummer during the later Middle Ages and the Renaissance. Far more urbanized by 1100 than the rest of Europe, northern Italy also had a large noble class living within the cities. It provided a cavalry force to be used with the city militia, which consisted of spearmen and, later, crossbowmen. Bitter rivalries among the cities, and often within them, provided ample opportunity for the Italians to hone their military skills.

In the twelfth century the northern Italian military was put to good use against the Holy Roman Emperor, who for 200 years had had some jurisdiction there. Frederick I Barbarossa was determined to make good his claim to real authority in the region. From 1160 on, Frederick almost annually led an army across the Alps to dispute control of northern Italy with a group of cities known as the Lombard League. It was centered around Milan, the major prize in most of the wars in the region. In 1176 Frederick, while marching with part of his army, all cavalry, to join up with the rest of it, ran into a large Italian force north of Milan near Legnano. The charge of the German knights easily broke the ranks of the Italian cavalry

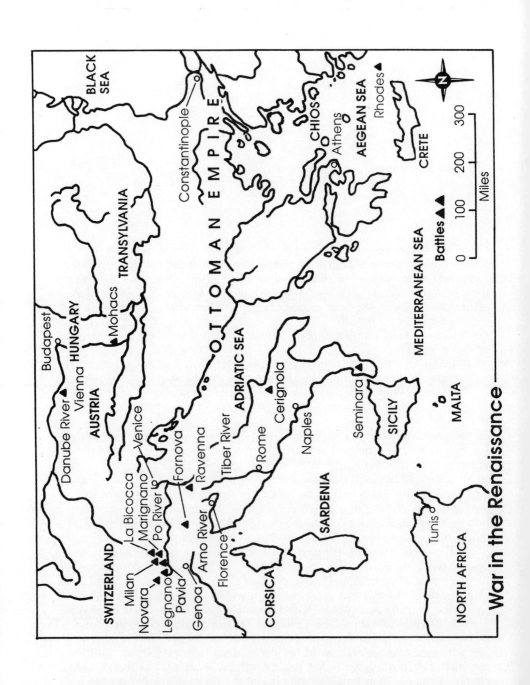

War in the Renaissance

and sent it reeling in retreat. Surprisingly, the infantry, largely Milanese, did not take flight as the Italian knights fled. They stood their ground despite repeated assaults by the Germans. The Italian cavalry halted some distance away; reinforced by a newly arrived company, it returned to strike Barbarossa's army on its flank, and routed it.

The Italian knights took all the credit for the victory, which elevated the reputation of the cavalry to the detriment of the infantry. The major consequence, however, was that northern Italian cities became truly autonomous. Despite another century of efforts by the emperors to reassert their authority, the Italian city-states were free to go their own way in politics and military affairs. Rivalries among the cities produced endemic petty warfare throughout the next two centuries. The merchants and artisans serving in the urban militias objected to the loss of time to military service and were not eager to expend much effort in training. Bitter social conflict in most cities between the middle and lower classes made it risky for the bourgeoisie to arm the lower classes, and difficult for the latter to be committed to the defense of the cities. Consequently the city-states began to turn to mercenaries.

THE *CONDOTTIERI*

As the number of mercenaries increased, the cities found it easier to sign a *condotta* (contract) for a small army with a *condottiere* (mercenary captain) than to recruit troops individually. In the fourteenth century, the captains and their men were largely non-Italians. There was a vast amount of manpower available across the Alps, and during the lulls in the Hundred Years War many free companies came to Italy to ply their trade. Despite Italy's reputation as a source of good crossbowmen, these mercenary companies were entirely cavalry. Generally the foreign condottieri did their duty without extensive interference in the affairs of the cities.

By 1400 a return to the use of native manpower had begun, but it little changed the style of military already in place. The condottieri, now mostly Italian nobles, were military capitalists whose product was war and whose capital was their manpower. The successful mercenary captain was a shrewd businessman who knew how to extract the best possible contract from the city-states. He had no compunctions about breaking a contract in order to accept another, even in the midst of a war. It was in his interest to drag a war out as long as possible to remain employed, but not to gain a reputation as a commander who engaged in bloody battles, for it would make recruiting more difficult. It was true that he had to win a certain number of battles to achieve a high reputation and earn top price, but an occasional surrender was not very damaging to a career. By surrendering when placed in an untenable position instead of fighting to the bitter end, a condottiere conserved his capital, his men, who could be ransomed for a reasonable sum. Thus the wars of the Italian Renaissance involved few bloody battles. The rival captains preferred to march and countermarch, hoping to place the other in a position where surrender would be quickly forthcoming. The losses would be more financial than human.

More serious a cause for concern among the city-states hiring native condottieri was their increasing interference in the politics of the cities. Being far more familiar with the system of government and more aware of the internal problems of the cities, they took advantage of their power as the only military force present in many cities and seized control. The term tyrant is used to designate such a ruler, who gained power outside of the usual system. The most significant of such condottieri-tyrants was Francesco Sforza. Hired by one faction in Milan in 1450, he seized power and declared himself duke of Milan. Upon his death in 1465, the title passed to his son, who was assassinated in 1476. That left an eight-year-old boy as the new duke under the guardianship of his uncle Lodovico Sforza, il Moro (the Moor). When the young duke reached the age of majority, il Moro refused to give up his power. The duke was supported across Italy, and especially by his father-in-law, King Alfonso of Naples. Il Moro, left without an ally in Italy, found one in Charles VIII of France (1483-98).

THE FIRST FRENCH INVASION OF ITALY

In 1494 Charles VIII was twenty-five years old and eager for the glory of military victory and conquest. Equally important the French royal family had an old claim to the kingdom of Naples, which il Moro urged Charles to make good. Accordingly he led an army across the Alps in September of 1494, initiating what is called the first French invasion of Italy. His army was huge for that era in western Europe, about 28,000 men in all. Almost one-half were cavalrymen, including some 8,000 men of the ordnance companies. The rest of the cavalry was made up of ill-disciplined and poorly equipped noble volunteers. Charles had 8,000 Swiss mercenaries and 6,000 arquebusmen and crossbowmen. What makes this army appear as a watershed in military history was the presence of a large artillery train. It consisted of about seventy guns, mostly bronze, on mobile gun carriages drawn by horse teams, which permitted them to be moved with the army. Although the three arms of an army—infantry, cavalry, and artillery— were not as well coordinated as in later armies, it was the first time that a field army included significant elements of all three.

The strength of the French king overawed the Italians, whose armies were far smaller and had little artillery. The French easily brushed aside the combined forces of several condottieri in Piedmont, and moved down Italy to Naples as if they were on parade. Charles proclaimed himself king of Naples, and King Alfonso fled to Sicily. However, what was so easily won was almost as easily lost. Neopolitan resistance quickly appeared; it was aided by Ferdinand of Aragon, since Alfonso was his cousin. Ferdinand sent a small force to Italy under Hernandez Gonzalvo de Cordoba, whose talent as a commander gained him the title of Great Captain.

Frightened by the possibility that he might get trapped in Naples, Charles divided his army and led half back toward France. In early 1495, Venice, which usually sought to be neutral in any conflict, had joined an anti-French league that included the pope, the Holy Roman Emperor, Ferdinand, and even il Moro of Milan, who had quickly repented of his dealings with France. In July an army of about 15,000 men, mostly mercenaries in the pay of Venice and Milan, moved to block Charles' passage across the Appennines. Charles' army had 900 gens d'armes, 8,000 infantrymen, and most of his artillery. The armies clashed near Fornovo on the Taro River.

The Italian captains had devised a complicated plan of battle, which along with their manpower superiority they believed would induce Charles to surrender. When they realized that they had to fight, their attack was hampered by having to cross the river in the face of the French artillery. They were taken by surprise by the ferocity of the French in battle and the heavy casualties they inflicted. The French won the battle in that they drove the Italians off with casualties of 3,300 men and cleared the way into the Po valley, but the Italians also were successful in that Charles became even more determined to return home. Once there he largely forgot about the army he had left in Naples.

THE RISE OF THE SPANISH INFANTRY

A week before the Battle of Fornovo, a combined Aragonese-Italian army had faced the French army that had remained in southern Italy in the Battle of Seminara. They were routed, as the Spanish had been nearly every time they had fought the French in the Middle Ages. During that period the Spanish had relied largely on light cavalrymen, called *genitors* who carried round shields and threw javelins. Their principal foes, the Spanish Muslims, also depended on light horse during the centuries of warfare the Christians called the *reconquista*.

The final phase of the reconquista began in 1481, after a long period of relative peace, with a Muslim attack on a Christian fort in southern Spain. Ferdinand of Aragon (1479-1516) and Isabella of Castile (1474-1504) committed their full resources to the renewed war. By April 1491, Muslim control of southern Spain had been reduced to the great fortress-city of Granada, which was put under siege by a 20,000 man army and 80 guns. After a fourteen-month siege, the Moors surrendered, ending eight centuries of Muslim rule in the Iberian peninsula. The conquest of Granada allowed the two monarchs to attend to momentous projects: Isabella to provide the final sum of money needed for Columbus' first voyage, and Ferdinand to intervene in Italy.

The army that Cordoba led to Italy in 1495 included 1,500 genitors, 100 gens d'armes, and 1,500 infantrymen. Spain had few heavy cavalry troops, in part because most Spanish nobles were too impoverished to afford the necessary armor and also because Spain could not breed enough great horses because of agricultural deficiencies. The Spanish infantry was ill-disciplined, which made their use of the short sword and buckler in the Roman style ineffective. Cordoba's army did include some crossbowmen and a few arquebusmen. At the Battle of Seminara the French heavy horse crushed the Spanish and Italian cavalry, while the mercenary Swiss pike easily disposed of the allied infantry.

Several times in history, a devastating defeat has led to a productive search for new tactics and weapons. Thus after Seminara, Cordoba recognized the need for a new type of army. He turned much of his infantry to carrying pikes, behind which he deployed the sword and buckler men. When pike jammed against pike, the swordsmen found it much easier to slip in among the ranks of the enemy pike than did the halberdiers with their long and clumsy weapons. More significantly in the long run, Cordoba also vastly increased the number of arquebusmen, and eliminated the crossbow.

Cordoba got his opportunity to use his greatly revised army in 1503 at the Battle of Cerignola, east of Naples. His force of 6,000 men, mostly infantry, was deeply entrenched on the lower slope of a hill and was fronted by a ditch and a palisade. His genitors were used to harass the French as they approached, while the small amount of heavy cavalry was held in reserve. The French chose to attack in an unusual formation: the gens d'armes formed the right, forward echelon, the Swiss pikemen the center, and the French infantry the left. The French cavalry made contact first and was brought to a halt within easy arquebus range by the ditch and palisade. As the infantry units reached the ditch, the front ranks scrambled across it and up the palisade, but devastating arquebus fire drove them back. With the entire French line in disorder, Cordoba ordered his heavy cavalry to strike at the French flanks. The French were routed, and the infantry, pursued by the Spanish cavalry, suffered very heavy casualties. Cordoba spent the next year mopping up the remaining French garrisons, and in 1505 Louis XII (1498-1515), Charles VIII's cousin and successor, agreed to recognize Ferdinand as king of Naples.

THE SECOND FRENCH INVASION

Louis XII, however, had not conceded all of Italy to his foes. Because his grandmother had been a member of the ruling family of Milan prior to 1447, he claimed the city. Louis occupied Milan in 1500, during the second French invasion. The twists and turns of the shifting alliances of the next several years need not concern us, since they produced no major battle until 1512. That year the young French commander, Gaston de Foix, who had been twenty-one years old when he received his command in 1511, invested the city of Ravenna, held by a Spanish garrison. A large Spanish army arrived to relieve the city, commanded by Raymon de Cardona, since Cordoba had been recalled to Spain. He followed Cordoba's tactics of entrenching his infantry and some thirty guns in a strong position in front of an unfordable river, and waiting for the attack. The Spanish cavalry was deployed in the open on both flanks.

De Foix pulled most of his men out of the siege lines to attack the enemy. He drew them up in a semicircle facing Cardona's lines and opened fire with his fifty-four guns, devastating the Spanish cavalry. Unwilling to take it for more than a few minutes, the Spanish horse on both flanks charged the French cavalry. After a sharp fight, the Spanish cavalry was broken up and driven off. As the Spanish cavalry was collapsing, the French infantry, which included a large number of landsknechts, was ordered to charge. It did so with enthusiasm, since it had been passively taking heavy artillery fire for some time. The heavy casualties the infantry took in front of the Spanish lines might have broken it, had not the French cavalry, returning from driving off the Spanish horse, attacked the Spanish flanks. Two cannon, dragged along the opposite bank of the river for several miles, also opened on the Spanish rear. The Spanish infantry soon broke and ran, suffering heavy casualties from the French pursuit. De Foix, taking part in the pursuit, was killed by an enemy company that turned on its tormentors, costing the French a very promising commander. The Battle of Ravenna is regarded as the first where systematic artillery fire was the determining factor.

If Ravenna can be considered a nearly modern battle, the next major confrontation saw a return to earlier tactics. The French could not follow up on their victory because Emperor Maximilian had declared war on France, forcing most of the Germans in French service to withdraw. A Swiss army in Maximilian's service moved into the region of Milan. In June 1513, the French and the Swiss clashed at Novara, west of Milan. The French had some 10,000 foot soldiers, 1,000 gens d'armes, and 1,000 light horse. Because the French had crossed the Alps much earlier in spring than the Swiss had expected, most of the 8,000 Swiss were still in the cantons. By forced marches, they quickly arrived in the vicinity of Novara. The French commander knew of their arrival but expected them to rest before attacking.

The Swiss, however, rushed on toward the French positions after only three hours of sleep. They arrived at dawn, catching the French by surprise. The Swiss were arrayed in their usual three columns, but the outside columns were both quite small and in front of a massive center column. The outside columns hit the flanks of the French army, setting it up for the main blow a short time later in the center. The French did use their artillery, and it caused heavy casualties in the massive block of charging infantrymen. But the speed of the Swiss enabled them to overrun the guns before their momentum was halted. The French infantry took the brunt of the attack; it was reported to have had over 5,000 casualties. The French cavalry was hardly engaged. The Swiss were said to have lost 1,300 men, mostly from artillery fire.

MACHIAVELLI'S *ART OF WAR*

One consequence of the French defeat at Novara was the ousting of the pro-French government in Florence. A Florentine official, Niccolò Machiavelli, lost his position and was forced into retirement. He turned his attention to writing political theory and history. His *Art of War* (1520) is not as well known as *The Prince*, but in the sixteenth century, it was far more influential. Machiavelli had watched the condottieri quickly succumb to the foreign invaders, and as an Italian patriot he was enraged at what he regarded as the betrayal of his homeland. In his work he set out his ideas for a potent Italian military that would drive the foreigners out of Italy and eliminate the need for the mercenaries.

Like so many of his contemporaries, Machiavelli looked back to the Romans for inspiration. He saw the Roman military system of the early Republic as the ideal, with its citizen soldiers who fought out of love for their homeland. Vegetius' description of the Roman legion was the basis of Machiavelli's proposed Italian army, but he made some changes in the Roman model to accommodate the new weaponry of his day. In general he was convinced that the training and tactics of the Roman legion were fully appropriate for his day. He largely equated the arquebusmen with the Roman light infantry, and did not believe that firearms would replace shock weapons. In particular Machiavelli emphasized the importance of a disciplined heavy infantry that was capable of forming tactical units. He felt that discipline could not be maintained in a mass army, and advocated dividing an army into tactical units of 600 to 800 men. He also believed that marching in step was an effective way to get the men to execute their tactical maneuvers on the battlefield.

Machiavelli's achievement was to reinterpret Vegetius' work in the context of the early sixteenth century, while emphasizing that the Roman's book was still a valid description of military practice. He thus added the military to the long list of areas in which the Romans served as authorities for the Renaissance. The *Art of War* was quickly translated into most European languages and had broad influence on future generations of commanders, most importantly Maurice of Nassau and Gustavus Adolphus.

THE THIRD FRENCH INVASION

The irony of the Battle of Novara is that it was the last battle in which the Swiss style of heavy infantry, which Machiavelli praised very highly, was successful. Like many of the Swiss victories, it had depended upon surprise and speed. Two years later in 1515, these were no longer sufficient for victory against the new king of France, Francis I (1515-1547). Twenty years old he was impetuous and dashing. He was determined to win military glory, gain revenge for previous French defeats, and make good his family's Italian claims. Francis secured an alliance with Venice and in June 1515 led a great army into Italy: 2,500 gens d'armes, 1,500 light cavalry, 18,000 infantrymen, and an artillery train of 72 guns.

Francis established his camp, which he entrenched, at Marignano, ten miles south of Milan. The Swiss assembled in Milan, but French gold persuaded a large number to return home. About 15,000 foot soldiers and 500 Milanese cavalrymen remained to do battle with the French. Francis decided to wait for the arrival of a Venetian army, giving the Swiss the opportunity to take the offensive. About noon they marched out of Milan, having spent the morning debating an even more generous offer from the king. They covered the ten miles in four hours, but Francis' scouts kept him informed of their progress.

The Swiss attacked in their traditional three columns, reaching the French lines before the artillery did much damage. Extremely bitter fighting occurred along the lines of the French infantry. They were kept from breaking by a counterattack of the French gens d'armes led by Francis himself. At dark the two armies disengaged; and they spent the night only a few yards apart. At dawn the Swiss, drawn up in two columns, attacked again. The French cavalry charged, bringing the Swiss to a halt and allowing the French guns to tear great gaps in their ranks. Nonetheless, the

Swiss might still have prevailed had not the lead elements of the Venetian army appeared on their flank. The Swiss carefully disengaged, taking their wounded and establishing a strong rearguard. Local gravediggers were said to have buried 16,500 bodies from both armies, and a good number of French nobles were embalmed and returned to France. Francis was so pleased by the showing of his gens d'armes he declared that no one could again call them hares in armor.

Marignano dealt a devastating blow to the Swiss style of war. It marked the last time that the Swiss fought as a national army outside of their borders, and thus it can be regarded as the beginning of Swiss neutrality. Nonetheless the battle did not remove the Swiss as a major factor in European war, for they continued to appear in large numbers as mercenaries. It resulted in the Treaty of Geneva, in which eight cantons agreed to allow the French to recruit in their lands. From that point on Swiss troops appeared largely as mercenaries in the French army.

THE FRENCH-HABSBURG FEUD

French access to Swiss troops became increasingly important in the next several years, as young Charles of Habsburg, already the ruler of the Low Countries and the Franche-Comté upon his father's death in 1506, began to accumulate the vast number of titles that came from his grandparents. King of the Spanish realms upon Ferdinand of Aragon's death in 1516, Charles gained the titles of duke of Austria and king of Bohemia when his grandfather Emperor Maximilian died in 1519. Charles faced strong competition in the election for Holy Roman Emperor from Francis I and Henry VIII, but he won the war of bribing the electors and became Emperor Charles V. As emperor, Charles had rather little real authority in Germany and became mired in the enormously difficult matter of the Protestant Reformation; but he did gain the right to call on the Germans for money and manpower for war, although both were usually granted only reluctantly.

Becoming emperor provided Charles with a pretext for war with France; he claimed the right to name the duke of Milan, on the ground that Milan was a fief of the empire. Distracted by a revolt in Spain, he could not attempt to make good his claim until late 1521, when he sent a Spanish force north from Naples and a German force south across the Alps. In the following spring, the two armies, some 29,000 men in all, joined up and moved on Milan. There a French army of 16,000 Swiss, 7,000 gens d'armes, and 10,000 French and Italian foot soldiers was waiting. In April 1522, the imperial army entrenched itself on the grounds of an estate called La Bicocca, three miles from Milan. The French commander, Odet de Lautrec, was not eager to attack, since he recognized the strength of the imperial positions. His Swiss, chafing to get into battle, demanded that he fight or they would return home.

Against his better judgment, Lautrec moved his army into position to attack. He agreed to the Swiss demand that they lead the assault; their confidence had been little damaged by Marignano. A force of French cavalry was sent forward first to clear the ground in front of the main imperial position. Then two columns of 4,000 Swiss apiece (it is not clear where the rest of the Swiss were) were directed at the imperial center, while the main body of French cavalry was to strike at the imperial right flank. A gang of sappers was attached to the Swiss to fill in the ditches and bring the artillery close enough to be effective. When Lautrec ordered the Swiss to wait for the artillery to be brought up and the cavalry to execute its flanking maneuver, they flatly refused.

Charging across a field crisscrossed by ditches, the Swiss took very heavy casualties from the imperial artillery. Just in front of the imperial lines a deep ditch had been dug and the dirt thrown up to form a rampart that was said to have been a pike's length from bottom to top. As the first ranks of the Swiss jumped down into the ditch, Spanish arquebusmen opened up with devastating fire. Scrambling over the dead and wounded of the first ranks, some Swiss made it to the top of the rampart, but German pikemen deployed behind the arquebusmen drove them back. After taking perhaps 3,000 casualties in all, the Swiss broke off and, as at Marignano, carefully pulled their columns off the battlefield. Few French units had been engaged up to that point, but they also pulled out. The next day the remaining Swiss abandoned the French entirely and returned home. A contemporary said about the Swiss after La Bicocca: "They returned to their mountains much diminished in numbers but much more so in audacity, for it is certain the losses they received at Bicocca so affected them that for several years they did not show their accustomed vigor."[1]

The battle was the last time the Swiss used their traditional charge of large columns of pikemen. They continued to appear in large numbers, mostly in the French army, for another century, but thereafter they made use of tactics similar to those of other infantry forces of the era. Those tactics involved the heavy use of firearms. La Bicocca was the first battle where firearms were the determining factor. That they were used in large numbers was largely because of the presence of the Spanish army. By 1523 the Spanish had largely completed the transformation of their army that had begun after the defeat of 1495. The sword-and-buckler men had been replaced by arquebusmen, so that pike and firearms were about equal in number.

THE BATTLE OF PAVIA

The arquebus played a dominant role in the last great battle of the three decades after 1494, an era unusually studded with major battles. Francis I was furious upon learning of the defeat at La Bicocca. He immediately began to make preparations to lead a larger army into Italy. In October 1524, he crossed the Alps at the head of a great army of well over 30,000 men. The imperial garrison in Milan quickly abandoned the city for more defensible strongholds such as Pavia south of Milan. By November the French had settled into a siege of Pavia. The city held out through the early winter while the imperial commanders collected manpower to relieve it. They were eager to attack the French, because the contracts of a large portion of their landsknechts were about to run out, and they lacked the money to pay them. They wanted to use them before these troops left their service. Consequently in early February the imperial army moved within close range of the French, and several weeks were spent probing and feinting.

Francis' army of about 25,000 men (some French had been dispatched toward Naples) was encamped in a large walled park whose walls provided an excellent defensive line, bolstered by fifty-three guns. Unable to draw the French out for a battle, the imperial commanders moved under the cover of darkness to a corner of the park. There sappers broke out three openings, and the imperials slipped in and took up positions. Exactly when Francis became aware of the imperials inside the park is a matter of dispute, but he had sufficient warning to get a number of guns turned in the right direction. He decided to attack with the units he had in hand, mostly cavalry.

The French guns began the battle, scoring effectively on the large squares of enemy infantry; but then Francis charged his cavalry in front of the guns, silencing them. The French gens d'armes easily broke through the imperial line of cavalry; but that exposed them to a solid line of Spanish arquebusmen, whose fire rapidly reduced them. By then Francis' Swiss had also advanced. Musket fire all but halted them, and they barely came to "push of pike" before pulling back. Other French units of infantry fought more bravely but only suffered annihilation for their courage. The king continued to fight at the head of a dwindling company of gens d'armes until his horse was killed under him and he was captured. Pavia was a true disaster for France: the king was a captive and his army virtually destroyed—8,000 men dead and 10,000 captured. The imperial army suffered 1,500 dead.

Francis wrote to his mother: "All that is left to me is my honor and my life, which is safe."[2] He was taken to Spain, where he was confined in the rude tower of a fortress. Deprived of his usual pastime of hunting and the company of women, he quickly agreed to a demanding peace treaty: Habsburg sovereignty over Burgundy, Flanders, Milan, and Naples was recognized; and Francis, recently a widower, was to marry Charles' sister. Francis persuaded his captors that he alone could effect the transfer of Burgundy, so it was agreed that he would be exchanged for his two older sons, ages six and eight, until the treaty was fulfilled. The story has it that when he again touched French soil in March 1526, Francis leapt on a horse, shouted "Now I am king again," and rode off without looking back at his sons being taken into Spain. He disavowed the treaty on the grounds that it had been coerced from him, and the war resumed.

The war was carried on with no major battles until 1529, when a new treaty called for the payment of 2 million gold crowns for the royal sons instead of the transfer of Burgundy. Finally returning home after four years in captivity, the younger son, who became Henry II in 1547, burned with hatred for Charles V. His hatred ensured that the Habsburg-Valois wars would continue after he became king.

THE SPANISH *TERCIO* SYSTEM

Having experienced forty years of nearly continuous warfare, the Spanish army by 1534 had finished the transformation of its infantry. Charles V's ordinances of 1534 were the culmination of the long era of change and established the form of the Spanish army for the next century. The key unit described therein was the *tercio,* "third." It was based on the traditional division of an army into three parts, but a tercio, while capable of serving as a division in a full army, also could operate separately. The ordinances set the tercio's size at twelve companies of 258 men apiece or 3,096 in all plus a staff of nineteen persons. There were to be six companies of pikemen and six of arquebusmen, each company consisting of 240 privates, a captain and four company officers, ten corporals, a drummer, a fifer, and a chaplain. The tercio's staff included the commander, called the *cabo de colunela* (head of the column), origin of the word colonel. There were six staff officers, a physician, a surgeon, an apothecary (druggist), a chief chaplain, a drum major, and eight halberdiers to serve as a bodyguard for the commander. Among the interesting features of the tercio's organization was the presence of thirteen chaplains but only three medical personnel. The monthly pay listed in the ordinance included forty escudos for the colonel, fifteen for a company captain, four for an arquebusman, and three for a pikeman.

The tercio was strictly an infantry unit; it did not include any cavalry. Squads of horse did often accompany them, but their numbers were quite small, and Spanish commanders learned to depend little on the cavalry. What the 1534 document does not reveal is how the arquebus and pike were deployed on the battlefield. From scattered accounts and drawings it appears that for a time after 1534 the two types of soldiers were drawn up in large blocks, each consisting of one type of weapon (hence the term Spanish square). The squares alternated across the line with a similar line of squares in reserve. It was soon recognized that such a formation made the arquebus squares in an open field very vulnerable to cavalry charges. Even with each rank of gunners stepping forward to fire, charging horsemen could be on top of them before their fire could halt the charge. If the pikemen rushed over from their squares to provide support, they would be disorganized and would have lost the depth and solidity of formation that was the pike's primary strength.

Consequently other formations were tried to better utilize the strengths of both weapons. The most successful appears to have been one in which a solid block of pikemen was enveloped in the front and on the flanks by several ranks of gunners. Their firepower would slow down the enemy's charge—whether cavalry or infantry—and occasionally halt it, but once the enemy came into close contact, the arquebusmen would retreat into the ranks of pike and to the rear, leaving a bristling front of pike to take the impact of the charge. Should the gunfire halt the enemy or should he refuse to charge, the pikemen could go on the offensive with their own charge. It was felt, however, that the Spanish squares were more effective standing on the defensive, at least at the beginning of a battle. Should the enemy choose not to charge, a group of experienced men was sent out to provoke him into attacking. The low survival rates of these squads gave rise to the term "forlorn hope" or the French *enfants perdus* (lost children) for them. Gradually the Spanish square system spread across western Europe, but each nation had its own variation on the Spanish model.

THE OFFENSIVE OF THE OTTOMAN EMPIRE

The one powerful army active in Europe that did not follow the Spanish system was the Ottoman. The Turkish infantry corps, the Janissaries, adopted firearms early on but never the pike, using their swords for hand-to-hand fighting. The heart of the Ottoman army continued to be the horse archers, complemented by an increasing corps of heavy cavalry, the spahis. After his army had recovered from the costly conquest of Constantinople, Sultan Muhammed II returned to the offensive against Christendom, landing a force on the heel of Italy in 1480 and promising his soldiers the sack of Rome. Fortunately for Europe, he died the next year, and his army was expelled from Italy. His successor was the only member of the Ottoman dynasty in its first three centuries who was not an aggressive military leader. The Ottoman army thus remained at home until 1512, when hot-tempered and aggressive Selim I the Grim (1512-20) gained the throne. His aggression, however, was directed toward Persia and Egypt, not Europe. He defeated those two Muslim states and annexed Mesopotamia and Egypt.

The conquest of Egypt from its Mameluk rulers vastly increased the strategic value of the island of Rhodes. Located off southwest Asia Minor and the last outpost of the crusaders, Rhodes controlled the sea lanes between Constantinople and Egypt. It was left to Selim's son, Suleiman II the Magnificent, (1520-1566) to strike at Rhodes. Sultan at age twenty, Suleiman was a first-rate administrator and important patron of culture as well as a great commander. For most of his reign his attention was focused on Europe, but first he turned on Rhodes. After Acre on the Palestinian coast fell in 1291, the Knights Hospitaler had escaped to Rhodes, which they massively fortified. A failed Turkish attack in 1480 gave them ample warning and forty years to build up their defenses further, so that by 1520 the city of Rhodes had probably the best defensive works in the world. Suleiman methodically prepared his attack, so the Knights had plenty of time to accumulate vast supplies of foodstuffs and ammunition.

Rhodes' garrison consisted of 700 Knights, 6,000 other troops, and nearly all of the able-bodied men of the island to serve as militiamen and laborers. In June 1522, 50,000 Ottoman troops crossed to the island to begin the siege; a great many more arrived over the next six months. The Knights' engineers had measured exact distances to all points within range of their cannon, which scored with exceptional accuracy when the Turks began to dig trenches and bring up their artillery. From the very beginning of this siege, therefore, the Turks suffered heavy casualties.

The major tactic that the Turks used was digging mines, fifty-four in all according to the defenders' count. Nearly all were detected and destroyed, but on September 4 a mine was successfully exploded and brought down part of the wall. Suleiman ordered several great assaults on the breach, but the Turks were thrown back with horrendous losses. However, the outnumbered garrison was also being reduced by the fighting; so when Suleiman, not eager to have his army winter in the siege lines, offered on December 1 to negotiate, the Knights agreed. After two weeks the negotiations broke down, and the sultan ordered another great assault. It put the Turks inside the wall, but prompt action by the defenders restricted the enemy's toehold to a few houses. The Knights requested renewed negotiations. Suleiman, well aware of the heavy casualties his army would take in house-to-house fighting, agreed. On December 21, 1522, the surrender of Rhodes was agreed upon. The 180 surviving Knights and some 1,500 troops were allowed to evacuate with honor, and Suleiman committed himself to protecting the lives and property of the residents. The Turkish losses are unknown, but they surely were very high.

The remnants of the Hospitalers sailed on to Venetian-ruled Crete. The Venetians, who had refused to provide any aid, forced them to leave after two weeks for fear of Turkish retaliation. They moved on to Italy, where they remained until 1530, when Charles V gave them the island of Malta. Thus the Knights of Rhodes became the Knights of Malta.

THE BATTLE OF MOHACS

With Rhodes secured, Suleiman turned his attention to Hungary, where several key forts along its southern frontier of Hungary had already been taken. There was little to prevent the Turks from striking into Hungary proper. Although the Hungarians and their young king, Louis, had clear warning, factionalism among the nobles made it impossible to prepare for the coming assault. Louis was married to Charles V's sister Mary, but he received no help from the Habsburgs. In July 1526 Suleiman crossed the frontier with some 80,000 men, mostly light cavalry but including 6,000 Janissaries and 2,000 spahis. Louis marched south to meet him with 12,000 gens d'armes and light cavalry and 13,000 infantry, mostly German mercenaries. The Hungarians reached the plain of Mohacs, about 120 miles south of Budapest, which they decided was a fit field for cavalry, and waited for the Turks to appear. On August 29, 1526, they did.

The Hungarians were arranged in a very long line in order to prevent being outflanked, placing their twenty pieces of artillery slightly forward. When the Turks appeared late in the day, they deployed into three lines: the first two were entirely horse archers; behind them was the artillery, of which Suleiman had much more than did Louis; and behind the guns were deployed the Janissaries, flanked by the spahis. Suleiman had also sent a detachment of 6,000 light horse on a very broad flanking movement designed to strike at the Hungarian left only after the battle had begun.

The battle began with a charge by the Ottoman light cavalry. It was easily thrown back, and the Hungarians went on the offensive. They drove through the two lines of light cavalry only to find themselves in the direct line of fire of the Turkish guns. Several sources suggest that Suleiman had ordered a tactical retreat for precisely that purpose. The Turks had chained their guns together, so that the Hungarians, mostly heavy cavalry, could not break through. Behind the guns the Janissaries opened fire, and the spahis counterattacked on the flanks. Even as the Hungarians reeled from the power of the Ottoman counter-attack, the 6,000-man Turkish detachment struck at their rear. Their lines collapsed in the worst disorder. Suleiman, aware that his army was also in serious disorder and had taken heavy casualties, forbade any pursuit beyond the Hungarian camp. Nonetheless, the Hungarian casualties appear extraordinarily high—10,000 infantry and 5,000 cavalry.

Few nations have suffered as complete a defeat as did Hungary at Mohacs. The long list of fallen leaders included the king himself, whose body was found in a bog two months later, where he apparently drowned trying to flee. Ten days after Mohacs, Suleiman reached Budapest, which was completely undefended. Rather than try to rule Hungary directly he offered the crown to John Zapolya, duke of Transylvania, who conveniently had begun his march to join Louis too late to fight at Mohacs. A fringe of Hungarian land along Austria and Bohemia remained in Christian hands. The nobles there offered the crown to Louis' sister Anne and her husband, Ferdinand of Habsburg, brother of Charles V. Serving as ruler of Austria for Charles, Ferdinand could provide considerable resources against the Turks. The agreement gave the title of king of Hungary to the Habsburgs, who kept it until 1918.

THE 1529 SIEGE OF VIENNA

In 1527 Ferdinand defeated John Zapolya and retook Budapest. This stung Suleiman, who gathered an army said to have been 120,000 men strong and marched northward in 1529. The wettest summer in memory slowed his progress and forced him to consume more of his supplies than expected. After retaking Budapest, he pushed on to Vienna in September. Ferdinand had been gathering resources for its defense, but Charles, deeply entangled in war with France, could provide only 700 Spanish arquebusmen. In all, some 16,000 soldiers formed the city's garrison, along with a few thousand local militiamen. Vienna was a strongly defended city; its defense was enhanced by the presence of the Danube on one side and a large tributary on another, making assault from two directions impossible. The Turks decided to concentrate on the southwest corner of the city.

On October 1, 1529, full-scale battering of the walls began, but mining appears to have been the Turks' main hope of creating a breach. On two occasions large mines were exploded, collapsing sections of the wall; but fierce fighting by the defenders drove the assault troops back. After only two weeks, Suleiman's officers persuaded him that it was getting so late in the season that he risked having his army caught in the open when winter set in. The Turks were already short of food. Their retreat to Budapest in heavy rains proved to be very costly, since the route had been thoroughly ravaged only a month earlier and the Austrian cavalry was in hot pursuit.

Suleiman's failure at Vienna was partly a consequence of pushing an attack too late in the year, which was in turn a result of Austria's being too distant from the Ottoman center of power. It was also the first time the Turks had confronted experienced Spanish and German troops.

Suleiman's brush with them caused him to be more cautious in the future. In 1532 when he raised another great army, he did not risk it against Vienna, where Charles V personally commanded a formidable army. Instead, he wasted it on a futile expedition into the mountains of southwest Austria. After that his attention was drawn to a new war with Persia for several years. Whether it was the long memory of his defeat at Vienna or because Suleiman thought greater gains could be made at sea, the center of war between Islam and Christianity shifted from the Balkans to the Mediterranean. Despite being only eighty miles from Ottoman-ruled Hungary, Vienna was not put under serious attack again for 150 years.

Although it failed, the significance of the Turkish attack on Vienna and the threat of a new attack must not be underestimated. It prevented Charles V from putting his full resources into the war against France, and forced him to call on the Lutheran princes for help instead of crushing the Reformation in Germany. The Turks played a significant role in the splintering of western Christianity, but it did not pay them any real dividends. The Lutheran princes were usually quick to respond to the emperor's calls for help against the infidel, while it was Catholic France that proved to be a more useful ally for the sultan against the Habsburgs.

NOTES

1. Francesco Guicciardini, quoted in R.J. Knecht, *Francis I* (Cambridge, 1982), p. 115.

2. Knecht, p. 172.

14

Naval War in the Mediterranean

In my judgment the troopers are right who say that you should never fire your arquebus until you are near enough to be splashed with the blood of your enemy; and I have always heard the most experienced sea-captains say that the crashing of a ship's iron beak and the first report of her guns should be heard at the same moment, and I think so too. But your people should be taught not to be considering the enemy, or who is to fire first or last, but to fire when Your Highness gives the word, and only then.

> Don Garcia de Toledo, quoted in Charles Petrie, *Don John of Austria* (New York: 1967), p. 153. Don Garcia wrote this letter on galley tactics shortly before the Battle of Lepanto in 1571.

The war between Christendom and the Islamic world had been fought in the eastern Mediterranean Sea from virtually the first appearance of Islam, but it reached its height in the mid-sixteenth century. Both emperors, Charles V and Suleiman, committed more and more resources to the naval war until it eventually overshadowed their conflict on land.

Through the Middle Ages war in the Mediterranean continued to be a matter for galleys. Unlike the ancient Greek galleys, late medieval fleets ranged across the entire sea. The large crew aboard a galley was not a great drawback, since numerous stops could be made during a voyage. The north-south distance across the sea is relatively short, and a galley could make it without straining its crew and provisions. The east-west distance is obviously far greater, but the many land features in the Mediterranean meant that the trip could be made in several legs. While a typical war galley had serious problems in the Atlantic, there was little reason for one to venture out into its rough waters, except as a speedy courier.

When Greek fire was lost at the time of the conquest of Constantinople in 1204, galleys rapidly changed. The decline in the need for protection against fire meant that ships could become lighter and faster. Boarding and hand-to-hand fighting again dominated naval warfare. A typical Italian galley of 1300, whose design would change very little for the next 250 years,

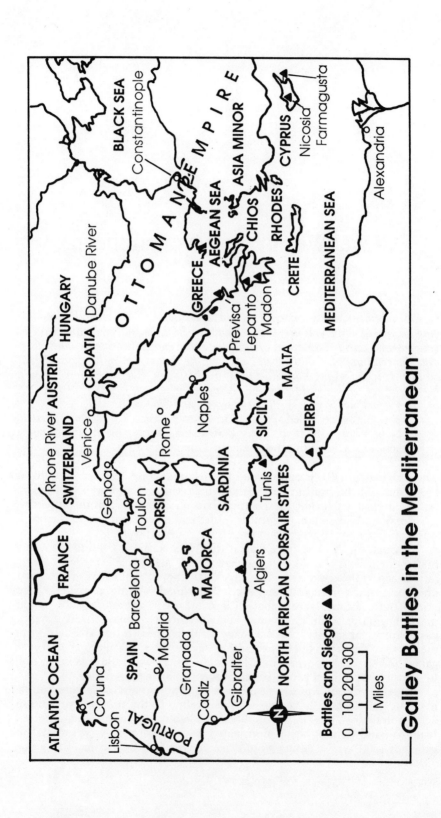

Galley Battles in the Mediterranean

had only one bank of oars, in contrast to the two of Byzantine ships. Two or three men pulled one oar. Such a galley had a long spur at the bow, whose primary purpose was to break apart the rowers' deck of an enemy ship as it ran into it at an angle. These galleys were about 180 feet long and 23 feet wide with a draft of about 4 feet and a displacement of 140 tons. They had a single mast with a large triangular "lateen" sail attached to a yard. With a favorable breeze they relied on their sails, but they were not good sailers in rough water, primarily because of the low bow.

Under oars a late medieval galley could hope to maintain a speed of three and a half knots for several hours, which was considerably slower than Greek triremes. Attack speed could reach seven knots, but it would exhaust the rowers in a very short time. At the bow was a catapult or two; by the late 1400s cannon had replaced them. The offensive and defensive capabilities of a galley, however, lay largely in its marines. Bows, slings, swords, and half-pikes were the usual weapons aboard. A late medieval galley usually had about 120 free rowers, who were expected to grab a weapon and join in the fighting once two boats had grappled. Another forty to fifty bowmen, officers, and sailors were also aboard.

NAVAL POWERS IN THE MEDITERRANEAN

During the 200 years before 1453, the Mediterranean was a jumble of shifting alliances involving the Italian cities, Aragon, and the Byzantine Empire. With their conquest of Constantinople and its great maritime tradition and resources, the Turks became a major player. Since the first appearance of Muslim ships, the Christians had always had the advantage over the Muslims in the struggle for control of the sea because the major routes passed along its northern coasts. A combination of winds, currents, trade patterns, and the limits of naval technology dictated that most sea traffic, and especially war fleets, follow a limited number of routes, which passed largely along Christian shores. That gave the Christians a decided advantage in the naval wars with Islam, and the Muslim states never were able to gain more than a temporary advantage.

With the Turkish conquest of Asia Minor and Greece, however, the Muslims were able to mount a far more powerful challenge to Christian control of the Mediterranean. The conquest of Egypt in the early 1500s added that region's naval resources to the Turkish fleet. As Ottoman influence spread along the coast of North Africa, the Muslim maritime states there acknowledged the sultan's sovereignty and put their fleets at his disposal as well.

The emergence of Spain as a major Mediterranean power came a little later. Aragon had been one of several nearly equal naval powers in the late Middle Ages; the union of the Spanish kingdoms and the vast influx of wealth from the New World enabled Spain to become an effective counterweight to the Ottoman Empire. The growing roles of the two empires vastly changed naval warfare in the sea, greatly increasing the size of the fleets and the stakes of battle. Among the changes effected by both empires was a rapidly increasing dependence on slave rowers instead of freemen—not that slave rowers were unheard of before 1500. Raids on enemy coastlines for manpower to fill the rowing benches became common in the sixteenth century.

Spain became a major naval power in large part because of the conquest of Granada. A large population of resentful, forcibly converted Moors was now concentrated in southwest Spain, easily accessible to Muslim power in North Africa. They were ready to rise in rebellion either in response to a Turkish invasion or upon promises of one. The Spanish were terrified at the prospect, while the sultans made it well known that it was one of their primary goals. Thus Spain needed a powerful fleet to stave off this threat. The Spanish conquest of Naples added a modest fleet to Spain's naval power, but it vastly increased its area of responsibility, since southern Italy and Sicily were highly vulnerable to Muslim seapower.

As the naval power of the two great empires at opposite ends of the Mediterranean grew, the Italian fleets became less and less important. Nonetheless, Genoa and Venice still remained major factors in the balance of power. On a ship-for-ship basis, the Venetians were the best in the sea, for Venice's place as a great power depended upon its ability to defend its shipping and its forward posts in the eastern Mediterranean. As a trading nation it needed to provide for its defense at the lowest cost. This generally can be achieved by concentrating on quality rather than quantity, since manpower costs have always made up the largest share of a military budget. One reason for the better quality of Venetian galleys was that Venice always made use of free rowers, who were expected to grab weapons and take part in combat. Venice's power also depended in good part on its great arsenal, created shortly after 1100, which was capable of turning out a fleet of well-built galleys in a few weeks and the weaponry for them.

As of 1500 Venice still held an impressive number of outposts in the eastern Mediterranean and the Aegean, including Crete and Cyprus, but most of them were highly vulnerable to Turkish attack. Since Venetian power and prosperity depended upon access to the eastern Mediterranean, Venice did its best to avoid conflict with the Turks; for example, it refused to come to the aid of Rhodes in 1523. That policy did not keep the Turks from picking off several Venetian bases in the early 1500s, but it did earn for the city the hatred of most of the rest of Christendom for refusing to cooperate in the war against the infidel.

The centers of Genovese trade in the late Middle Ages had been the Black Sea and Constantinople itself. The Genovese presence was largely eliminated by the Ottoman conquests, although Genoa did hold on to the island of Chios off of Asia Minor until 1566. Nonetheless the Genovese fleet remained a potent one. In 1528 the admiral of Genoa, Andrea Doria, signed a contract with Charles V, taking Genoa out of the French orbit and into in the Spanish. He was essentially a naval condottiere, who rented his galleys to Charles for 500 ducats apiece per month. He also was to be paid inflated prices for supplies. For the next century, Genoa was completely tied to Spain.

There were also in the Mediterranean two fleets whose legal status and behavior were truly ambiguous. They were the *ghazis* of North Africa, known as corsairs, and the Knights of St. John, known after 1530 as the

Knights of Malta.   Both groups had a nominal allegiance to an overlord—the sultan and the Holy Roman Emperor respectively— but both operated largely independent of any authority. Their fleets were manned by some of the best seamen available, and their captains were especially well regarded. After 1540, corsairs regularly emerged as admirals in the Ottoman fleet. Both fleets raided the coasts and shipping of the opposite religion relentlessly; they were regarded as pirates by their enemies and as heroes of the faith by their allies.

GALLEY TACTICS
     By 1500 all galley fleets had begun to make use of gunpowder artillery. The presence of banks of rowers and the fragile construction of the galleys meant that heavy guns could not be mounted amidships. The stern could not be heavily armed because of the large steering oar and the cabin. So the only place where heavy ordnance could be mounted was at the bow. In the early 1500s large bombards throwing stone balls of up to eighty pounds were mounted on the center line. After 1530 a typical galley had a large cannon mounted on a recoiling carriage on the center line flanked by two "half-cannons." These pieces were flanked by several small pieces mounted on sturdy posts, allowing them to swivel. On larger galleys several decades later, a raised fighting platform over the bow guns and the rowers held a number of swivel pieces.
     In calm water experienced gunners had some hope of hitting an enemy ship at 500 yards with large balls, and possibly sinking it; a few examples of that are known. Most of the time such long-range gunnery was of little value, and a galley captain who attempted it could find the enemy galley on top of him before his gunners could reload. The ability of a galley to close very rapidly at battle speed meant that the guns had to serve a different purpose: to do as much injury as possible to the defenders of a galley a moment before contact. Therefore the guns usually were discharged at "cloth burning" range. The Turks are known to have used scatter shot (later called grape shot) on occasion, while there is no reliable evidence that the Christians did so. The English sailing ship, the *Mary Rose*, sunk in 1545, did have it aboard.
     The essence of galley combat was the neutralization of the armed men defending the enemy ship. Therefore, the first priority of a galley was the quality and quantity of its marines. For battle a galley would be crammed with fighting men, several hundred on the larger galleys. As two galleys closed on one another, missile weapons were used to reduce the enemy's manpower. In Christian fleets the arquebus replaced the crossbow beginning about 1480, but the Muslims remained committed to the composite bow until the 1570s. The superior penetrating power of firearms balanced the much greater rate of fire for archers. Once two galleys had grappled, hand-to-hand combat with half-pikes, halberds, and swords decided the issue.
     Fighting battles at sea was only part of a galley's raison d'être. More crucial was a galley fleet's ability to conduct amphibious operations. Galleys brought siege forces to their targets or relief forces to forts under siege.

Galleys' bow guns could be used as a gun platform to batter a coastal fort. They could bring in supplies or attack the enemy's lines of communication. Their ability to move in and out of a harbor quickly without waiting for a favorable wind enabled them to give support to land forces, even a besieged fort, in a way that was not possible for sailing ships.

The symbiotic relationship between a galley fleet and coastal forts was at the heart of Mediterranean warfare in the sixteenth century. A galley equipped for battle could spend a very limited time at sea before it ran out of supplies, especially water. Since tides in the Mediterranean are low and there are plenty of good beaches, a galley could always pull up its steering oar and beach itself, send men off to find water, and then use its rowing crew to push itself off the beach. But on enemy shores that was highly dangerous, since shore patrols could discover it and bring a larger force to capture it. Certainly one could not count on obtaining food and ammunition that way. Thus for a Mediterranean state to project its naval power into enemy waters required a series of forward bases. Both Venice and Genoa had such bases in good number before 1500, but the Turks worked diligently to reduce them.

In order for Spain and the Ottoman Empire at the extreme ends of the sea to make effective use of their growing fleets and project their naval power in the other's waters, they had to secure forward bases in the central Mediterranean. The weather pattern of the region was also a factor, since rough weather occurred from October to March and no galley wanted to be at sea then. Thus they needed large fortified harbors in the central Mediterranean where a fleet could winter, which would give the fleet a full summer to operate against the enemy's coasts.

The dependence of galley fleets on coastal forts created a circular situation in that a large fleet was needed to defend the forts against an enemy, since most of the bases in question were islands. With a few exceptions, mainland forward bases were difficult to defend. Most naval battles of this era in the Mediterranean involved sieges of shoreline forts on small islands, with the galleys carrying a siege force or a relief army to the site. The manpower and ordnance on a galley could be used aboard ship or unloaded to fight on shore. Fleet encounters at sea were relatively unusual.

WAR BETWEEN EMPEROR AND SULTAN

The Turks early in the 1500s made effective use of their fleet to reduce the eastern bases of Venice and Genoa, thus rapidly swinging the balance of power their way. The accession of Charles V, however, brought to the fore a ruler with the determination and the resources to restore the balance. In particular, his contract with Andrea Doria of Genoa in 1528 gave him the use of a good galley fleet and made him more adventuresome in the Mediterranean. Four years later a Spanish-Genovese fleet of forty-four galleys landed a force that took Coron at the southern tip of Greece.

Suleiman responded to the increased threat by naming as his pasha (admiral) the leader of the corsairs in Algiers, Khair ed-din, a Greek converted to Islam. Given the task of rebuilding the Ottoman fleet, he brought to the job unusual boldness and a half-century of experience. He quickly recaptured Coron and in 1534 captured Tunis, held by a Muslim vassal of Charles V. The next year Charles personally led a fleet of 65 galleys and 150 transports to North Africa. Andrea Doria, commanding the galleys, drove Khair ed-din's fleet away from the fort of Goletta in Tunis harbor and laid siege to it. Once it fell, the city of Tunis quickly capitulated.

Khair ed-din and the remnants of his fleet fled to Algiers. Charles planned to strike there in 1536, but a French invasion of northern Italy distracted him, and the opportunity to crush the corsairs slipped away. The French attack was part of a strategy Francis I worked out with Suleiman in which the Turks would invade southern Italy in cooperation with the French fleet. The French galley fleet was quite small but not inconsequential. The joint operation was the first open demonstration of the decade-old tacit alliance between France and the Ottoman Empire. Venice was also invited to join but refused. That refusal, along with an attack on a galley carrying a Turkish ambassador, led Suleiman to attack the Venetian-held island of Corfu off the west coast of Greece. The attack failed, but Venice now joined the anti-Ottoman alliance. In 1538 a Christian fleet of 130 galleys—Spanish, Genovese, papal, and Venetian—under Andrea Doria gathered in the south Adriatic, while Khair ed-din led a fleet of 140 ships, many of which were smaller galiots.

Andrea Doria found the Ottoman fleet sheltered in the Gulf of Arta on the west coast of Greece, the site of the Battle of Actium. The narrow entrance into the gulf was well defended by a fort and shore batteries at Prevesa. Aware that it would be extremely risky to try to force the entrance, Andrea Doria landed men to assault the castle, while using his galley guns to batter it. The danger of such an undertaking on a hostile coast was demonstrated by the quick appearance of a powerful Ottoman army. Deciding to withdraw, Andria Doria hoped to get his fleet away in the dark, but it had not gone far when the Turks recognized what was happening. Khair ed-din brought his fleet out to catch the Christians from behind. A drop in the wind meant the *nefs* (sailing transports) were open game, and most were lost. But because of their head start, only seven Christian galleys were lost. The Great Galleon of Venice, also becalmed, fought off a daylong attack by Turkish galleys—a portent for the future.

The Christian alliance soon was fractured by Venetian accusations of treachery against Andrea Doria for his decisions at Prevesa. It was claimed that he was motivated by the traditional Genovese rivalry with Venice. Venice signed a peace with Suleiman, which endured for thirty years. The Ottoman-French alliance also collapsed when Francis and Charles signed a treaty. With his resources freed from war with France, Charles again gave full attention to the naval war. Despite warnings from his advisors about the lateness of the season, he led a great force, some 22,000 troops, against Algiers in October 1540. The army quickly put Algiers under siege; but four days after it had disembarked, a tremendous storm lasting three days caught the fleet unprotected. Fourteen galleys and 140 other ships were wrecked. The army was left without supplies, and Charles had to withdraw. A third of his men were lost.

The catastrophe at Algiers, very revealing of why sailors feared being at sea out of season, badly affected Charles' confidence in dealing with the Turks. He lost interest in the naval war, permitting Khair ed-din to bring the Ottoman fleet into western waters in 1543. After ravaging the Italian coast, he wintered in Toulon, a French harbor. From Toulon Turkish galleys raided nearby shores for plunder and slaves. The scandal was enormous, but when Francis I was criticized, he replied: "When the wolves attack my flock, I don't hesitate to call on the dogs."[1]

Yet the criticism may have been a factor in Francis' sudden decision to make peace with Charles in 1544. Khair ed-din was forced to return to the Aegean, where he died in 1546; he was about eighty years old. His death brought to the fore another Christian-turned-corsair, Turgut Reis (Dragut), who was even more enterprising and bold. He had been a galley slave on a Genovese ship for four years until ransomed, and he burned for revenge. Becoming an Ottoman admiral in 1546, he began to raid Christian coasts with apparent impunity. By 1551 Turgut Reis was confident enough to strike at the Knights of Malta, the implacable enemy of the North Africans. In 1553 his fleet helped put a French force on Corsica, a Genovese possession, which the French quickly overran. For the most part, however, the French-Ottoman alliance resulted in missed opportunities, perhaps because many French leaders resented being asked to work with the infidel.

PHILIP II'S MEDITERRANEAN POLICY

By 1556 Charles V, worn out by his heavy burdens and incapacitated with gout, had begun to abdicate his titles. His son Philip became king of Spain and Naples, duke of Milan, and prince of the Low Countries, while his brother was chosen Holy Roman Emperor. Philip II was freed of his father's problems with the German Lutherans, and made peace with France in 1559 (Chapter 14). He was more determined than his father to crush Muslim power in the Mediterranean because he was more truly a Spaniard. His first concern was the corsair fleets of North Africa, because they were raiding the coasts of Spain and Italy. In 1558 Turgut Reis had captured the island of Djerba off the coast of Tunisia, creating a clear threat to Spanish control of Tunis.

In response Philip named Gian Andrea Doria the commander of his fleet. He was the twenty-year-old nephew of Andrea Doria, who had just died. Why Philip accepted him as admiral is unknown, but perhaps he had to in order to keep control of the Genovese galleys. In late October 1559, fifty galleys and fifty-five transports carrying 5,000 troops left Sicily. They avoided winter storms by making the voyage in very short legs from one harbor to another. By February the fleet arrived at Djerba. The superior Christian force had little trouble occupying the fortress of Djerba, since the Muslims were taken by surprise by the arrival of a fleet so early in the year. When word of the attack reached Constantinople, a fleet of eighty-six galleys under Piali Pasha sailed immediately. The Christian force now was taken by surprise when Piali appeared off Djerba in May.

The only explanation for what followed is that Gian Andrea Doria and the other Christian captains panicked. Instead of forming a tight line close to or even on the beach, with the guns of a friendly fort behind him, he ordered his ships to make a run for it. The precipitous flight left the fleet in serious disorder. Piali Pasha's fleet was coming in under sail. He was about to strike the sails and masts in preparation for battle, when he realized how disordered the enemy was. So he ordered a pursuit with sails up—a highly risky situation for a galley in battle—to give his galleys extra speed to catch the Christians. A galley caught from behind was exceptionally vulnerable. Accordingly the Christian losses at Djerba were very high—some thirty galleys and numerous transports. The garrison Andrea Doria left behind on Djerba was badly undercut by lack of water. After a siege of eight weeks, the 5,000 men surrendered. The ships lost at Djerba were easily replaced; it was the enormous loss of experienced manpower that truly hurt Spain. Land-based arquebusmen were sent to sea because of the lack of marine arquebusiers; the trouble they had adapting to sea duty was clear. In the next three years, Spain suffered a series of defeats at sea.

THE SIEGE OF MALTA

Everyone knew that Suleiman would follow up the victory at Djerba with a major strike at an important Christian position. An attack on the Spanish mainland was appealing to him, because Philip's determination to enforce religious conformity on the Moors was stirring up rebellion. But it was too far from the Ottoman center of power for a great force to be sent there except at very great risk, especially since Malta with its corps of elite Knight of Malta stood in the way. Malta in Muslim hands would provide an excellent base to strike at Spain. It would also eliminate a constant irritant, for the Knights did much the same work in a more limited way for Philip as the Corsairs did for the sultan. It took some time for Suleiman to assemble the forces needed for a full-scale attack on Malta; he may also have needed time to realize how badly Spain had been hurt at Djerba. Finally in April 1565 a fleet of 130 galleys and 35 other ships under Mustafa Pasha left Constantinople. They carried 30,000 troops including 9,000 spahis and 6,000 Janissaries. During the first weeks at Malta they were joined by fifty North African galleys and 6,000 more men. Their heavy artillery consisted of sixty "double cannons" taken off their galleys, and two huge bombards carried to the island in galleys designed for that purpose.

The Knights had been busy since 1530 fortifying Malta. After Djerba they were well aware that it was the likely target of Ottoman attack. The call went out to Knights across Europe to come to its defense. By the time the Turks arrived, there were 700 Knights on Malta along with 2,000 other troops and several thousand locals, who were used largely as laborers. The defenders had about fifty artillery pieces. The small number of guns relative to the length of the walls, considering the time the Knights had to prepare and their wealth, indicate the difficulty of procuring guns in this era.

The heart of the defense of Malta were the twin forts of St. Angelo and St. Michael, which guarded the Grand Harbor. At the head of the point of land between the Grand Harbor and another inlet, Marsamuscetto, stood Fort St. Elmo, small but modern. Rightly anticipating that the Turks would want to take it first, the Knights' grand master, Jean de La Vallette, placed twenty of his guns there. Mustafa Pasha has been severely criticized for expending so much of his supplies and manpower taking Fort St. Elmo, but it was necessary before he could assault the main forts. The closest alternative to the inlet that it blocked was six miles away. To anchor the fleet that far away greatly increased the work needed to bring guns and supplies to the site of the siege, and it vastly increased the force needed to guard the ships. Assaulting the main forts was all but impossible until Fort St. Elmo was taken, and the fleet brought close at hand. No one could have anticipated how long the fort would hold out.

Fort St. Elmo was defended by 65 Knights and 200 arquebusmen. Every night men were sent across the Grand Harbor by boat to replace those fallen in the day's fighting. For five weeks the Turks assaulted the fort, at the cost of 6,000 men, until it fell on June 24. Turgut Reis was killed in one of the last assaults. By enduring as long as it did, the little fort took the siege of Malta into the heat of the summer and wore the edge off the enemy's forces. Equally important, by then the inevitable spread of disease in the Turkish army had begun.

Having taken Fort St. Elmo, Mustafa Pasha brought his fleet into Marsamuscetto Inlet, where the remaining cannon were unloaded and dragged into place to batter the main forts. On August 7, after a breach was opened in the wall of Fort St. Angelo, the Turks mounted a general assault. They gained control of the breach, and La Vallette himself led his last reserves in a counterattack. As the fate of the fort hung in balance, word suddenly came from the Turkish camp that it was under attack. Thinking that the Spanish relief force had arrived, the Turks pulled back from the walls to protect their camp and ships. It was in fact a tiny force from a fort in the center of Malta that the Turks had not bothered to reduce. Its captain, whether by design or chance, chose precisely the right moment to strike at the enemy. Mustafa Pasha, after driving off the raiding party, returned to wearing the Knights down by bombardment and sapping rather than by assault.

Rumors had constantly swept through both camps that a Spanish relief force was on its way. On August 20, it finally sailed. The viceroy of Sicily, Garcia de Toledo, had delayed going to sea, partly because of Philip II's orders to be most cautious in using the last force available to defend Italy and Spain, but also because the relief of Malta by a much smaller force than that of the Turks had to be timed perfectly. Philip allowed him to send only twenty-eight galleys and held the rest back to defend Sicily. So the enemy had to be sufficiently worn down before Toledo could hope to be successful.

Despite later complaints from the Knights that he had tarried unnecessarily long, the arrival of the relief force off Malta on September 5, having been delayed at sea for nearly two weeks by contrary winds, probably would not have been effective any earlier. Mustafa Pasha was ready to admit defeat when he heard of the coming of the relief fleet. Toledo was not willing to risk an attack on the Turkish ships, so the Turks were able to reload most of their men and guns and effect an orderly withdrawal. Because of the loss of manpower, however, they had to leave forty ships behind. They also left as many as two-thirds of their original force behind. The defenders lost about half of the manpower available to them.

The Knights of Malta were hailed as the saviors of Europe, and volunteers and money poured in. La Vallette used the money to begin an enormous project of fortification building, which by 1600 gave Malta the best defensive works in Europe. The new defenses were never tested.

THE BATTLE OF LEPANTO

When Suleiman received word of the defeat, he ordered 200 galleys built to show that "the sword of Islam is still sharp." The next year, however, he died waging war against the Habsburgs in Croatia. Suleiman's successor, Selim II the Sot (1566-74), was elevated largely because of palace intrigue. Two more capable older brothers had been executed on charges of treason. Selim preferred life at court to leading his forces and had become very fond of the wines of Cyprus. For some, that has been sufficient reason to explain his decision to conquer the island, which was held by Venice. More likely motives include his need to conquer territory early in his reign (one reason why Suleiman attacked Rhodes in 1523) in order to win the respect of his fighting men, and the effrontery of Christian rule over land so close to his realm.

Since 1540 Venice had maintained a strict neutrality in the conflict between Islam and Christendom—for example, refusing to give any aid to Malta in 1565. The other Christian states regularly denounced Venice. Selim and his advisers were certain that they would not come to the aid of Venice, and so in early 1570 he declared war. But Selim had not counted on the presence of Pope Pius V, a man whose zeal in opposing Islam succeeded in temporarily overcoming the intra-Christian hatreds and rivalries.

Selim sent 116 galleys to Cyprus with some 50,000 troops. The Venetians concentrated their resources in the coastal fortress of Famagusta and the inland one of Nicosia. Perhaps recalling how the ignored fort in the interior of Malta had helped to ruin that campaign, the Turks attacked Nicosia first. It was no match for the enormous attacking army, and surrendered after seven weeks under siege. The severed head of the Venetian commander of Nicosia was shot into Famagusta, setting the stage for that long siege, which began in mid-September 1570. The Turks blockaded Famagusta by land and sea during the winter, and in early spring resumed battering the walls. The Venetian garrison, led by Antonio Bragadino, put up an excellent defense, and the siege dragged into the summer without any sign of a relief force.

Pope Pius had declared a holy league to rescue Cyprus, but France flatly refused to join. Bickering between Spain and Venice delayed signing an alliance until May 25, 1571. Don Juan of Austria, Philip's half-brother, was named commander of the allied fleet. He was only twenty-six years old and had never fought at sea, but he was well respected as a captain and had the high status needed for command of such an alliance. Philip had also insisted on it as a condition of Spanish participation. Don Juan must be given great credit for overcoming the rivalries and squabbling natural in such combined forces and turning them into a unified fleet. The fleet consisted of ships from Venice (the largest contingent), Genoa, Spain, Naples, the papacy, and the Knights of Malta, totaling about 200 galleys. Some twenty large sailing ships were also present, but they were left well behind at the time of battle because of calm winds.

In addition Venice contributed six galleasses. Built on the hulls of large merchant galleys, they were much larger than typical galleys, especially in width—forty feet versus twenty-three feet. Galleasses were also much higher above the water. They carried a much greater number of rowers, but still were extremely slow under oar. Because of the need to save the energy of their rowing crews, they carried a great deal more sail; but in battle they were rowed exclusively. The most significant feature was the amount of artillery the galleasses carried—five large pieces and fifteen medium sized ones as well as twenty swivel guns. Several of the heavier guns were not directed straight ahead but were set at an angle to the side, so that galleasses had a much wider field of fire than ordinary galleys. The difficulty that an enemy would have in boarding them because of their height meant that their guns could be fired repeatedly during a battle.

By the time the Christian fleet had assembled, word came that Famagusta had surrendered on August 1, 1571. Having been offered very attractive terms, Bragadino opened the gates only to find that the Ottoman commander, enraged by the heavy losses he had taken, had reneged on the terms. Bragadino's surviving men were hauled off as galley slaves, while he was tortured and killed. Word of this Ottoman perfidy spread through the Christian fleet and created a unique uniformity of will. Nonetheless it was only on September 16 that the fleet sailed from Sicily, its assembly point.

Even before the fall of Famagusta the Ottoman fleet had left Cyprus and gone to Greece in order to confront the enemy fleet known to be assembling. Commanded by Ali Pasha, the Ottoman fleet consisted of 210 galleys and 64 galiots. By the time Don Juan had made any headway out to sea, Ali Pasha had reached the Gulf of Lepanto, 100 miles south of the Gulf of Prevesa and much like it in geography—a very narrow mouth commanded by batteries on both sides opening up into a large bay. Once the Turks had anchored in the gulf, there was no pressing need for them to go out to meet the Christians; they could have repeated the Battle of Prevesa. But Sultan Selim had commanded that the Christian fleet be destroyed in order to open the way for a full-scale invasion of Italy the next spring. So Ali Pasha, learning that the Christian fleet had arrived in the region, brought his ships out of the gulf on October 7.

Don Juan had accepted two recommendations from Gian Andrea Doria, who was present with the Genovese galleys. One was to load the galleasses with arquebusmen. The other was to cut the spurs off the bows of the galleys. The spurs made the center guns fire high, while their removal allowed the guns to be depressed further. It made a difference because the Ottoman galleys were lower in the water than the Christian ones.

The Christian cannon fire became much more effective because of this move.

Don Juan already had his fleet in battle formation when the Turks appeared. His fleet was divided into three divisions with a small reserve behind. They formed a large near-crescent. The Christian left, consisting of fifty-three galleys, mostly Venetian and commanded by the Venetian Agostino Barbarigo, came as close to the beach as thought possible. The Venetians were concentrated there because it was expected that the Turkish galleys, having a shallower draft than most Christian ships, would try to outflank the line by slipping by inshore. The Venetian galleys came closest to matching the Turks in draft. The center, commanded by Don Juan, had sixty-four galleys, and the right under Doria had fifty-four. Each division was to be led into battle by two galleasses; one in the center served as Don Juan's flagship. Except for the left, where the Venetian ships were in the majority, ships of each nationality were spread as equally as possible among the divisions so as to give a sense of cohesion and common purpose to the whole fleet.

Ali Pasha's fleet was organized in largely the same formation. His right had fifty-four galleys and two galiots, his center had sixty-one galleys and thirty-two galiots, and his left eighty-seven galleys and eight galiots. The size of the Ottoman left was apparently intended to allow their faster galleys to swing outside the Christian line and outflank it. The manpower for both sides was about equal—roughly 80,000 men, counting the rowers.

At about ten in the morning, the two fleets closed on each other. The two galleasses on the Christian left made first contact. While they did heavy damage to the Ottoman ships with which they made contact, most of the galleys of the Turkish right swept by. It soon became clear that they were trying to get through between the beach and the end of the Christian line in order to outflank it. Barbarigo then executed one of the greatest tactical maneuvers in naval history: he was able to pivot his entire line, like a door, it was said, and drive the Turkish galleys onto the beach. The difficulty in achieving such a maneuver with some fifty galleys was enormous, and it completely surprised the Turks. After an hour, the Turkish right collapsed. Barbarigo himself was killed by an arrow in the eye near the end of the battle.

In the center the fighting was concentrated between the two galleasses and several large Turkish galleys. Ali Pasha's and Don Juan's ships locked together in a bitter battle. Reserve manpower was fed onto both ships by smaller boats tied up behind them. After an hour and a half of continuous fighting, the superior firepower of the galleasses, both artillery and small arms, took its toll. Ali, who used a bow in the thick of the fight, was killed. His death and the dropping of the great standard of Islam from the flagship's mast took the fight out of what was left of the Ottoman center.

Andrea Doria on the Christian right saw that the Turkish line facing him was much longer than his. In order to avoid being outflanked, he began to edge his line away from the center. The Turkish left's commander, Uluj Ali, was also moving his line outward, and as a result contact between the two wings was delayed by as much as two hours. The inner-

most fifteen galleys in Doria's wing, fearful that they would miss the fighting, dashed across the growing gap to take part in the fighting in the center.

Uluj Ali, seeing the great gap now opened up between Christian divisions, quickly dashed for it to outflank both Christian right and center.
By sheer coincidence Doria's two galleasses, which had been well behind
his line at ten o'clock, also were moving into the space in their effort to
reach their assigned places. They effectively plugged the gap until Doria
realized what was happening and brought his line back into the battle. The
Christian reserves, assured that the center was victorious, also came over.
By two o'clock, the major fighting was over. Uluj Ali's galley and 46
others escaped, but they left behind 117 ships in Christian hands and 60
more sunk or too badly damaged to take as prizes. Ottoman losses in
manpower may well have reached as high as 15,000 dead and 7,200 prisoners. The victors freed 12,000 to 15,000 Christian galley slaves. Christian
ship loses were few, as generally was true for the victor in a galley
battle—twelve sunk. As was also true in such a clash, their manpower
losses were quite high, some 7,700 men, nearly two-thirds of whom were
Venetians.

AFTER LEPANTO

Don Juan wanted to lay siege to the fortress of Lepanto, but his advisers convinced him it was too late in the season to risk the fleet. The galleys
returned to various harbors in Italy for the winter. After a period of gloom
in Constantinople, the Ottoman government went to work to rebuild its
fleet. Over the winter, 150 new galleys were constructed, although not of
the quality of those lost. More seriously the new crews were badly inexperienced. The Christian fleet was expected to make an all-out effort the
next spring to take a major Ottoman position, perhaps even Cyprus; but
political factionalism, momentarily overcome for Lepanto, reappeared.
The death of Pius V in May 1572 removed the glue from the Christian alliance. Philip II, expecting war with France, refused for a time to allow
Don Juan to take the Spanish galleys eastward. When he relented in July
it was too late to go any further than Greece.

In September 1572 the Christian fleet reached the southern tip of
Greece, where it encountered the rebuilt Ottoman fleet. The Christian
commanders hoped to repeat Lepanto by putting six galleasses and twenty-four heavily armed nefs in the first line. This shows that the Christians
recognized the extent to which their victory the year before had depended
on firepower. The wind failed at the crucial moment of first contact, and
the nefs became useless. Attempts to tow them forward with galleys only
tired the rowers. Uluj Ali backed off from battle, and the Christians could
not force him to fight. He retreated into the harbor of Modon under the
protection of its shore guns, backing his galleys onto the beach with their
bow guns to the sea. Recognizing the strength of the Turkish position, the
Christian captains agreed that it was too late in the season to risk anything,
and they returned to Italy.

Thus the victory of Lepanto came to naught. The Christians had not
seized a major Ottoman base, the necessary second phase for any naval

victory in the Mediterranean to be complete. Yet Lepanto is a major turning point nonetheless. The Turkish losses in experienced officers and naval archers were enormous. Both groups required long training to be effective. The Ottoman government bought 20,000 arquebuses to try to make good quickly the loss in archers, but the Turkish strength had been in archers using the composite bow. The many Turkish victories before Lepanto attest to how well the bow matched up to the arquebus.

The Christian failure to gain more from Lepanto was more political than military. Venice signed a peace treaty with the sultan in early 1573 and withdrew from the war. Philip II was by then deeply committed to crushing the Dutch revolt at a tremendous cost in Spanish resources. Already by 1574 the decline in Philip's involvement in the Mediterranean allowed the Turks to take Tunis, the last significant change in possession in the region until 1669, when Venetian-held Crete fell to the Turks. The conquest of Tunis was also the last time the North African Corsairs fought as part of an Ottoman fleet. While they never renounced Ottoman sovereignty, they drifted out of effective control. By 1577 the Turks were involved in a bloody war with Persia that lasted until 1612.

Lepanto was the last great galley battle in history. Because of the success of the galleasses there, larger and larger galleys were built. But the larger galleys lost their speed over short distances, the principal characteristic that had allowed them to compete with sailing ships in the Mediterranean. The larger galleys also cost the fleets much of their strategic mobility, since the proportionally greater increase in number of rowers reduced the space for provisions. The increase both in size and number of galleys required an enormous amount of timber, and by 1575 most of the easily accessible forests in the Mediterranean basin had been cut. The principal source of timbers large enough for masts now was the Baltic. The larger crews also added to the expense of galleys at a time when the Mediterranean basin was slipping into a prolonged economic depression.

It was a technological development reducing the cost of cannon that was the final factor making galleys obsolete by 1600. The discovery of a new method of casting iron culverins, which made them both cheaper and more reliable, allowed the Atlantic nations to outfit large numbers of broadside-firing sailing ships. Great fleets of English and Dutch ships began to appear in the Mediterranean after 1590. While galleys were capable of coping with a small number of sailing ships by using their sprint speed to escape from them or their greater numbers to swarm all over them, they were ineffective against large numbers. Soon the galleys became consigned largely to harbor defense, a role they kept until 1789.

NOTE

1. Quoted in Jean Jacquart, *François I* (Paris, 1981), p. 278.

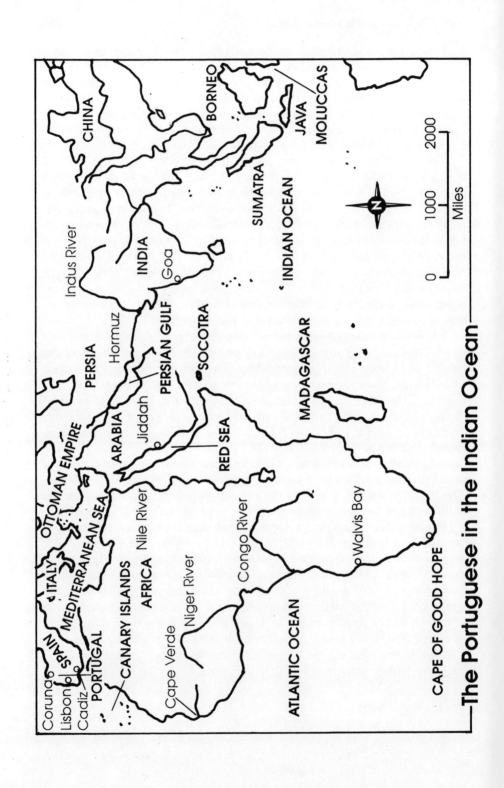

The Portuguese in the Indian Ocean

15

The Rise of the Atlantic Fleets

When Vicente Sodré saw the enemy fleet, he ordered the caravels to come one astern of the other in a line and to run under all the sail they could carry, firing as many guns as they could....Each of the caravels carried thirty men, and four heavy guns below, and above six falconnets, and ten swivel-guns placed on the quarter deck and in the bows, and two of the falconnets fired astern. The ships of burden were much more equipped with artillery....When they had discharged their guns, they made such haste to load again that they loaded the guns with bags of powder which they had ready for this purpose so that they could load again very speedily....The Portuguese ships kept their steerage way, keeping aloof from the Moorish ships, passing amongst them all, doing wonders with their artillery, firing both broadsides and their poop and forecastle guns, as in all directions it was not possible to miss...but the Moorish ships were much ill-treated, they were shattered and stove in, and many had the masts and yards shattered, which was the greatest advantage our men obtained.

> Gaspar Correa, *The Three Voyages of Vasco Da Gama* (London, 1869), pp. 367-70.   Correa was describing a sea battle with Arab dhows off the coast of India in 1502.

Even as the galley fleets were reaching the peak of their size and power in the late sixteenth century, major advances in the design of sailing ships were laying the foundation for the sudden displacement of galleys as the dominant European naval force. The rapid improvement in sailing ships in the fifteenth century had nearly as profound an impact on European war as did contemporary advances in gunpowder weaponry.

Although the development of the sailing ship was more advantageous by far to the nations on the Atlantic coast, the process involved the contributions of both Atlantic and Mediterranean shipbuilders and sailors, with several key elements from the East. The dominant medieval vessel of northern waters, the cog and its successors, was a square-sailed, round-bottomed ship. Its most important innovation was the permanent stern-post rudder, which was in use by 1400. The rudder gave the helmsman more control over the ship, especially in the rough waters of the northern seas, but it did pose an increased risk of snapping off close to shore. Careful attention to the tides made it possible to settle such a vessel gently on the beach, but that kind of rudder increased the value of deep harbors, of which the Atlantic coast had rather few.

Crucial developments also occurred in the Mediterranean, where large sailing ships were used for bulk cargo throughout the Middle Ages. The key change was the adoption of the lateen sail. This triangular sail was probably Arabic in origin, since it was and still is used in the dhows of the Indian Ocean, plying the coasts from Arabia to India. Set on a yard that can be swung from parallel to the boat's center line to perpendicular to it, the lateen sail can propel the boat when the wind is blowing obliquely to the desired direction of the boat as well as from directly behind. The yard and sail are free to swing from side to side of the mast, allowing the ship to tack and thus greatly improving the maneuverability of a ship.

THE CARRACK AND THE CARAVEL

A clear description of two ships, eighty-four feet in length and twenty-one in width, which were built at Venice in 1268, reveals that they had two masts with lateen sails. The masts had "crowsnests" or fighting platforms near the top. By the late 1300s, the northern sternpost rudder began to replace steering oars, at least on sailing ships. About the same time, ships with lateen sails and a large square sail amidships appeared. Large merchantmen with that combination of sails, which ventured out into the Atlantic, were called carracks. A Portuguese drawing from 1466 shows a carrack with a small square sail in front of the mizzenmast with its lateen sail. The foresail quickly increased in size, and the three-masted carrack became common in both the Mediterranean and the Atlantic.

The *Santa Maria* of Columbus' first voyage was a small carrack. According to his log it had five sails— the common ones by then of mainsail, mizzen sail, and foresail, plus a small sail atop the mainmast, later called the gallant, and another small sail, the sprit sail, set in front of the bow. Columbus complained that the *Santa Maria* was slow and difficult to maneuver, and that her draft was too deep for working close to shore in uncharted waters. She in fact went aground off Hispaniola in 1492, and was abandoned.

Columbus much preferred his two smaller ships, the *Niña* and the *Pinta*, which were caravels. That type of ship was developed in Portugal as a coastal boat, with lateen sails to work against the wind. In the early 1400s, the Portuguese had begun to explore the coast of northwest Africa with caravels. The return voyage put them against a prevailing wind, for which lateen sails were necessary. The voyages were a product of both the powerful crusading spirit in fifteenth-century Portugal and the search for the source of the gold that the Portuguese knew was coming across the Sahara to North Africa in Muslim caravans. Seeking to outflank the Moors, the Portuguese sailed further and further down the coast of West Africa.

The Portuguese maintained a strict policy of secrecy about their ships and voyages, spreading stories about the dangers of the southern seas to scare off competition. They also wanted it believed that only the caravels were capable of making the voyages. When a brash captain declared that he could make an African expedition in any kind of ship, he was admonished that foreigners must be made to believe that only the caravels would do. Because of this attitude, little is known about the construction of the early caravels and their early voyages.

It is known that Prince Henry of Portugal, while not initiating the Portuguese expeditions, provided royal patronage and encouragement for them. Step by step his captains ventured further down the coast, returning with slaves, ivory, and exotic foodstuffs, which were enough to keep up interest in the expeditions. In 1444 they reached Cape Verde, the westernmost point of Africa, and subsequent voyages showed that beyond there Africa curved to the east. By the time of Henry's death in 1460, his captains had reached the mouth of the Niger River. His death slowed the push for exploration, and it was only at the accession of King John II in 1481 that regular expeditions were resumed. In two voyages of 1484-85, Diogo Cão explored the African coast from the Congo River to Walvis Bay in Southwest Africa. By then the voyages had become so long that the next expedition, under Bartolomeu Dias, took a supply ship along with two caravels. Leaving the supply ship behind near Walvis Bay the two caravels continued southward. Strong winds pushed them well out to sea. By the time Dias was able to turn eastward, he had gone beyond the southern tip of Africa. He landed about 100 miles east of the Cape of Good Hope, and followed the coast until it was clear that it now swung to the northeast. The warm currents also confirmed that he had rounded Africa. In 1488 Dias returned to Portugal with the news.

For nearly a decade the Portuguese prepared for the final push to India. Vasco da Gama's voyage of 1497, which took ten months to reach India, included two features unknown to earlier expeditions: a long period of time (thirteen weeks) sailing in the south Atlantic out of sight of land, and a hostile reception by the local populace, largely Muslim. The Portuguese overcame the two problems by major improvements in navigation and the use of cannon aboard ship.

NEW NAVIGATION DEVICES
Navigation in the Middle Ages consisted largely of the memory of experienced pilots. They knew the coastal features of the waters they sailed, and kept close enough to the shore to see them. In the Mediterranean such navigation was fairly easy, and it was greatly aided by the appearance of *portolani*, chart books of the coasts and harbors. In the northern seas such piloting was more difficult, in large part because pilots had to learn the location of many more rocks and shoals, as well as worry about tides and unpredictable winds. The major piloting aid in the north was a lead fathoming device that indicated shallow waters. Accumulated knowledge of the location of the shoals, the nature of the bottom, the soundings along the coast, and the tides were collected in books called *rutters*. Distances

were kept by estimates of sailing time and speed. Sailing out of sight of
land for several days, such as for the voyage from Spain to England, was
done by dead reckoning.

The fifteenth century saw the development of several major navigational devices. One was the log, which was literally a log tied to a long line
with knots at regular intervals. The log was thrown off the stern, and the
number of knots that were pulled out were counted for a given time set by
a sandglass. The device gave a rough estimate of speed adequate for that
era. Hence the term knots for a ship's speed. At about the same time an
astronomer's instrument, the quadrant, began to be taken to sea. It provided a fairly accurate reading of the altitude of a star, usually the North
Star, above the horizon. That in turn could be translated into the ship's
latitude (north-south position). The astrolabe was an improved version
that did not have the problem of a swinging plumb line. It provided an
adequate method of determining latitude at sea. As the Portuguese worked
down the coast of Africa, they found that the North Star disappeared beneath the horizon. They soon fixed on the Southern Cross as a substitute
in southern waters.

Determining longitude (east-west position) was far more difficult and
was in fact impossible to do accurately until a clock suitable for use at sea
was invented in the eighteenth century. Until then, the practice of sailing
to the desired latitude and then due east or west along that latitude was
generally followed for long voyages across the oceans. An accurate written
record of the readings of the ship's log (which appropriately became known
as the log) helped, but by no means solved the problem of determining
longitude. The appearance of the magnetic compass, probably from China,
enabled sailors to set their direction when clouds obscured the skies for
days on end.

SHIPBOARD GUNS

By 1500, Portuguese navigation had improved to the point that their
ships sailed due south to the southern tip of Africa and then turned east to
enter the Indian Ocean. In entering that ocean, the Portuguese were en-
croaching on a sea dominated by Muslims determined to keep Christians
out. Da Gama's three ships of 1497 had only twenty guns, but they were
enough to carry him through several fights with Arab dhows. The next
expedition of 1500 was far better prepared for trouble. The ships were
bristling with guns, and they had little trouble making their way to India
and back despite Arab opposition. King Manuel's instructions to the fleet
included the advice that "you are not to come to close quarters with
[Muslim ships] if you can avoid it, but you are to compel them with your
artillery alone to strike sail."[1] This is clear evidence of the use of long-
range artillery fire to defend a ship. The next expedition to Indian waters
reported fighting the locals by lining up one ship astern of the next and
rapidly firing their guns.

The mounting of guns on ships had begun in the late 1300s. However,
the Portuguese were the first to make them an essential part of a ship's
defense. The mounting of guns was equally important to trans-oceanic

exploration and trade as were the improvements in shipbuilding and navigation. Shipboard guns solved the crucial problem of how to defend a ship without a huge crew, whose bodies and supplies would take up nearly all its cargo space. If the same small crew needed to sail the ship could defend it with its guns, then a great deal of space would be available for supplies for a long voyage and cargo for trading. The first European ships that went into the distant seas found no forces capable of standing up to even the small guns they carried. Those guns were mounted on the railings or on posts beside the railings, and were effective in repelling boarders, although they did little damage to a enemy vessel. The Portuguese began to build higher and higher castles on their caravels in order to gain more advantage in fighting off the small but numerous hostile boats that they encountered in eastern seas.

IBERIAN OVERSEAS SUCCESSES

With this type of ship the Portuguese found it possible to sail to India and back with valuable cargos. But the Arabs continued to control the route from India to the Mediterranean via the Middle East, which kept Portuguese profits from being as large as they wanted. In addition the Arabs, with Turkish help, were organizing themselves to drive the interlopers out. The Portuguese response was to seize control of key points along the Arab route.

The new admiral of the Indian Ocean, Affonso d'Albuquerque, set about the task. In two years, with an impossibly small force of six ships, he seized the islands of Socotra at the mouth of the Red Sea and Hormuz in the Persian Gulf, and the city of Goa on the west Indian coast. Goa gave him a collecting point for Indian goods, while Hormuz closed off the Arab route through the Persian Gulf to the Mediterranean. Socotra proved to be less effective in closing off the Red Sea, so in 1516 a Portuguese fleet was sent into the Red Sea to stop Muslim shipping. An Arab-Turkish galley fleet assembled at Jiddah, the port for Mecca. The battle went against the Portuguese because they found themselves facing a galley fleet working under the protection of shore batteries. After inconclusive skirmishing, they were forced to withdraw.

That defeat was not too costly to the Portuguese since they had already seized a foothold on the Moluccas Islands in Indonesia, the major source for spices, in 1513. Their base there also gave them a forward position to sail on to China and Japan in the next decades. In twenty years, Portugal had built a vast maritime empire that extended to Brazil as well. That this small nation was able to do it was a tribute to Portuguese daring and the technical superiority of their navigation and ships.

The Portuguese, of course, were not the only Europeans sailing unknown oceans in the late 1400s. Columbus' voyage of 1492 under the auspices of the Castilian crown depended on Portuguese technical advances, but he also owed a great deal to an error in ancient astronomy that estimated the size of the earth some 6,000 miles as smaller then it is. The error convinced Columbus that he could reach China by sailing west for a month or so. With a carrack and two caravels, he first sailed to the Canary

Islands. He left the islands in August and had fair winds for the six-week voyage to the Bahamas. The careful log he kept shows he was a knowledgeable navigator. After sailing to the coast of Cuba and losing the *Santa Maria* in shallows, Columbus caught the westerlies at the latitude of Bermuda back to the Azores. There the Portuguese became the first to hear of his discoveries. They objected that he was an interloper in regions they had claimed. Once Ferdinand and Isabella heard of Columbus' success, they rejected Portuguese claims. Papal mediation resulted in the Treaty of Tordesillas, which divided the newly discovered oceans between Portugal and Spain at a line in the mid-Atlantic. Portugal later received an adjustment to the west, which placed Brazil in its jurisdiction.

EUROPEAN COMPETITORS

In occupying the lands assigned to them by the treaty, Portugal and Spain held clear military superiority, especially in the western hemisphere. The two Iberian states, however, were not so superior to the other European states on the Atlantic coast. They were quick to reject the Treaty of Tordesillas. As France's King Francis I asked: "Where in Adam's will was the world thus partitioned?"[2] European interlopers in the waters claimed by the Iberian states appeared by 1500. From early on French pirates were using carracks as oceangoing ships.

Better known in the details of their construction and armament were the early sixteenth-century parade ships of the French and English monarchies. They were enormous for their time, with four masts and as many as 200 guns, which were mostly small railing pieces. The most famous is Henry VIII's *Mary Rose*, built in 1509 and extensively rebuilt in 1536. In 1545 it sank in Portsmouth harbor on its way to battle a French fleet. Largely preserved in the mud, it has become a museum for naval warfare for that era, having been raised in 1981. The *Mary Rose* was one of the first to have gunports, which probably first appeared on French ships just after 1500. With them ships could carry large guns on the main decks instead of small pieces just on the castles. That in turn meant that at close range the guns could damage an enemy's masts and hull. Numerous heavy bronze pieces were found in the wreckage of the *Mary Rose*, along with the weapons and armor of about 285 soldiers. Added to the regular crew of 485, this suggests that the ship was top-heavy, and capsized when a gust of wind brought her over so far that the gunports began to take water. Her heavy guns were on carriages, the first known to be used on a ship. The carriages allowed the guns to be pulled back from the ports and the ports closed, but obviously that was no help when she sank. The *Mary Rose* also carried a large number of archers: 2,500 arrows and 139 longbows were found in her.

The *Mary Rose* was still essentially a large carrack in design, although built from the first as a warship. About 1530 a new design appeared called the galleon. The word is assumed to have come from galley, perhaps because the galleon was so much narrower and sleeker than a carrack that in its basic lines it resembled a galley. Galleons carried a beakshead similar to the spar of a galley. Their castles were lower and within the lines of the hull. They had four masts—two with square sails and two with lateens. The masts, except the mizzen, carried gallant sails and even top gallants. With up to forty heavy guns and improved sailing characteristics, the galleon was capable of projecting naval power a long distance from home.

The Spanish began to use the galleons —perhaps developed them—to serve as escorts for the fleets to and from the New World and to carry American treasure back to Spain. A successful French pirate raid in 1549 that captured four treasure ships was said to have persuaded Charles V to initiate the *flota* system: two fleets left Seville every spring for Mexico and Panama, and in August the ships assembled at Havana for the return voyage as a single fleet carrying a fortune in bullion.

THE ENGLISH SEA DOGS

Two decades later English pirates or privateers (the distinction is often very hard to make) were the more serious problem for the Spanish. Among the worst was John Hawkins, who in the usual fashion of seamen combined trade with piracy. He carried slaves from Africa to the Caribbean, where despite Philip II's prohibition he traded with the Spanish colonists. In 1568 he led a fleet of ten ships, including a small vessel captained by his cousin Francis Drake, into the Caribbean, stopping at several Spanish ports. A feigned display of force permitted the locals to trade with him in good conscience. A severe storm forced him to put into the harbor of San Juan de Ulua on the Mexican coast. The day after he anchored, the fleet from Spain arrived with eleven armed merchantmen and two galleons. The new viceroy was aboard with orders from Philip to stop illegal trade with foreigners. He was not willing to be accommodating, although he did enter the harbor under a truce with Hawkins.

The next day a battle erupted in the narrow confines of the harbor in which the English gunners sank two Spanish ships and the Spanish one English vessel. The close confines of the harbor probably account for the exceptional success of the gunners. Hawkin's largest ship was severely damaged and had to be left behind when the English fled. The Spanish record of its armament included eight great pieces, three of which shot stone balls, and sixty smaller pieces. The battle of San Juan was not the first between broadside-firing sailing ships; one off the Guinea coast of Africa in 1557 between a Portuguese fleet and a combined English-French fleet, which had joined for convenience, rates that designation. It was the first, however, in which a ship was sunk by broadsides. Hawkins and Drake returned to England fired with hatred for the "treacherous Spaniard" and were quick to go back to sea as full-fledged pirates.

The slaving, smuggling, and raiding of these English sea dogs did much to increase antagonism between Spain and England. By 1580 English ports were crowded with pirates and smugglers. Regardless of which activity was presently being engaged in, they required fast ships that were easily maneuverable and well armed. The small company of men aboard a handful of ships at sea, often for a year at a time, could not afford bloody hand-to-hand battles on the decks of ships as a routine part of their expeditions.

Accordingly enormous innovation took place in English shipbuilding and naval tactics.

ENGLISH NAVAL INNOVATIONS

Major changes in the design of ships occurred. The Spanish galleon was considerably trimmer than a carrack, but it still carried castles fore and aft for repealing boarders. The castles were detrimental to maneuverability under sail, for they caught the wind and acted as rigid sails, seriously reducing the ability of a high-charged ship to tack. The English shipwrights began to raze the castles, producing race-built ships with more speed and maneuverability. The lower center of gravity of these ships improved their stability as gun platforms, and that increased the emphasis on gunnery in English naval warfare. Major improvements in the casting of iron guns, achieved in the 1540s by German founders working for Henry VIII, meant that cheap but reliable iron culverins became available in large quantities. English ships began to carry more ordnance than did ships of other nations.

These pieces were muzzle loaders, which could take large charges and iron balls. That meant they could do damage to a ship from a greater distance. But before long-range gunnery could become a standard tactic, another innovation was required—retractable gun carriages. Without them, the pieces, except for the smallest ones, had to be lashed securely in the gun ports, usually after being loaded. In the heat of battle reloading would be most difficult and time consuming. Without carriages, the gunners would hold their fire until the enemy was in point-blank range (no elevation for the guns) with a view to doing as much injury as possible to the defenders before boarding the ship, as in galley warfare. The English by 1588 had developed moveable carriages that used the recoil of the guns' discharge, controlled by strong ropes, to propel the guns back inside the hull after firing. There they could be reloaded and returned to firing position safely and quite quickly. The English ships now could hope to damage an enemy ship as well as its defenders by standing off and firing repeatedly, breaking its masts, tearing up its sails, and holing its hull. Unlike galleys, sailing ships could not usually close quickly enough to prevent the guns from being fired repeatedly.

A third area of innovation arising from the English experience in piracy was the taking of command of ships by seamen. Ships had been and continued elsewhere to be commanded by soldiers of high rank, often with little experience at sea; the highest-ranking seaman was essentially a navigator. Francis Drake may not have been the first to move up through the ranks of seamen to take command, but his example and influence were most important in making it a common practice among the English.

Having a seaman in command meant that the problems of navigation, sailing, and fighting would be the concern of one man, instead of being divided between two or more with the ensuing disagreements. It also meant that the ship's captain would be far less likely to think of fighting at sea in the same terms as land battles, thus accelerating the trend among the English away from boarding as the basic tactic. The English voyages of plundering and trading, like those of the Vikings 600 years earlier, required that everyone in the small crews be able to man the sails and the guns and fight hand to hand if necessary. The desire of men who have not been trained to fight in close combat to avoid such combat further explains the move of the English navy toward the long-range battering of the enemy's ships as its tactic of choice. In short, the English fleet that found itself confronting the great Spanish Armada (war fleet) in 1588 had been greatly transformed in the previous twenty years.

THE CAUSES OF THE SPANISH ARMADA

The raids of Drake and the other sea dogs were one factor in persuading Philip II to dispatch the Armada against England. Another was English aid to the Dutch rebels (Chapter 15). Elizabeth had moved from providing moral support to financial aid to military help in the form of a force of 6,000 men in 1585. Philip's response was to support rebellion in Ireland and efforts to overthrow Elizabeth by English Catholics. The latter had greater appeal to the careful Philip, who wanted to avoid the expense of another war. As long as the Catholic Mary Queen of Scots, the great-granddaughter of Henry VII and therefore Elizabeth's heir, was alive, albeit in an English prison, Philip decided against the "Enterprise of England" in hope of a nonmilitary resolution in his favor. In February 1587, however, Mary was executed for her involvement in a plot to assassinate Elizabeth. Her execution removed Philip's hesitation. The invasion was on.

Don Juan of Austria, as governor of the Low Countries in 1577, probably devised the basic plan for the invasion. Its essence was that a Spanish fleet would sail into the Channel and secure it while the Spanish army in the Netherlands would cross over and occupy England. In 1580 the plausibility of the plan vastly improved when Philip became king of Portugal and took control of the Portuguese fleet. Two years earlier King Sebastian had been killed, along with much of his nobility and army, fighting the Muslims in North Africa. His aged uncle became king, but he died in 1580 without an heir. Philip claimed the Portuguese throne through his Portuguese mother. He sent a Spanish army to Lisbon to clinch his case. Although he agreed to rule Portugal as a separate kingdom with only Portuguese officials, his accession proved to be very costly to Portugal. Spain's many enemies were now Portugal's, and they were quick to strike at its overseas empire. In 1583 an English fleet raided the Moluccas. More seriously in the long run, the Dutch actively began to infringe on Portugal's claims, not only in the East but also in Brazil. In thirty years Portugal lost two-thirds of its colonial trade and most of its positions in the East, although Brazil was recovered after 1640.

ASSEMBLING THE ARMADA

The immediate impact of Philip's becoming the king of Portugal was his taking over the Portuguese fleet. Ship for ship, it was clearly superior to the Spanish fleet, although not to the English. The Portuguese galleons became the core of the Armada, including the flagship; but Philip believed that he needed still more ships. From across his vast empire he brought together some forty large carracks from the Mediterranean trade, which were given high castles and large guns, and twenty-five smaller urcas (merchantmen) from the Baltic routes, which served as supply ships. Another thirty-two small ships were added, the fastest of which served as dispatch and scout boats. The most controversial element, at least for modern historians, were four Neopolitan galleasses and four Portuguese galleys. The latter were sent along probably because they were already at Lisbon, but they were far too lightly built for the Atlantic. The galleasses, well built, well armed, and well masted, were expected to give valuable service in the Armada, since the operation was at the end to be an amphibious landing.

The presence of the Mediterranean ships, especially the oared ones, has been used to argue for the obsolete style of the Spanish navy in contrast with the modern English fleet. As we have seen, however, Spain had vast naval commitments in the Mediterranean. It was only natural that Philip would draw on his resources there for the Armada. Moreover, the oared boats could have provided crucial service at a key point of the expedition, the landing on the English shore. It was not their fault that the Armada never got that far.

Once Philip decided in early 1587 to send the Armada, ships began to collect in various Iberian ports, with Lisbon as the final assembly point. He publicized his plans in hope that word of the great fleet would frighten England into concessions. The English response was hardly what Philip could have expected. Francis Drake led a squadron of twenty-five ships to Spain to impede the assembling of the Armada. Hearing that the harbor of Cadiz was full of ships, Drake sailed into it on April 29, 1587. The harbor was defended by eight galleys and a galliot. There had been enough confrontations between well-armed sailing ships and galleys to have made it clear that the galleys could hope to be victorious only if they had a clear numerical advantage. The only hope the Spanish had to defend the Cadiz harbor was if the galleys could lure the English under the guns of the harbor fort. They achieved that much, but the fort's gunnery failed badly, scoring only one hit on the English ships. Thus Drake was free to destroy the Spanish ships and stores, among them a new galleon being outfitted.

Drake spent another month harassing shipping along the coast of Portugal, while Philip was forced to reassess his situation. Whether the Armada could have sailed in 1587 without Drake's raid is impossible to say, but the raid ensured that the Spanish would not try. The most significant result of the delay was the death of the old admiral, Spain's best naval officer, who had been appointed as the commander of Armada. Philip chose as his successor the duke of Medina-Sidonia, who had the high noble status required for such a command but little experience in war at sea. The few times he had been to sea, he had become badly seasick. He wrote a poignant letter to Philip begging to be spared the duty, but Philip would not hear of it. In the months to come the duke did his duty as well as was humanly possible, but he knew little of naval war.

Possibly an experienced sea captain could have overcome the inherent problems of the Armada's strategy and tactics, but even such a commander would have faced enormous difficulties. One was the fact that the Armada was an army at sea, not really a navy. There were about 19,000 soldiers crowded aboard the ships, with 8,000 sailors and 2,100 galley rowers. Army officers, who included Medina-Sidonia, made the major decisions. A second problem was that the duke of Parma, the Spanish commander in the Netherlands, lacked faith in the plan: the Armada was to protect his army as it crossed the Channel in small ships that had been collected at Dunkirk to invade England. However, the vast number of men that were abroad the Armada itself, more than was needed to defend it at sea, and the recent discovery by underwater archeology of scaling ladders on sunken ships, strongly indicate that the force on the Armada was to take part in the invasion. Regardless, from the first Parma did only what was necessary to be able to tell Philip that he was following orders.

A third major problem was the weather. The Armada's departure from Lisbon was delayed by two weeks because of contrary winds. Once out of the harbor on May 30, it was stalled for another two weeks off the Portuguese coast. When finally it began to make progress northward, a severe storm struck and scattered the fleet. The ships were so banged up that they had to put into Corunna in northwest Spain for repairs and more stores. Much of the food and water on board was clearly spoiled. Finally on July 22, the Armada sailed again.

THE VOYAGE OF THE ARMADA

By that time the fleet's sailors had learned that the Armada had atrocious sailing characteristics. A fleet is only as good as its worst ship, and many of the converted merchantmen were very bad indeed. They had not been designed to tack against the wind; their sailors would simply wait for the wind to change. The high castles, added to convert them into warships, further reduced their seamanship. The terrible sailing characteristics meant that for most of its voyage the Armada's progress was very slow, and that once it had passed a point, there was no hope of returning unless the wind shifted completely about. After leaving Corunna, however, the Armada had largely favorable winds to the English coast. The rough waters did force the four galleys to return to Spain or run for the French coast. On July 29 the southwest English coast was sighted. The fleet turned east to follow the coastline to the Channel and across to Dunkirk.

As the Armada sailed past Portsmouth harbor, it passed a large part of the English fleet safely in the harbor. The English admiral was Lord Charles Howard. He had the high status necessary for command but had more experience at sea than Medina-Sidonia. Drake was his vice admiral, and he had a major voice in most decisions. The English fleet consisted of about 190 ships, and like the Armada they varied greatly in quality. The number of true warships was about the same as the Spanish, but the heart of the fleet were the twelve race-built galleons. The view that the confrontation was between the Spanish Goliaths and the English Davids was based in large part on the tonnage figures that appeared to make the Spanish ships much larger. But the modern realization that the Spanish ton was at least 25 percent smaller than the English has shown that the largest ship in the two fleets was English. The high castles on the Spanish warships also helped to give the impression they were larger.

Recent scholarship and underwater excavations have also demonstrated that the Armada was well armed with guns, quite possibly with more per ship than the English, contrary to nineteenth-century British historians. The type of gun, however, differed between the two fleets. The English had largely the culverin type, which provided range and accuracy but threw relatively small balls. English full culverins used seventeen-pound shot, and their demi-culverins, far more numerous, nine-pound shot. Only the larger ships had room to mount these guns, so the smaller English ships were very lightly armed.

The Spanish did have some culverins and were actively seeking more when the Armada sailed, but their dominant gun was the cannon type. The full cannon shot fifty-pound balls and the demi-cannon, thirty-two-pound ones. The gun most in evidence on the Spanish ships was one with a very short barrel that fired twenty-four-pound stone balls. Its range was very limited. The Spanish clearly intended to throw heavy weight at short range, while the English expected to throw much lighter shot at greater range. Whether this difference really constituted a difference between English "ship-killing" weaponry and Spanish "man-killing" guns is debatable, since at close range the Spanish pieces were more likely to do serious damage to ships. But it did dictate a major difference in tactics: the English could stand off and fire at a distance, while the Spanish had to close with the enemy in order to accomplish anything.

As the Spanish sailed past Portsmouth, the English came out behind them and followed them down the coast of England. Each fleet attempted to make use of its preferred tactics, and each was frustrated because they did not work. The English failed to do any damage with their long-range gunnery, and the Spanish could not get close enough to any English ship to board. Medina-Sidonia's orders were to proceed directly to his rendezvous with Parma, and so his attention was focused largely on keeping his fleet closely together in strong defensive formation. The precise formation is unknown, but it appears to have followed a contemporary plan published at Rome. At the head were several galleons and the galleasses. In the center were the transports. On the wings were squadrons of warships, while in the rear were the rest of the galleons. From the view of the English behind it, the formation easily could have looked like the crescent shape they attributed to it. It was an excellent defensive formation, and the Spanish lost no ships to the English guns before reaching the Flemish coast. But the powder magazine of an armed carrack blew up and forced it to be abandoned, while a galleon collided with another ship and was too damaged to continue. (It is surprising there were no more such incidents.) Both ships were towed into port by the English, and the contemporary descriptions of their size and guns are important for understanding the Armada.

THE BATTLE OF GRAVELINES

After little fighting, the Armada reached Calais on August 6. There the pilots told Medina-Sidonia that the fleet could not anchor at Dunkirk, its appointed anchorage, because the harbor was too small and shallow. He ordered the fleet to anchor outside of Calais harbor to wait for word from Parma that he was ready for the crossing to England. Parma in fact was utterly unprepared for it. His boats and barges were small and unseaworthy, and his men were not in position to board them. Clearly Parma was doing only as much as was necessary to say that he was obeying the king.

The two dukes had little time to argue, via messengers, over what was to be done. During the Armada's second night off Calais, the English sent eight fire ships, full of tar, oil, and other combustibles, drifting on the tide and wind into the anchorage. The Spanish were expecting such a tactic, and it may well have been precisely the expectation that caused greater problems. In 1585 the Dutch had used a fire ship, loaded with gunpowder, to blow up a fortified bridge and kill some 800 Spaniards. The men on the Armada expected these to be the same "infernal machines." In a matter of perhaps fifteen minutes the Spanish sailors had cut their anchor cables, set their sails, and gotten out of the way. It was hardly a panic, since none of the fire ships did any damage. Yet the loss of their anchors was the greatest injury inflicted on the Spanish. The immediate consequence was that their ships were not able to hold their position at the new rendezvous point set by Medina-Sidonia. When morning came, the duke found only a handful of galleons in sight. The rest of the fleet was scattered for miles northeastward along the coast.

When the English saw the deserted anchorage, they came charging after the Spanish. Howard's squadron was distracted by a beached galleass, so the bulk of the fighting in what is called the Battle of Gravelines was done by some forty ships led by Drake. About thirty Spanish ships, mostly galleons, were close enough to take part in the fighting, but only a few could assemble in a defensive formation. The English found it possible for the first time to get into close range and pound the enemy with their guns. We know of one clear case of a line-astern attack by twelve or thirteen English ships against a galleon. It is not clear, however, if that was the galleon that was sunk in the battle. Two more were so badly damaged that they had to be beached. It is also known that eventually the English came in close enough that they were within shouting range. That suggests that the Spanish had stopped firing their guns. Whether it was because they had run out of shot or, as has been proposed recently, because they could not reload in the heat of battle because of the absence of retractable gun carriages, can not yet be fully answered.

By late afternoon, the English began to break off, partly because they were running out of shot and partly because the wind was pushing the Spanish toward the shoals along the coast. After a day-long ordeal in which the Spanish desperately fought to keep their ships off the shoals, the wind shifted and pushed them into the North Sea. There was no hope of beating southward against the wind for the rendezvous with Parma. As the wind continued to blow in that direction for several days, the Armada, still nearly intact in terms of the number of ships, found itself at the latitude of central Scotland when the wind calmed. Some Spanish officers wanted to return to the Channel and take on the English again, but most, including the duke, agreed that they were too short of supplies and their ships too battered for such an attempt. The decision was made to return to Spain around Scotland.

THE RETURN TO SPAIN

Well-designed navigational instructions were given to each ship, intended to keep the fleet well away from the dangerous coasts of Scotland and Ireland. Many of the ships, however, were desperately short of food and water. A large number were badly leaking, especially the Mediterranean ships, which were not built for the rough seas they were in. The battering many ships had taken from the English and the shaking of the ships from firing their own guns, in many cases guns far too heavy for the ships they were on, also caused severe leaking. Several ships sank at sea, but most of those lost were wrecked on the Irish coast. Some came into shore because of a desperate need to reach any land; others because of navigational errors. The loss of their anchors at Calais proved catastrophic for many of these ships as they came in to shore.

On September 21 the first surviving ship reached the Spanish coast. By the end of October sixty-four ships had come in, while by best estimate fifty-nine were lost. The largest proportion of those lost were the armed merchantmen. Because of their size, they carried the most soldiers, and so the manpower losses they represented were considerably higher. Furthermore on the ships that did return to Spain, the number of dead and dying was very high. It is probable that only one-third of the men who sailed in June were still alive in December, including a small number who after many narrow escapes and adventures in Ireland returned home, and a smaller number who settled among the Irish. Of the ships that did return, many were too badly damaged to sail again. English losses, on the other hand, were truly negligible: perhaps a hundred men killed, but no ships lost or even badly damaged.

The failure of the Spanish Armada hardly saved Protestant Europe from destruction, as traditionally has been maintained. The Dutch revolt did not depend upon English help; also it is hard to believe that a victorious Spain could have held England for long, although it is probable that a decent-sized Spanish force would have reached and taken London with ease in 1588. Certainly the defeat was not, as often has been said, the end of Spanish seapower. To the contrary, it caused Philip to invest a great deal of money in building a new fleet much more like the English one. In 1594 he gave the navy its own administration and captains. When a large English fleet found the Spanish treasure fleet at sea in 1602, thirty new galleons easily drove it off.

As for England, Elizabeth seems to have learned little from her victory, as has usually been true in history. In 1589 she sent a fleet under Drake with 120 ships and 25,000 men to Portugal in hope of stripping it from Philip's control. Unlike the Armada, it did land its men, but Spanish resistance and, more importantly, disease reduced it rapidly. After two months ashore, some 11,000 men had died, and the rest were withdrawn. In 1595 an expedition to raid the West Indies cost both Drake and Hawkins their lives.

Yet the failure of the English to follow up their Armada victory should not detract from the long-term consequence of the confrontation. It persuaded the English that a powerful royal fleet was necessary to defend their island. From that point of view, the events of 1588 can be regarded as the true beginning of the English royal navy, even if Elizabeth and James I did little to build it in the decades after 1588.

NOTES

1. Quoted in Geoffrey Parker, *The Military Revolution: Military Innovation and the Rise of the West, 1500-1800* (Cambridge, 1988), p. 94.

2. Knecht, p. 333.

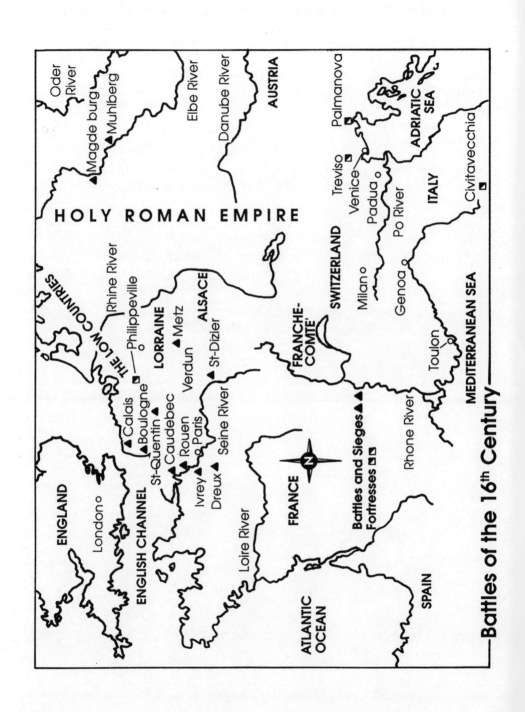

Battles of the 16th Century

16

The Sixteenth Century

*But the French made much more manageable pieces and only out of bronze,
which they called cannons, and used iron balls where they used to be of stone
and incomparably larger and heavier; and they moved them on carts which
were drawn not by oxen as was the custom in Italy, but by horses. The men
and equipment assigned to this work were so skillful that they could almost
always keep up with the rest of the army; and when brought up to the walls
they were set up with unbelievable rapidity. With only the briefest intervals
between shots, they shot so rapidly and powerfully that they could do in a few
hours what in Italy used to take days.*
    Francesco Guicciardini, *The History of Italy*, trans. Cecil Grayson,
    (New York, 1964), p. 153. Guicciardini was a Florentine historian
    of the early sixteenth century.

Just as guns profoundly changed war at sea, so they required drastic
changes in siegecraft and fortification design. Guns were in use at sieges
from their first appearance, but only after 1430 did they begin to have a real
impact on siegecraft. It took another generation before they affected the
design of fortifications.

It was in Italy that fort building first began to reflect the destructive
power of artillery. The increasing use after 1470 of iron balls, which were
more effective in battering the high walls and towers of medieval castles,
required a reduction in their height. The lower trajectory of cannon in
comparison to mechanical artillery meant that the lower part of a wall was
more likely to be hit by cannonballs. That in turn meant that the rubble
from a collapsed wall would probably fill the moat and make an assault
on the breach easier. Lowering the walls, however, increased the likelihood
of a successful escalade. The response to these problems was to make the
ditch deeper and wider, so that only a small portion of the wall was raised
above ground level. Machicolation atop the walls was replaced by rounded
shoulders to allow balls to deflect off without doing as much damage. Gun
openings, called casemates, were cut into the base of the wall to aid the
defense of the ditch.

These features, except casemates, had appeared in Italy by 1494, although no one fort had them all. The invasion of the French army in 1494 with its powerful artillery train exposed the weaknesses of Italian forts, even the modified ones. The French reduced some of the older structures in a matter of hours. The Italian responded by putting some of the best minds in history— Michelangelo, Da Vinci, Machiavelli—to work on new fortification designs. Da Vinci's work in particular was too advanced for his time. The more acceptable solutions came from lesser known men such as Fra Giocondo and the Sangallos.

THE BASTION

The Italian architects remained committed to masonry structures, although it was well known that brick was easily shattered by cannonballs, while earthen structures reinforced by timbers absorbed much of their shock. It may have been simply a preference for the age-old Italian tradition of masonry structures, but it was reinforced by the temporary nature of earth works, which eroded and settled. In continuing to use brick, the Italians had to find ways to reduce the destructive power of cannon against it. One was to use angled walls so that balls deflected off, causing less damage than balls that struck directly perpendicular. A few forts were built in which every surface was obliquely angled, so that they appeared serrated in outline. Another response was to build guns platforms called bastions, which projected outward from the wall and pushed the attackers further from the curtain wall. The basic idea of bastions was already 2,000 years old.

For some fort builders the rounded bastion was the design of choice, on the grounds that a circular structure was inherently stronger and that projectiles glanced off them. In rebuilding the walls of Treviso and Padua near Venice around 1510, Fra Giocondo used round bastions in conjunction with a very advanced design. He cleared a 1,500-foot space in front of the wall to give the defenders a clear field of fire; such a feature became known as the glacis. His round-shouldered walls were only twenty feet high and were set in a fifteen foot ditch.

The rounded bastion is best known for its use in the series of forts that Henry VIII built along the southeast coast of England against the threat of a French invasion. He engaged Albrecht Dürer, the German artist, to design several forts. In what is regarded as the first book devoted to fort design, published in 1527, Dürer provided plans for round bastions bristling with gun casemates. Those forts were never tested, since England was never invaded throughout the era of masonry forts.

Had they been assaulted, Dürer's circular forts probably would have been found vulnerable, as round bastions on the continent were. The circular design made it difficult to bring more than two or three guns to bear on one point, but rather scattered the fire of the guns around a broad circle. Second and more serious, there was a blind spot at the front of a round bastion that could not be covered by guns on the bastions on either side. The use of triangular bastions solved both problems. The first example of

La premicre charge de la bataille de Dreux, la ou M. le Conneftable fut prins le 19. Decembre 1562.

The Battle of Dreux of 1562. Note the Spanish Squares with their sleeves of musketmen around the pikemen in the center left, and the units of pisto-leers at lower left.

a fortification with triangular bastions was built by Antonio da Sangallo in 1501 at Nettuno, south of Rome. It was a small square fort with a trian-gular bastion at each corner. The fort's geometry was calculated so that guns situated at the protected flanks of each bastion could sweep the ad-joining sections of the curtain wall and the faces of the neighboring bas-tions. Every point on the outer surface of the fort could be seen and covered by gunners on the bastions. The men and guns at the flanks were well protected by protruding *orillons* (shoulders) of the bastions. This de-sign became known as the Italian trace when Italian engineers carried it northward. With them they carried their preference for masonry structures, which gradually replaced the earthen structures of the northern architects.

THE ITALIAN TRACE

In 1515 Sangallo's nephew applied his design to the Italian city of Civ-itavecchia, using a series of triangular bastions to defend the large, irreg-ularly shaped city. In the hands of a competent architect the Italian trace proved to be easily adaptable to cities of any shape or size. To keep the cost down, governments would keep as much of the old structure as pos-sible and place new bastions in front of it, or in some cases replace the most vulnerable towers with bastions. By the mid-sixteenth century, the Italian trace had been combined with low walls set in a deep ditch to create the basic design of forts until well into the nineteenth century. Engineers set to work to improve on the basic design, for example, by increasing the defensive capacity of the outside wall of the ditch (the counterscarp). It was faced with masonry, and guns and men were placed on a narrow terrace a little below the rim, called the covered way, on which men and equipment could move in relative safety. Gun casemates were cut in the counterscarp to catch anyone who entered the ditch in a deadly crossfire. To add to the difficulty of reaching the ditch, the glacis was improved from simply being an open field of fire to becoming an artificial slope down from the rim of the counterscarp. Often it was laid with masonry to make the work of digging trenchs up it more difficult.

Rarely did a besieging army have the capacity to lay siege lines around an entire fortified city. Instead the army's engineers would determine which side would be most vulnerable or easiest to approach. Once it had become clear what bastions and portion of the curtain wall were to be bombarded, the defenders could move guns from the other bastions to those under attack. The gun carriages and their horse teams often had trouble negotiating the narrow, crooked streets of medieval towns and the steep climb up to the bastions.

Accordingly when governments intended to build an entirely new fortified town, it was carefully designed to avoid those problems. Governments often decided to build a new fortified town instead of a simple fort because it was believed that the commerce of a town would help pay for the construction and would support a large garrison. In the center of the town a large plaza provided room for the guns to turn easily. From the plaza straight broad streets radiated out to the bastions. Gentle slopes up to the bastions eased the work of moving the heavy guns. Two major new fortified towns of the sixteenth century were Philippeville on the Flemish border with France, which was built by Spain in 1555, and Palmanova, begun in 1593 by the Venetians to defend their city from the north. Both serve as excellent examples of the simple geometry found in sixteenth-century fortifications and of how that geometry became increasingly complicated in the next century.

The result of all of these changes was to enhance the defenders' use of artillery, which appeared in greater and greater amounts. Sieges became more and more difficult, costly, and time-consuming. The new design of the curtain walls and bastions meant that cannon fire could be effective against them only if the guns were mounted at the rim of the counterscarp and fired directly into them to create a breach. To achieve this, trenches, which had to zigzag to avoid giving the defenders a clear line of fire down them, had to be dug from beyond effective cannon range up the glacis. The process of digging the trenches was slow and costly. Even when that job was done, and guns dragged up and a breach opened, the crossfire from neighboring bastions made assault of the breach murderous. On numerous occasions until as late as 1602 commanders assaulted modern fortifications without the necessary trenches. Their men paid extremely dearly for such stupidity. Consequently, starving out the fort's garrison continued to be used.

The nature of warfare changed rapidly in the three decades after 1530, as the changes in fortification design were being implemented. The presence of powerful forts much decreased the movement of armies, since their artillery trains could no longer be counted on to reduce quickly any fortification in their path as had been true for the half-century before 1530. An army dared not leave a force behind to mask (surround) a fort and go past it, since leaving a powerful garrison at one's rear was highly dangerous. An army well equipped to execute long sieges was not well prepared to fight major battles in the field. For a century after 1530 there were few major field battles; great sieges dominated the period. Because of the dramatic reduction in the speed with which a decision could be gained, wars were said to have "smoldered like a wet match."

The Anglo-imperial invasion of France in 1544 from the north and the west gave an early indication of how warfare was changing. Both invading armies quickly bogged down before powerful forts—the English before Boulogne and the imperial army at Saint-Dizier. Both forts were taken, but only after delaying the invading armies for two months. Henry refused to go any farther; taking Boulogne may have been his goal all along. Charles decided to push on to Paris, as Henry was supposed to do. In mid-September, his army reached the half-way point between the frontier and Paris, but by then it was short of supplies and the campaigning season was close to an end. Charles had to withdraw. By the end of the year, one of those futile peace treaties between Francis and Charles was signed.

RELIGIOUS WAR IN GERMANY

Charles V was willing to accept peace with France rather than take advantage of the continuing French war with England in order to turn his forces against the German Lutherans. Ever since Martin Luther had first gone public with his demand for church reform in 1517, Charles had opposed his movement. A devout Catholic, Charles was also motivated by the operative political theory of the time: religious dissent necessarily led to political rebellion. In a society that still depended upon personal oaths of loyalty and service, how could someone be trusted to fulfill his oath if it were sworn on a false bible or to a false god? Heresy was treason to God, and a traitor to God could only become a traitor to his king. Thus the ruler had an obligation to maintain religious conformity; political unity required religious unity. Very few people of the sixteenth century disputed that view; even Protestants persecuted by Catholic rulers enforced it once they gained political power. Consequently religion was added as a cause of war and factionalism in Europe, and few wars are as bitter and bloody as religious wars.

Charles V truly regarded it as his sacred duty to repress Lutheranism by force if necessary, but his attention to the problem kept being distracted by war with the Ottoman Empire and France. Only in 1546 upon peace with France and a truce with the sultan was he able to assemble a force to take on the Lutherans, who had gained control of most of northern and central Germany. The only noteworthy event in the war that followed was the Battle of Mülhburg in April 1547. The two armies were separated by a broad river. The Lutherans, apparently lacking experience with the great range of the Spanish musket, were little concerned when Charles marched several companies of musketmen into the shallows of the river. Their effective fire from a considerable distance so confused the Lutherans that Charles' army easily forded the river and routed them.

With this victory, Charles imposed a compromise religious settlement on Germany. The more ardent Lutherans refused to accept it, and the northern city of Magdeburg became their center of resistance. Lutheran resistance was actively supported by Henry II of France, who succeeded his father in 1547. In 1550-51 Magdeburg was put under siege, but it held out and served as a rallying point for Lutherans elsewhere. In exchange for a large subsidy and the promise of his direct intervention, the Lutheran princes offered Henry II possession of those lands in the Holy Roman Empire where French was spoken, namely Lorraine. In 1553 he led an army into the province to take possession of the cities of Metz, Toul, and Verdun in Lorraine. From there Henry marched on to the Rhine in hope of occupying Alsace and joining up with the Lutherans. During this "promenade to the Rhine," Henry used a map to determine the route of his army; he may have been the first commander to do so. In Alsace, he found the German-speaking locals sharply opposed to him, and he returned to France with no further gains.

Charles V was enraged by this attempt to take advantage of his religious troubles in Germany, and he gathered an army of 80,000 men to recover Lorraine. Despite the lateness of the season, in November he led his army to Metz, which was ably defended by François de Guise. Forty great guns were brought up and battered a section the curtain wall until it collapsed. The elation of the imperial troops was crushed when they saw that Guise had erected an earthen rampart behind it. They refused to assault the breach, and with the end of December fast approaching, Charles gave up the siege and the effort to defeat the Lutherans as well. Negotiations resulted in the Peace of Augsburg in 1555, which allowed the German princes to choose between Catholicism and Lutheranism as the religion for their states. The signatories of the treaty swore eternal peace; eternity in Germany lasted until 1618.

PHILIP II AND HENRY II
    Totally exhausted by his wars and badly crippled by gout, Charles abdicated his titles in 1556. His brother Ferdinand, already king of Hungary and Bohemia, had been elected King of the Romans in 1531, designating him as the next emperor. Charles gave him the Habsburg lands of central Europe to provide a power base to govern the empire. Charles' son Philip received the Spanish kingdoms, Naples and Milan in Italy, the Franche-Comté, and the Low Countries. The Habsburg family and lands thus were split into Austrian and Spanish branches, but the two cooperated closely and intermarried constantly.

    Upon becoming king of Spain Philip found himself in the midst of war with France. In 1556 Henry II sent an army under the duke of Guise to drive the Spanish out of Naples. Philip responded by sending a force of 47,000 men south from Flanders toward Paris in August 1557. It halted before the fortified town of Saint-Quentin. The French army sent to relieve the town was quite green, since the best captains and units were with Guise in Italy. Attacked by the larger Spanish force, some of the newly recruited companies of French infantry panicked and crashed into the others, ending any chance of an orderly retreat. About half of the French army was killed or captured.

The way to Paris was open, but Philip, called by the Spanish the Prudent King, felt that he dared not send his army on while Saint-Quentin remained untaken. By the time it capitulated, much of the French army in Italy had returned home. Since it was now late September, the Spanish returned to Flanders. Henry meanwhile had collected a vast army to defend Paris. He was determined to use it during the winter before the contracts of the mercenaries ran out, and he lacked the money to pay them. He settled on Calais as an opportune target. England was then an ally of Spain, since Queen Mary Tudor was married to Philip (she was the second of his four wives). Regaining Calais was the dream of every Frenchman, in part because it gave the English excellent access for invading France at any time and in part because of the boast they had placed over its main gate: "The French Calais shall win. When iron and lead like cork shall swim."

Henry II ordered a winter attack on Calais because the garrison was reduced for the winter months, the cold weather would have frozen the shallower marshes around it, and the English would be taken by surprise. Perhaps the most amazing thing about the attack on Calais was how well the secret was kept, until a week before the French army reached it on January 1, 1558. The attack fulfilled all of the king's expectations. Eight days after the first bombardment, Calais surrendered, removing the last vestige of the Hundred Years War.

With each side having a major victory and a major defeat, peace negotiations began in late 1558, resulting in the Treaty of Cateau-Cambrésis of April 1559. France conceded sovereignty over Naples and Milan to Spain while retaining the cities of Lorraine and Calais. To seal the peace, Henry's daughter was to marry Philip, since Mary Tudor had died in late 1558. The duke of Alba arrived in Paris to swear the peace and serve as Philip's proxy for the marriage. Henry, who loved to joust, arranged for a grand tournament for the festivities and took to the jousting lanes himself. An opponent's lance shattered on his breastplate and bounced upward, catching him in the face of his helmet and driving splinters through his eye opening. Ten days later he died of blood poisoning.

CHANGES IN THE FRENCH ARMY

Among the consequences of Henry II's death was the hastening of the decline of the armored lancer as the mainstay of the French military. Henry's widow Catherine de' Medici outlawed jousting at the court. With the virtual cessation of tournaments, the style of fighting for which they provided practice declined rapidly as well. Certainly other factors contributed to the dwindling numbers of the armored lancers on the battlefield—their vulnerability to gunfire, their expense at a time of increasing economic trouble, the difficulty of breeding horses strong enough to carry the heavy plate armor—but the tournaments and the romances had served to emphasize the traditional values and skills of the knight. With knightly combat in disfavor and lacking the opportunity to practice their skills in tournaments, the French nobles let the old style of combat die out. In the rest of Europe many of these developments in the military had already occurred, but it was in France, the birthplace of the knight and the romance, that the code of medieval warfare had lasted the longest.

Another development dating from Henry's reign that contributed to the decline of the lancer was the use of pistols from horseback. Soon after the appearance of handguns, mounted men were using primitive pistols, but the smoldering match frightened the horses and made pistols impractical for cavalry. About 1520 the invention of the wheel lock pistol changed that. The wheel lock was a steel wheel attached to a spring that could be pulled back and locked into place. When the trigger was pulled, the spring was released and spun the wheel against a flint, throwing sparks into the pan of powder and firing the ball. The pistol could be loaded and cocked and then carried in a holster until needed. It was a one-handed weapon, a feature important for a man trying to control a horse. But the wheel lock was very expensive, nearly three times the cost of an arquebus, and consequently its use was restricted to the nobility, who still insisted on their right to fight mounted.

The first to use the pistol on the battlefield were German light cavalrymen called *reiters*. By 1557 Philip II had recruited several thousand reiters, and they played a major role in his victory at Saint-Quentin. Since the battle was largely the pursuit of panicked French forces, their speed was a major factor in the destruction of the French army. Henry II decided to rebuild his shattered forces with a large number of reiters. He was reported as saying that the greatest advantage his enemy had was his reiters, "all of whom are found loaded with pistols and seemed to have been invented for the stunning and breaking up of the French men-at-arms."[1] By August 1558 the French army included 8,000 reiters from Germany.

THE FRENCH RELIGIOUS WARS
Pistoleers were present in large numbers in the French civil wars known as the Wars of Religion, which lasted from 1562 to 1598. The wars were in part a consequence of Henry II's death, which passed the French throne to his young sons Francis II (1559-1560) and Charles IX (1560-1574). Francis' short reign was dominated by the Guises, uncles of his wife Mary Queen of Scots. Other prominent families deeply resented their exclusion from power. Some, already attracted to Protestantism, began to provide political and military leadership for the Huguenot (Protestant) party. When organized hostilities began in 1562, both the Huguenots and the ardent Catholics, led by the Guises, had little trouble in recruiting manpower in France, especially among the nobles. The peace treaty of 1559 and the financial crisis of the French government had led to the disbanding of much of the army. Because neither party had much money, however, the masses of foreign infantry formerly recruited for the French army were not found in the French civil wars.

In December 1562 the first major battle of the civil wars took place at Dreux, west of Paris. The battle, marginally a Catholic victory, is notable for two features. One is an event unique in military history: both commanders were captured by their foes. The second, more significant in the long term, was the first known use of the cavalry tactic known as the caracole. Pistoleers in the Huguenot army at Dreux formed up in bodies of considerable depth, perhaps as many as sixteen ranks deep. As each rank approached the Catholic lancers, they fired their pistols, then wheeled away to their left, since they carried their pistols in their right hands, and returned to the rear of the company to reload. Meanwhile the next rank came up and repeated the procedure. Against a resolute body of lancers, the tactic would have been ineffective. But since the quality of French gens d'armes was declining rapidly, at Dreux the caracole was quite successful.

Being a pistoleer required less training; the horses used were smaller and thus cheaper; and a reiter, depending more on speed, needed less armor. Meanwhile the lancers had to carry heavier and heavier armor to protect themselves against the pistol balls, to the point that they and their horses were exhausted after brief activity. These factors led the French nobles to turn to the pistol.

Against an infantry force with little or no firepower, the caracole was effective because the horsemen could do injury to the foot soldiers without driving into the line of pikes. Against companies of firearms, however, the far greater range of the arquebus resulted in the pistoleers discharging their pistols from a distance at which they were totally ineffective. In warfare, like usually fights like, and the pistoleers generally took on the enemy's reiters.

By 1568 the conversion of the French cavalry to the pistol had reached the point that Marshal Tavennes, a commander of the Catholic forces, recommended that his cavalrymen carry pistols. He also required that companies of mounted men march together in the formation they would take on the battlefield so they would become accustomed to holding their positions. While the German reiters were prepared to depend largely on their pistols, the French pistoleers did not give up the ingrained taste of the French nobles for shock combat. They fired their pistols and then charged into the enemy's ranks.

The French Wars of Religion dragged on through the 1560s and 1570s. They were marked by incompetent leadership and atrocities on both sides, but the worst was the Saint Bartholomew's Day Massacre of 1572, which eliminated much of the Huguenot leadership. In 1584 a new dimension to the civil wars appeared when Henry III's younger brother died childless. Since Henry (1574-1589), the third of Henry II and Catherine de' Medici's sons to rule, was himself childless, the next in line for the royal succession was Henry of Navarre, leader of the Huguenots. Determined to prevent his succession, the ardent Catholics formed the Catholic League, which ended the often uneasy alliance between the Catholic party and the monarchy. Henri de Guise, son of the earlier mentioned duke, emerged as the leader of the league. Having his own ambitions, he was prepared to fight the king.

THE VICTORY OF HENRY IV

Henry of Navarre was first of all a dashing cavalry captain who preferred to have his men combine the sword with the pistol. He won his first major victory at Coutras in 1587, with a cavalry charge that was carried into the enemy with the sword after the pistols were discharged. He had a tendency, however, to fail to follow up his victories, and the Catholic League's army was able to escape largely intact. As a result Guise, a few months later, was able to defeat a largely German army that had entered France in support of the Huguenots.

Guise's victory raised his reputation among the French Catholics, especially in Paris, always an ardently Catholic city, to the highest possible standing. Ignoring Henry III's order not to enter Paris, he did so in early May 1588, and was hailed as a conquering hero. The king had prepared for this by bringing Swiss troops into Paris. Already a most unpopular king, Henry sparked open rebellion. In an uprising known as the Day of the Barricades, the Parisians made barricades of carts, paving stones, and so forth in the streets to cut off the and surround the Swiss. The king was forced to flee Paris, but he got his revenge by arranging the assassination of the duke of Guise in December 1588. Denouncing Henry as a tyrant, the league avenged Guise by assassinating the king the next August.

Henry of Navarre was now king of France, at least by the usual laws of succession. Most French Catholics refused to accept him on the basis of a "law of Catholicity"; but enough of the captains who had served Henry III recognized Navarre to give him a good-sized army. In March 1590 Henry gave battle to the league's forces at Ivry, very near Dreux. The two armies were arrayed in the same manner: blocks of cavalry and infantry interspersed across a single line. The Catholic forces were somewhat larger and thus had a larger line. The chronicles of the battle all note that the Catholic cavalry still included many lancers, while Henry's was entirely made up of pistoleers. The battle was largely decided when his pistoleers drove a smaller body of Catholic reiters back into the lancers. That disrupted their lines and cost them their momentum, allowing Henry's cavalry to drive them off the field.

Again Henry was slow in following up his victory, but after several weeks he marched on Paris. By the time he reached it, the city was prepared for a siege. Henry's forces were hardly equipped for an assault on the walls, which were still largely medieval in design. Throughout the civil wars, commanders from both sides, despite lacking siege guns and experienced sappers, dissipated victory after victory in the field by laying siege to nearby towns. At Paris Henry quickly abandoned the idea of assaulting the walls and settled into a siege to starve it into submission.

Philip II had been watching the successes of Henry IV with rising fear. A Protestant-ruled France would have been a far greater threat to Spain's interests than England had ever been. He ordered the duke of Parma to relieve Paris with 15,000 men from his army in the Low Countries. The direct intervention of Spain in the French civil wars brought into confrontation the two most respected commanders of their generation: Parma, the cautious master of the tactics of the Spanish square, and Henry, the dashing cavalry captain.

Parma's relief of Paris in August 1590 required little fighting, since Henry quickly pulled out. It was not until 1592 that the two faced each other in the field. Henry had put Rouen under siege, and Parma came to relieve it. The king decided to use only his best cavalry units, perhaps 7,000 men in all, to impede Parma's approach, leaving his infantry and poorer cavalry to maintain the siege lines. Parma was leading a force of both cavalry and infantry, 30,000 men in all, so Henry's decision created an interesting situation: could a pure cavalry force led by a first-rate commander defeat or at least stall a complete army led by an equally good commander? The answer proved to be no, although Henry gave it a good try. Parma kept his forces tightly together and under control, so that Henry's attempts to find units separated from the main body and destroy them failed.

Breaking the siege of Rouen, Parma moved on westward to take the fortress of Caudebec, which controlled the lower Seine. Recognizing that a successful Spanish campaign in Normandy would be very damaging to his cause, Henry called all of his available manpower to Normandy. Once it had assembled, his forces outnumbered Parma's. Henry caught up to Parma at Caudebec. A superior army now blocked Parma's retreat to Paris or Flanders; movement eastward would only trap him against a sea controlled by his enemies; and the broad Seine blocked his way to the south with no bridge over it for more than 100 miles. Parma's solution was both brilliant and daring: he brought up boats and pontoons from Rouen to bridge the Seine, about 1,000 feet wide at that point. At night Spanish engineers chained the boats together, and before dawn most of the heavy guns were brought across. A small force of light cavalry and infantry was left in the lines while the rest of the army crossed in early daylight.

Henry had no idea what Parma was doing, but when his men reported that the Spanish lines were very lightly held, he sent a light cavalry company to probe. By the time it reported what was happening and Henry brought his full army forward, the last of the enemy was crossing the bridge, which they destroyed behind them. Parma, through his great faith in his engineers, saved his army. He quickly marched back to Flanders, leaving 1,500 men to strengthen the garrison in Paris. Six months later he was dead from complications of a wound suffered at Caudebec.

Parma's brilliant escape over the Seine meant that the military and political situation in France remained a stalemate. It was broken in March 1593, when Henry announced his intention to accept Catholicism. In the words attributed to him, "Paris is worth a Mass." A year later he entered Paris in triumph. A few Catholics still opposed him, but the war now became largely a conflict with Spain. Despite several Spanish successes, the dying Philip II offered to open peace negotiations in early 1598. The Treaty of Vervins reestablished the status quo of 1559; all captured places were to be returned. Quickly following the peace came the Edict of Nantes, by which Henry gave religious toleration to the Huguenots. With the end of nearly forty years of civil war, the French monarchy could return to its century-old struggle to destroy Habsburg power, although the assassination in 1610 of Henry IV delayed direct French involvement in the anti-Habsburg wars until 1635.

NOTE

1. François de Rabutin, *Commentaires des guerres* (Paris, 1932), 2, 195.

17

The Dutch Revolt

Therefore, despairing of all means of reconciliation and left without any other remedies and help, we have been forced (in conformity with the law of nature and for the protection of our own rights and for those of our fellow-countrymen....so that they should not fall into Spanish slavery) to abandon the king of Spain and to pursue such means as we think likely to secure our rights, privileges and liberties.

Therefore we make it known that for all these reasons, forced by utter necessity, we have declared and declare herewith by a common accord, decision and agreement that the king of Spain has ipso facto forfeited his lordship, jurisdiction and inheritance of these provinces, that we do not intend to recognize him in any matters concerning him personally, his sovereignty, jurisdiction and domains in these countries, nor to use or to permit others to use his name as that of our sovereign. Consequently we declare all officers, judges...and all other inhabitants of these provinces, whatever their conditon or quality, to be henceforward released from all obligations and oaths they may have sworn to the king of Spain.

> Quoted in Ernst Kossman and Albert Mellink, editors, *Texts Concerning the Revolt of the Netherlands* (Cambridge, 1974), pp. 225-26. The Dutch Declaration of Independence was approved by the States General of the six Dutch provinces in 1581.

A dying Philip II was willing to make peace with Henry IV, his long time foe; but even on his deathbed he was not prepared to treat with a more bitter enemy, the Dutch, whom he regarded not only as heretics but also as traitors. By 1598 the Dutch revolt was already thirty years old, but the fighting would continue for another fifty years, leading the Dutch to refer to their war of independence as the Eighty Years War. Especially in its middle years, it was far more productive of innovation in warfare than were the French Wars of Religion.

THE DUTCH REVOLT

Battles and Sieges ▲▲

Miles
0   25   50

N

Texel Island

GRONINGEN

Coevorden ▲

Zuider Zee

Ijssel River

Haarlem

Amsterdam

HOLLAND

Rotterdam

Nijmegen

NORTH SEA

Zealand

▲ Breda

Sluys

Ostend

Antwerp ▲

Dunkirk

Nieuwpoort ▲

Scheldt River

Maastricht ▲

Rhine River

FLANDERS

Ghent

Brussels

LIEGE

Cologne

Gravelines

Namur

Lille

BRABANT

Maas River

ARTOIS

Cambrai

LUXEMBOURG

Luxembourg

Amiens

St-Quentin

Moselle River

FRANCE

HOLY ROMAN EMPIRE

—Defensive Line Between Dutch and Spanish 1590.

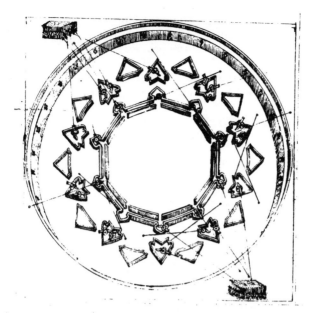

A drawing of a fort of the late sixteenth century, showing the precise geometry of the bastions, ravelins, and demi-lunes.

Philip II held responsibility for the Dutch revolt in a way that was not true of his numerous other conflicts. While Charles V had always been regarded as one of their own by the people of the seventeen provinces that made up the Low Countries, Philip was seen as an outsider, a Spaniard, whose policies were highly detrimental to the Netherlanders. He found that the governing body for the Low Countries, the States General, which was dominated by the nobility and distracted by feuds among the provinces, was a hindrance to his goal of gaining greater control over the Netherlands. Having served as regent for his father in the Netherlands since 1549, Philip was determined to establish effective rule when he gained sovereign power in 1556. The Netherlands began to chafe under his plans for increasing his control and taxes and imposing Spanish officials.

Religion was also a factor. Protestantism had quickly become strong in the Netherlands, although no one sect dominated until after 1560. Even the Netherlanders who remained Catholic were more tolerant of religious dissent than was true of most other Europeans. Philip made it clear that he intended to enforce the largely ignored laws against heresy that his father had decreed, and he introduced the Inquisition in 1559. In this repressive atmosphere the more militant branch of Protestantism, Calvinism, rapidly gained strength.

ORANGE AND ALBA

In 1565 a group of prominent nobles, led by William of Nassau, the Prince of Orange, known as William the Silent from his taciturn manner, began to organize resistance against Philip. Many militant Calvinists quickly outstripped their noble leaders by rioting in the cities of Flanders and Brabant and destroying church property. Philip's response was to order the duke of Alba, his best commander, and 10,000 men to the Low Countries. Since France refused free passage and Philip dared not risk the army at sea, he decided to send it by galley to Genoa and march it northward from there.

A route through Savoy, the Franche-Comté, Lorraine, and into Flanders was chosen because those lands were friendly or neutral. (The Franche-Comté was Philip's.) Because of the need to retain the cooperation of the locals, foraging was strictly prohibited, and a series of depots a day's march apart were established. The army was divided into three parts each a day's march apart, in order not to overwhelm the depots at one time. After the Spanish troops left Genoa in June 1567, it took two months to reach the Netherlands, somewhat above the average of forty-eight days for the 120,000 men who took the route northward over the next eighty years. The route, known as the Spanish Road, remained essentially unchanged until 1622 when the French pressed the duke of Savoy into ending free passage through his duchy. The route was then moved to the passes of the eastern Alps.

Once Alba reached Brussels, the administrative center of the Netherlands, he took control of the government and proceeded to institute the harsh Council of Troubles to deal with heresy and rebellion. Better known as the Council of Blood, it quickly convicted and executed a number of Netherlander nobles for treason. Alba also alienated the middle classes by imposing a hefty sales tax. By 1568 the Iron Duke found all segments of Netherlander society in rebellion. The Spanish troops he had brought with him, originally 8,650 infantrymen and 1,250 cavalry, were augmented by local levies and mercenaries from numerous other lands so that he had about 15,000 men in the Army of Flanders.

The heart of the rebellion in its early years was in the cities of the southern provinces—what today is Belgium. The northern provinces remained quiet for several years, and in fact the northernmost, Groningen, remained loyal to Philip until conquered by the rebels in the 1580s. Early on the rebellion was more political than religious, as many Catholics were present in the rebel forces. William of Orange, emerging as the principal leader of the rebels, had accumulated a large body of soldiers, mostly German mercenaries. They numbered close to 30,000, but were poorly trained and ill-disciplined. Alba had little trouble in defeating that army in several battles during 1568 and 1569. The southern provinces—the Cockpit of Europe—were well suited for the movement and maneuvering of armies, at which Alba was a master. By 1570 he had regained control of the south and embarked on a program of stringent repression of the Protestants.

Most of the surviving rebels were forced to flee northward, where the land, thoroughly waterlogged by the sea and the deltas of the Maas and Rhine rivers, was far more defensible than in the south. The provinces of Zealand, largely made up of islands along the coast, and Holland, north and west of the "waterline" created by the Maas, the Rhine, and the Zuider

Zee, were all but unapproachable except by sea. The security of these Dutch provinces was made fast by the rebels' control of the sea. From the first days of the rebellion, rebel seamen—called Sea Beggars from an off-hand comment by a Spanish official: "What do these beggars want?"— had wrestled control of the sea from the few Spanish ships in the region. Elizabeth allowed them for a time to use English ports, but when she shut them out in 1572, they returned home to capture the Zealand towns of Brill and Flushing. The presence of the Sea Beggars made any attempt to invade the north by sea impossible, and added enormously to the difficulties of reinforcing the Spanish forces.

Largely secure from attack, Holland and Zealand became the heart of the rebellion. Thousands of refugees, mostly militant Calvinists, fled there for refuge, and the conflict more and more became a religious war. The ardent Calvinists of Holland refused to accept anything less than full toleration for their religion. Their determination not to concede to Philip II kept the revolt alive on several occasions when less motivated men might have accepted a compromise. Although Alba won all but one encounter with the rebels between 1568 and 1572, his harsh methods only increased hatred for Spain and the number of sympathizers for the revolt. As a military man, Alba became extremely weary of the roles of policeman and inquisitor that he had taken on. In September 1573, he asked to be recalled. Since Philip and his advisers were convinced that he was bungling the job in the Netherlands, they were quick to agree.

THE SPANISH FURY OF ANTWERP

Just before Alba left, he was faced with a mutiny by 2,600 Spanish soldiers. This was the first of some forty-five mutinies, which probably were the most important factor in the failure of Spain to crush the revolt. The mutineers' principal demand was always for their pay, which was as much as forty-six months in arrears before one mutiny. The Spanish monarchy rarely had the money to pay all of its men, and the mercenaries had to be paid first. That left the Spanish troops unpaid for long periods. What makes the Spanish mutinies unique in military history is that they usually occurred after a Spanish victory and largely negated the advantage achieved in the victory.

On the battlefield the troops from Spain were always well-disciplined and were capable of prodigious feats of courage. One of the most amazing occurred in October 1572, when 3,000 Spaniards crossed the tidal flats of the Scheldt estuary at low tide to attack one of the Zealand islands. The water was up to their chins at places. If there had been any delay in the crossing, which took five hours, they would have been caught in the high tide. The Spanish government, however, hardly appreciated the quality of such men, while the chaotic situation in the Spanish military system meant that some units received their pay fairly regularly while others went for years without it. It was often the best companies that went unpaid and mutinied; but the whole Army of Flanders never mutinied, as much as the Spanish government dreaded the possibility.

The first significant mutiny, which occurred in July 1573, involved the 2,600 troops who had taken the city of Haarlem after an eight-month siege. Alba had decided to try to placate the rebels by prohibiting the sack of the city. The Spanish units, unpaid for twenty-eight months and now deprived of their right to plunder a city for which they had paid with their blood, mutinied. After three weeks Alba secured the money for a portion of their back pay, and the mutiny ended. It prevented Alba from following up on his victory at Haarlem deep in Holland. Some of the units involved, whose morale remained very low, were sent to Antwerp where they mutinied again in 1574, for they had not been paid since the earlier mutiny.

A second mutiny of Antwerp in 1576 was the most significant. In 1575 Philip II defaulted on his loans, which made raising money most difficult for the next several years. The Spanish troops who had taken the fortified town of Zierikzee in Zealand in June 1576 were twenty-two months in arrears in pay. The town was not rich enough to satisfy the soldiers with plunder, so they abandoned it, and it quickly returned to Dutch control. Marching southward they picked up supporters from other garrisons on the way. Alba's replacement had just died, and there was no one in authority to settle with the mutineers, 5,500 strong. They marched on Antwerp and easily overran it, aided by mutineers in its garrison.

The Spanish Fury of Antwerp in November 1576, a week-long orgy of plunder and rape, forced the king to come up with most of the back pay in March 1577. The damage the mutiny did to the Spanish cause in the Low Countries was enormous. An entire campaigning season was lost at a time when the Spanish army was making real progress against the Dutch; more seriously, the mutiny cost Spain all of its positions in Holland and Zealand. The two provinces were never again seriously threatened, and largely secure after 1576, they became the foundation of the new Dutch nation.

Furthermore, the Spanish Fury aroused a strong upsurge in hatred for the Spanish, which deeply influenced the delegates of the provinces then meeting in the States-General at Ghent. They signed the Pacification of Ghent, which suspended all decrees against heresy and demanded the recall of Spanish troops. The new governor, Don Juan of Austria, accepted most of its demands, but Holland and Zealand refused to accept it. The war was resumed.

THE DUKE OF PARMA

In 1578 Don Juan suddenly died, and Alexander Farnese, duke of Parma, son of Philip's half-sister Margaret of Parma, became the new governor. The most respected commander of his generation, he was also a skillful diplomat. Upon his arrival in 1579, he was forced to negotiate because Philip had pulled a large part of the Spanish troops back to Spain for the impending invasion of Portugal, led by Alba. Parma secured an agreement with three Walloon-speaking provinces of the south to return to loyalty to Philip and Catholicism. The response of the Dutch was to organize the Union of Utrecht among seven northern provinces and create a separate government. Two years later, the same seven provinces denounced the sovereignty of Philip II in what is called the Act of Abjuration. It is remarkably similar to the American Declaration of Independence of 200 years later in its denunciation of tyrannical kings.

The search for a prince to rule the new United Provinces of the Netherlands involved Henry III of France, his younger brother, and Elizabeth of England. But nothing worked out, and the new state emerged as a republic in the control of wealthy merchants. Both France and England in turn did send forces to the Netherlands, but they proved to be more a hindrance than a help: in 1583 the French perpetrated the French Fury of Antwerp, and in 1589 an English garrison sold a key fort to the Spanish. The possibility that William of Orange, the major architect of the new state, might have emerged as its monarch was ended when he was assassinated in 1584 by a bounty hunter seeking to collect the high price Philip had put on William's head.

After several years of confusion about the direction the new Dutch state would take, William's son, Maurice of Nassau, emerged as commander in chief of its army. By then the nature of the war had changed from a revolt to a war between two states, although the Spanish continued to regard the Dutch as rebels. Spain had far greater resources but also vast other commitments, while the Dutch Republic had the advantage of geography and the ability to concentrate its resources on the war.

In the first years after the definite split between north and south in 1579, the war was fought for control of the central provinces. Since the region was largely dry and flat, the Spanish army made steady progress in securing final control. In 1585 Parma recaptured Antwerp, despite the Dutch use of an "infernal machine," a boat crammed with gunpowder, stones, and bricks, which blew up a Spanish bridge across the Scheldt and killed 800 Spaniards at the bridgehead. The fall of Antwerp brought Parma back to the Waterline, which had foiled Alba earlier.

DUTCH FORT BUILDING AND SIEGECRAFT

After that the war became largely a matter of fort building and siegecraft. The Dutch had been busy fortifying a line from Antwerp along the Ijssel River to the Zuider Zee. At many points there were Dutch and Spanish forts on opposite sides of the Ijssel. The fortifications built by the Dutch were usually earthen structures designed on the plan of the Italian trace. Many were simply new bastions built in front of old walls, but others were entirely new. The Dutch proceeded to improve on the principles of Italian fortification by introducing more detached fortifications, or outworks.

The original outwork was the ravelin, of which there are a few examples from the end of the fifteenth century in Italy. The ravelin was a separate, usually smaller, triangular bastion placed in front of the curtain wall. The increase in the range at which cannon was effective against walls required that the attackers be kept further away from the curtain walls, which were more likely to suffer a breach than the bastions. The ravelin was already in fairly common use by 1580, but the Dutch were the first to make use of outworks called demi-lunes and hornworks. A demi-lune (half-moon) was a small bastion placed in front of a main bastion. The concave face of the demi-lune facing the point of the bastion was responsible for its name. Hornworks were structures that extended further out and came to two sharp points or horns.

The waterlogged topography of the region enabled fort builders to make extensive use of water-filled ditches. At Coevorden, rebuilt from scratch by Maurice of Nassau in 1605, the magistral line, that is, the curtain wall and main bastions, was surrounded by a ditch 180 feet wide. Then came a line of ravelins and demi-lunes, and another ditch thirty feet wide; and finally came the glacis. Defense in depth became the trademark of Dutch engineers in the early seventeenth century.

Attacking such a fort was made more difficult by the high water table. Trenches could not be dug very deep before they began to fill with water. Dirt had to be thrown up to build a protective line above the surface, making the trenches more vulnerable to cannon fire. A huge number of gabions—cylindrical structures made of sticks and stakes bound together and filled with dirt—had to be available to protect the trenches and siege batteries. After taking enormous casualties trying to rush a breach at Maastricht in 1579, the Spanish generally settled into sieges intended to starve out the defenders. On many occasions, however, when a siege truly began to pinch the defenders, the Dutch would cut the local dikes, and the besiegers would be flooded out.

Despite the enormous difficulties he faced, Parma made progress from 1585 to 1588. But the year's interruption for the Armada debacle cost him dearly, and he had hardly returned his army to the field when he was ordered to relieve Paris in 1590. The eight-year period during which the Army of Flanders fought more in France than in the Netherlands not only cost Parma his life, it probably cost Spain its last chance to defeat the Dutch. By the time the Spanish army had returned fully to the Dutch war, the Dutch had greatly extended and strengthened their line of fortification. More significantly, Maurice of Nassau had completed his apprenticeship and was now ready to make his mark as one of the most innovative military leaders of early modern history.

MAURICE OF NASSAU'S INNOVATIONS

A university graduate, Maurice was highly knowledgeable of history and military systems. Numerous editions of Roman history and military works had been printed in the previous decades, and Justus Lipsius, a member of the faculty of a new Dutch university at Louvain, had published *On Military Wisdom* (1589) and *On Roman Military Science* (1595). Since the Romans had dug their own entrenchments to protect their camps, Maurice also insisted that his soldiers, mostly mercenaries, do their own digging instead of relying on impressed labor from the local population. He ensured that they would do it, despite the tradition that it was below the dignity of a soldier, by paying them extra. Siegework already involved digging zigzag trenches toward the defensive works, but Maurice made it much more systematic. Having his soldiers do this digging not only improved the quality of the trenches, it also kept them busy, largely eliminating the enormous amount of idle time soldiers usually had during sieges.

A second feature of the Roman military that Maurice adopted was an emphasis on drill. Recruits had always spent some time learning how to move as a unit and hold their pikes or reload their muskets; but once this basic training was over, there was no further drill. Maurice insisted on continuing drills even for his veterans, in particular his handgunners, whom he required to have a standard weapon. He broke down the motion of loading and firing a matchlock gun into forty-two steps and gave a word of command to each. The sergeants could now drill men to load and fire in unison by these words of command, and they could be used on the battlefield as well to get their men to move and fire as a unit. Each rank could fire a volley and retire to the rear to reload in proper order. In the Spanish square the confusion caused by retiring ranks bumping into those coming forward to fire prevented anything resembling a true volley after the first two or three ranks had fired. Maurice's system created the conditions for fairly continuous volleys over a considerable length of time.

The increased effectiveness of both the pike and the arquebus under Maurice's system enabled him to deploy his infantry in smaller units, and over a longer and shallower line. These features had two consequences—bringing a higher proportion of the men into action against the enemy, and improving maneuverability. Because the risk of a long, shallow line being broken is quite high, Maurice deployed his army in two and sometimes three lines. The improvements required many more officers and sergeants. They needed in particular a commanding officer who was truly in control of his forces during the battle, and was neither a direct participant nor a bystander. Maurice's new infantry could not be effective with short-term enlistments and rapid turnover of men and officers, and certainly not without regular pay. Keeping the companies together year after year and paying the men well and regularly were necessary. The success of the Dutch economy even in the midst of the war ensured that the money would be available.

The size of a Dutch company was reduced from the 250 men of the Spanish army to 135. Instead of separate companies for pike and musket, the Dutch placed both in the same company, so that it became a tactical unit in itself. Maurice also increased the ratio of handgunners in his army from the ratio of three pikemen for every musketman in the Spanish forces to one pike to two muskets. This greater emphasis on firearms was probably a result of the fact that extensive drill could vastly improve the performance of handgunners, while it did far less for pikemen or other shock combat types. Furthermore, drill allowed vast numbers of men with only ordinary physical abilities, and perhaps less than ordinary mental capabilities, to become competent soldiers. The heroic tradition had little place in a well-drilled company of handgunners.

While the long-term consequences of Maurice's innovations were enormous, he had little opportunity to demonstrate their value on the battlefield because he fought few battles. After 1590, the Eighty Years War was largely a matter of sieges. Maurice preferred to take a fortified place by stratagem rather than by assault. Of the many different stratagems he tried, the most successful was sending grain barges filled with his men into the the key town of Breda—a sort of early modern Trojan horse. Breda's fall put the most important position on the west end of the Waterline in Dutch hands. During the years the Army of Flanders was fighting in France, Maurice cleared the Spanish from their forts along the Ijssel River and eastward along the Rhine. With his judicious use of entrenchments and well-protected batteries brought in close to the walls, he was able to gain breaches quickly at little cost in men.

THE SIEGE OF OSTEND

After Philip II died in 1598, his successor Philip III (1598-1621) was more willing to negotiate. It was now the Dutch who were more adamant about pursuing the war, being determined to reunite the Netherlands. In 1600 Maurice moved his army southward along the Flemish coast to cut off Flanders completely from the sea. The Dutch already controlled the mouth of the Scheldt River cutting Antwerp off from sea traffic. Maurice easily dispersed the mostly German and Walloon forces at the Battle of Nieuport, since the Spanish troops were in the midst of a mutiny. However, he could not take the town of Nieuport and retreated to Ostend.

Ostend was a Dutch enclave on the Flemish coast that posed a real problem for the Spanish. From there Dutch forces raided deep into Flanders, and Dutch seamen attacked Spanish shipping. In 1601 Archduke Albert of Austria, who had been appointed governor after Parma's death, resolved to take it. The Dutch had spent ten years building up its defenses; it was one of the first places to have extensive outworks. Their strength was vastly enhanced by the sea and wide marshes. In July 1601, Albert's forces in the number of 12,000 men invested Ostend. Assaulting the outworks without proper preparation cost Albert thousands of men. An assault on a bastion in January 1602, for example, cost 2,000 casualties with no progress to show for the losses. The climate of the region was cold and damp, and the Spanish losses from disease and exposure were particularly high during the three winters that the siege was maintained. The Dutch garrison of 7,000 men was easily reinforced and resupplied by sea, and the sick and wounded could be taken away for treatment.

After two years of useless assaults and battering, a young Italian, Ambrosio Spinola, arrived at the Spanish camp in July 1603. His commission had been purchased by his father's promise of a huge loan to Philip III. He had no experience at all in war, and had learned everything he knew about it from books. Yet he quickly proved to be an excellent siegemaster and field commander. Restoring the morale of the troops in the siege lines, Spinola systematically began reducing the outworks on the west side of Ostend. In August 1604, he placed a battery on the counterscarp of the main wall. His progress was aided by a summer of foul weather, which made resupplying Ostend by sea very difficult. In September the Dutch commander agreed to accept honorable terms of surrender. In the siege of more than three years, the Spanish may have lost as many as 80,000 men, while the Dutch casualties have been loosely assessed at 30,000.

Enormously bolstered by their victory, the Spanish under Spinola were back in the field the next year, west of the Ijssel. The loss of Ostend and the presence of the dynamic Spinola persuaded the Dutch now to negotiate, while another major mutiny in 1607 dulled the optimism that the same factors had raised in the Spanish government.

THE TWELVE-YEAR TRUCE

In April 1608 an armistice was agreed upon, and a year later a twelve-year truce was signed. By then the Dutch Republic had become a viable, economically vibrant state despite a chaotic governmental structure that did not provide for a true executive. The lack of strong government allowed the Dutch merchants to do business without government interference. Their business included raiding Spanish and Portuguese shipping and colonies; by 1618 they had gained almost complete control over the Moluccas in the East Indies and had planted colonies in Brazil, the Caribbean, and New York.

Dutch success in trade depended heavily on their use of the *fluyt* (flyboat). It was a broad-beamed and flat-bottomed ship that has been called a floating hold. It was designed to hold a great amount of cargo in proportion to its size, and to be sailed by a small number of men. According to Walter Raleigh in 1603, an English ship of the same size required thirty men compared to the ten of a Dutch fluyt. A fluyt carried few guns, because the goods they carried, such as grain from the Baltic, was in bulk and of low value. Those ships working the spice trade were more heavily armed. Dutch warships were relatively small and light, even in comparison to English galleons. Their principal virtues were speed and maneuverability. They had shallow drafts to allow them to run closer to the shore, a crucial attribute in the waters off their homeland with its wide shoals and numerous sandbars.

In the 1590s, Dutch galleons joined several English expeditions against Spain and its colonies. After 1600 Dutch fleets began to operate alone, and in 1607 Admiral Jacob van Heemskerck won a brilliant victory off Gibraltar (although he himself was killed). In this battle, the Dutch apparently divided their smaller fleet into units that attacked individual Spanish ships in a line-astern formation, and then boarded them after they had been sufficiently damaged. Half of the twenty-two large warships in the Spanish fleet were sunk, burned, or captured. The threat that the Dutch fleet now posed to the Spanish treasure fleet was another reason for the truce of 1609.

Maurice of Nassau, who opposed the truce and expected it to be broken, continued to work on improving the Dutch army. Already in 1596 his cousin William Louis of Nassau had commissioned an artist to draw illustrations of the positions that corresponded to the steps of Maurice's drill. In 1607 the illustrations were published in a drill book that included the words of command. Copies of the drill book began to spread across Europe, as did some of the sergeants of the Dutch army. Even the Swiss city of Bern reorganized its army on Dutch lines in 1628. In 1616 another cousin, John of Nassau, opened a military academy, generally recognized as the first. New officers were given six months of training in the use of maps, weapons, and drill. Maurice also was probably the first to use the telescope, invented shortly after 1600, for military purposes.

RESUMPTION OF THE WAR

By the time the twelve-year truce was up in 1621, the Thirty Years War was already raging in the Holy Roman Empire. The Spanish government had been discussing for three years the issue of whether to negotiate a renewal of the truce. The decision not to renew was based on three motives: a strong sense in Spain of being the champion of Catholicism, which expressed itself in a demand for toleration of Catholics in the Dutch Republic; the need to reopen the Scheldt River to revive Antwerp's trade; and the continuing Dutch penetration of the Portuguese trade empire. When the Dutch, who had their own war party led by Maurice of Nassau, refused any concessions on these points, the war resumed in 1621.

The Spanish had been preparing for renewed war by pouring men and money in the southern Netherlands. In 1617 the army had actually received its pay a month in advance. Once the war resumed, Spinola, who was still in command, quickly took the offensive. But the wall of Dutch forts on the frontier proved to be a formidable barrier to any advance. After probing at several forts, he settled his army around the great fortress of Breda in August 1624. Spinola planned to starve Breda out, since its defensive works were too strong to assault. In order to prevent the Dutch army from driving him off, he had extensive field works dug. It was said that when Maurice of Nassau realized that Breda was not going to be relieved, he became ill with discouragement; he died in April 1625. Two months later the fortress surrendered on honorable terms. The great Spanish painter Diego Velázquez produced one of his best works commemorating the surrender of Breda.

The year 1625 was a splendid one for the Spanish. Besides Breda they recaptured Bahia, the major Dutch fortress in Brazil, and an English fleet was beaten back from Cadiz. However, the presence of the English in the war from 1624 to 1630 ended the trickle of supplies and reinforcements that had been coming to the Army of Flanders by sea. More seriously in 1622 the French had persuaded the duke of Savoy to deny Spanish troops passage through his duchy. The Spanish Road was moved to the passes of the eastern Alps, but the new route was longer and more difficult and involved the Spanish in the complicated politics of the eastern Swiss cantons and southern Germany.

The momentum gained in 1625 quickly stalled, and 1628 proved to be as bad a year for Spain as 1625 was good. Spinola resigned his command, and Spain had no one to replace him for six years. Much worse, Admiral Piet Heyn of the Netherlands caught the Spanish treasure fleet in the Bay of Matanzas in Cuba and captured all but three ships. The Spanish ships were run aground in the bay and apparently surrendered with little resistance, in part because they were so crammed with merchandise that many guns could not be used. The 8 million florins that fell into Dutch hands enormously bolstered their ability to conduct the war, while equally hurting Spain's. To cap the year off, Spain became involved in a brief but sharp

war with France over the duchy of Mantua in northern Italy. The war siphoned resources and troops away from the conflict in the Netherlands,
and the presence of a French army in northern Italy prevented the dispatch
of Spanish units on the Spanish Road.

Spain soon lost the gains it had made in 1625. The Dutch captured
Pernambuco in Brazil in 1630; in the Netherlands, the major fortresses of
Maastricht fell in 1632, and Breda in 1637. The recapture of the latter place
was the last significant exchange of territory in the Eighty Years War. It
largely settled the border between the Dutch republic and the Spanish
Netherlands, that is, modern Belgium. The Spanish failures after 1628 were
also caused in part by Spain's involvement in the Thirty Years War. By
1648 Philip IV (1621-1665) was willing to recognize the independence of
the Dutch republic as part of the Peace of Westphalia.

The Eighty Years War in its last phase was far less productive of military innovation than it had been before the Twelve Years Truce. Spain in
particular was drawing on its last reservoir of strength to fight on, and like
a punch-drunk boxer, it could only continue by relying on what it had
learned to do earlier. The Spanish situation in this war is unique in history:
attempting to defeat a determined and capable enemy while lacking both
direct territorial contact with the arena of war and control of the seas. At
one time or another virtually all the states within the wider region were at
war with Spain and aided the Dutch, but fortunately for Spain they rarely
cooperated with each other. That Spain fought the war for eighty years
despite the enormous difficulties and cost testifies to the vast resources it
could draw on and to the dogged determination of its monarchy not to
concede an inch. The fact that Spain emerged from the war with more
than half of the original Netherlands still under its control is, after everything is considered, proof of the quality of the Spanish military of the early
modern period.

Battles of the 30 Years War

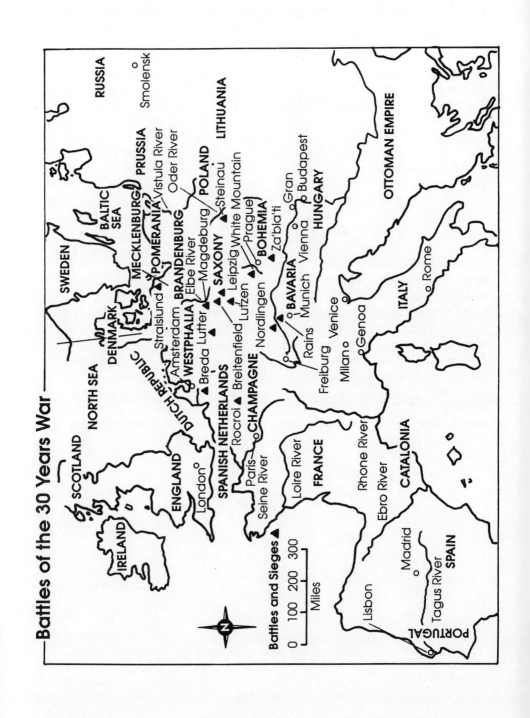

18

The Thirty Years War

If it is true that the Bohemians are about to depose Ferdinand [of Habs-burg] and elect another king, let everyone prepare for a war lasting twenty, thirty or forty years. The Spaniards and the House of Austria will deploy all their worldly goods to recover Bohemia; indeed the Spaniards would rather lose the Netherlands than allow their House to lose control of Bohemia so disgracefully and so outrageously.

> Count Solms, quoted in Geoffrey Parker, *Europe in Crisis, 1598-1648* (Ithaca, N.Y., 1979), p. 163. Solms, who wrote those words in 1619, was a German diplomat.

In its last decades the Dutch revolt was subsumed into a much broader international conflict called the Thirty Years War. The event that touched off that war, a revolt in Bohemia in 1618, was highly similar to the beginning of the Dutch revolt in that it was both a Protestant rebellion against a Catholic ruler and a nationalistic uprising against a Habsburg prince.

Like several monarchies of central and eastern Europe, Bohemia's was elective. Members of the Habsburg family had been elected king since 1440. A majority of the Bohemian nobles had become Protestant, but the Habsburg kings of the late sixteenth century were not very zealous Catholics. There was little thought of electing a king from a different family, and in 1617 Archduke Ferdinand was chosen as king-designate by the estates of both Bohemia and Hungary to succeed Emperor Matthias, his cousin. Ferdinand had a reputation as a Catholic zealot, but Protestant misgivings were overcome by bribery and diplomatic pressure. Almost immediately the new officials he installed in Prague began to reduce Protestant privileges. The Protestant nobles made contact with the Protestant rulers of Europe and asked for foreign support.

In March 1618, the Bohemian Estates met to denounce Ferdinand's religious policy. When he ordered the meeting broken up, the Protestant members marched to the Castle of Prague, forced their way into the chamber of the royal council, and threw the two most notorious Catholic officials out of a third-story window. Although the officials survived the fall by landing on a garbage pile, the "defenestration of Prague" was a blatant act of rebellion. The Estates voted to create a provisional government and raise an army.

THE BOHEMIAN PHASE

Aided by money from several Protestant rulers, the Bohemians took the offensive in July 1618, defeating an imperial army at the Bohemian frontier. In the same month, Emperor Matthias sent an urgent request to Madrid for money and manpower. The government of Philip III, which had been planning an expedition against the Algerian corsairs, debated long and hard about its course of action. In the end it opted for supporting Austria. Some Spanish troops dispatched from the Netherlands reached Vienna in late 1618, but the initiative remained with the rebels. One army, mostly Bohemian, under Count Thurn crossed into Austria and reached Vienna in June 1619. Another, mostly German mercenaries under Count Ernst von Mansfeld, systematically reduced the imperial fortresses in Bohemia.

However, a Spanish army of 7,000 arrived in late spring and joined with twice as many Austrians in attacking Mansfeld in Bohemia. The little-known Battle of Záblatí in June 1619 was a major Habsburg victory. Mansfeld lost 1,500 men and most of his guns. With Prague open to attack, Thurn had to retreat from Vienna. Záblatí likely prevented a quick success for the rebellion, as Vienna probably would have fallen to Thurn. It also ensured the election in August 1619 of Ferdinand II as emperor, Matthias having died in March, despite strong opposition to him among the German princes. Three days earlier the Bohemian Estates had voted to depose him as king and had elected Frederick, Count of the Palatinate, the German prince who had been strongest in support of the rebellion. He was a Calvinist, as were the majority of the Bohemian Protestants, which made the German Lutherans less interested in cooperating with him.

Ferdinand again appealed to his Spanish cousin, and Philip agreed to send 20,000 troops from the Army of Flanders to invade the Palatinate in early 1620. The key decision in prolonging the war and turning it into more than a rebellion of a Habsburg province was probably made by Duke Maximilian of Bavaria. A devout Catholic, he was also a strong rival of the Habsburgs and closely allied to France. In 1619 the Huguenots in southern France revolted, and Louis XIII, believing a general Protestant conspiracy was afoot, urged Maximilian to aid Ferdinand. Thus the Bavarian army and the rest of the forces of the German Catholic League joined the Habsburg army in marching on Prague under the command of Count Johann Tilly. Born in Belgium, he had served for eight years in the Army of Flanders. After moving on to Bavaria, he received the command of the Bavarian army in 1610. Tilly was regarded as one of the best commanders of his generation and a strict disciplinarian. That his troops would be involved in some of the worst atrocities of the war demonstrates the difficulty commanders of this era had in controlling their men.

Eager to fight before winter set in, when he would lose much of his army through desertion, Tilly pressed on to Prague in late 1620. Just west

A soldier of the Thirty Years War and his female companion. Note the plunder of war spilling from her open saddlebag.

of the city his 28,000-man multinational force came upon the Bohemian army entrenched in a strong defensive position. That army was commanded by Prince Christian of Anhalt; it included Germans, Hungarians and Austrians as well as Bohemians. His line was flanked by White Mountain on one side and a castle on the other, and fronted by a stream and marsh. Christian chose to wait for Tilly's attack, confident of the strength of his position. However, he had little artillery, and he had spread his troops out in three long shallow lines in the Dutch style. His soldiers lacked the training to be successful in that formation. Tilly's army assembled in the massive squares of the tercio system. The Bohemian army did not have the firepower either from artillery or muskets to halt the powerful surge of Tilly's squares. Tilly's right easily broke through the enemy's left, and rolled up the Bohemian army. In two hours of fighting, the Bohemian cause was ruined.

Tilly's great victory at White Mountain quickly returned Ferdinand II to control of Bohemia and his other rebellious provinces, but it did not end the war. In fact it expanded it, for the German Lutheran princes had no desire to see the Habsburgs completely victorious. They encouraged Count Frederick and Mansfeld to remain in the field. But the Germans provided them with very little money, and Mansfeld in particular turned to supporting his army by heavy exactions on the towns and villages of southeast Germany, even the friendly ones. The burden of the war on the civilian population began to go beyond being plundered, if they happened to be

on the losing side, to a systematic pillaging by friend and foe alike. After
1621 that became the usual way for armies to support themselves.

   In August 1623, Tilly badly defeated Frederick on the lower Rhine and
forced him to sign a truce. England, the Dutch republic, France, Sweden,
Denmark, and Savoy all agreed to keep the war going. King Christian IV
of Denmark was to aid the Protestant cause in Germany by invading from
the north. He was a devout Lutheran who also hoped to dominate
northern Germany and the whole Baltic region. With one of the deepest
treasuries of Europe to draw on, he assembled an army of 21,000 mercenaries and marched south in the summer of 1625. His triumphant march
was brought to an abrupt halt the next year by a new player in the already
long war— Albrecht Wallenstein.

WALLENSTEIN

   Wallenstein's appearance as a commander was largely a product of the
anti-Habsburg coalition's success in 1624-25 in impeding the movement
of Spanish troops into northern Europe. The emperor decided that he
needed to raise a large army of his own, since Tilly's was still largely funded
by the German Catholic League. He offered Wallenstein a contract to raise
50,000 men. Born a Protestant in Bohemia, Wallenstein had fought for the
Habsburgs against Venice and the Turks. After the Battle of White
Mountain, he received numerous estates confiscated from rebel nobles, and
bought more at low prices. Most of the properties were around the town
of Friedland, and in 1627 he was rewarded with the title of duke of Friedland. An excellent manager of his lands, he soon was taking an income
from Friedland that was four times what Charles I was gaining from Scotland. Wallenstein set to work to organize his estates to produce as much
as possible of the goods needed for his new army, thus increasing his profits
from his contract with Ferdinand. He also applied his keen business sense
to the operation of war. If mercenary captains can be described as military
capitalists, then Wallenstein was the ultimate condottiere.

   Wallenstein established an efficient military organization. He commissioned other officers to recruit regiments under his control, much like a
sovereign. Aware that unpaid soldiers were ill-disciplined, and often deserted, he made sure his men were paid regularly. He had nothing against
his men plundering a newly conquered town or region, and even reduced
their pay in consideration of the plunder taken. Once a territory was under
his control, however, he ensured that his men did not disrupt commerce
and agriculture so that production of goods could continue and taxes could
be collected— although the taxes were often so high that plunder is as appropriate a term. Taking large profits from his contract with Ferdinand
and the sale of goods from his own estates to his army, by 1628 Wallenstein
was living the life of a wealthy prince with a household of 899 persons.

THE NATURE OF MERCENARY ARMIES

   Wallenstein's army was a mercenary army par excellence. Nationality
and religion were of no interest to the recruiters. Virtually the entire range
of European nations were represented, although Germans were the major-

ity. All of the armies of the Thirty Years War were heavily mercenary, although the Spanish and the Swedish armies usually had a majority of native troops.

A large number of those serving as mercenaries were attracted to army life by the freedom it offered from the humdrum life of a peasant or urban worker. Although a soldier was subject to the harsh discipline of officers, he had a great deal of liberty in comparison to other lifestyles. Not only was he free from most of the bonds of society, he also could become wealthy through plundering. For many the threat of death in battle paled before these considerations. The recruiters' drummers summoned the restless and the lawless to a life of adventure and freedom. The officers provided the weapons for new soldiers, for which payments were docked from the soldiers' pay. Uniforms were not in use yet, and the soldiers dressed in their own clothes, which were usually brightly colored and bedecked with ribbons and bows. They identified themselves as part of an army by wearing scarves and sashes of the same color. The absence of uniforms made it easier for a soldier to desert and join another army.

In addition to those who would have been attracted to army life in any era, vast numbers more became soldiers out of sheer necessity. The Thirty Years War coincided with one of the worst economic depressions ever. Contemporaneous with the depression and contributing to it was a worsening of the climate, which is called the Little Ice Age. Beginning about 1585, the colder weather caused European-wide crop failures on a much more regular basis than had been true since the 1300s. The 1620s and 1640s were particularly bad.

Between economic depression and agricultural catastrophe, great numbers of people took to the roads to eke out a bare existence. They came from the lowest levels of both rural and urban society; joining an army was often the only alternative to starving. Much of the manpower available for recruiting was from groups that had little attachment to social mores and traditional constraints. For them the freedom of the soldier was license to plunder, pillage, and rape. The devastation of war zones also contributed to recruitment, as the ruin of many regions produced impoverished and desperate men ready to enlist. That factor became more and more important as the war progressed.

The plentiful manpower available —which extended to the officers since the economic bad times made the nobles more eager to serve—helps to explain why the war dragged on as long as it did, despite heavy losses in battle and to disease and desertion. The ease of refilling the ranks also explains why the war was so bloody, despite the heavy use of mercenaries, whom their captains have usually tried to conserve. The presence of so many mercenaries further explains why victorious commanders often recruited troops from the army they had just defeated. The ease of recruiting meant that commanders spent little time in training their troops, for that required time and expense. The economics of the war made it more expedient to use many unskilled men instead of fewer well-trained ones. And since little expense had been invested in training their men, the commanders were not reluctant to waste them in large numbers in bloody battles.

Far from home and with little hope of returning there, the soldiers often married women among the camp followers, the numbers of whom also were swelled by the hard times. Others brought their families with them upon enlisting. Thus another feature of this war was the enormous size of the baggage trains and the camp followings, which included great numbers of whores, gamblers, hustlers, ill or wounded soldiers, and deserters from other armies. At one point in the war, an army of 40,000 men had 100,000 people in its train. These mobs of people needed food and shelter, but they usually had to fend for themselves. Many turned to marauding—plundering the territory through which they passed. It was often true that the marauders did more damage to villages and towns than did the soldiers. A further consequence of the huge trains was to make the movement of armies extremely slow.

THE DANISH PHASE
Despite the vast difficulties an army of that sort presented to its commander, Wallenstein proved capable of using his effectively, in large part because he paid it regularly. In April 1626, he fought his first major battle. He had caught up to Mansfeld's Protestant army of 12,000 men at Dessau on the Elbe in northeast Germany. Using the best artillery yet seen in the war and cleverly concealing much of his manpower so his foe did not know how badly he was outnumbered, Wallenstein soundly defeated Mansfeld, who was fooled into a frontal assault. Mansfeld retreated into Brandenburg, previously untouched by war, to wait for Christian of Denmark to make his move into Germany.

When the Danish king had decided to get involved in Germany, he had seen himself as part of a grand alliance. But England contributed almost nothing, while the extensive Huguenot uprisings of 1625 forced Cardinal Richelieu, first minister for Louis XIII, to back off. The Dutch had suffered serious reverses in 1625 and could provide little help. Furthermore, Christian was unaware of the existence of Wallenstein's army until he was deep in Germany. Tilly's army had been in northern Germany for some time, and it was against Tilly that Christian led his forces in the Battle of Lutter of August 1626. Christian charged Tilly's lines three times, despite Tilly's superiority in numbers and quality. The result of his folly was the loss of half of his army. Christian rebuilt his army, only to suffer further defeats in 1627 and 1628. After the second defeat, in the Battle of Wolgast against Wallenstein, the king admitted failure. He accepted peace terms in the Treaty of Lübeck of June 1629. The German Protestants were to restore all church lands seized since 1552, and Wallenstein gained Mecklenburg from its deposed Lutheran duke.

The Habsburgs and their general Wallenstein now dominated Germany. Encouraged by Spain, they hoped to push their advantage further by occupying a portion of the Baltic coast and building a fleet there. Spain's interest was to destroy the profitable Dutch trade in the Baltic. But a six-month siege of the port of Stralslund failed to win the planned base for the fleet. The reason for Wallenstein's failure was an ominous portent for the future: a Swedish army had been dispatched from a war in Poland to relieve the city. In October 1629 Cardinal Richelieu mediated a truce between Poland and Sweden to allow Sweden to enter the German war.

GUSTAVUS ADOLPHUS

King Gustavus II Adolphus of Sweden (1611-1634) was by 1629 a thoroughly experienced commander. He had been fighting from early in his reign with Denmark, Russia, and Poland. The conflict with his cousin King Sigismund III of Poland was the most bitter because it was a family dispute. Sigismund, the eldest son of John III of Sweden (1568-92), had converted to Catholicism in order to be elected king of Poland in 1587. After he inherited the Swedish throne in 1592, his uncle Charles, a devout Lutheran, led a revolt that succeeded in ousting Sigismund by 1600. Charles IX was succeeded in 1611 by his son Gustavus, who was seventeen years old at the time.

Fortunately for Gustavus, Sigismund, who never accepted the loss of his Swedish throne, was then involved in Russia. The Time of Troubles in Russia allowed Sigismund to occupy Moscow in 1610 for two years, but his failure to win the election of his son as Russian czar illustrates the problem the Poles had in fighting anything but a purely defensive war. In 1609 the Polish Diet had voted money to raise an army to recover the city of Smolensk, taken by the Russians in 1514. While the Polish army besieged the city for two years, Sigismund detached a large part of it to occupy Moscow. When Smolensk surrendered in 1611, the Diet, satisfied with the gain, ended the subsidy. The Poles in Moscow were left without resources and were abandoned to their fate of mass execution after surrendering in 1612.

With Sigismund at war with Russia, Gustavus had time to mature and learn military craft before declaring war on Poland in 1617. He received a solid education in military history and in the military styles and trends of his era. Once war with Poland broke out, Gustavus demonstrated that he had learned his lessons well. It was the conventional wisdom of the time that professional mercenaries were vastly preferable to conscripts. Gustavus recognized, however, that native conscripts had certain advantages if time were taken to train them adequately, and as an advocate of the Dutch system, he intended to do that. Native conscripts cost less, were more loyal since they were fighting for their king and country, accepted discipline better, were quicker to follow orders, and were more willing to inflict and take heavy casualties.

In 1620 Gustavus established a system of conscription and administration for his army. Each province was to raise a regiment and support it through local taxes. The provincial regiments were permanently established, and several still exist today. The population base of Sweden was too small, however, to provide all the soldiers the king felt he needed, and from the first he filled out his army with mercenaries. Their numbers increased rapidly after his bloody battles in 1631-32, but the Swedes always formed the core of the army.

In adopting the Dutch system, Gustavus made a higher proportion of his infantry pikemen than was true of other armies of the time, returning

to the one-for-one ratio found in the original tercio. He recognized that
handgunners were vulnerable to a hard assault by enemy pike or heavy
cavalry, and he realized that the changes he proposed to make in the way
handgunners fought would increase their vulnerability. Gustavus further
appreciated how the pike in the hands of a well-drilled and spirited infantry
could be an effective offensive weapon. The opportunity for the pike to
reach the enemy's lines and carry home the charge had to be prepared by
gunfire. Gunfire would be far more effective if it were a concentrated blast
that shattered the enemy's ranks, after which the pike would charge.
Gustavus therefore insisted that his musketeers carry an eleven-pound
musket, which was about half as heavy as the standard piece and did not
need the fork, and that they learn to fire salvos. His musketeers were
formed into six ranks. Once they had loaded and were ready to fire, three
ranks combined into one line. The first rank knelt; the second stooped;
and the third fired over the top of the other two. At the sergeant's signal
they fired simultaneously. The concentrated blast of the three ranks would
break up the enemy's lines and give the pikemen openings to exploit in
their charge. But if the salvo failed to accomplish the desired result, the
pike was needed in strength to defend the musketeers until they had reloaded.

The activities Gustavus expected of his infantrymen required thoroughly drilled, well-disciplined, and regularly paid troops, and he ensured
that all three were the norm for his army. The constant drill of the
musketeers in particular sped up reloading, and the king further increased
the speed by introducing the paper cartridge, which contained a measured
amount of powder and a ball. Lastly Gustavus felt that soldiers who
looked alike would act alike; he began to encourage the the use of similarly
colored coats for his infantry regiments, each regiment having a different
color.

Gustavus also sought to increase firepower on the battlefield by greatly
improving battlefield artillery. Guns were still too large to be moved once
put in place before a battle. It was hoped that their powerful blast at the
beginning of the fighting would do considerable damage to the enemy, and
artillery fire often had the desired effect of enticing the enemy into attacking
well-prepared lines. Often, however, artillery had little or no impact once
the battle was underway. Gustavus adopted a light field piece, the three-
pounder, which fired a three-pound ball or its equivalent in grape shot and
which could be easily moved during the battle by two or three men. With
these changes, artillery could be used in close cooperation with the infantry
as another regular source of firepower to open holes in the enemy's lines.
The effective coordination of infantry and artillery was improved by Gustavus' insistence that the gunners be military men under the orders of the
infantry officers and not civilians. The development of the iron industry
in Sweden in the early 1600s gave Gustavus the capacity to produce the
large number of high-quality guns he needed for his reforms to work.

During the wars with Poland, the Swedes had confronted a cavalry that
still depended upon the lance and the sword in shock combat, and had not
adopted the pistol. At Kirkholm in 1605, the Polish cavalry devastated the

Swedish army by getting inside the ranks of musketeers, who were unsupported by pike, and massacring them with the sword. Gustavus did not abandon the pistol entirely; he allowed his cavalrymen to carry a pistol apiece. It was to be discharged as the horsemen closed with the enemy, but instead of wheeling away in the caracole to reload, Gustavus' horse was to charge into the enemy with the sword.

Charging into a mass of disciplined pikemen was, however, not likely to produce positive results. Gustavus began to attach mounted musketeers to his cavalry, who would dismount and fire salvos into the enemy's ranks to open holes for the heavy cavalry to exploit. He soon began to attach three-pound guns to his cavalry for the same purpose. In both his infantry and cavalry Gustavus' basic principle was that shot, whether from handguns or artillery, was to open up opportunities for shock troops, whether pikemen or heavy cavalry, to carry the attack into the enemy's lines with cold steel.

GUSTAVUS AT WAR

In the war with Poland, the Swedish army fought in wide open spaces where fortresses were few and far between. Gustavus came to believe that victory in the field was the purpose of war, and he eagerly sought battle. Although Germany was lightly fortified compared to the Netherlands and northern Italy, most of the captains in the first decade of the Thirty Years War had trained in those theaters and had the cautious attitude toward field battles typical of early modern war in those regions. The Polish war gave Gustavus the opportunity to work out the weaknesses of his theories and demonstrate to his men that they worked. Furthermore it enabled him to train a solid corps of officers and NCOs for his linear system of small tactical units, which required large numbers of experienced officers. In the war he also developed the system of logistics that some have called the first quartermaster corps.

Gustavus recognized that he needed to control the Baltic if Sweden was going to win the empire he planned for it. Despite conceding Poland in 1627 its only naval victory in history, by 1630 Gustavus had built a first-rate fleet to transport his army, supply it, and dominate the Baltic. However, his intended flagship, the *Vasa*, with over 100 guns, sank on its maiden voyage in 1628. The beautifully preserved ship was raised in 1973.

In June 1630 the king of Sweden issued a declaration of war, which listed his own grievances and those of the German Protestants against Emperor Ferdinand II. He declared that his sole purpose was to defend "German liberties." The next month 13,000 Swedish troops and their commander landed on the north German coast. German Lutherans and mercenaries flocked to his banner, so that his army reached 40,000 men in a matter of months. But the German states, except for the northern city of Magdeburg, were reluctant to ally themselves openly with him in order to avoid open treason against the emperor. In January 1631, France and Sweden signed a secret agreement under which France provided Sweden with a large sum of money and Sweden pledged to tolerate Catholicism in any Catholic lands it occupied.

Meanwhile Emperor Ferdinand had dismissed Wallenstein in August 1630. Unaware of the danger Gustavus presented, the emperor had become frightened by Wallenstein's power and had been pressed by the German princes to remove him from his office as imperial commander. Tilly was appointed imperial commander, and he brought his army to lay siege to Magdeburg in November 1630. After six months in the siege lines, his men were suffering more than the besieged city was, and the residents were confident they had weathered the siege. In May 1631, one of Tilly's lieutenants, Count Pappenheim, led a desperate assault on the walls. It caught the defenders by surprise and low on ammunition, and secured a gate. According to established practice the victors now had three days to sack the city.

The sack of Magdeburg differed from other cases in the size of the city: at 30,000 people, it was the largest city taken by storm in the early modern period. That explains in part the huge casualties suffered by the civilian population at the hands of the imperial troops, but the massacre of the Magdeburgers went far beyond the usual level of brutality. Only 5,000 people were said to have survived. Many were killed in a fire that all but destroyed the city. Whether it was an accident or was set by drunken imperial soldiers, or by defiant Lutherans determined to deprive Tilly of his prize, is not known. It can be said that Tilly did not set it, since he had planned to use the city to shelter and feed his army.

THE GREAT BATTLES OF THE WAR

The burning of Magdeburg meant that Tilly had to abandon it and lead his army across northern Germany in the face of enraged Lutherans. The duke of Saxony, neutral in the war until now, joined his 16,000-man army with the Swedes. In September 1631, Tilly and Gustavus clashed at Breitenfeld in Saxony, just north of Leipzig. Gustavus had a manpower advantage over Tilly of 42,000 men to 36,000, but a third of his force was made up of untested Saxon troops. Tilly drew up his men into the huge squares of some 3,000 men typical of the tercio system, with his relatively small amount of cavalry on both flanks. Gustavus formed his Swedish infantry into a shallow linear formation, with the Saxons en bloc on his left and most of his cavalry on his right, although some cavalry was interspersed between the infantry units. The battle opened with a two-hour cannonade, which greatly benefitted the Swedes, because they had many more guns and a much faster rate of fire. Unwilling to take the cannon fire for long, Tilly's cavalry on his left rode forward to execute the caracole against the Swedish infantry. The unexpected heavy firepower from the Swedes devastated their ranks, and a charge by the Swedish cavalry with naked swords drove them off the field.

Meanwhile several tercio squares moved forward against the Saxon lines, and the inexperienced Saxons quickly broke and ran, totally exposing the left flank of the Swedish infantry. Although any change of direction of his massive squares was slow and ponderous, Tilly must have thought that he was about to win a great victory. Against any other foe of the era, he would have. But at this point all of Gustavus' innovations proved their value. His cavalry was rushed in to slow the imperial advance, charging into the lines of musketeers. A vast number of three-pounders was wheeled into new positions to blast the enemy squares, while the Swedish infantry quickly turned and re-formed its lines to pound the imperial infantry with devastating musket fire. Charging into the gaps created by their musketeers, the Swedish pike threw the imperial tercios into panicked flight. The Swedish cavalry pursued for a considerable distance and inflicted many more casualties. Tilly, himself badly wounded late in the battle, left 7,600 dead and 9,000 prisoners at Breitenfeld, while the Swedish dead were put at 2,500 men.

Besides demonstrating the value of his new tactics, the Battle of Breitenfeld opened up all of Germany to Gustavus. He had three options: pursue and destroy Tilly's beaten army as it fled toward northwest Germany; march on Vienna; or move into wealthy and largely Catholic lands of the Rhine valley. In large part because he expected the war in Germany to pay for itself through plunder and taxes, he chose to invade the Rhineland. It had been barely touched by the war until then, so the Swedes spent a comfortable winter there. While they wintered in the Rhine valley, Tilly resolutely rebuilt his army in Bavaria, his home base. In the spring of 1632, Gustavus marched into Bavaria after him. Crossing the Lech River near the town of Rains on a bridge of boats in the face of the enemy, Gustavus, now with the manpower advantage of 37,000 men to 22,000, crushed Tilly's forces. Tilly himself was killed. Bavaria, also largely untouched by the war until then, was thoroughly ravaged.

After the Battle of Rains, Emperor Ferdinand was truly desperate. His army in Germany was completely wrecked, and there was no hope of immediate help from Spain. He had to turn again to Wallenstein, who had spent the time since his dismissal repairing his finances and calculating his opportunities. He had been highly upset with Ferdinand for his curt dismissal in 1630, and he recognized how desperate the emperor now was; so his demands for returning to service were high indeed. Essentially Wallenstein became the viceroy of the empire. Even with the remnants of Tilly's army, Wallenstein could raise only 20,000 men, largely because the battles of the past year temporarily had reduced the manpower available.

Wallenstein began his new campaign by driving the Saxons out of Bohemia and invading Saxony. That forced Gustavus to give up his planned attack on Vienna and go to the rescue of his ally. Wallenstein's superb logistics system enabled him to keep his men in his camp, while Gustavus' passage in the fall of 1632 through regions already thoroughly plundered cost him a good deal of his manpower. By the time Gustavus approached Wallenstein's camp in Saxony, the two armies were about the same size. After waiting for two weeks for an attack, Wallenstein decided that the Swedes had gone into winter camps, and he dispersed his men for the winter. Suddenly word came that the Swedish army was marching on his headquarters, which was at Lützen twenty miles south of Leipzig. Wallenstein quickly gathered about 18,000 men, but some 3,000 cavalry under Count Pappenheim were in Leipzig. With the men he had, Wallenstein formed up his infantry behind a road edged by two deep ditches.

His infantry was no longer formed in massive squares but in shallower
rectangles, ten ranks deep. He anchored his right flank on the village of
Lützen, while on his left he left space for the missing cavalry, on its way
back from Leipzig.

Gustavus moved his 17,000 man army into battle lines early in the
morning. Heavy fog and smoke from Lützen, which had been set afire,
shrouded the field, and hid how weakly the imperial left was held. Early
gains by the Swedish infantry were halted by the arrival of Pappenheim's
cavalry filling in on the imperial left. Regrouping, the Swedes charged
again. Gustavus led a cavalry unit into the center of the enemy line, hoping
to break it. He was hit in the back by a pistol ball, which knocked him
off his horse. A musket ball to his head killed him as he lay on the ground.

Enraged by his death, the Swedish infantry drove into the imperial right
and seized the guns there. By then fog and darkness halted the battle. It
was a standoff, but Wallenstein, despite being reinforced by 4,000 infantrymen, decided to pull out and retreat, allowing the Swedes to claim victory. The Swedes lost 4,200 men, while the imperial army lost 6,000. The
death of the king by no means ended Swedish involvement in the war.
Command of the army was taken by Gustave Horn, who was well trained
in Gustavus' tactics. The body of the Swedish army was still solid, since
it had a core of well-trained men and officers; but its heart was gone.

Wallenstein now towered over Germany. In September 1633, after a
summer of inactivity, he suddenly swooped down on a small Swedish army
at Steinau in northeast Germany and captured 8,000 men. His victory only
increased his sense of being ill-treated by the emperor, who was late as always in paying him. Even before Lützen he had been in contact with
Gustavus to see what sort of deal he could get from him. After Steinau,
Wallenstein contacted the Swedes again. When Ferdinand got wind of the
negotiations, he ordered that Wallenstein be arrested and brought to
Vienna. The emperor gave the officers commissioned to arrest Wallenstein
permission to kill him if necessary. Whether Ferdinand intended his death
from the first is in dispute, but there is no doubt that his officers saw it as
the only solution. In February 1634, Wallenstein was assassinated as he
fled toward his Bohemian estates.

Taking advantage of imperial weakness, Horn moved the Swedish army
into Bavaria in the spring of 1634. At the same time, however, a Spanish
army of 15,000 men was leaving Milan to take the Spanish road northward.
After five years without sending reinforcements to the Army of Flanders,
the Spanish government had assembled a potent force in Italy. Now that
the Spanish Road passed through the eastern Alps, Spanish troops on the
way to the Low Countries marched through Bavaria. Appraised of the dire
situation for the Habsburg cause in Germany, Philip IV agreed to allow
his troops to be used against the Swedes before marching on to Brussels.

When the Spanish troops entered Bavaria, an imperial army was besieging the city of Nördlingen, while the Swedish army was marching to
relieve it. The Spanish linked up with the imperial forces only two days
before the Swedes arrived. The Catholic captains decided that their manpower advantage—about 30,000 men to 20,000—and the strong defensive

position they occupied made a battle desirable. The imperials were entrenched on a high hill, while the Spanish used the hill as the anchor for their right flank. When the Swedes arrived, they concentrated on assaulting the imperial lines on the hill, while their German allies attacked the Spanish. After bitter fighting, the Swedes took the hill, but the Spanish easily drove off the Germans.

The Spanish were freed to counterattack the Swedish positions before they were set. The Spanish quickly learned to kneel down when they saw that the Swedes were going to fire a salvo, allowing the balls to pass overhead. Then leaping up, they charged with their pikes while the Swedes were reloading. Driven off the hill, the Swedes collided with their allies, who had re-formed to attack the Spanish. The Protestant lines collapsed in chaos. They lost some 12,000 men and Horn himself, while the Catholic dead was put at 2,000. The Battle of Nördlingen cleared the Swedes from Bavaria, and the Spanish army moved on to the Low Countries. The battle badly damaged what had remained of Gustavus' army. Although Sweden did not pull out of the war, its army was now mostly mercenaries, with a core of native troops. It was little different from the other armies in the war, which were rapidly adopting Gustavus' tactics.

THE FRENCH PHASE

Nördlingen had the effect of convincing Cardinal Richelieu of France that if he were going to achieve the French goal of destroying Habsburg power, he would have to get directly involved in the war. In November 1634, France gave the German Protestants 12,000 men and a large subsidy in exchange for their recognition of French rights in Alsace. In May 1635, France declared war on Spain. Its involvement vastly increased the scope of the war, as the French army went on the offensive across western Europe. In 1636 Spain responded by invading France and coming within twenty-five miles of Paris, but a Swedish offensive in Germany siphoned off the imperial units accompanying the Spanish, and the attack stalled.

The following year it was France's turn to go back on the offensive. A French invasion of Flanders occupied Spanish forces, which contributed to the Dutch capture of Breda. While that was the only success of the French offensive, it drained Spain of its last reserves of money. Heavier and heavier taxes across the Spanish Empire failed to raise the necessary sums, since it was gripped in a deep depression; and the popular resentment raised the specter of revolt. The first Spanish province to erupt was Catalonia in early 1640. A year later, the rebels, determined to free their homeland from Castilian rule, accepted aid from France.

As if the revolt of Catalonia were not threat enough to Spanish unity and war effort, later in 1640 Portugal declared itself independent of the Spanish monarchy. Heavy taxation was a motive, but more so the rebellion was a consequence of Spain's failure to defend the Portuguese colonies, especially Brazil. In 1636 the Dutch had captured the region of Pernambuco, costing the Portuguese their lucrative sugar industry and threatening the fall of all of Brazil. In October 1639, a Spanish fleet of fifty-three ships, intended for the reconquest of Brazil, was diverted for a

quick dash to Flanders with reinforcements and pay. The Dutch destroyed
the fleet in the Battle of the Downs off the coast of England. The Portuguese were enraged at Spain's failure to defend Brazil, and they revolted.
A Portuguese nobleman was proclaimed King John IV, and in 1641 he
began negotiations with the Dutch for a ten-year truce. The Dutch not
only granted it, they even sent a fleet to defend Lisbon. Conflict over
Brazil did not stop a rapid expansion of trade between Portugal and Holland. Profits from the trade helped both nations continue the fight against
Spain and win their independence.

Amazingly Spain was able to fight its enemies to a standoff on its other
fronts—Italy, the Rhine valley, the Low Countries, and Catalonia. Spain
was helped by popular revolts in France that sapped the French war effort.
In Germany the war continued, largely between the imperial and the
Swedish armies. Most of Germany suffered repeated pillagings from the
passage of mercenary armies. If one includes the popular revolts across
western Europe, only Castile and parts of France were free from the direct
impact of war.

By 1642, Cardinal Richelieu, who by then was seriously ill, had considerably transformed the French army. In hope of saving money by emphasizing quality over quantity in his manpower, he had forced the army
to adopt Gustavus' principles of drill and discipline and to concentrate on
recruiting native troops. His death in late 1642, the illness of Louis XIII,
who died in May 1643, and internal disturbances in France convinced
Francisco de Melo, commander of the Army of Flanders since 1641, that
an invasion of France was good strategy. Melo assembled an army of
18,000 infantrymen and 8,000 cavalry and crossed into France in early
1643. His intended route was to move south into Champagne and then
strike westward to Paris,. That route, although much longer than going
directly to Paris from Flanders, was less well fortified except for several
forts on the frontier.

One of those frontier forts was Rocroi, which Melo invested in early
May 1643. The French commander, Prince Louis d'Enghien, only twenty-two years old, rushed his army of 23,000 men to its relief. When Melo
was informed of the approach of the enemy, he formed his army into lines
between Rocroi and the French army. He was eager for battle because he
was sure he had a clear manpower advantage, and he had full confidence
in his veteran infantry. The tactics of the Spanish army had changed little
during the war. The victory at Nördlingen had kept the Spanish convinced
of the superiority of their traditional style. The French had adopted much
of the Swedish style, but most crucial in the coming battle was the reem-
phasis on shock combat in the French cavalry.

Enghien used his cavalry to drive off the enemy horse during the
opening stages of the battle. The Spanish tercios were left unsupported,
but they had rarely depended on cavalry support anyway. The French infantry charged them three times, but was thrown back. After the third
time, however, the French cavalry exploited the gaps opened in the Spanish
lines. Active French artillery fire also took its toll. As casualties rapidly
mounted, the Spanish signalled for quarter. When Enghien and other of-

ficers rode forward to discuss it, some Spanish musketeers, thinking they were making another cavalry charge, fired on them. The enraged French fell on the Spanish and inflicted huge casualties before the surrender was accepted. The dead in the Spanish army, mostly among the infantrymen, was put at 8,000, while 7,000 were captured. French casualties numbered 4,000.

The stone monument the French much later allowed the Spanish to erect at Rocroi has been called the gravestone of Spanish military greatness. This is not entirely true, since the Spanish continued to fight on with several minor successes, but the heart of the Spanish army had been destroyed. The veteran infantry units in the Army of Flanders had for nearly a century fought well and usually successfully, sometimes against great odds. Now they were largely gone. The deep depression in Spain and the depletion of the Castilian peasantry, the Spanish army's major source of recruits, made it impossible to rebuild the army to the level of the force lost.

Yet the war continued. France was determined to fight to the complete ruin of the Habsburgs. In 1644 a large French army crossed the Rhine River and fought three battles in a week's time with the Bavarians under Franz von Mercy, around the city of Freiburg. Although the Bavarians were able to retreat in good order after the third battle, this left the middle Rhine in French hands. For two years most of the fighting occurred in Bavaria, as the French, German Protestant, and Swedish armies, at times fighting alone, at times as a combined force, pursued Mercy back and forth across the duchy. In August 1645 he was killed at the Battle of Allerheim, which eliminated the last competent Catholic commander in Germany. After Allerheim, the Catholic side was left with virtually no forces. Meanwhile the French and the Dutch, fighting separately but in concert, were systematically reducing the lines of powerful forts that protected the Spanish Netherlands.

THE END OF THE WAR

It would be impossible to describe the misery and war-weariness of the peoples of Europe, especially in Germany, by 1647. An English diplomat crossing Germany with a mounted escort that year related how the peasants ran in terror from his small body of horsemen. He described also the utter devastation of the countryside and the extreme poverty of the towns and cities. The clamor for peace finally reached Emperor Ferdinand III (1637-1657), but only after the defeats of 1645 made it impossible for him to continue the war. He agreed to grant amnesty to those who had rebelled against imperial authority and to send representatives to a peace conference. The first peace conference in history began in November 1645, at Münster in the duchy of Westphalia. The Dutch had unexpectedly also agreed to discuss peace with Spain, and delegations from both states arrived in January 1646.

The process of hammering out a peace was naturally slow and contentious. French demands, such as for a duchy in the Holy Roman Empire so the French king could sit in the imperial Diet, were the most troublesome. But with the outbreak of serious violence in Paris in May 1648 in what became known as the Fronde, the French government decided it needed peace as soon as possible. By then the Dutch republic and Spain had agreed on peace terms that recognized Dutch independence. Another key issue was the close alliance between the Austrian and the Spanish Habsburgs. Under tremendous pressure from his enemies, including a potent Swedish army poised to invade Austria, Ferdinand III agreed in September 1648 to renounce the alliance. That broke the logjam. The remaining issues involving Germany were quickly settled, largely to the profit of Sweden. The Peace of Westphalia was finished in October. But Spanish hatred for the French, especially for aiding the revolts in the Spanish Empire, prevented a peace settlement between them. Their war continued until 1659.

In the Peace of Westphalia the emperor acknowledged the independence of the Dutch republic and, three centuries after it was a fact, of Switzerland. The numerous states within the empire were given true autonomy, and were now free to carry on their own foreign policy including war without the permission of the emperor. The title of Holy Roman Emperor no longer conveyed any authority. Bavaria, by gaining a large part of the Palatinate and the title of Elector, and Brandenburg, getting half of the duchy of Pomerania, came out the best among the German states. Sweden retained control of western Pomerania and the mouths of the Oder and Elbe Rivers. For its part France gained special rights in Alsace, which set the stage for absorbing the province into France thirty years later. Most important the war had brought about the ruin of Spain as the major power in Europe. France was now in position to play that role in the decades to come.

HUGO GROTIUS AND THE LAWS OF WAR

The unbridled atrocities and destruction of the Thirty Years War gave rise to a search for a way to control warfare and a new moral imperative to regulate soldiers' behavior. Traditional religion no longer seemed adequate. The man most responsible for a new theory of warfare was Hugo Grotius, a native of Holland. In 1625, he published *On the Laws of War and Peace*. He began the work by complaining of the "license in making war of which even barbarous nations would have been ashamed...when arms were once taken up, all reverence for divine and human law was thrown away; just as if men were thenceforth authorized to commit all crimes without restraint."[1]

Grotius' solution was to proclaim that a law of nature controlled the waging of war. While his distinction between a just war and an unjust one was not new, he declared that a just war cannot be fought against the innocent, among whom he included virtually everyone not directly involved in the fighting. The obligation to avoid harming the innocent included the requirement that commanders prevent the sack of cities taken by storm. Rape was to be punished in every circumstance.

Grotius argued that the use of certain methods of killing in war, such as the use of poison, was illegal. Prisoners of war legally could be made slaves but not killed, and the Christian officer had the obligation to exchange them or allow them to be ransomed. Standard procedure for POWs in the era was to release them on their word that they would not fight against their captors for a specified period of time; anyone found violating his parole (pledge) was summarily executed.

Grotius' achievement was to provide what was essentially a secular theory on which to base arguments that the impact of war on noncombatants must be limited. If there were no law governing behavior in war, then human society would be destroyed. War and its participants therefore had to be controlled. Grotius' work had no impact on the Thirty Years War, but his views fit the tenor of the time after 1648 and helped to change the perception of how war should be fought. Combined with changes in the nature of the armies themselves, the new view made war a more gentlemanly affair again, until the French Revolution.

NOTE

1. Quoted in Michael Howard, *War in European History* (Oxford, 1976,) p. 74.

England During the Puritan Revolution

IRELAND

The Boyne ▲

SCOTLAND

NORTH SEA

Newburn ▲

Marston Moor ▲

○ Dublin

Preston ▲

IRISH SEA

Aughrim ▲

ENGLAND

Naseby ▲

WALES

▲ Edgehill

▲ Oxford

London ○

The Downs ▲

Dover ○ Ostend ○

Calais ○

Lowestoft ○

Amsterdam ○

Texel ▲

THE DUTCH REPUBLIC

Rhine River

ENGLISH CHANNEL

FLANDERS

Antwerp ○

SPANISH

NETHERLANDS

Paris ○ Seine River

FRANCE

LORRAINE

Battles and Sieges ▲▲

0 30 60 90

Miles

19

The New Model Army and Navy

1. In all cases of fight with the enemy the commanders of his majesty's ships are to endeavour to keep the fleet in one line, and as much as may be to preserve the order of battle which shall have been directed before the time of fight

2. If the enemy stay to fight us, we having the wind, the headmost squadron of his majesty's fleet shall steer for the headmost of the enemy's ships.

3. If the enemy have the wind of us and come to fight us, the commanders of his majesty's fleet shall endeavour to put themselves in one line close upon a wind.

4. In the time of fight in reasonable weather, the commanders of his majesty's fleet shall endeavour to keep about the distance of half a cable's length from the other.

5. None of the ships of his majesty's fleet shall pursue any small number of ships of the enemy before the main [body] of the enemy's fleet shall be disabled or shall run.

6. In case of chase none of his majesty's ships shall chase beyond sight of the flag, and at night all chasing ships are to return to the flag.

> *Fighting Instructions 1530-1816*, ed. John Corbett (London, 1905; reprint New York, 1967), pp. 126-27. These instructions were issued by the duke of York, later King James II, in 1665.

The Thirty Years War was very productive of innovation and change in warfare. Gustavus Adolphus' work in particular had a great impact on the way war was conducted. His influence was obvious in Oliver Cromwell's New Model Army when it was created in 1644 to fight for the Parliament in the English Civil War.

Prior to 1642, the date of the first violence of the civil war, or the Puritan Revolution as it is also called, an English army can hardly be said to have existed. Well aware of how monarchs on the continent used standing armies to dominate their subjects, Parliament refused to fund an army, although the navy received considerable support. What land-based forces were found in England in the early seventeenth century were militia units based in the counties. They drilled one day a month during the summers, which was hardly adequate even to form a competent militia. The absence of an army and the isolationism of most Englishmen of the era prevented any significant participation in the Thirty Years War, despite great sympathy for the Protestant cause.

The failure of the monarchy to aid the Protestant states after Charles I (1625-1649) took the throne was one of the complaints of the Puritans. More serious was his refusal to "purify" the Church of England of Catholic practices; opposition to royal religious policy was one of the factors in the rebellion. But it was also a political struggle between crown and Parliament for control of the government, and the Puritans strongly identified with the cause of Parliament.

While the conflict over religious policy became worse under Charles I, since he was more pro-Catholic than his father had been, the clash over taxes also became more heated. Charles hoped to build up both the army and navy; it was he who made the first large commitment to building a royal fleet, for which the Spanish Armada had been the inspiration. In particular, he built the *Sovereign of the Seas* in 1637. This was not only probably the largest ship built to that date, it may well have been the most lavishly decorated warship ever. With 104 guns on three gun decks, the 1,500-ton ship could have served as an admiral's flagship a hundred years later had she not burned in 1696. The ship cost 65,586 pounds to build.

CHARLES I AND PARLIAMENT

Parliament's refusal to vote the new subsidies he wanted had led Charles to try to govern without Parliament for eleven years after 1629, collecting old taxes to the fullest legal extent and often beyond it. One such tax was the ship tax, which coastal towns paid for the defense of the coasts. Charles extended it to the entire realm, on the very reasonable grounds that the fleet defended the whole kingdom. The complaints from places newly taxed were furious.

In 1639 Charles suddenly found himself with a war on his hands. His efforts to impose Anglicanism on the Presbyterians of Scotland had led to rebellion. The Scots were always ready to invade England, and were able to draw on a large number of veterans from the continental war, as Scotland was an important source of mercenaries. The king was forced to recall Parliament and had to make broad concessions to the Puritans, who controlled it. Having been voted a large subsidy, he raised an army of 20,000 men. But far fewer Englishmen had fought on the continent, so few of the recruits had military experience.

In August 1640, the Scots soundly defeated Charles' force, more a mob than an army, in the Battle of Newburn. The king quickly agreed to terms, which required him to halt his attempt to change the Church of Scotland, and pay the Scots army. Faced with rebellion in Ireland as well, he had to go back to Parliament for a new subsidy. Charles gained the money he needed in exchange for an extensive transfer of authority to Parliament. With the money in hand, Charles moved in June 1642 to recover his lost

A fleet in the line of battle. The second and fourth ships from the right are armed merchentmen.

authority by trying to arrest the parliamentary leaders. Both sides immediately turned to collecting forces.

Parliament could call on a number of officers who had served with the Dutch and the Swedish armies, but had access to little trained manpower. Through its Militia Ordinance it called up the militia companies and in a month had assembled 20,000 foot and 4,000 horse. Command of this force was given to the earl of Essex. Although the tag of Roundhead used for the parliamentary forces implies social inferiority to the Cavaliers of the royal army, there was a large number of gentlemen among the Puritans.

Charles issued his Commissions of Array to raise an army, and many experienced officers joined him. They had seen service across Europe, including the Habsburg states, for many English Catholics rallied to the king. Charles' chief lieutenant was his nephew, Prince Rupert of the Palatinate, who was primarily a cavalry captain.

In October 1642, the first battle of the civil war was fought at Edgehill, north of London. Using the Swedish cavalry tactics, Prince Rupert drove his foe's cavalry off the field. While Rupert was pursuing the beaten cavalry, Essex rallied the parliamentary infantry and gained a small edge until Rupert's cavalry returned to the field. Essex was forced to retreat to London. Neither side suffered many casualties, but Charles never again had the manpower advantage of three to two that he held at Edgehill. In London Essex had access to supplies, money, and the city's militia units, the largest source of manpower in the realm.

OLIVER CROMWELL

After a year of inconclusive scrimmaging, Parliament signed a treaty with the Scots, who committed 18,000 infantrymen and 3,000 horsemen to the cause. The next major battle quickly followed the arrival of the Scots. The Battle of Marston Moor was fought in July 1644. The Puritans had the clear advantage in numbers, 20,000 men versus 11,000, but the two cavalry forces were about equal at about 7,000 men each. The battle, a clear victory for Parliament, was noteworthy for revealing the ascendancy of Oliver Cromwell among its officers.

Already forty-five years old, Cromwell had never been in battle before Edgehill. He had been a member of Parliament and had ardently supported its cause. When the break with the king came, he volunteered to raise a cavalry unit in eastern England using his own money. Imposing rigorous discipline and demanding that his men neither curse nor drink, he created a powerful force that emphasized shock over pistol fire. His regiment was so successful that it became known as Old Ironsides.

At Marston Moor Cromwell was the commander of 1,400 horse on the parliamentary right. As the battle developed, Cromwell had success with the tactic of having his men wait until they were in amongst the enemy before firing their pistols, and then using swords. While his men were securing the right, the parliamentary left, both infantry and cavalry, was being thrown back. Cromwell led his regiment around to the opposite flank and routed the royal units. The fact that his men were disciplined enough to execute such a maneuver after considerable hard fighting showed the caliber of the regiment.

Despite the parliamentary victory, the Roundheads failed to profit from it. Discord among the generals on how to proceed allowed Charles to regroup his forces and fight again in October at Newbury in central England. The king was outnumbered two to one, but continued disagreement among the parliamentary commanders allowed him to get away with small losses. The squabbling so enraged the leaders of Parliament that they decided to change the command structure of the army. The result was the Self-denying Ordinances of early 1645. These required that all members of Parliament give up their commissions and that all appointments to the higher officer posts be based on merit. Sir Thomas Fairfax was named commander in chief, or general. Cromwell was supposed to give up his commission, but his talent gained him the office of lieutenant general of the cavalry, and he was made Fairfax's second-in-command.

THE NEW MODEL ARMY

At the same time, a bill creating a "new-model militia" was also passed. It called for a standing army of 22,000 men. About half of the manpower was to come from existing units; the other half was to be raised by conscription. The infantry was made up of twelve regiments of 1,200 men apiece. The regiment, commanded by a colonel, consisted of ten companies. The colonel's company had 200 men; the lieutenant colonel's, 160; and the major's, 140. The remaining companies had 100 men and were led by captains, who had their lieutenants and ensigns. There were five NCOs in a company—two sergeants and three corporals. This was the first time that all of the modern titles of officers and NCOs appear in one document, although the titles themselves had been used previously.

In the infantry of the New Model Army, the ratio of musket to pike was two to one, as the emphasis on drill had improved firepower to the point that fewer pikemen were needed. This army has the distinction of being the first army to have a uniform, although some regiments on the continent had earlier used coats of the same color. In 1645 the famous scarlet coat was adopted, largely because it was the cheapest dye available. The cost of the uniform was deducted from the soldiers' pay, but buying them in bulk reduced the price. The ever-increasing emphasis on the use of the musket was one factor in the adoption of uniform dress, as close hand-to-hand combat in which friend could easily be distinguished from foe became less common. Numerous incidents of regiments firing on their own units had occurred in the Thirty Years War. Uniform dress was also seen as enhancing esprit de corps, which was of greater importance in the new style of warfare dependent on drill. The decreasing use of armor also helped make the adoption of uniforms possible.

The New Model Army acquired a reputation for strict discipline both on and off the battlefield. Fairfax and Cromwell were insistent that their men not plunder civilians or rob and mistreat prisoners of war. The ordinances against such behavior were much more rigidly enforced than in most armies of the era. The system of military justice for accused soldiers began to become more regularized, as the whim of the commanding officer to punish offenders was replaced by a court-martial, admittedly brief, before a "judge-advocate." (The English did owe something to the Swedish army in this respect.)

CROMWELL'S VICTORY

The creation of the New Model Army with Thomas Fairfax as its general ended the problem of dissension in the parliamentary ranks, while the royal army had become badly split by a dispute between Prince Rupert and Sir George Goring, Charles' most prominent English officer. Unable to solve it Charles sent Rupert northward with half his army and Goring to the west. Fairfax hoped to take advantage of the divided enemy by placing the royalist stronghold of Oxford under siege. Charles responded by sending Prince Rupert to relieve it. The two armies clashed at Naseby, virtually the exact center of England. The New Model Army had a decided edge in manpower—13,500 versus 9,000— and in artillery, but Charles decided to fight rather than retreat and ruin the morale of his troops.

The battle began with a cavalry charge on both flanks. Prince Rupert and Cromwell commanded their own right flanks. Both succeeded in breaking the lines of their foes and driving them to flight. While Rupert and his cavalry pursued the fleeing cavalry on their wing far off the battlefield, Cromwell regrouped his men and led them in a charge into the flank of the Cavalier infantry. By the time Rupert's cavalry returned to the fight, the royalist infantry had broken. A hard but brief fight by Rupert failed to recover the situation for the royalists. They left 1,500 dead and 4,500 prisoners.

Although the small royalist army led by Goring remained intact, Charles could hardly challenge the New Model Army again. The next year saw the parliamentary forces systematically pick off the royalist strongholds in short sieges. The strongholds were nearly all unreconstructed medieval castles and town fortifications. Some, however, did stand up well to the small number of heavy guns the New Model Army had. Since most did not have any outworks, the use of petards—a bell-shaped device loaded with gunpowder and attached to a gate or wall and exploded—was common. The danger in using petards is made clear in the saying "hoisted on your own petard."

In June 1646, Oxford, the major royalist stronghold, surrendered. By then the king had given himself up to a Scots force in northern England, preferring to take his chances with them rather than the Puritans. The Scots, however, sold him to Parliament. Yet, when Charles escaped in November 1647, he again joined the Scots. Persuading them to invade England to restore him to power, Charles led a 24,000-man army across the frontier in July 1648. Cromwell led the New Model Army north and soundly defeated Charles at Preston in August. Capturing the king, Cromwell took him to London to be tried for treason because of the Scots invasion. After Parliament was purged of its more reluctant members, the small number of members left sitting found Charles guilty. On January 30, 1649 King Charles I was beheaded.

By then Cromwell had clearly taken control of the army, as Fairfax had opposed the execution. Thus he also dominated the Commonwealth of England, as the new state was called. In that he held power through the support of the army, he has been called the first modern dictator. For the first three years after Charles' beheading, however, Cromwell fought in Ireland and Scotland against forces loyal to Charles' son. Cromwell's atrocities against the Irish left behind a long legacy of bitter hatred for the English.

THE NEW MODEL NAVY

Returning victorious to London in late 1651, Cromwell became a strong advocate of the passage of the First Navigation Act. It was intended to restore the finances of the state and the English merchants; most had supported Parliament in the civil war. The act prohibited the importing of goods on ships other than English or those of the country of origin of the goods. This was directed largely against the Dutch, who had developed a very profitable carrying trade between England and the continent and England and its colonies. The Act also gave the English navy the authority to stop Dutch ships at sea to determine whether they were carrying third party goods. Attempts to search Dutch ships were resisted, and the mounting hostility between the two Calvinist republics, who ought to have been natural allies, led to the first Anglo-Dutch war in 1652. The fighting was entirely at sea.

For the previous half-century, the Dutch had been the major innovators in naval affairs. The tasks given their fleet in the second half of the Eighty Years War were to carry the fight to Spanish and Portuguese waters and colonies, blockade the ports of the Spanish Netherlands, and drive off the Spanish fleet when it made its occasional attempts to bring men and supplies to Flanders. These varied responsibilities required ships that were fast, had shallow drafts, and carried heavy firepower. Those requirements were met by the frigate, a long, narrow vessel, which became standardized at 300 tons and forty guns. Few Dutch warships of the seventeenth century were larger than that, although there were many huge "Indiamen" for trade with the Far East, which were well armed and capable of carrying much more armament.

In 1639, the Dutch frigates under Admiral Martaan Tromp used line-astern tactics to devastate a Spanish fleet during the Battle of the Downs on the English side of the Channel. Forty of the fifty-three Spanish ships were sunk. An English fleet was nearby at the time, having failed in its assignment of keeping the foes apart; its captains were given a convincing demonstration of the value of the line-astern.

The English Parliament ordered seventy-seven ships built after the victory over Charles I. Reforms were instituted in the navy consistent with those in the New Model Army to improve discipline and tactical maneuvering. A Commission of the Admiralty was created to direct war at sea, and three former army officers were made admirals, the most important being Robert Blake.

In any conflict with the Dutch republic, England had a clear geographical advantage. The English fleet could cut off passage through the Channel and blockade the Dutch ports with relatively few ships, while a Dutch blockade of England required an enormous navy. The prevailing westerlies in the region also aided the English, for they usually had the advantage of the wind in battling a Dutch fleet.

The first Anglo-Dutch war began in May 1652, when Blake fired on some Dutch merchantmen who refused to stop and be searched. In the next ten months, four major sea battles were fought, which were evenly split. The English admirals, advocates of the line-astern, found that their efforts to use the tactic were hampered by the tendency of individual ships to veer off the line and attack the enemy piecemeal. The Admiralty accordingly issued the "Instructions for the better ordering of the fleet in fighting," in March 1653. The Instructions required that as soon as the admiral engaged the enemy in battle, "the ships of every squadron shall endeavor to keep in line with the chief."[1] They called for the severest punishment for captains who failed to stay in the line except in case of serious damage to their ships.

For the first time, a clear system of signalling at sea was devised. Outside of the use of a few signalling flags for which there was no regular system, communications between ships from the time of the Greeks was limited to shouting or dispatching boats. The 1653 battle instructions listed the five flags that the admiral was to use to signal different maneuvers. By

1700 another five flags were in use to increase the number of messages possible.

After several minor tests of the battle orders, they received a major trial in the Battle of Texel in July 1653, when Dutch and English fleets of about 100 ships apiece clashed in an all-day battle off the Dutch coast.   Both fleets used the line-astern in the battle; the two lines sailed alongside each other and blasted away with their broadsides. The English fleet included a number of ships more heavily armed than the Dutch, with up to sixty guns; their greater firepower seems to have made the difference in the bat- tle. The Dutch lost thirty warships and Admiral Tromp was killed, while the English lost fifteen ships. With the defeat the Dutch asked for negoti- ations, which produced a treaty in April 1654. They agreed to adhere to the Navigation Act.

THE STUART RESTORATION

In September 1658, Cromwell died and was succeeded by his son Richard as Lord Protector. He lacked his father's standing with the sol- diers, and the huge national debt accumulated in the last years of Oliver's rule made it impossible to pay them. In May 1659, Richard resigned. General Monck took control of the army and the government; but when he could not suppress the popular unrest, he invited Charles II to return from exile. In May 1660 the king landed on the English coast. His ship originally named the *Naseby* had been quickly renamed the *Royal Charles.*

The Stuart restoration did nothing to solve the growing antagonism with the Dutch, who had taken advantage of the instability in England to recover its position lost in 1654. Charles accepted a new Navigation Act of 1660 aimed directly against the Dutch. Incidents mounted, such as the English seizure of several Dutch posts in Africa in 1663 and the occupation of New Amsterdam (New York) in 1664. In May 1665, war was declared.

The second Anglo-Dutch war began the next month with the clash of two powerful fleets in the Battle of Lowestaft. Charles' brother, later James II, commanded the English fleet, assisted by Prince Rupert, the erstwhile cavalry captain. The Dutch had increased the size of their war- ships in the previous decade, and many ships in their fleet had more than forty guns. The English, nonetheless, badly defeated the Dutch, sinking thirty ships. A French priest Père Hoste, who was chaplain to a French admiral later in the century, provided in his *Naval Evolutions* of 1697 a good description of this battle and the line of battle. He described how the two lines "cannonaded each other from three o'clock in the morning until eleven with great fury";[2] then the Dutch flagship blew up and sank, with the loss of all hands but five. The loss of their admiral and the heavy damage they had suffered persuaded the Dutch to run for their coast. The English pursued and destroyed twenty-two more ships, including twenty said to have had over fifty guns. The English losses were put at one ship.

The English victory, however, was more than offset by the entry of France in the war as an ally of the Dutch. Louis XIV was obliged to do so under a treaty of 1662. The French fleet as yet could not match the English or the Dutch in size and quality, but it swung the balance of power to the Dutch. In June 1667 a Dutch fleet sailed up the Thames to within twenty miles of London, burning ships and docks and towing off the *Royal Charles*, the English flagship. That raid, along with the effects of the Great Plague and the Great London Fire of the previous year, convinced the English to make peace on terms slightly favorable to the Dutch.

Charles II had been greatly upset by the French alliance with the Dutch republic, since he regarded himself as a close friend of Louis XIV. Consequently, when Louis indicated a willingness to form an alliance, Charles seized the opportunity. In May 1670, the secret Treaty of Dover was signed. Charles committed himself to another war against the Dutch republic in concert with France and the reestablishment of Catholicism in exchange for a large annual subsidy.

The third Anglo-Dutch war, actually the naval part of the larger Dutch War (Chapter 18), began in March 1672 with an English attack on a Dutch merchant convoy in the Channel. Although the French fleet now fought with the English, the skill and daring of Admiral Michael de Ruyter of the Netherlands balanced the allied numerical advantage. In August 1673, in a brilliant defensive engagement against the much larger combined French-English fleet, he saved his fleet from destruction and prevented the invasion of Holland by 6,000 English troops. Since the French ships had disengaged before the English had, all of England blamed France for the failure of the project. Charles was pressed into making peace with the Dutch republic, which reestablished the status quo.

NAVAL ORGANIZATION

The three Anglo-Dutch wars, although fairly brief in duration and essentially stalemates, nonetheless saw a great deal of hard fighting at sea and vast development in the navies, particularly the English. Hard experience had shown that the type of ship that best combined maneuverability and firepower for duty in the line of battle was what was called a third-rate ship, carrying between sixty-four and seventy-four guns. A first-rate ship had 100 or more guns; the few of these that were built served as admirals' flagships. Second-rate ships had between seventy-four and 100 guns. The first three rates were used almost exclusively in fleet action in the line-astern. A fourth-rate ship, with fifty to sixty-four guns, became the standard convoy escort. The fifth and sixth rates had two gun decks instead of three. Fast single-deck frigates also were in use; they carried up to fifty guns.

The success of the line-astern tactic in the Anglo-Dutch wars ensured that the Fighting Instructions of 1653, which required its use, would remain in effect. Two schools of thought had developed in the English navy. The mêlée advocates, while willing to open the battle in the line-astern, were eager to allow captains the freedom to break out of the line to take advantage of whatever opportunities might appear in the battle. The formalist school of tactics saw the line-astern as sacrosanct: any deviation from it was sure to result in disaster. Since James II was a dedicated formalist as admiral and as king, his influence made this view the official one. Even after James' abdication in 1688, the admirals who now dominated the navy had risen to the top in the formalist school. They ensured that it would remain official tactical doctrine through new sets of fighting instructions in 1691 and 1703, which emphasized even more the obligation of the captains to fight in the line-astern. This policy had the result of stifling personal initiative. In particular, it inhibited captains from breaking from the line in pursuit of a defeated enemy.

The administration of the English navy also underwent improvement during the Anglo-Dutch wars. The English government had established two bodies to supervise the navy. The Admiralty dictated naval policy, while the Navy Board had responsibility for the building and supplying of ships. The very capable Samuel Pepys, the noted diarist, emerged as secretary of the Admiralty in 1660, and clerk of the Navy Board in 1665. With one man having great influence on both boards, strategy and the acquisition of materials to implement it were well coordinated. Pepys built up the royal dockyards and created a separate victualling board in 1683 for supplying the ships. Pepys' policy, imitated by his successors, of maintaining a high quality fleet in peacetime and the resources for vastly expanding it for war played a major role in the future successes of the British navy.

THE GLORIOUS REVOLUTION

Pepys was one of the casualties of the Glorious Revolution. Having been closely identified with James II, he was immediately dismissed by the new king, William III. After James had become king in 1685, his support of Catholicism and France discredited him in the eyes of most of the English. When his second wife, a Spanish princess, gave birth in 1688 to a son who would succeed to the throne before his Protestant half-sisters, English political leaders made contact with William of Orange, the Dutch leader. Annoyed by the pro-French position of James II in the War of the League of Augsburg and eager to bring England into his anti-French coalition, William agreed to come to England to "protect the liberties of Englishmen." In November 1688, William and a Dutch force of 15,000 men landed on the English coast. This last successful invasion of England was made possible by easterly winds that blew the Dutch ships quickly across the Channel while keeping the highly royalist English fleet in harbor; meanwhile the English army, far less loyal to James, deserted him. Losing his nerve, James fled to France in December.

The sudden collapse of James astounded Louis XIV, who had not attempted to interfere in William's enterprise in the expectation that the Dutch leader would be bogged down in a bloody war in England. Louis quickly moved to undo the damage in late 1689 by transporting James and 7,000 French troops to Ireland. There they joined 20,000 Irishmen trying to wrest control of Ireland from the English to serve as a base for James to retake England. After initial success in Ireland, the Jacobite army was faced in July 1690 with a force of 35,000 men. It was led by William III, who had been recognized as king by the English Parliament the year before.

The two rival kings clashed near the River Boyne, north of Dublin. James' army was within a large loop of the river. It was a dangerous position, since it could permit his enemy to trap him within the loop if William could cross the river above or below the bend. After an afternoon of trading fire across the river, William sent about a third of his army to cross the Boyne at a ford upstream from James' forces, while the rest made an assault directly across the river. The Jacobites failed to defend the ford strongly enough, and after a brief, sharp fight, the English detachment made its way across. Made aware of the presence of the enemy on his left flank, James sent units to meet it. That, however, weakened his main forces, which were already outnumbered. After three hours of bitter fighting, the Jacobites retreated. Breaking the encirclement, they saved most of their forces. The major mystery of the battle is why the veteran French units, certainly among the best in either army, failed to become heavily involved in the fighting. They lost only six men, compared to 1,000 for the entire Jacobite army. The English lost about 500.

James himself was back in France in three weeks, his dream of regaining his throne shattered. The Battle of the Boyne, however, was not the end of the war in Ireland. Despite losing most of the French troops, whom Louis XIV recalled in September 1690, the Irish regrouped and fought again at Aughrim in central Ireland in July 1691. A much larger English army captured the strong defensive position of the Jacobites by direct assault. The Irish forces were nearly destroyed, suffering 7,000 casualties.

The English victory at Aughrim permitted them to pacify Ireland for a full century. More important it put the final seal of success on the so-called Glorious Revolution. William III was free now to turn the forces of England against Louis XIV, who by failing to support the Irish adequately lost his opportunity to stop William. What could be called the Second Hundred Years War ensued, lasting until the final defeat of Napoleon in 1815. The presence of England in the anti-French coalition swung the balance of power away from France, individually the most powerful state in Europe, to its enemies in this long series of wars. They collectively entailed more years of warfare over 125 years than had occurred in the original Hundred Years War.

NOTES

1. *Fighting Instructions*, p. 127.

2. Quoted in Geoffry Symcox, *War, Diplomacy, and Imperialism, 1618-1715* (New York, 1973), p. 216.

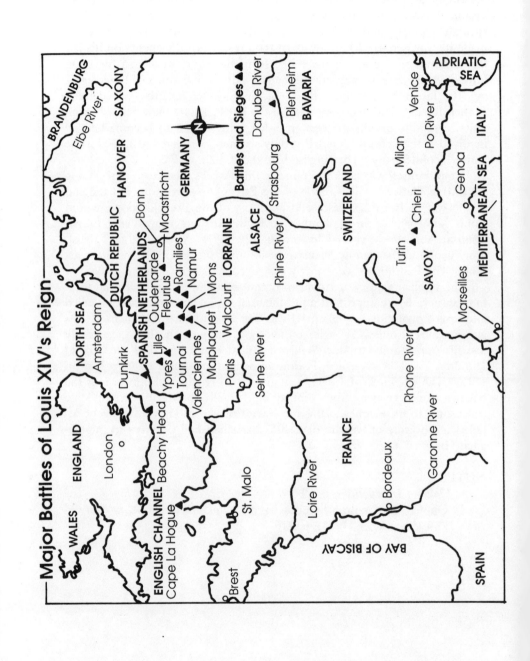

Major Battles of Louis XIV's Reign

20

The Wars of Louis XIV

The King [Louis XIV] with an unbelievable coolness placed his army in battle formation as it arrived, extending his right near to Valenciennes and his left to the woods of Saint Armand. Nothing escaped his Majesty's skill and foresight. He sent Marshal de Lorge with thirty squadrons and a thousand musketeers to the heights behind the woods. He established his artillery in an advantageous post. He had the dragoons and the infantry occupy the houses which were in his first line....The King wished to command the right wing and his first line....In this position the King ordered the firing of three cannon shots to tell the enemy of the desire and the intention that he had to give battle, and to assure them that he waited and sought the opportunity.

Louvois, quoted in John Wolf, *Louis XIV* (New York, 1968), pp. 250-51. Louvois, the French minister of war, was describing the preliminaries to the Battle of Valenciennes in May 1676.

While England was taking great strides toward becoming a major naval power, France was making even more progress toward becoming the dominant land power in Europe. France's natural wealth had only to be focused on war in order for it to outstrip its rivals. That focusing was largely done early in the reign of Louis XIV (1643-1715). As was true for Philip II of Spain in the previous century, Louis would overreach when he was at the height of his power and suffer major reverses, although French power would not decline as badly as Spain's had.

Before France could assert the political dominance created by its military success in the Thirty Years War, it had to undergo the ordeal of civil war. In the 1640s, economic depression and bad harvests, coupled with the heavy taxes needed for the war against the Habsburgs, led to popular revolts across France. The uprisings, known as the Fronde, persuaded France to make peace in the Thirty Years War, although Spain refused the peace terms and continued the war. Fortunately for France, Spain was in no position to take advantage of the French troubles. The return home of the French armies in 1648 merely added more men to the rebellion. The situation became truly dangerous for the government when the hero of Rocroi, now known as the prince of Condé, joined the rebels. In 1652 he entered Paris with broad support in the city, forcing young Louis XIV to flee. Louis never forgot the terror and humiliation inflicted on him by the great nobles and the Parisians.

Without a clear program and badly compromised by Spanish aid, the rebels floundered before loyalist forces led by Marshal Turenne. Turenne showed that he was the best general in France by badly defeating Condé in 1653. Condé fled to the Spanish Netherlands and agreed to serve Philip IV. In 1654 he received command of a Spanish army that tried to invade France. Turenne took the offensive and crossed into western Flanders with the aid of an English army and fleet. The two armies met on the coast east of Dunkirk in what is known as the Battle of the Dunes. The presence of the English fleet just offshore kept the Spanish army well back from the shoreline to keep from being bombarded from the sea. Turenne took advantage of the wide expanse of beach uncovered at low tide to send his cavalry to outflank the Spanish infantry. The French rolled up the enemy lines and won a brilliant victory in which the Spanish lost 1,000 dead and 5,000 prisoners while Turenne lost 400 men.

Spain was so demoralized by the defeat that it finally accepted peace. In the Peace of the Pyrenees, Philip IV's daughter Maria Theresa was pledged to wed Louis XIV. She was the elder of his two daughters from his first marriage, but the heir to the Spanish throne was Philip's infant son from his second wife. Maria Theresa's marriage contract required her to renounce all claim to the Spanish crown for herself and her descendants in exchange for a large dowry. Very little of the dowry was ever paid because of the virtual bankruptcy of the Spanish monarchy, giving cause for future war.

REFORM OF THE FRENCH ARMY

When Louis XIV was old enough to rule on his own, he declared that he would be his own first minister. To a large extent he was, but he still needed the aid of several capable ministers to rule successfully. In respect to the military his principal ministers were Michel Le Tellier, François de Louvois, and Jean-Baptiste Colbert. Le Tellier had been secretary of state for war since 1643. Because of his middle-class origins, he did not command the respect of the noble officers whom he was supposed to control. It was only after much of the nobility had been discredited in the Fronde that he was able to implement his ideas of military reform.

The most important development was the use of the office of *intendant* in the army. Intendants originally had been used to supervise tax collection and the courts of justice. Le Tellier assigned a civilian intendant to each of the provincial regiments. The regiments had been controlled virtually as autonomous fiefdoms by their colonels, who were members of powerful local families. While technically subordinate to the colonels, the intendants took control of the administrative structure of the regiments, especially their finances. The sorry state of the regiments had provided vast opportunities for fraud and waste. In the 1640s a Venetian ambassador reported that 60 percent of the money provided by the monarchy to the regiments was not used as intended. The intendants were to ensure that there were no "ghost soldiers" whose pay went into the pockets of the colonels. They were required to inspect the regiments for proper drill and weapons. Expenditures for supplies, rations, and fortifications also came under the purview of the intendants.

As a commoner himself, Le Tellier was not sympathetic to the tradition that officers come only from the nobility, but his efforts to change that met much stiffer resistance. A number of talented commoners were promoted to the middle levels of command, but never to the top. His most successful move in respect to the French officer corps was the creation of a model regiment under a Colonel Martinet, in which young officers were drilled in the use of the musket before they received their commissions. Martinet's emphasis on constant drill and rigid discipline caused his name to become a synonym for a strict disciplinarian. By requiring that officers learn the intricacies of drill, Le Tellier ensured that most French soldiers would be well drilled, which was becoming more and more essential in battle.

In 1668 Le Tellier passed his office to his son, whom Louis XIV named the Marquis de Louvois in recognition of his father's service. Louvois continued and extended his father's work of increasing royal control over the army and expanding its size. By tightening royal authority, the military now could be used as an enforcement tool for the tax system. Not that the soldiers were put to work collecting taxes, but they could be used to crush quickly and ruthlessly the numerous tax revolts that occurred in the provinces. By 1680, tax collections had risen significantly. A large portion of the new revenues went to the army to increase the number of soldiers and provide higher and more regular pay.

The French military increased from under 100,000 men in 1648 to about 300,000 by 1680. Most of the men were volunteers for terms of four years, which were usually renewed several times. Foreigners continued to make up a large part of the army's manpower, as much as one-third at several points after 1680. With higher and more regular pay, the commanders could insist on regular drill for their regiments. That in turn improved discipline, both on and off the battlefield. Better pay also allowed Louvois to insist that French soldiers wear uniforms, for which they still had to pay out of their wages. By 1670 the French army was fully in uniform, although the style varied among regiments. The color for the French infantry was white.

The increased revenues also allowed Louvois to improve the army's logistics. In the past the army had depended on contracts with private individuals who agreed to sell the supplies and rations directly to the troops at a profit. That system was open to widespread fraud and frequently led to severe shortages, especially when the army was on campaign. Le Tellier and Louvois began to create a bureaucracy to control the logistical system. The intendants negotiated and oversaw the contracts for supplies and rations. Standardization of the production of many items became possible, thus reducing their cost, for even artisans working with hand tools could produce more of a certain item if all pieces were made the same. Economy of scale was a major reason for the introduction of uniforms. State-owned industries were also established to provide some crucial supplies.

The two secretaries of war also began a system of permanent depots where huge quantities of supplies and rations could be stored. While the depots were located all across the realm, the majority were near the frontiers that were most likely to be the focus of campaigns. When the army began a campaign, supplies would be moved up from the depots by a system of transport called rolling magazines.

An important consequence of the system of depots and rolling magazines was that it reduced the need for soldiers to forage among the local people. That in turn reduced the terror of the passage of an army through a region, and increased the officers' control of their men on the march. Few things have been more destructive to discipline than foraging and looting, even if the officers have approved. However, the age-old tradition that an occupied region should help support an occupying army did not disappear; it was converted into a system of levies imposed by the army's bureaucracy. And the difficulty of moving supplies from the depots in bad weather frequently required that the troops live off the locals. But overall the new system was far less harsh on civilians than allowing the soldiers to forage.

Supplying the much larger armies of the late 1600s was made easier by a dramatic reduction in the size of their trains, especially in the number of women. Previously soldiers wanted women with them in order to nurse them when ill or wounded. Le Tellier developed a system of field hospitals, which were a decided improvement over the prior policy of total neglect. He felt that he could now prohibit women from accompanying the army and even forbid soldiers to marry. While far from successful in eliminating camp followers, these acts did greatly reduce their number.

THE FRENCH NAVY

Much of what Le Tellier and Louvois achieved in reorganizing and expanding the French army was made possible by Colbert's work. Behind his success in increasing the crown's revenues was his ardent belief in mercantilism. This was an economic theory that argued for extensive government regulation of economic activity in order to increase the power of the state. Since the best measure of a state's power was its reserves of bullion (gold and silver), it could increase its power by accumulating bullion. That could be done either through the possession of bullion-producing colonies, such as Spain had, or by a favorable balance of trade, which brought bullion into a realm. Colbert strongly supported colony building, and the French presence in Canada and the Caribbean expanded greatly under his encouragement. The French colonies were barely profitable, however, so Colbert turned to achieving the favorable balance of trade that mercantilists advocated. Regulation of the economy was part of a zeal for government control that was also reflected in the regulation of the army. It benefited the army not only by making much more money available for it but also by the government's directing resources to the production of military goods.

As a mercantilist, Colbert also was convinced that the well-being of the state required that foreign cargo be carried in French ships, so that profits from the carrying trade would accrue to France. Therefore, he actively encouraged the growth of the French merchant marine and a fleet to protect French commerce. Although Richelieu had put considerable resources into the navy, two decades of neglect had reduced it to impotency by 1660. Colbert largely had to start from scratch. Establishing a system of shipyards, arsenals, and schools for training seamen, he built the French navy from eighteen poor ships to 276 high-quality vessels by the time of his death in 1683. A large fleet was also needed for control over the French colonies overseas. The colony in Canada began in 1608 with the founding of Québec, but the tiny colony was barely hanging on when Colbert took office. He envisioned it as the hub of a vast French empire in North America, and recruited 4,000 peasants to settle there. In general, however, despite the heavy taxes the French monarchy imposed on its commoners, they were very reluctant to leave their homeland.

LOUIS XIV'S FIRST WARS

With these three very capable men serving him, Louis XIV soon acquired the military power to be the great conqueror that every young king aspired to be. Louis in fact was rather slow in becoming involved in war after he acquired full authority in 1661. His first war was fought in the name of his wife. In 1665 Philip IV of Spain died, leaving his titles to his infant son Charles II. Louis claimed several provinces of the Spanish Netherlands for his wife on the grounds that a "law of devolution" in these provinces gave them to her as the first-born child of the dead king, rather than to his son. The clause in her marriage contract giving up her rights of inheritance was declared null because her dowry had not been paid.

When Louis' claims for his wife were ignored, he ordered Turenne to invade Flanders with an army of 70,000 men in May 1667. Despite low manpower and morale, the Spanish garrisons resisted and slowed the progress of the French. Moreover, the Dutch became badly frightened at the prospect of having France as their neighbor. They realized how badly Spanish power had declined since 1648 and preferred that Spain have control of the southern provinces, since they still had hope of reuniting the Low Countries. In January 1668, the Dutch republic, England, and Sweden formed an alliance to counter French ambitions.

Louis was not eager to fight a larger war, and in May 1668 accepted the Peace of Aix-la-Chapelle. It extended the French border to Lille in Flanders and allowed Louis to keep five fortified towns within the Spanish border that his army had captured. The result was a confused frontier that demanded adjustment. The treaty was barely a truce, but what made the next war certain was the attitude of the French toward the Dutch. Louis was deeply angered at the Dutch support for Spain; it appeared to him as gross ingratitude for French aid in the Eighty Years War. Colbert the mercantilist advocated war as a way of destroying the enormous trade advantage the Dutch had in France, and Louvois was eager to win the great victory that had been denied to the army in 1668.

Louis' diplomats set to work to break up the anti-French coalition of the War of Devolution. Charles II of England was bought off. Spain was assured that France had no further designs on the Spanish Netherlands. This was demonstrated by a strategy that called for the French army to avoid Spanish lands by marching down the Rhine to strike at the Dutch republic from the east. Louis went with the army of 130,000 men as it moved down the Rhine valley in the spring of 1672. The Dutch frontier was well defended with forts and rivers, but the French army successfully crossed the Rhine into Dutch territory, reducing the forts along the frontier. A young military engineer, Sébastien de Vauban, caught the king's attention in these operations and gained his confidence. As the French surged on toward Amsterdam, the Dutch cut the dikes and flooded the land between the invaders and the city. The French ought to have been aware of that possibility, but poor intelligence prevented the quick victory that appeared in sight. The Dutch did offer generous peace terms to Louis; still convinced that a total victory was possible, he demanded more.

Blaming their leaders for the French invasion, the Dutch turned on them and killed several. William III of Orange, twenty-two years old in 1672, was made *stadtholder* of the republic. He nursed a bitter hatred of Louis XIV, which made him the prime force behind the broad anti-French coalition of the next thirty years. His search for allies had quick success as Brandenburg, the Holy Roman Empire, and Spain joined the Dutch. Louis was forced to disperse his forces to be on guard for any moves by the members of the coalition.

Only 40,000 French troops were left in Holland to wait for the winter freeze, which would allow the French to march to Amsterdam. A mild winter foiled that strategy. In the spring of 1673 Louis turned his attention to the great fortress of Maastricht, which the French had bypassed the previous year. The siege was put under the command of Vauban. It was the first time in history that a siegemaster had the authority to conduct a siege as he thought best. Louis was present for the siege, which made it easier for Vauban to give orders in the king's name. Vauban's systematic digging of siegeworks was so well done that the men in them were all but invulnerable to the defenders' artillery (Chapter 21). After only twenty-two days under siege, Maastricht fell to an assault led by the king himself. The attackers lost fewer men than the defenders, a truly rare event in history. The French had expected the siege would last the entire summer. Despite that impressive victory, the tide began to turn against the French. The anti-French alliance continued to expand, adding several German states and Denmark. The French army in Holland was threatened with being cut off, so Louis ordered its withdrawal. The war zones now moved to the Spanish Netherlands and the Rhineland. Turenne, after a successful campaign in Alsace in 1674-75, was killed in July 1675 by a cannonball.

Vauban became the major strategist for the French army. He was developing his theory of clear defensive lines anchored by strong fortifications, and he regarded it as crucial that the frontier between the Spanish

Netherlands and France in particular be straightened out. He complained of the chaotic mixture of enemy and friendly forts there and argued that the situation required three times as many forts and men to be maintained properly.

The campaigns of 1676 and 1677 were directed against the Spanish forts. The prize was Valenciennes, the central anchor of the Spanish defensive line. Vauban's system of besieging forts was clearly demonstrated for the first time, and despite atrocious weather, the fort fell in eighteen days. Over the next year several great cities were taken in short sieges; Ypres, for example, fell only five days after the trenches were open.

SHORT-LIVED PEACE

Despite these successes, the cost of the war accelerated the financial crisis in France, which was compounded by several years of poor harvests. Louis decided to begin negotiations with the Dutch, the enemy most likely to accept terms. In August 1678 peace between France and the Dutch republic was signed; without their ally, Spain and the empire also quickly came to terms. The peace was largely at the expense of Spain, which conceded the Franche-Comté and most of the cities the French had occupied in the Spanish Netherlands.

Louis XIV took advantage of peace to pursue two projects close to his heart—the annexation of Alsace and the revocation of the Edict of Nantes. In regard to Alsace, he established special courts called the Chambers of Reunion to determine the highly complicated historical and legal jurisdiction in Alsace and Lorraine. Piece by piece, all of Alsace and much of Lorraine were declared to be under French sovereignty. Only the city of Strasbourg attempted to resist, but the appearance of a large French army at its gates settled the issue in September 1681. Across Europe there was an outcry against the French, and William of Orange made the rounds of the European capitals seeking to revive the anti-French coalition.

Louis had always resented the presence of the Huguenots in his realm, for he was a firm believer in the principle of "one king, one law, one faith." After 1661 he began to use the power of the state to coerce them into converting. By 1685 Louis' ministers could tell him that the Edict of Nantes was no longer necessary, since there were so few Protestants left in France. The new edict withdrew religious toleration for Protestants but forbade their emigration from the realm. Nonetheless some 200,000 Huguenots did flee France, settling largely in the Dutch republic, England, and Brandenburg. They spread their deep hatred for Louis in their new homelands. They stirred up further the anti-French feelings in Protestant Europe and pushed for a renewal of the anti-French alliance, believing that if Louis were defeated, they could return home.

THE WAR OF THE LEAGUE OF AUGSBURG

French behavior in the 1680s made the exiles' task easier. Not only did Louis refuse to go to the aid of Vienna when it came under Turkish attack in 1683, he had actively encouraged the Turks, expecting to pick up the pieces in Germany after Habsburg power was smashed. The Ottoman defeat foiled those hopes, while resentment toward France was immense. It culminated in 1686 in the creation of the League of Augsburg. The league, along with Austrian successes against the Turks in Hungary, which promised to increase the emperor's power, led Louis to decide on a preemptive strike in the Rhine valley. The French army was at full strength and ready for war. Perhaps equally important was the strength of the French navy; the admirals wanted to use it to demonstrate its capabilities.

In September 1688, Louis issued a declaration of war against the League and sent his army into the Rhineland. Louis intended it to be a short war with limited goals. What resulted was nine years of warfare known as the War of the League of Augsburg, or the Nine Years War. It could as easily be called the First World War, for it was fought wherever the European powers had colonial and commercial interests. In North America it is known as King William's War.

The French waged a campaign of terror in the Rhineland, largely destroying several cities that resisted. Much worse, Louis and his advisors decided to turn the Rhine into a defensive perimeter for France. A number of fortified places were greatly strengthened, while other cities were to be destroyed to deny a German army their use in any attack on France. Only a few cities among the designated places were destroyed, since the task of totally destroying a city was immense and many French officers refused to obey the order. This ruthless policy aroused further the hatred of most Europeans toward France. The League of Augsburg became a military alliance of all the states of western and central Europe against France. When Louis miscalculated the situation in England and allowed William of Orange to cross the Channel late in 1688, England also became a part of the alliance. William III proved capable of mobilizing the resources of England for war in a way the Stuarts never were.

The main theater of war was again the frontier between France and the Spanish Netherlands. In August 1689 the first major battle was fought at Walcourt, in Brabant. Marginally an allied victory, it was important because John Churchill, later the duke of Marlborough, led an English contingent of 8,000 men in the allied force of 35,000. Churchill and many other Englishmen had fought on the continent before, but it was the first time in over a century that so large an English force had fought there under its own flag. The allied commander expressed his pleasure at the unexpected taste for combat shown by the English.

FRENCH VICTORIES

The principal result of the battle was that it persuaded Louis to replace the defeated general with the duke of Luxembourg. A far better commander, Luxembourg showed his aggressiveness in the Battle of Fleurus in 1690. He won the battle largely through the superiority of the French cavalry over the allied cavalry, which was usually the case in this war. Ten days after Fleurus, the French won an equally complete victory at sea. When Colbert died in 1683, his fleet included 117 ships of the line and 140 other ships, although the strength of those numbers was reduced by their division into Mediterranean and Atlantic fleets. Colbert's son, the marquis

de Seignelay, became naval minister, but he failed to win the office of secretary of finance, to the ultimate detriment of the French navy. Nonetheless in 1688 it was superior to its rivals in both numbers and quality.

Seignelay was eager to use the fleet when the War of the League of
Augsburg broke out, but it took two years for the opportunity to present
itself. In 1690, in order to send help to the Irish fighting William III, Admiral de Tourville was told to seek out and destroy the Anglo-Dutch fleet
in the English Channel. Tourville found the allied fleet off of southern
England. His opponent, Admiral Torrington, with fifty-seven ships compared to seventy-seven for the French, declined battle and headed for the
safety of the Thames. On July 9, however, he received orders from his
government to give battle, so the next morning off Beachy Head on the
southeast coast of England, he formed the line-astern and advanced on the
French. Torrington's Dutch ships formed the vanguard of his line, and
they took the brunt of the superior French firepower. Taking advantage
of his greater numbers, Tourville was able to place ships on both sides of
the Dutch line, raking the Dutch ships from two sides.

The beating the Dutch ships took was shown by the sinking of one ship
of the line during the battle and a second the next day. Three were so badly
damaged they were abandoned. The French boarded and captured another
five. Torrington broke off and retreated into the Thames, leaving Tourville
in control of the Channel. However, Seignelay's death soon after the battle
put the direction of the navy under Louis de Pontchartrain, who was inexperienced in naval affairs. Unable to decide what to do next with
Tourville's fleet, and in tune with the king's fixation on the war on land,
he let the opportunity presented by the victory at Beachy Head slip away.

The victories at Fleurus and Beachy Head put the French in a good
position to make a favorable peace, but Louis' demands were excessive.
Then in July 1691, the French received a sharp blow when Louvois died.
Although the office of secretary for war went to Louvois's son, Louis
himself took over much more of the direction of the war. Louvois' death
removed the most uncompromising person from the court; after 1691,
Louis was far more willing to negotiate.

THE CHANGE TO *GUERRE DE COURSE*

Nonetheless the war dragged on. In 1692 there were two major events.
The first was the siege of Namur, which was perhaps the best fortress in
the Spanish Netherlands. Louis personally commanded the 130,000-man
army that invested Namur, but Vauban directed the siege, which lasted
from May 25 to June 30. The quick fall of Namur showed the great
siegemaster at his best. Earlier in June 1692, however, the French had lost
a major naval battle. Louis had approved of a plan to invade England by
using the combined Mediterranean and Atlantic fleets. The Anglo-Dutch
fleet put to sea to prevent their joining. Unfavorable winds had delayed the
arrival of the Mediterranean fleet when the allied fleet appeared off Brest
in western Brittany, the main harbor for the Atlantic fleet. Admiral de
Tourville was ordered to attack the ninety-nine ships of the enemy with
his forty-four ships. The two fleets had moved off the western point of

Normandy, Cape de la Houge, before contact was made. Holding the wind
gauge, the French fleet in tight formation made for the center of the allied
line, which was badly strung out.

For a time the concentrated French fleet had the better of the fight, but
eventually the numerical advantage of the allies took effect. The rise of a
heavy mist allowed Tourville to break off without losing a ship, but overnight a strong wind badly scattered the French ships. The majority of them
reached the harbors of Brest and Saint-Malo, but those that had been
damaged had to put into several small harbors on the Normandy coast.
The allied fleet gave up its pursuit of the main body to burn fifteen ships
in the harbors.

Not only had the French navy suffered a serious defeat, it was now split
between two ports. The continued presence of the allied fleet made it impossible for the French to join up. Without any possibility of threatening
Anglo-Dutch control of the Channel, Pontchartrain decided to turn the
smaller ships in the fleet into commerce raiders, or corsairs, until the fleet
was was rebuilt. Privateers were also engaged to carry on this *guerre de
course* (war of commerce raiding). It was perceived as a temporary measure, since in the next two years seventeen first- and second-rate ships were
built, which were too slow for commerce raiding. However, the expense
of rebuilding the French navy to make it again competitive was too great
for Louis. He never had much interest in the sea, and when fiscal problems
forced a decision between the navy and the army, he chose the army
without hesitation.

The French battle fleet remained in existence and on occasion after
1692 did challenge its enemies, but more and more of France's maritime
resources were directed to guerre de course. Most of the smaller ships of
the line were contracted out to privateers, which made it difficult to pull a
powerful fleet together. By 1695 French naval activity was largely commerce raiding. It was highly successful in the last years of the current war
and the War of the Spanish Succession, ruining a large part of English and
Dutch commerce. Nonetheless, commerce raiding had its disadvantages.
It made it impossible to give adequate aid to the Irish in their fight against
William III; what had been a major diversion of English resources was all
but over by 1694. And in the wars of the mid-eighteenth century, the
emphasis on guerre de course rendered hopeless the French efforts to defend their colonies.

In general the French effort in the War of the League of Augsburg was
hampered by severe financial problems, which were compounded by a disastrous harvest in 1695. The result was a stalemate, and serious peace
negotiations were begun in 1696. Pressure for peace in England forced
William III to agree to terms in September in the Peace of Ryswick without gaining for the emperor his key demand, the return of Strasbourg. The
Habsburgs' attempt to continue the war without Anglo-Dutch aid failed,
and late in 1697 they agreed to largely the same terms. The peace returned
the borders of western Europe to those of 1678, except for Alsace, which
remained under French control. Louis also recognized William III as king
of England and Scotland.

THE WAR OF THE SPANISH SUCCESSION

The Treaty of Ryswick was again little more than a truce between wars, but the immediate cause of the next war was far more significant than for most other wars in history—nothing less than the rule of the Spanish Empire. After thirty-five years of rule, sickly, impotent, and feeble-minded Charles II died in November 1700. Two princes had good claims to the Spanish throne: the son of Louis and Maria Theresa, Charles' half-sister; and Leopold I of Austria, the grandson of Philip III of Spain. The death shortly before of the young grandson of Charles' other half-sister had eliminated the choice of most of the other states of Europe and an acceptable compromise for Louis and Leopold. Both Louis and Leopold knew that they could not propose a candidate who would unite their crowns with Spain; so Louis supported his second grandson Philip of Bourbon, while Leopold backed the claim of his younger son Charles.

Louis, however, was holding a trump card: a month before his death, Charles II had signed a will that recognized Philip of Bourbon as his successor. Well aware that if he accepted the will unconditionally, there would be war, Louis hesitated for a moment. But there really was no possibility that he would pass up such an opportunity to add to the glory and power of his dynasty. On November 16, 1700, Louis announced that he recognized his grandson as Philip V of Spain. Louis further declared that Philip would keep his place, then third, in the line of succession for the French throne. That was as sure a cause for war as ever was to be found.

In 1701 the War of the Spanish Succession began. The first fighting occurred in northern Italy. The Holy Roman Emperor had sent an army under Prince Eugene of Savoy to occupy the Spanish holdings there. Eugene, who made his reputation battling the Turks in Hungary, had gone to the French court as a young man in hope of a military career. In one of the worst mistakes of his life, Louis XIV had rejected the frail young man with the cutting slight that a church career was more appropriate for him. Deeply embittered by this, Eugene offered his services to the emperor and quickly proved Louis wrong. After Eugene had several quick successes in northern Italy, Louis sent out a vastly superior army under Marshal Villeroi to drive him out. In September 1701, Villeroi found Eugene's forces well entrenched at Chiari but, trusting his numerical superiority, attacked anyway. The result was a massacre of the French. Villeroi took his badly reduced army into winter quarters only to have Eugene pull off a surprise attack in February and capture the marshal himself.

THE BATTLE OF BLENHEIM

While Eugene was proving in Italy that he was a brilliant commander, more bad news for Louis arrived from London. The death of William III in March 1702 had given rise to hopes that England would stay out of the war, but the succession of Queen Anne gave control to the duke of Marlborough, who was eager for war and conducted it far more energetically than William would have. In May England declared war, and the duke was sent to the Netherlands as the commander of a combined Anglo-Dutch army of 50,000 men. Marlborough quickly demonstrated why he had such an excellent reputation as a general, stressing mobility at a time when a turtle's pace was the norm, and keeping the French off-balance with unexpected attacks.

These characteristics were best demonstrated in the campaign of 1704 that culminated in the Battle of Blenheim. In 1702 and 1703, Marlborough had cleared the French from the forts on the Meuse and lower Rhine rivers. With these waterways secured, he could quickly transport his army and supplies over a considerable distance. Later in 1703, Prince Eugene was recalled from Italy to lead a campaign against Bavaria, France's ally. Louis sent a large French army under Marshal Tallard to Bavaria in the hope that the combined Franco-Bavarian army of 60,000 men would be able to attack Vienna.

Marlborough had concentrated nearly 100,000 men on the Rhine south of Bonn. The build-up of men and supplies made it obvious to the French that he was planning a major campaign, but his position offered the possibility of striking at any point on the northern and eastern frontiers of France. The French forces were frozen in place waiting for Marlborough to strike. With a third of his army, Marlborough suddenly began to move southward up the Rhine; the rest of his Anglo-Dutch forces remained in place to guard against a French strike in the Netherlands. Since he could have been planning a strike into Lorraine or Alsace, the French still could not react until he suddenly turned to the east. His objective was then clear enough—to join Eugene in driving the French out of Bavaria.

Eugene and Marlborough joined their forces on August 12. The cooperation and coordination between these two generals was exemplary, perhaps the finest example in European history. Tallard had taken up a position across the allies' line of communications. His right flank rested on the Danube at the village of Blenheim, while at his front was a small river whose bank on the French side rose some ten to fifteen feet. Despite the French army's excellent defensive position, Eugene and Marlborough decided to attack, with Eugene's army on the right and Marlborough's on the left. By attacking on the flanks first the allied commanders pulled the French reserves from the center. After three hours of fighting, Marlborough struck at the center of the French lines with a powerful force of both cavalry and infantry. Despite heavy casualties, he broke the French center. The broken units from the French center, especially the cavalry, fled to the Danube where a great many men drowned trying to cross.

Consequently the Franco-Bavarian casualties were extremely high: 21,000 dead and wounded, and 14,000 prisoners, including Tallard. The allies lost 4,500 men. In respect to casualties, Blenheim was the largest battle of the early modern era, and it is the major reason for Marlborough's brilliant reputation. The allied victory enabled them to occupy Bavaria and ended any threat to Austria, but it also gave rise to complaints about Marlborough's high "butcher's bill," especially among the Dutch, who had not agreed to his march into Bavaria. For the next year he was reined in and was unable to follow up on Blenheim. He returned to the lower Rhine Valley, while Eugene returned to Italy.

CONTINUED ALLIED VICTORIES

The only significant naval event of the war also occurred in 1704. The French emphasis on guerre de course left few opportunities for the Anglo-Dutch fleet. In 1702 it had captured or destroyed seventeen Spanish treasure galleons that had been caught at anchor in Vigo Bay, along the northwest coast of Spain, but the action was hardly a battle. In 1704 the fleets fought a drawn battle off the southeast coast of Spain, but the Franco-Spanish fleet was forced to withdraw, leaving the allies free to occupy Gibraltar. While crucial for controlling traffic in and out of the Mediterranean, Gibraltar lacked a large enough harbor and enough water to post a large fleet there. So in 1708 a British naval force occupied the island of Minorca, giving them an excellent base for operations.

In 1706 Marlborough was back on the offensive in the Low Countries. The French sent 60,000 men under Marshal Villeroi to prevent the expected siege of Namur. Marlborough, always eager to fight, moved to intercept Villeroi and found him at the village of Ramillies. The ensuing battle was very similar to Blenheim. The armies were equal in size to that battle; the French had time to locate a good defensive position on high ground; and Marlborough's tactics were virtually the same. He struck at the flanks, drawing the French reserves out of the center, and then attacked the center with a force very strong in cavalry. Again the French center broke. The defeat demoralized the French garrisons in the Spanish Netherlands, and there was no army available to serve as a relief force. Numerous strongholds surrendered after only a show of resistance. Antwerp and Dunkirk were the most notable of the places taken, and control of most of the Spanish Netherlands passed to the allies.

Meanwhile in Italy, French forces had laid siege to Turin, where about 40,000 men faced a garrison of 15,000 troops. Eugene of Savoy brought an army of 30,000 to try to relieve the city. Not wishing to give up their hard-won positions close to Turin's defenses, the French built a strong line of circumvallation. After a lengthy reconnaissance, Eugene settled on an attack point in the circumvallation. The need to defend the entire line reduced the number of troops that could be concentrated opposite Eugene's army. Furthermore the French commander was convinced that Eugene would not attack. But he did attack, in careful coordination with a sortie by Turin's garrison, and broke through the circumvallation. Not only did the French suffer very heavy casualties in the ensuing envelopment of their lines, they also lost nearly all their artillery and equipment. By the end of 1706, the French had abandoned Italy entirely and were being driven back into Savoy.

Early in 1707, with the war on the two major fronts going disastrously and another allied army making good progress in Spain, Louis began to put out peace feelers. His enemies, convinced that the total defeat of France was at hand, refused. However, Marlborough could do little in 1707, since he again had been reined in by the politicians he served because of his long casualty lists. He was also waiting for Eugene to join him from Italy.

Before Eugene's army reached the Netherlands, a major battle was fought at Oudenarde in July 1708. The French were hampered, as they frequently were throughout the war, by a split command consisting of an old veteran, in this case the duke of Vendôme, and Louis XIV's eldest grandson, the duke of Burgundy. When they heard that Marlborough was six miles away, Vendôme wanted to fight; but Burgundy, frightened by Marlborough's reputation, wanted to retreat. Vendôme eventually convinced him to fight by pointing out how the enemy was in a position to cut off their communications with France. The vacillation delayed their preparations for Marlborough's attack. Vendôme's experience enabled him to pull out most of his army after several hours of hard fighting, but again the French had far greater casualties—4,000 dead and 9,000 prisoners.

The allies followed up this victory by laying siege to the city of Lille, within the borders of France itself. Eugene, who had arrived with 40,000 men, conducted the siege, while Marlborough's army of 70,000 men made sure that no French army could come to Lille's relief. The French garrison of 16,000 men, defending one of Vauban's best set of works, made Eugene pay dearly before surrendering four months later.

The war was now carried into northern France as allied cavalry raised contributions of food and money from the towns and villages there. The winter of 1709 was the coldest in memory, and the exhaustion of France forced Louis again to propose peace talks. Yet again the allied demands were excessive, including a demand that Louis use his own troops to drive his grandson from Spain. So the war continued into 1709.

The strategy of the allies was to continue to reduce the powerful fortresses on the frontier near Lille. Eugene in particular was opposed to driving into France with those forts untaken behind him. Tournai fell in late July, and the allies moved on to Mons. Marshal Villars had replaced Vendôme, who could no longer work with the Prince of Burgundy. Villars brought 90,000 French troops into position to challenge the 110,000-man allied army at Mons. He drew the allies to the village of Malplaquet where he had prepared a strong defensive line with both flanks resting on woods. The battle plan of Marlborough and Eugene was the same as it had been for several previous battles: strike at the French flanks to draw the reserves from the center and then break the center. The old veteran Villars was ready for the tactic; he strongly fortified his left flank and kept his reserves in the center when Marlborough began the battle with a strong assault on the flank. The numerical advantage of the allies eventually pushed the French out of their lines and off the field, but the allies took very heavy casualties, 6,500 dead versus 4,500 for the French. Villars wrote to Louis: "If it pleases God to give your majesty's enemies another such victory, they are ruined."[1] But another such battle was never fought. Marlborough's superiors again found the bill in lives and money too high and curbed his aggressiveness; in 1711 a change in government in England cost him his command entirely.

THE END OF THE WAR

In 1711 serious peace negotiations were opened at Utrecht. Both Emperor Leopold and his eldest son had died by then, and the new emperor, Charles VI, had been the allied candidate for the Spanish crown. Neither England nor the Dutch republic was willing to fight for his right to both thrones. In April 1713, the two sea powers signed the Peace of Utrecht. As in the previous war, the emperor refused to sign, and fought on alone. Prince Eugene found himself fighting an army twice the size of his in the Rhineland. A year later, Charles VI agreed to the same peace terms.

The terms of the Peace of Utrecht included the mutual recognition of Queen Anne in Great Britain and Philip V in Spain, although Philip had to agree to renounce his rights to the French throne. The Emperor received the southern Netherlands and the Spanish lands in Italy as compensation for the loss of the Spanish throne. The duchy of Brandenburg-Prussia was recognized as a kingdom. England received Gibraltar and Minorca, plus Newfoundland and the Hudson's Bay Territory in North America. Holland gained several major fortresses on its southern frontier.

Old King Louis lived another year after the peace. When he finally died in 1715, he had outlived his son and eldest grandson, leaving a five-year-old great-grandson as Louis XV (1715-1774). Of his seventy-two year-reign, forty-six years had been spent in war. These wars saw a dramatic transformation of European warfare, which then remained largely unchanged until 1789.

NOTE

1. Quoted in John Wolf, *Louis XIV* (New York, 1968), p. 282.

Central and Eastern Europe in the Early 18th Century

FINLAND

St. Petersburg

SWEDEN   Cape   GULF OF FINLAND
Oslo   Hanko   Narva Novgorod
NORWAY   ESTONIA
Stockholm   Moscow

NORTH SEA   Riga   Smolensk   RUSSIA

DENMARK   BALTIC SEA   LITHUANIA

                    PRUSSIA   Niemen River

            BRANDENBURG   Minsk
DUTCH   Battles and Sieges ▲
REPUBLIC   SAXONY   Warsaw Vistula River   0   100   200   300
SPANISH   POLAND   Miles
NETHERLANDS GERMANY   Elbe River
Namur   BOHEMIA   UKRAINE
        Weser River   Oder River   Kiev
                                                    Poltava
            Neuf-Brisach   AUSTRIA   Gran
FRANCE   BAVARIA   Vienna Budapest
        Rhine River   HUNGARY
    SWITZERLAND   Drave River
Rhone River   Zenta   TRANSYLVANIA
    SAVOY   Venice   BLACK SEA
Po River Genoa   Belgrade
            ADRIATIC SEA   Danube River
        ITALY   OTTOMAN EMPIRE
                        Constantinopole

21

War in the Early
Eighteenth Century

After the experience of above a century...the pike has given way to the improved musket and bayonet, as to a weapon more universal and adapted to all varieties of situation. The thin order of formation (bringing more men into action where fire is now so material) has become the fundamental one in preference to that on a greater depth....Defensive heavy armour has been laid aside as insufficient against musketry, and productive of more inconvenience than advantage. The lance is also disused, as requiring a man to be covered with heavy armour, and as incompatible with the closeness and vigour of the charge in which the strength of cavalry is allowed to consist. Artillery has been increased, and the use of it improved in a surprising manner.

The internal discipline and economy of the troops have been well established, and the authority of the officers fully founded: nor is there a modern instance of great mutiny or defection; which were so common, when corps and armies were the property of individuals, rather then of the state or prince whom they served.

David Dundas, *Principles of Military Movements* (London, 1788), p. 2. Dundas was a colonel in the British army in the mid-seventeenth century.

The wars of Louis XIV's reign were highly productive of change, especially in weaponry and siegecraft. By the mid-eighteenth century these developments had spread to eastern Europe, and the military forces of the major eastern states became factors in the European balance of power.

One very obvious difference between the armies of 1648 and 1713 was their size. The largest armies in the field during the Thirty Years War were at best 40,000 men, while in the War of the Spanish Succession armies of over 100,000 men were common. The total number of men the large states had under arms surpassed 300,000; France armed 440,000 men in the War of League of Augsburg. In the early eighteenth century, mercenaries troops were less common than previously, and they tended toward long-term service in one army. The rapid changes of allegiance of the earlier era were less usual. The cosmopolitan officer corps remained as aristocratic as ever; the differences in class and culture between it and the private soldiery were perhaps the greatest they had ever been. In battle the differences became even greater. The officer on horseback was permitted to fight his private battles against his opposite number in hand-to-hand combat, or fight a rival within his own army in a duel. The ordinary soldier was obliged to fight as part of an anonymous mass of musketmen.

THE INFANTRY

The infantry composed well over three-fourths of the manpower in the armies of the eighteenth century, a sizeable increase in its proportion of the army. The weapons the infantrymen carried had changed a great deal. One new weapon was the grenade, which was in fact a very ancient weapon, if one thinks of jars of incendiary liquids as grenades. The first known use of a gunpowder grenade dates to 1536. These early devices, which weighed about three pounds, were made of cast iron or thick glass containing several ounces of gunpowder. They resembled a pomegranate, hence the name. They had a slow fuse that usually allowed the grenadier time to throw, but the grenades were nearly as much a threat to him and his fellows as to the enemy. The grenade proved to be unreliable in the field but was reasonably effective in siegework.

The grenadier, who generally carried three devices in a leather pouch, had to be a large and powerful man to throw them far enough to be effective. Their companies came to be made up of the tallest and biggest men in the army. Because they needed to throw easily, grenadiers abandoned the broad tricorn hat standard among eighteenth-century infantrymen for a tall, mitred one. This became their trademark, and made them appear even taller. The Spanish spread the use of the grenade in the seventeenth century. The high point of its use was the War of the League of Augsburg. The difficulties in using it, however, caused a decline in the next century. The distinctive grenadier companies continued to exist, but were turned into elite infantry units.

A far more important change in weaponry was the adoption of the flintlock, or snaphance. The flintlock mechanism, similar to the wheel lock, appeared around 1600. It was a device by which a flint on a trigger was made to strike a piece of steel. The sparks produced fell into a pan full of fine priming powder; this in turn fired the coarser powder in the chamber and propelled the shot. While the flintlock had many of the same problems as the matchlock, such as numerous "flashes in the pan," it was easier to use and more effective. It required only some twenty-five steps to load and fire, compared to forty-three for the matchlock. The proportion of misfires was lower than for a matchlock, and the absence of the smoldering match was a major advantage. On the other hand, it had the problem of the expensive flints breaking, falling out, or wearing down rapidly, and the early flintlock musket was far more costly than the arquebus.

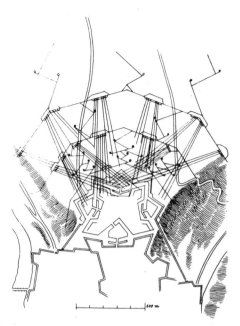

A drawing showing the ideal geometry of Vauban's System of the Three Parallels for laying siege to a fort of around 1700.

For most of the 1600s the cost of the flintlock limited its use to the nobility, who used it for hunting. At mid-century it began to be used by troops assigned to protect the artillery; the absence of the sparking match was the major reason. Adoption by regular musketeer companies was delayed by the cost, and because it required different motions for loading and firing than the matchlock's. Piecemeal adoption was not possible because of the necessity of uniform motion in drill. In 1668 Le Tellier forbade the use of flintlocks by French troops and ordered the intendants to inspect for its use and break the flints of any found. But as improvements in the flintlock were made, James II ordered the English army to adopt it in 1685. Yet, five years later Louis XIV prohibited its use on the penalty of death, largely because of its cost. At virtually the same time, however, the French generals were reporting that their musketmen were picking up flintlocks left on the battlefields by the English and the Dutch, the latter having adopted it in 1690. The French moved to incorporate the flintlock regiment by regiment, since it was now felt that as long as a complete regiment had a standard weapon, the needs for drill were met.

A great variety of flintlocks were produced, but the two major types were the French fusil and the English brown bess. The fusil was four feet, ten inches in length, weighed nine pounds, thirteen ounces, and fired a ball that weighed eighteen to the pound. The larger brown bess reached its final form by 1730; over the next century 7 million were made. The "longland" version was five foot, ten inches in length, weighed eleven pounds, and used a one-ounce ball. There were also a smaller "shortland" model and a still smaller "sea service" version.

The comparative merits of the British and the French muskets have been debated endlessly, but there probably is no answer to the question of whether a lighter weapon or one with greater impact is better on the battlefield. On the parade ground, a musketeer using either model was expected to get off up to five shots in a minute, but there was no chance that number could be achieved on a battlefield. The development of the greased cartridge with both ball and powder helped increase the rate of fire. After the powder and then the ball were dropped down the barrel, the greased paper was used as a wad and tamped down with a ramrod. Most muskets of the era did not have gun sights. The soldiers were not given time to aim; they simply pointed their muskets and fired.

Nearly contemporaneous with the shift to the flintlock was the appearance of the bayonet. This weapon, said to have been developed in the French city of Bayonne, was originally the plug type— a long knife with a tapered handle was stuck into the muzzle of a musket. The device had its problems: it could not be put in place until after the musket had been fired, by which time it was often too late; the men often badly cut themselves trying to shove the bayonet in during the heat of battle; and it frequently fell out. By 1687 the socket bayonet had appeared. The handle of the blade was formed into a sleeve, which fit over the barrel, and tightened on a lug. It was now possible to fix bayonets and continue to load the musket, although musketmen frequently cut themselves while loading. With up to sixteen inches of steel at the end of a five- or six-foot musket, the infantry had for the first time a weapon that combined shock with missile fire. the bayonet was nearly as effective as the pike in keeping heavy cavalry off the infantry, and better when fighting against other infantry. The use of the bayonet meant that the pike could be replaced, a process that began in the French army in 1689. By 1710 the bayonet had spread to all the armies of Europe, although at that date the pike still had its defenders among some of the era's best generals.

At first glance the adoption of the bayonet appears to be merely the substitution of one bladed weapon for another, but it had a major impact on infantry tactics. Drill was simplified, since no longer were two types of infantrymen forced to learn to work together. On the other hand, the soldiers did have to learn two very different actions. The enhanced ability of the infantrymen to defend themselves and the improved firepower of the flintlock allowed the use of an even thinner line, eventually reduced to three ranks and even two in the British army during the American Revolution. At the same time, the distance between each man was reduced considerably, because the flintlock removed the problem of the burning match that had required musketmen to keep a prudent distance between themselves.

By 1700 the English had adopted the tactic of firing by platoons of forty-two men each. The three ranks in a platoon would fire a volley— the first rank kneeling, the second stooping over their shoulders, and the rear rank standing up. Each battalion formed up into sixteen musket platoons and two platoons of grenadiers at the flanks. Having advanced to about sixty yards from the enemy, every third platoon along the line would fire a volley at the colonel's order; then the second group; and then the final third. By then the first group was expected to have reloaded and be ready to fire again—not that it often worked that well on the battlefield. The French for a time after 1700 continued to form up in five ranks and fire by battalions. However, that system largely wasted the rear two ranks and could not muster the continuous fire of the platoon system. By 1740 the French had adopted their own version of the platoon system.

THE CAVALRY

The great firepower possible with the flintlock and the platoon system, and the development of the bayonet for hand-to-hand combat, made the cavalry far less effective in frontal assaults on the infantry. Previously a determined cavalry force often had exploited the infantry's two different weapons which often failed to provide the intended mutual support of musket and pike. After 1700 the cavalry's best use was to exploit its speed and mobility in turning the flank or striking at the rear of the infantry.

By then there were three distinctive types of cavalrymen— dragoons, hussars, and cuirassiers. The dragoons developed out of the mounted arquebusmen of the sixteenth century, and were still regarded as essentially mounted infantrymen. They were armed with carbines (a type of small musket), bayonets, and pistols. In battle they fought mounted or dismounted, and depended on their mobility to strike at the flanks or rear of the enemy. More often they were used for such duties as reconnaissance, seizing bridges and fords, and raiding.

Since dragoons did not have the status or pay of true cavalry, they were recruited from the lower classes. This fact, along with their mobility and the usual ability of mounted men to dominate people on foot, persuaded governments to use them for the dirty business of controlling civilian populations, both in occupied lands and their own. From this came the modern verb dragoon, meaning to force by threat of violence. By the late 1700s, the dragoons made up well over half of the cavalry in most European armies.

The second type, the hussars, was based on the light cavalrymen of eastern Europe. The word itself is Hungarian. Their weapons were generally curved sabers, carbines, and pistols. The hussars' use was similar to that of the dragoons; but in battle their value was primarily harassment and pursuit, since neither in discipline nor in weight could they stand up to heavy infantry and cavalry. The hussars also were used to prevent desertion by patrolling around the camp or line of march. It was their style of dress that most distinguished the hussars. They retained the dress of the Hungarian originals: highly colorful, greatly exaggerated, and with plenty of fur. Both on and off the battlefield the hussars had a reputation for being ill-disciplined and difficult to control. Young noblemen found belonging to the hussars particularly attractive.

Third, there were the heavy cavalrymen, whom the French called cuirassiers and the English the royal horse guards. The French name came from the word for leather because of their extensive use of leather for protection, although they also wore steel breast plates. They also wore a steel helmet, which was not true of the other cavalry types. Their weapons were straight swords and pistols. Some also carried carbines. In addition, by the mid-1700s, the lance had been revived as a weapon for heavy cavalry.

The cuirassiers were the heirs in spirit as well as in blood of the medieval knights, but their effectiveness in battle depended on a high degree of discipline. The first purpose of the heavy cavalry was to drive off the enemy's horse. If that succeeded, and it often took most of the battle, the cavalry turned on the flanks and rear of the infantry. Against both cavalry and infantry, the cuirassiers moved at a trot toward the enemy, firing their pistols or carbines, then charged into the line with cold steel in hand. Only in the later 1700's did the practice of charging into the enemy at full gallop only with a shock weapon, often a lance, return to common use. As had always been true in battles involving mixed forces, eighteenth-century cavalry was most effective in the pursuit of a beaten infantry. Their onslaught on fleeing foot soldiers was often sheer butchery.

THE ARTILLERY

The third branch of every army in this era was the artillery. By then the use of the three- or four-pounder was well integrated with the foot. It was agreed, however, that a well-equipped army also had to have heavier guns, such as sixteen-pounders, for tasks like blasting fieldworks. Case shot and grapeshot were in common use, but the bulk of the shot was still in the form of balls. One of the greatest needs of any army was for a huge number of horses to pull the guns and the wagons with shot and powder. A shortage of horses often was the major reason why armies could move only short distances in the course of a campaigning season.

In battle the guns generally were set on the flanks of the infantry and fired at an oblique angle into the enemy's line, in the expectation that enfilading the enemy would cause more casualties than firing straight into his line. Mortars and howitzers, which were more truly siege weapons, were in common use by 1700. Both guns could use hollow balls packed with powder, which were lit just before touching off the piece. Bad timing or a faulty fuse often resulted in the explosion of the ball a few feet out of the piece or even in it, with devastating results to the gun crew. In the mid-1700's the British developed a bomb fuse that was lit by the windage around the ball as the piece was fired. While far from perfect, it made mortars and howitzers much more useful.

THE CRISIS IN STRATEGY

All of the above developments, especially the great increase in the size of armies, required that generals learn how to handle the new-style armies. The long learning time was one reason for the "crisis in strategy" that has been said to have existed for the forty years after 1680. The wars of that period had few major battles, and even such great battles as Blenheim and Malplaquet were far from decisive. Campaigns often appeared to have been conducted with little clear purpose and a lack of energy. The English writer Daniel Defoe observed that two armies of 150,000 men would pass the campaigning season within sight of one another and spend it "in dodging—or, as it is genteelly termed—observing one another, and then march off into winter quarters."[1]

Certainly the vast size of the armies in that era was one factor in that situation. The logistical requirements for 100,000 men were enormous. The need to bring along the necessary provisions or bring them up from the rear badly slowed the pace of an army. In particular the need to set up and break down portable grain mills and baking ovens was a real restriction on an army's speed. The system of rolling magazines and depots largely ensured that the armies could get their rations, but it greatly restricted the distance that they could cover in a campaign. If an army pushed 300 miles from its base in a season, a general would regard it as a worthy accomplishment. One reason why Marlborough's Blenheim campaign was so highly regarded was the distance he covered and the speed with which he did it. Interdiction of an enemy's supply lines was a task for which dragoons and hussars were well suited.

Another reason for the crisis of strategy was the sheer difficulty of finding a field large enough to deploy 100,000 men in the linear formation of the era. By 1700 an army in battle deployment could stretch for three miles. Even well-drilled troops had problems maintaining their order while marching across open terrain to establish their battle formations. Generals feared being attacked before their army was in complete order; proper formation was regarded as a must. The problem of dragging an artillery train along terrible roads and the lack of horses for moving everything an army would need also slowed its movement.

But the most important reason for the crisis of strategy was the presence of an overwhelming amount of fortification in the key zones of warfare. The threat that the garrison of a bypassed fort presented to the supply lines of an army on the move was greater than ever. The generals almost always decided that they had to halt and take a fort before moving further into enemy territory. This meant that there were more sieges than field battles and many of the battles that did take place were brought about by the arrival of a relief force. Military engineers, who had steadily been increasing in importance, now came into their own as a key component of an army.

VAUBAN

Probably the greatest name in the entire history of military engineering is that of Sebastien de Vauban. Vauban initially had followed a simpler style of fortification, in contrast to the elaborate outworks of the Dutch school. His designs became increasingly complicated as his career progressed, so that he is often said to have had three systems. However, if the terrain demanded it, he often returned to a simple plan late in his life. What is described as Vauban's first system, the work of his early career, was a relatively simple line of defense with ravelins and demi-lunes.

Most of Vauban's forts are placed in his second system, which made greater use of outworks. He returned to the use of towers on the bastions. These bastion towers were a response to an effective siege weapon Vauban himself had developed—ricochet fire. To creat ricochet fire, an artillery piece was loaded with a small charge and elevated; the ball would clear the forward edge of the defensive work, drop down on its top, and bounce for some distance. This type of fire was far more dangerous to the defenders than the full-charged, horizontal fire that was used to blast the masonry of the structure. As ricochet fire became more widely used, Vauban protected the defenders by erecting bastion towers. These were two stories high, with thick walls and roofs, and were equipped with gun platforms and casemates. Improvements in the venting of gunsmoke through flues made the use of guns inside such structures bearable.

The only example of Vauban's third system to be built is the fortress of Neuf-Brisach. Its construction was begun in 1697 on the west bank of the Rhine to protect Alsace. It took fifteen years to complete. Since it was a completely new fortress on level terrain, Vauban was free to implement all of his ideas. Neuf-Brisach is a perfectly symmetrical octagon with eight bastions topped by bastion towers. Powerful in its own right, the main trace was fronted with extensive outworks that extended for 1,000 feet. Both the cost and the amount of land occupied made it difficult to copy Neuf-Brisach.

Vauban's reputation as a builder of fortresses depended heavily on his ability to match his basic plan to any type of terrain and to take advantage of the local topography. He had a great many opportunities to demonstrate this talent; he built or rebuilt fortresses on virtually every type of terrain in every part of France, ranging from forts on the peaks of the Alps and the Pyrenees to ones set directly on the beach. He applied the same principles to the defense of the kingdom as he did to individual fortresses: provide for defense in depth and opportunities for an active defense by the garrisons. On those frontiers where France could expect frequent and powerful attacks, most obviously Flanders, Vauban constructed three lines of forts in the expectation that an invader would exhaust himself before he could break through. The fortresses were also planned so their garrisons could give support to a nearby one under attack.

The fortresses of Vauban's great rival, the Dutchman Menno van Coehorn, the heir of the Dutch school of the Eighty Years War, were even more complicated, with greater use of outworks and wet ditches. Like Vauban, he is known for developing a new weapon, the Coehorn mortar. Since both men were at their height of influence during the War of the League of Augsburg, on several occasions they were asked to reconstruct fortresses originally designed by the other. In particular that was true of Namur in the Spanish Netherlands, which changed hands several times.

EIGHTEENTH-CENTURY SIEGECRAFT

In their own time both Coehorn and Vauban were more highly regarded as siegemasters than as architects. Coehorn's style of attack consisted of a heavy cannonade intended as much to silence the defender's guns as to open breaches, followed by an assault on the bastion, even if the trenches had not reached the covered way. It was very costly in casualties, but by keeping a siege short it probably saved an equal number of men from death by sniper fire and disease.

Vauban regarded such bloody assaults as inhumane. His style of besieging a place was slower and far more methodical, so much so that the term scientific has been used to describe it. Generally he would personally reconnoiter a fortress and decide on the portion of its defenses that appeared the weakest. Usually the targeted section consisted of two bastions and the outworks between them. A siege park was established perhaps a thousand yards away to provide shelter for some 60,000 men who generally made up a siege force in this era. Supplies and equipment for a major siege might have been collected for six months or more. Moving men and materials to the site was a slow and costly process, unless a waterway could be utilized. Vauban had a twenty-mile canal constructed during one siege to facilitate transportation.

The siege park was set within lines of countervallation and circumvallation; both were field works consisting of a ditch and earthen works. When these were completed, the main elements of the siege force moved in. The train included perhaps eighty heavy siege guns, generally twenty-four-pounders, and a great number of lighter guns and mortars.

When all had arrived, the engineers would direct the laborers and soldiers in digging the first parallel about 600 yards from the outermost point of the defensive works. This was called the opening of the trenches and was considered the official beginning of the siege. It was done at night so that some protection for the diggers was created before the enemy gunners could open fire. A well-stocked fortress, however, might fire random shots during the night at points where the first parallel was expected to be built in order to disrupt the work. An enormous number of gabions, which were cylinders made of sticks, and fascines, bundles of sticks, would have been prepared in advance. The gabions were placed at the inside edge of the first parallel and filled with dirt from the trench. Fascines were placed atop them. When completed, the first parallel was four to five feet deep and six to ten feet wide. It was now a covered way where men and equipment could move quite safely.

Then six to ten emplacements for the batteries were prepared just in front of the first parallel, and the siege guns were dragged into place and fired. The purpose at this point was more to reduce the garrison and damage its artillery rather than to batter the works. Once all this was done, the first trenches were dug forward from the first parallel. Those who dug the trenches, the sappers, were well paid, but they rarely had any opportunity to spend their wages. The trenches were zigzagged so the defenders could not get a clear shot down them. The best engineers could lay out zigzags that moved forward the most directly without exposing them to enfilading fire.

After pushing forward about 300 yards, the sappers then dug the second parallel, and the siege guns were dragged up to new emplacements. By now the trenches had come close enough to the defenders that sorties could quickly reach the sappers and the guns. Should they get control of the guns, if only for a few minutes, they would render them useless by driving spikes into the touchholes. Spiked guns were not destroyed, but took a long time to repair. To counter sorties, units of infantry were kept in ready in the second parallel. The sappers again pushed forward another set of zigzags, even tighter than the first set, and then dug the third parallel about sixty or seventy yards from the covered way. The siege guns were brought forward to point-blank range, and serious battering of the defensive works began. Two or three days of continuous firing usually created a breach. If the mortars, small guns and the infantrymen with their muskets had been doing their job, the garrison would have been greatly reduced.

Coehorn usually launched an assault at this point. Vauban, however, was more cautious. He pushed a third set of zigzags up the glacis toward the covered way. As they approached the covered way, grenadiers and musketmen in the trenches took on the defenders on the covered way. Once the covered way was "crowned" and lodgements secured on it, the heavy guns were brought up to silence any of the defenders' pieces still firing, and to open more breaches. A great number of fascines were thrown into the ditch to make the passage of the breach easier. Then came the moment for the assault on the breach, usually at daybreak in order to assemble men and materials during darkness. Often it was the only time when the outcome depended on hard fighting between sizeable forces. Such an assault was so costly in manpower, especially to the attackers, that a failed assault could cause the siege to be given up. Generally, however, the attackers had an overwhelming advantage in manpower and successfully pushed the assault through the defensive works.

Yet sieges rarely reached the point of an assault in this era. It was widely agreed that continued resistance after the attackers had crowned the covered way was hopeless. The governor of the fortress, declaring himself to be caught in the toils of geometry, would ask for and be given honorable terms of surrender. Such terms allowed the garrison to march out with their standards flying, and perhaps with their heavy guns, and preserved the lives and property of the townspeople. If the defense was continued to a successful assault, the lives of all inside were at the disposal of the commander of the siege force.

Vauban estimated that a proper siege should take forty days from the opening of the trenches to the assault on the breaches. Given the tremendous amount of preparation time needed before the opening of the trenches could occur, it is easy to see why an army could hope to carry out only one major siege in a summer.

The War of the Spanish Succession was the ultimate war of siegecraft. Even Marlborough, justly famous for his eagerness to fight and his ability to bring his foes to battle, engaged in only seven major battles in that war, while conducting thirty sieges. The war was carried on in the Spanish Netherlands, the Rhineland, and the Po valley; all were very extensively fortified. It is easy to see why progress in these war zones would be very slow, and it gives support to the theory of a crisis of strategy during the era.

TURKISH-HABSBURG WARS

If indeed there was such a crisis during the years 1680-1720, by the time of the next major war in 1740, it had largely disappeared. A major reason was the movement of the war zones away from those of Louis XIV's time.

The emergence of Austria, Prussia, and Russia as major military powers and allies of the powers of western Europe created new zones of conflict that were far less heavily fortified.

The Habsburg states of central Europe had been a significant factor in war since 1500, but their resources had always been heavily diverted to the nearly constant war with the Ottoman Empire. Even in the Thirty Years War, when Habsburg forces concentrated on Germany, they were several times distracted by Ottoman attacks. Fortunately for the Habsburgs, however, that war coincided with a period of political instability in the Turkish state. In 1648 Mohammed IV became sultan. While not a strong ruler himself, during his reign there emerged a a series of able grand viziers from the Kiuprili family, who restored Ottoman military might for several decades. By 1663 the Turks felt strong enough to resume the offensive against Habsburg Hungary. The Habsburgs had spent considerable money in building modern fortresses along the frontier and the invasion routes, while Turkish siegecraft, and especially the quality of their artillery, had not kept up with western advances. Thus the Ottoman advance of 200,000 men into Habsburg territory stalled. In late 1664 an eighteen-year truce was signed.

In 1676 the third of the Kiuprili grand viziers, Kara Mustafa, took office. He was determined to resume the war against Christendom. Once the truce with Austria ended, he spent a year gathering a huge army. In March 1683, for the first time in a century the sultan himself led the army into the field. In the same month, the Holy Roman Emperor Leopold I formed an alliance with John Sobieski, King John III of Poland. Sobieski had been elected king in 1674 largely because of his reputation for battling the Turks. Besides the pope, he was the only Christian leader eager to organize a new crusade against the Turks.

THE SIEGE OF VIENNA

In June 1683, the Turks commanded by Kara Mustafa (the sultan had remained at Belgrade) left Budapest and marched to to Vienna. They reached the city on July 14. An Austrian army of 30,000 men led by Duke Charles of Lorraine retreated to the west of the city, while inside Count von Starhemberg commanded a 15,000-man garrison. Vienna's defenses had been largely built in the late 1500s, with a few outworks added after 1650. As they had in 1529, the Turks concentrated their siegeworks at the southwest corner of the city. Their attack was hampered by a lack of siege guns, but they still put more faith in mining anyway. On August 12,the Turks were able to secure a lodgement on a ravelin, and they held it despite fierce counterattacks. By September 1, the Turks were attacking the main bastions. A breach was opened in one, but an assault was driven back. By September 8 the garrison had been reduced to 4,000 men.

Preparations were being made for hand-to-hand combat in the houses and streets of Vienna, when, in the most dramatic fashion, word came of the arrival of a large relief army to the west. King John Sobieski, although completely committed to the relief of Vienna, had had difficulty gathering an army. Generally the Poles assembled in midsummer and fought until

November. It was only in early August that the Poles began to move toward Austria. Being mostly cavalry, the Polish army did move fast, reaching the Danube on September 5. They crossed on a pontoon bridge, and linked up with Charles of Lorraine's army and forces from Saxony and Bavaria. Sobieski took supreme command of the allied army of about 76,000 men. A week later, the vanguard of his army descended from the hills of the Vienna woods.

Mustafa's lack of knowledge of siegecraft revealed itself in his failure to build a line of circumvallation for his siegeworks. Despite that Sobieski's army had a great deal of hard fighting, but it finally broke into the Turkish camp. Sorties by the garrison added to the Turkish problems. By dark the Ottoman forces had collapsed in disarray. Sobieski refused to push a hard pursuit, so the grand vizier and about half of his 150,000 men escaped. After taking several days to savor their great victory, Sobieski and his army chased after the retreating Turks. In late October they took the major fortress of Gran and gained control of northwest Hungary. That was the last straw for the sultan; he ordered the execution of Kara Mustafa. Sobieski, under pressure from his own men and the Habsburgs, returned to Poland in December. He remained committed to the war against the Turks, but waged it in the Ukraine. At his death in 1696 he had made no major gain. Niether he nor Poland gained anything directly from the relief of Vienna, although his fame is firmly fixed in history.

EUGENE OF SAVOY
    The boost that the victory at Vienna gave the Habsburgs continued into the next years, despite the outbreak of the War of the League of Augsburg. For the next fourteen years, the war zone moved back and forth across central Hungary. By 1697 Emperor Leopold had found a most capable young general in Eugene of Savoy. After Louis XIV slighted him, Eugene offered his services to Leopold and rapidly rose to command the Austrian army. Like Marlborough, he was eager to give battle to the foe and was determined to create a mobile force.

In 1697 he led an Austrian army of 50,000 men to counter an Ottoman force twice that size that had crossed into southern Hungary. The new sultan, Mustafa II, was not eager for battle, but Eugene was. When Eugene heard that the Turks were crossing a river near Zenta on a makeshift bridge, he rushed his forces there. When he arrived, he found that the Ottoman infantry and some cavalry were still on his side of the river. Despite the exhaustion of his men, he decided to attack at once. Sultan Mustafa ordered his spahis back across the bridge, preventing the escape of his troops still on Eugene's side. The Turks lost 30,000 men versus 2,100 for Eugene. The devastating defeat at Zenta forced the Ottoman state to do something it had never done before: negotiate a peace treaty with the Christians. In January 1699, the Treaty of Karlowitz established Habsburg sovereignty over Hungary.

Despite Zenta, Ottoman power was far from crushed; but the Ottoman Empire was nearly always on the defensive for the remainder of its existence. The decline of Turkish power was largely the consequence of their failure to keep up with western military developments and changes in their own army. By 1700 the Janissary corps had lost its unique character and discipline. Now the recruits came largely from the Muslim population, and positions had become hereditary. The corps frequently mutinied and had become a major factor in the rise and fall of sultans and grand viziers. The Turkish cavalry had also declined, partly because Turkish landlords, still the source of the cavalrymen, were becoming reluctant to serve, and partly because, having changed little in three centuries, it was vulnerable to the flintlock and bayonet of the Christian armies. More and more the sultan had to draw on the Tartar horsemen of Crimea, a vassal state north of the Black Sea. The Ottoman Empire continued to be a player in the wars in eastern Europe, but the days when the Turks posed a clear threat to Central Europe were over.

PETER THE GREAT

While Austria largely filled the void created by the decline of Ottoman power, Russia also took advantage of Turkish decline to become a major power. The Russian army in the early 1600s was truly in dismal shape. The Russian nobles, who formed the cavalry, still used the bow, rode horses that were gun-shy, and totally lacked discipline. Czar Ivan IV (1534-80) had created a corps of musketmen, the *streltsy*, who were somewhat more effective. But when Russia found itself in wars against Sweden and Poland in the early 1600s, even the streltsy were badly overmatched. After 1630 the czars began to hire westerners to introduce drill, siegecraft, and gun casting to their people. Nonetheless, for the remainder of the seventeenth century, the Russians relied on massive numbers of barely trained conscripted peasants. They died in masses in any war, but their sacrifices did enable Russia to expand its borders in every direction.

It was Peter the Great (1689-1725) who turned Russia into an important military power. Beginning with a play army of make-believe soldiers who drilled and fought mock battles, the young Peter began to create a modern army by integrating his now-skilled play soldiers into the regular army. Convinced that Russia had a great deal to learn from the West, Peter embarked on his famous trip to Holland and England in March 1697. In particular he learned the craft of shipbuilding in Holland, but was also busy hiring officers, sergeants, and technicians to take back to Russia. Forced to cut his trip short because of a mutiny by the streltsy in July 1698, Peter set to work to modernize his army. He broke up the streltsy regiments and created western-style ones with both volunteers and conscripts. The regiments were drilled by western sergeants and largely commanded by western officers.

Well before his new army was ready for war, Peter found himself involved in a major conflict called the Great Northern War. Its cause was the succession in 1697 of fifteen-year-old Charles XII to the Swedish throne. Sweden's neighbors—Denmark, Poland, Russia, and Saxony—smarting from a century of defeat at Swedish hands, formed an alliance to take advantage of the young king's inexperience. They could not have made a worse mistake. Charles was obsessed with the military. One story about him relates that he was so convinced that he was the next Alexander the Great that he tried to learn Greek. When the allies invaded Sweden in 1698, he became totally dedicated to the complete destruction of the two men he regarded as the instigators: Augustus the Strong, duke of Saxony and the elected king of Poland, and Peter of Russia.

In 1700 a Polish-Saxon force attacked the Swedish stronghold of Riga on the eastern Baltic Coast, while Peter personally led 34,000 men to lay siege to Narva in eastern Estonia. Two westerners served as siegemasters for the Russians. Charles landed with 16,000 men on the Baltic coast in November and moved to relieve Narva first. The Swedes charged out of the woods surrounding Narva at full speed and easily broke the line of circumvallation. The Russian cavalry fled at first contact, and the infantry was quickly overrun. The next spring Charles relieved Riga and pursued the fleeing Saxon-Polish army into Poland.

These two victories established Charles' reputation for speed and decisiveness, which was further proven in the next five years as he occupied Poland, deposed Augustus the Strong, and had his own candidate elected king of Poland. Charles, however, largely ignored the Russians, despite their capture of Narva in 1704. Thus Peter was given the time to build a potent army with the help of numerous foreigners, especially Scotsmen. His army was soon transformed into a reasonably modern and effective force.

Peter took advantage of the period of Swedish neglect to occupy the land at the head of the Gulf of Finland. He began to build a powerful fortress on the future site of Saint Petersburg. Having gained access to the sea, he also began to build a navy. Because the Gulf of Finland and the Baltic are much like the Mediterranean, many of the ships built were galleys, which proved invaluable in the battle for control of the many islands and bays of the Baltic.

In 1708 Charles turned his attention back to Russia. Driving due east from Poland, he intended to take Moscow and split Russia in half. The Russians staged a fighting retreat toward Moscow while destroying everything of any use to the Swedes. Faced with the terrifying prospect of trying to reach Moscow in the late fall over a route devastated by the Russians' scorched-earth policy, Charles decided to turn south to the Ukraine. There he expected to find forage and get aid from the Cossacks and the Turks.

In April 1709 the Swedes laid siege to the fortress of Poltava, southeast of Kiev, which sat on the route between Moscow and the Black Sea. In June Peter arrived with a relief force of 45,000 men. Leaving 5,000 in the siege lines, Charles moved out with 25,000 men to give battle to the Russians before his manpower disadvantage became worse. Halting some distance away, Peter had time to build a sophisticated set of field works before the Swedes attacked. Skillfully using their field defenses, the Russians brought the Swedish attack to a halt. They then moved out into the open field to repulse a second assault and drive the Swedes off the field. The ability of the Russian soldiers to leave their defensive works and successfully form their lines was convincing evidence of Peter's transformation of his army.

The 15,000 Swedes who escaped from Poltava were forced to surrender two days later 100 miles to the south, where they were trapped against the Dnieper River. Charles and some of his officers escaped into Ottoman territory. There he spent five years trying to convince the Turks to declare war on Peter. Meanwhile, Peter had occupied much of the eastern Baltic coastline. In 1714 the Russian fleet, Peter's real pride and joy, defeated the Swedes, which had dominated the Baltic for a century, off Cape Hanko, the southwest point of Finland. The battle is also significant for the extensive use of galleys. In fact the Russian fleet had 416 galleys by 1720.

Shortly after the Battle of Hanko, Charles returned to Sweden and restored Swedish power. The Danes had taken advantage of his absence to invade Sweden. After driving them out, he invaded Danish-ruled Norway. There he was killed in 1718 by a musket ball while supervising a siege. His death in the trenches was a sad demise for the last European king who personally led his troops into battle.

Having taken control of the Baltic, Peter sent raids against the Swedish coast in 1719. This prompted the Swedish government to open peace negotiations, which resulted in the Treaty of Nystad of 1721. The treaty largely restored the prewar status quo, except in regard to Russia, which kept its conquests on the east Baltic coast. This gave Peter his "window to the West," where he built a new capital city, Saint Petersburg. Before his death in 1725, Peter had also turned his new war machine against the Persian Empire, which ruled the land north of the Caspian Sea. Russian successes there laid the foundation of the Russian empire in central Asia.

Peter the Great turned the Russian military into a force to be reckoned with in the wars of Europe, even if it still stood in the second rank. The survival of the Russian army as a powerful force despite the fifteen years of political instability that followed his death makes the level of his achievement even more outstanding. And when in 1756 Russia did get involved in a major war against the best general of the century, it had notable success despite having as its commander in chief Czarina Elizabeth, who had little interest in the military.

NOTE

1. Quoted by David Chandler, *The Art of Warfare in the Age of Marlborough* (London, 1976), p. 14.

Frederick The Great's Wars

22

The Wars of Frederick the Great

The greatest force of the Prussian army resides in their wonderful regularity of formation, which long custom has made a habit; in exact obedience and in the bravery of the troops. The discipline of these troops...has such effect that amidst the greatest confusion of an action and the most evident perils their disorder still is more orderly than the good order of their enemies. Consequently, small confusions are redressed and all evolutions made promptly. A general of other troops could be surprised in circumstances in which he would not be if commanding Prussians, since he will find resources in the speed with which they form and maneuver in the presence of the enemy. Prussians' discipline renders these troops capable of executing the most difficult maneuvers, such as traversing a wood in battle without losing their files or distances, advancing in close order at double time, forming with promptness, reversing their direction suddenly to fall on the flank of the enemy, gaining an advantage by a forced march, and in surpassing the enemy in constancy and fortitude.

Frederick II, *Instructions for his Generals,* trans. Thomas Phillips (Harrisburg, Penn., 1960), p. 22. Frederick wrote these instructions in 1747 intending to keep them secret. The Austrians captured a copy and published them in 1761.

The modernization of the Russian army became an increasingly important factor in the European balance of power after 1750. Yet even this development was overshadowed by the stupendous rise of the Prussian military. The real heart of the state called the kingdom of Prussia was the duchy of Brandenburg, centered around Berlin in eastern Germany. Through inheritance and successful alliances in the wars of the seventeenth century, Brandenburg's ruling family, the Hohenzollerns, gained lands to the east (the duchy of East Prussia), to the west (several small principalities on the lower Rhine and the Dutch border), and to the north (western Pomerania on the Baltic coast). Except for Pomerania, these lands were widely separated from Brandenburg itself. The Hohenzollerns were eager to win con-

trol of the lands in between in order to make their state a contiguous unit.
With their lands stretching across northern Europe from the Netherlands
to Russia, the Hohenzollerns became involved in every war from 1618 on.

The father of Prussian militarism was Duke Frederick William I.
Taking the throne in 1640, at a time when his state was near collapse in the
Thirty Years War, he rebuilt his army and came out of the war with significant territorial gains and a veteran army. Rather than disband his army,
as most German princes did after 1648, he was determined to strengthen
it. In order to get the estates of his various lands to agree to levy a permanent tax, he agreed in 1653 to confirm all existing privileges of the nobility and other elites. In turn they allowed the ducal officials to assess and
collect taxes instead of doing it themselves, as was traditional. By the end
of his life in 1688, Frederick William had increased the size of his army to
45,000 men, large enough to be a factor in the European balance of power
and huge in respect to his lands' population and wealth. The next duke,
Frederick III, was not the militarist his father had been, but he did agree
to join the anti-French coalition in the War of Spanish Succession. He
gained the title of king in Prussia in the peace of 1713.

The now King Frederick I died the same year, and his son Frederick
William I, called the Royal Drill Sergeant, took the throne. He was obsessed with the need for obedience, discipline, and hard work from both
his subjects and soldiers. The General War Commissary created by his
grandfather now became the bureaucracy for the entire state. It oversaw
every aspect of the state's activities, including religion and education. The
purpose was to direct virtually all of the Prussian state's energies and money to the army. The army itself collected the taxes.

Frederick William also tightened the alliance between the monarch and
the nobles of East Prussia, known as the Junkers. The tradition of military
service became so engrained in these families that the word "Junker" became a synonym for Prussian officer. The nobles agreed that every peasant
would be conscripted into the army at age twenty for two years of service
and after that spend several months in drill. Prussian officers and sergeants,
many of whom were foreigners, soon gained a reputation for brutality in
drilling their men and instilling strict discipline.

Frederick William was closely involved in every aspect of military life.
It was he who chose the plain Prussian blue uniforms, regarding the old
ones as too French. He also was largely responsible for adopting the iron
ramrod to replace the wooden one in use. Wood had been used because
it feared that iron rods would throw sparks and touch off the powder in the
chamber, but wooden rods often broke in use. His very frequent presence
on the drill field gave him the nickname of Royal Drill Sergeant, but his
greatest obsession was for tall soldiers. He formed a grenadier regiment of
3,000 men all over six feet tall. The surest way to curry favor with him
was to send him some giants for the regiment.

Yet despite the king's obsession with his army, he never sent it to war.
It was said that he loved his soldiers too much to bear to see any of them
die in war. That was certainly not true of his son, Frederick the Great,
who within six months of his succession in 1740 was involved in a bloody

Eighteenth-century Musketmen at drill.

war with Austria. That Frederick would become one of the most famous names in military history could hardly have been anticipated when he was young. He was far more interested in French philosophy and culture, and did not look and dress like the giant grenadiers his father so admired. Frederick William literally beat these characteristics out of his son and turned him into a soldier, although the son never gave up entirely his interest in French learning. The young prince was given a regiment to command, and he worked his way up the chain of command. By the time he gained the throne, he was highly knowledgeable in military matters.

THE WAR OF THE AUSTRIAN SUCCESSION

Frederick had been king for only a few months when an opportunity to use his 83,000 man army presented itself. The death of Emperor Charles VI left the Habsburg crowns without a direct male successor. Charles had arranged that the estates of his many lands and the nations of Europe would recognize of the right of his daughter Maria Theresa to succeed him. Prussia was one of the states that had agreed. But upon Charles' death, Frederick, while recognizing Maria Theresa's right to rule most of the Habsburg lands, claimed the large and wealthy duchy of Silesia, to the southeast of Brandenburg, on the grounds that its law of succession prohibited a female from ruling. He proclaimed that he was a relative of the last duke of Silesia. In December 1740 he sent his army into the duchy.

The far better prepared Prussian army easily mopped up the small and surprised Austrian garrisons. Frederick, convinced that the successful four-month campaign was over, offered to recognize Maria Theresa as ruler of all the other lands of Charles VI if she recognized him as duke of Silesia. Maria Theresa responded by sending an army to retake the duchy and seeking allies across Europe. The old Habsburg rivalry with France prevented an alliance with that realm, although France had no interest in seeing Prussia become more powerful. Maria Theresa had better luck with Britain and the Netherlands. In early 1741, an Austrian force of 17,000 men, one-third cavalry, moved into Silesia.

Frederick had not expected such a move, and found his route back to Brandenburg had been cut off. He commanded 23,000 men, of whom 5,000 were cavalry. The king decided he had to fight to break through to safety. In April 1741, the two armies clashed at Mollwitz. The Austrian cavalry struck much more quickly than the Prussian and drove it off the field. The Austrian cavalry then turned on the enemy infantry and began to drive it back. Frederick's officers persuaded him to flee the battlefield before he was captured. Despite the flight of the king, the Prussian infantry rallied and used its numerical advantage to drive off the Austrians. Thus Frederick won his first real battle even if he was not present for most of it.

Frederick reacted sharply to the failure of his cavalry at Mollwitz. He decided that it had been caused by the slowness of its charge, and ordered the horsemen to strike into the enemy lines at full gallop. In 1744 he further ordered that the gallop was to begin 200 paces from the enemy so that the horses would be at top speed at contact. During their charge the cuirassiers were to stand up in their stirrups and hold their swords overhead. At contact they were to bring their swords down in a powerful stroke on the foe. Almost always opening the battle in that way, the Prussian heavy cavalry became a significant factor in Frederick's many victories.

After the battle of Mollwitz, it was clear that Austria would not concede Silesia without a hard fight. The war quickly spread. France, in alliance with the duke of Bavaria, who had a claim to the entire Habsburg inheritance, invaded Bohemia in October 1741. Britain and the Netherlands joined the war as allies of Austria.

Britain had already been involved in a naval conflict with Spain, which is humorously known as the War of Jenkins' Ear. Jenkins was a sea captain engaged in smuggling goods into the Spanish colonies, as were many Englishmen. Spanish efforts to stop them were often violent and were much resented. In early 1739 Jenkins returned from a smuggling expedition with his ear in a bottle. He claimed the Spanish had cut it off. The claim enraged a large part of the British merchant class, who were eager for a war to open the Spanish colonies to trade. In October Britain declared war on Spain. Still another old rivalry flared into war when Sweden, pressed by France, declared war on Russia, an ally of Austria's. But the clash of the titans, Britain and France, did not officially begin until 1744.

The main theater of war in 1741-42 continued to be the Austrian lands. In May 1742, two battles in Silesia, ten days apart, revealed that the changes that Frederick was effecting in his cavalry were paying off—his cavalry drove the foe off the field in both battles. In June the Austrian government conceded the loss of Silesia, which ended temporarily the war between Austria and Prussia. The war continued, however, with most of the fighting for the next two years taking place in Bavaria and the Rhine valley. Tempted by the absence of so large a part of the Austrian army, Frederick marched back into Bohemia in August 1744. In a brief siege he took Prague at the cost of only fifty men. This easy success was soon counterbalanced by his inability to bring the Habsburg forces to battle. The Hungarian light cavalry, the original hussars, who were fighting for the first time for the Habsburgs in large numbers, effectively harassed Frederick's army, which had little light cavalry. He was forced to retreat into Silesia with heavy losses. There he set to work to strengthen his hussar corps.

THE BATTLE OF CULLODEN

With formal war between France and Britain clearly impending, Louis XV decided to create a distraction for the British. He encouraged Charles Stuart, grandson of the deposed James II, to go to Scotland to lead a revolt of the Highlanders against "German George," who was duke of Hanover as well as George II of Great Britain. It must be said, however, that the support France gave to the Jacobites, as the Stuart supporters were called, was very limited. In August 1745 Bonnie Prince Charlie landed with a few retainers in northern Scotland. In two weeks he had collected 4,000 clansmen and began to move southward. Easily slipping past the British army sent to deal with him, Charles entered Edinburgh in mid-September. The British army rushed back to the city, only to be soundly defeated. The ferocious charge of the Highlanders using the broadsword easily reached the British lines and broke them.

Rather than consolidating his control of Scotland, Charles crossed into England, whose crown he also claimed. He was convinced that most Englishmen supported him, and he also needed a solid success in battle if he wished to get meaningful French aid. With a force of about 6,000 men, including many Irishmen, he reached Derby 130 miles north of London, in early December. The Jacobite force had raced by two British armies, but they were in hot pursuit, and a third was in position north of London. Charles very reluctantly agreed to retreat to Scotland without giving battle. But the decision broke the heart of his cause, because many of the men with him had joined in anticipation of pillaging the capital of their ancient enemy. Back in Scotland, Charles engaged a British army at Falkirk in January 1746, and was victorious. Instead of pursuing it, he laid siege to Stirling Castle. Quickly tiring of the inactivity of a siege, many of his men slipped away from his army. A month later, he agreed to a strategic retreat back to the Highlands.

George II's son, the duke of Cumberland, had taken command of the British forces in Scotland, a total of about 10,000 men. By April he had caught up to the Jacobite army near Inverness, where Charles decided to make a stand. Against the advice of his Highlander officers, he chose Culloden Moor as the site to take on Cumberland. A flat, open field, it was highly suitable for cavalry and artillery, of which he had little and the British had a great deal. Perhaps realizing his disadvantage, Charles decided to attempt a surprise attack on the British camp. His men marched through the night, only to find that they were still two miles away at daybreak. They returned exhausted to Culloden, where most fell asleep on the wet ground.

When Cumberland heard of the overnight march, he rushed his army to Culloden to take advantage of the Jacobite weariness. Informed that the British army was four miles away, the Jacobite officers made frantic efforts to wake their men and form them into a line. About 4,000 Scots faced 9,000 regular British troops. The Jacobites had six guns, while their foes had five battalions of artillery, mostly three-pounders.

The Scots opened the battle with a few stray cannon shots; the British answered with a devastating barrage. Prince Charles, at the rear of his army, could not see what was happening, and his men had to take a bloody pounding until he ordered a charge. The dreaded Highlander charge never reached its full potential. Exhaustion, uncertainty about orders, and pique on the part of one clan that was not given its usual place of honor in the line all reduced the weight of the charge. Thunderous volleys of musket fire easily broke the charge before more than a handful of Jacobites reached the British line. The battle quickly became a slaughter of the Highlanders. In the months that followed, the British government exacted a brutal revenge on the Scots. For his part, Prince Charles managed to reach France after five months of wandering in northern Scotland.

Culloden was the last battle ever fought on British soil. It can also be called the last battle in Europe in which the discipline formed by kinship and clan ties was a factor. The battle provided a strong contrast between kinship-based discipline, found in the Jacobite army, and modern drill-based discipline of Cumberland's men. Yet it should not be taken as clear proof of the superiority of drill. Had the numbers been more equal and the Jacobite army handled better, the outcome might well have been different.

THE WAR ON THE CONTINENT

Having crushed the Scots revolt, Britain formally entered the war in alliance with Austria, Saxony, and the Netherlands against France, Bavaria, and Prussia. Flanders again became a major theater of war. Marshal de Saxe, author of a valuable commentary on war, the *Reveries*, advanced on Tournai with 70,000 French troops. The duke of Cumberland arrived with an army of 52,000 men. Leaving 20,000 men in the siege lines at Tournai, de Saxe brought out his forces to block the enemy's advance. The two armies met at Fontenoy. The French had time to build a set of field works. After initial contact, Cumberland decided to force the center of the French line with 16,000 infantry, mostly British. Before the charge began, a British colonel stepped to the front of his line, saluted the French and drank a toast, and, according to one source, even offered to allow them to fire first.

This episode is often used to demonstrate the high level of chivalry in this era, but many historians fail to mention that while the French were returning the salute, the British fired a murderous volley. With the advantage thus gained, they broke the French lines. However, with effective use of cavalry and artillery, de Saxe was able to reestablish his line and drive the enemy off the field. He proceeded to take Tournai and several other large cities in Flanders.

Meanwhile in central Europe, the Austrians and the Prussians had spent the spring of 1745 in maneuvering, until they clashed at Hohenfried-burg in Silesia in June. Frederick followed the retreating Austrians back into Bohemia but could not force another battle before they had been re-inforced. In late September Charles of Lorraine, Maria Theresa's husband, caught Frederick by surprise. After a forced night march, Charles was in a strong position on the rear of the Prussian army at daybreak. In this Battle of Soor, Charles had a decided manpower advantage—41,000 men versus 22,000. Charles, however, was slow to move to the attack, and Frederick regained the initiative. He started his army in a huge right-hand wheel, but before the wheel was completed, he ordered his forces to attack. The result was a formation in which his right wing, much stronger than his left, acted as a spearhead, while the left wing remained behind, or was "refused." The Austrians had expected the Prussians to retreat and hoped to catch them in the disorder of a retreat. The sudden attack caught them by surprise. The Prussian right easily broke the Austrian left, and pro-ceeded to roll up their center

This battle was the origin of Frederick's "oblique attack" formation. In its final form it consisted of a powerful advance guard in one wing. The rest of the regiments were set back on a diagonal some twenty to fifty paces behind the previous regiment. The opposite wing was deployed well be-hind the forward elements of the first wing. The well drilled Prussian in-fantry was capable of quickly forming the oblique formation on either wing upon the commander's assessment of which of the enemy's flanks appeared the more vulnerable.

The Prussian victory at Soor, and three more in 1745, persuaded Maria Theresa to sign another peace treaty with Frederick in December. Fighting continued for another two years in the western theater, where de Saxe continued to push his advantage in the Austrian Netherlands and even crossed the frontier into the Dutch republic in late 1747.

French victories there were balanced, however, by British successes in the colonial and naval war (King George's War). Well supported by the British navy, the colonial militia took the great fortress of Louisbourg on Cape Breton Island in the Gulf of Saint Lawrence in 1745. That siege was probably the first time siege artillery was used in North America. The British also had considerable success in India, but when peace terms were worked out in 1748, the status quo in the colonial lands was reestablished. In Europe the same was true, except that Prussia's control of Silesia was recognized. Maria Theresa was confirmed as ruler of all the other Habs-burg lands, while her husband was elected Holy Roman Emperor.

THE DIPLOMATIC REVOLUTION

The peace was hardly more than a truce, for the major contentions amongst the European powers were left unsolved. A new resentment was one the Austrians had against Britain for what they regarded as the miser-able level of support Britain had provided during the war. Still determined to recover Silesia, they began to make diplomatic overtures to France, since the old rivalry did not have the hold that it once did. By May 1756 Austria had persuaded France to enter into an alliance, which Russia also joined. Czarina Elizabeth was motivated largely by a deep hatred of Frederick II, whom she often called "that atheist." Meanwhile, the British negotiated with Frederick, since George II was eager to protect his homeland, the duchy of Hanover. Thus occurred the so-called "Diplomatic Revolution." Perhaps that term is a little over-dramatic for what happened, but it seems appropriate enough for the end to 250 years of constant Habsburg-French hostilities.

With Russia and Sweden also committing themselves to the Franco-Austrian alliance, Frederick, well aware of its purpose, decided to strike at his enemies first. Since 1748 he had been improving his forces, especially his cavalry, and had fortified the frontiers of Silesia. He planned a quick strike into Saxony, still an Austrian ally. He expected that Austria and France would not be able to cooperate well after so long a record of conflict, and felt that Russia was not strong enough to be a real factor in a war. Therefore, in August 1756, without a declaration of war, he led a force of 70,000 men into Saxony. An Austrian army of 50,000 men moved into Saxony to help defend it. In October the Prussians defeated the Saxon-Austrian forces on the border of Bohemia. Frederick occupied the duchy and impressed 16,000 Saxon troops into his own army.

THE SEVEN YEARS WAR

In April 1757, the Prussian king invaded Bohemia in order to keep the initiative. His army crossed into Bohemia in four widely separated columns and gathered before Prague in early May. Charles of Lorraine decided to make a stand outside the city. The two armies were about equal, with 65,000 men each. Frederick decided to push an attack on his foes despite their holding the high ground where they had set a large number of field pieces. He sent most of his cavalry to envelop the Austrian right flank. Although it took heavy casualties, the Prussian horse succeeded in driving off the Austrian cavalry. Charles had to turn part of his line to meet the threat on his flank, and a gap opened at the pivot point in his line. Frederick recognized the opportunity and drove eighteen battalions into the gap, splitting the enemy army in two. The Austrians were forced back to Prague. As often was true in his battles, Frederick lost more men than his foe, 14,300 men versus 13,400. Frederick put Prague under siege, but a month later Marshal von Daun of Austria came to its relief. Daun won the battle of Kolin and so reduced the Prussian army that it had to return to Silesia.

By July 1757 the anti-Prussian alliance of France, Austria, and Russia had three large armies moving on Prussia. An English army trying to protect Hanover was badly defeated in Hanover in July, allowing the French to move on eastward. Four days later the Russians defeated a Prussian force in East Prussia. Expecting that bad roads and poor logistics would greatly slow the Russian advance, Frederick divided his forces in two. His plan was to meet the French coming from the west and the

Austrians from the south, and prevent their conjunction. In early November, the army he led came upon the 64,000 men of a combined force of French and Germans at Rossbach near Leipzig. Despite having only half that number of men, the Prussian king decided to attack, in order to catch the enemy on the march. The speed of his infantry enabled it to wheel in a right-angle turn and drive into the allied forces while they were attempting their own flanking motion. The allies were totally routed in half a hour. The Prussian cavalry pursued vigorously and inflicted 8,000 casualties, compared to 300 for their own side.

The Prussians had no time to savor their victory, for Daun had moved into Silesia. Frederick rushed back to meet him. The Austrian commander had time to choose a proper field for his 65,000-man army, and selected a plateau near the village of Leuthen. The field chosen had a marsh at one flank and a river at the other, but the Austrian line had to be nearly four miles long to fill the field. Furthermore, the field was fronted by a row of low hills, which masked the maneuvers of the advancing Prussians, 35,000 strong.

Frederick's method of raising morale among his troops is revealed in a short talk he gave his generals. After telling them that he intended to attack the much stronger Austrian army as soon as he could, he declared:

> If any regiment of cavalry shall fail to crash straight into the enemy, when ordered, I shall have it dismounted immediately after the battle and turned into a garrison regiment. If any infantry battalion so much as begins to waver, it will lose its colors and its swords, and I shall have the braid cut from its uniform.[1]

That stirring address produced what many historians regard as Frederick's most brilliant victory. As his army approached the Austrians, the row of hills in front of the Austrians prevented them from seeing how he was deploying his men. He decided to make a feint at their right flank, while rapidly moving most of his force behind the hills to strike at the left. The feint at the right persuaded Daun to send his reserves there. When the mass of Prussians crashed into his left, it broke after a hard but short fight.

Frederick pushed the pursuit for two hours after dark, resulting in very heavy losses for the Austrians—10,000 dead and 12,000 prisoners. The Prussians, however, lost 11,600 men, another example of Frederick taking heavier casualties despite being victorious. The Battle of Leuthen is seen as Frederick's finest moment: he used his tactical skill and the fighting spirit of his men to drive off a vastly superior and well entrenched enemy. Napoleon called it the nearly perfect battle plan.

By the beginning of 1759, the constant bloody fighting had badly reduced the Prussian army. The British had not provided much help, except for considerable gold, and several regiments of Prussians had been sent to defend Hanover. On the other hand Frederick's enemies had not cooperated well with each other. However, in 1759, a large Austrian force did join with the Russians in Poland. The allied forces nearly destroyed the Prussian eastern army in July at Kay. Frederick rushed eastward with his main force, but he was routed in August at Kunersdorf on the Oder River, because he lacked the manpower to pull off the oblique attack. The 20,000 men lost as casualties and prisoners, along with the loss of 172 guns, reduced his army to near impotency. Most fortunately for Frederick, his enemies, who also had been badly bloodied with 15,500 casualties, failed to pursue vigorously. Had they done so, they might have finished him off.

The Prussian army had lost some 100,000 men in two years. Frederick managed to replace most of them, although the new recruits were not nearly as well-drilled and well-disciplined. Even more amazing than replacing his manpower was the fact that Frederick was able to continue to supply his army despite enormous losses in material. While that can be attributed to the efficient Prussian bureaucracy, it is noteworthy that the Austrian army, which had taken even heavier losses, also was able to refill its ranks and supply depots. Clearly the nature of war was changing, for the major states of Europe were able to supply their armies on a more regular basis despite the frequent battles.

THE FRENCH AND INDIAN WAR

The British contributed little to the war effort on the continent, beyond gving Frederick large amounts of gold. In 1759 the British infantry showed what it could have contributed when 10,000 elite foot soldiers broke three lines of French cavalry in the Battle of Minden, preventing a French invasion of Hanover. However, Prime Minister William Pitt had decided to concentrate on the naval and colonial theaters of war. In North America, fighting had already begun in 1754 in what is called the French and Indian War.

Both the French and the British relied on their local militias for defense of their colonies. The century-long conflict with the Indian tribes had considerably changed the way both groups of colonists fought. The Indians used the forest tactics of hit-and-run, ambush, and firing from behind cover. Using such tactics, the Indian tribes could make the European penetration of their lands costly, but could not stop it from continuing. In part because the militiamen had to face an undisciplined enemy who used those forest tactics, and in part because colonists did not like to spend much time drilling, their militias lacked discipline. Nonetheless they were more than a match for the Indian warriors, who fought entirely as individuals. Largely out of necessity, the French were more willing than the British to make alliances with the Indian tribes. Their Indian allies helped for a long time to disguise the fact that the French were badly outmanned in America. The number of Europeans in the British colonies was nearly 2 million compared to only 80,000 in French Canada.

In 1754 the militia of Virginia under Colonel George Washington had been sent to the present locale of Pittsburgh to build a fort that would control the upper Ohio valley. The French were already present in strength in their Fort Duquesne, and they easily repelled Washington. With the defeat of the Virginia militia, which was regarded as the best in the British colonies, Britain sent two regiments of regulars under General Braddock to Virginia, while a fleet was sent into the Gulf of Saint Lawrence to blockade Canada. Braddock led 1400 regulars and 450 militiamen toward Fort Duquesne. A force of 900 Frenchmen and Indians ambushed them about nine miles from the fort. Firing at will from behind trees and from a ravine, the French force scored heavily on the British regulars, who were utterly unable to respond to that kind of attack. The militia responded better and was able to withdraw to the safety of a second British column several miles behind. The British lost 800 men, including Braddock.

The principal result of the battle was the British decision to form four regiments of light infantry, called the Royal Americans. They actually were largely Germans and German colonists, who used rifled firearms— that is, guns with spiral grooves cut in the barrels. The idea of rifling musket barrels had been known since the early 1500s, but there was a problem with it: the ball had to be driven by brute force down the barrel, an act that took too long for such a weapon to be used in regular units. A rifled firearm was far more accurate than a smooth-bore musket, and rifled muskets had become common in the Rhine valley for hunting. The Germans who used these weapons were organized first by the Austrians as military units to skirmish in advance of the main force. Their style of fighting was known as "little war." They had given good service in many battles of the era 1740-63. Many German Protestants had migrated to the English colonies, where they began to use the Pennsylvania rifle, longer than the German model. In the style of warfare in North America, the riflemen often were highly effective.

For two years after Braddock's defeat, the French remained on the offensive both at sea and in the colonies. A French amphibious operation landed 15,000 men on the island of Minorca in April 1756. A British fleet under Admiral Byng arrived off Minorca a month later to give battle. Both fleets formed the line-ahead and proceeded to blast the other with broadsides. A lucky shot felled the mainmast of a ship in the British center, and it blocked the progress of the ships behind it. The French were able to concentrate on the five lead British ships, damaging them heavily before sailing away. Byng decided to return to Gibraltar without attempting to relieve Minorca. When the admiralty heard of his failure, it recalled Byng to London to be court-martialed for failure to do his utmost. He was convicted and shot. While a disgraceful verdict, it did inspire other admirals to do their utmost in future battles.

THE BATTLE OF QUEBEC

The British navy did much better for the rest of the war. It cleared the French from the Gulf of Saint Lawrence and landed 9,000 regulars and 500 militiamen to lay siege to the fortress of Louisbourg in May 1758. The fort fell after a two month siege. The fall of Louisbourg opened the Saint Lawrence River to the British fleet. In the spring of 1759 a fleet carrying 9,000 soldiers worked its way up the river toward Québec; it anchored under the cliffs of the city in late June. The French fortress stood high above the river and was nearly unapproachable from every direction. There General Montcalm and his 3,800 men, half regulars and half militiamen, waited, confident that no British force could reach the fort in enough strength to be a threat. For two months General Wolfe, only thirty-two years old, searched for a way to get his troops up to the fortress. By mid-

September, aware of the approach of winter, Wolfe decided to take a gamble: he would send half of his men up the cliffs on a narrow footpath at night. By dawn, 4,800 British troops had formed battle lines on the Plain of Abraham in front of the fort.

General Montcalm, awakened with the news, faced a difficult choice: allow the British to attack his strong defensive works, or attack the British while their number was still little larger than his force. He chose the latter course because he did not have the supplies for a long siege. Bringing his men out of the fortress, Montcalm ordered them to advance on the British line. He did not appreciate that half of his army consisted of militiamen who lacked the discipline to charge an enemy line. Much too far from the enemy, the militiamen fired their muskets and then dropped to the ground to reload. This disrupted the lines of the regulars as they approached the British. The British stepped forward, and at a distance of forty yards delivered what one British officer called "the most perfect volley ever fired." They then charged with bayonets. The French militiamen broke and ran, and the regulars were too badly broken by the volley to give a strong fight. They retreated into Québec, which surrendered five days later. Both generals had been killed in the battle. A year later, the French surrendered Montréal.

THE WAR IN INDIA

British naval supremacy also was a major factor in their victory in India. The four European powers—Portugal, Holland, France, and Britain—competing for influence in India had been reduced to Britain and France by 1750. What makes the war in India unique in history was that private companies, the British and the French East India Companies, carried on the military activities on land. Founded for commercial exploitation of the East, they formed their own companies of soldiers, but depended on the royal fleets for support.

The French had the early advantage in the war in India because they made an effort to drill native recruits in the use of the musket and the bayonet. The Europeans had made use of native troops since the 1500s, but this was the first time they had been trained in western tactics. The British, however, had found a first-rate commander in Robert Clive. He had arrived in India as a young clerk in the East India Company. Given command of 500 soldiers in 1751 in an action involving a native ally of France, he revealed a talent for military matters. By 1756 he was an experienced officer in command of the company's forces in India.

Serious fighting commenced with the declaration of war in June 1756. The major event of the war occurred a year later, at the village of Plassey north of Calcutta. The Indian ruler of Bengal, a French ally, with some 50,000 men led by French officers attacked Clive's army of 1,100 British and 2,100 Indians. A sudden storm dampened the powder of the French; Clive's men had taken care to cover theirs. Aided by the defection of several Bengali officers, Clive's forces easily halted charges by both cavalry and infantry. After the Indian troops broke and ran, the British easily handled the few Frenchmen left and took control of Bengal. Clive's army then moved southward along the eastern coast of India, capturing the powerful fortress of Pondicherry in the far south in January 1761. The French were unable to reinforce their army because of British naval supremacy. The fighting in India ended in early 1761 in the complete defeat of France.

THE END OF THE WAR

Back in Europe, the steady onslaught of the three powers against Prussia continued to wear down Frederick's army. The year 1760 saw constant hard fighting in which the Prussian king showed again and again his talent as a tactician, but he was unable to prevent a temporary occupation of Berlin in October by Austrian and Russian forces. The hard-fought battle of Torgau in December forced the allies to pull back from Berlin, but it also reduced the total manpower available to Frederick to under 100,000 men. His enemies had well over three times that number.

In order to conserve his manpower, Frederick spent the summer of 1761 in an excellent defensive position on the border between Silesia and Bohemia. Neither the Austrians nor the Russians were willing to attack him, but even the limited skirmishing of the summer cut further into his manpower. More serious, the new British king, George III (1760-1820), was recalling much of the force that Britain had committed to the continental war. Such was Ferderick's dire situation when word came from Saint Petersburg in January 1762 that Czarina Elizabeth had died. Her heir, Peter III, immediately began peace negotiations, which led to a treaty in May. Peter then lent troops to Frederick.

With France also reducing its commitment to the war, Frederick was able to concentrate on Daun's Austrian army and chase it from Silesia in July 1762. By then both sides were ready to discuss peace terms. Two separate treaties, of Hubertresburg and Paris, ended the war in early 1763. In the first treaty, Austria again recognized Prussia's rule over Silesia. In the second, France conceded Canada, the Ohio valley, and the land east of the Mississippi to Britain, while several islands in the West Indies were returned to France. In India the several posts left to the French were demilitarized and their fortifications razed.

Frederick II's achievement in the Seven Years War is all but unique in the history of warfare. Only Alexander and Hannibal have comparable records of brilliant victories won largely through the tactical genius of the commander against enormous odds. Frederick's battlefield success was due largely to the speed and discipline with which his army moved both while going to and while on the battlefield. Prussian drill and discipline enabled Frederick to attack with his entire line, or pivot it, or refuse one flank while concentrating his forces at one point in the enemy line.

The other armies of Europe began to imitate the Prussians, especially in respect to moving more quickly in battle. However, since they were not capable of imposing the extremely harsh drill of the Prussian sergeants, they looked for other ways to achieve the same goal. The French responded by organizing their armies into divisions. Each of the four divisions of a French army approached the battlefield under separate command, in the belief that the smaller units could move with the same speed as the entire line of the better trained Prussians. The French division could deploy even more quickly when the French developed a drill for marching to the battlefield in a column, which facilitated speed in the march to battle. Approaching the field, it could quickly deploy into a line facing the direction of the march. Rough terrain on the way to a battlefield was consequently not as serious a problem as it had been. The creation of divisions also made striking at an enemy from several directions more feasible—a tactic that Napoleon would use with great success. The mobility of the division and its firepower were also enhanced by improvements in the casting of guns, which made them lighter and faster to move and capable of taking a larger charge. These developments became an essential part of the battlefield tactics during the French Revolution and the Napoleonic Wars.

NOTE

1. Quoted in Christopher Duffy, *The Army of Frederick the Great* (London, 1974), p. 176.

23

To the French Revolution

We open our campaigns with armies that are neither adequately recruited nor properly paid. Whether they win or lose, both sides are equally exhausted....Peace is made. A few colonies or provinces change hands. Often the cause of the conflict remains unresolved and each party remains sitting among its ruins and busies itself with paying off its debts and sharpening its weapon.

But suppose that there should arise in Europe a people vigorous in its genius, its resources and its government; a people in whom austere virtues and a national militia were joined to a settled policy of aggrandizement; one which did not lose sight of its purpose, which knew how to make war cheaply and to subsist on its victories, and was not reduced to laying down its arms through financial need. We would see such a people subjugate its neighbors and overthrow their feeble constitutions as the north wind shakes the tender reeds.

Jacques de Guibert, quoted in Michaël Howard, *War in European History* (Oxford, 1976), p. 74. Guibert wrote this attack on contemporary European warfare in 1772.

While the French thirsted for revenge for their defeat in the Seven Years War, the British were faced with repaying the enormous debt they had incurred for the war. The British government was eager to raise money from those who benefited the most from its victory, the American colonists. Various taxes and tariffs were set for the colonies soon after 1763. The new rates were modest compared to those in Britain itself, but the colonists deeply resented the new taxes. They ignored the new security from French attacks that the British war effort had brought them. In fact, it was precisely that new security that explains the eventual outbreak of the American Revolution, for the colonists were now free to express their resentment over the new taxes. Had the French stayed in Canada, there would have been no revolution, since the colonists would have never thought to defy British authority.

When resentment led to violence in 1774, the only organized military force available to the rebels was the militia. The militia had gained some experience in the French and Indian War, but once the war was over, it returned to its usual limited drill. Its weaponry was obsolete or worn out equipment handed down from the regular army. It was, nonetheless, the very lack of discipline in the militia companies that gave the rebels what successes they had in the first three years of the revolution. If they had been of better quality, they probably would have tried to fight the British regulars in formal battle, and been badly defeated. For the most part they did not try, instead using hit-and-run tactics that kept the British off balance and cost them steady casualties.

While irregular tactics could deny control of huge expanses of land to the British, they could not prevent the British regulars from dominating the major cities and strategic locations. Fortunately for the Americans, in 1777 the British high command played into their hands. A three-pronged attack was planned to separate New England, the heart of the revolution, from the rest of the colonies. One British force was to head north from New York, a second east from Lake Ontario, and a third south from Canada. They were to meet at Albany.

The third column, some 8,000 men under General Burgoyne, reached the vicinity of Saratoga, twenty-five miles north of Albany, in mid-September. An American army of about 7,000 men under General Gates had occupied a strong defensive position reinforced by earthworks. Gates used a force of 500 riflemen to hinder the British approach, and inflicted heavy casualties. The Americans then launched six assaults against the British, but were thrown back with heavy losses on both sides. Although Burgoyne remained in control of the field, he no longer was strong enough to fight his way to Albany. He decided to set up a fortified camp to wait for reinforcements. After three weeks it had become clear that none were coming, and Burgoyne decided to fight his way out after all. Thus on October 9 occurred the second Battle of Saratoga. Now with a large numerical superiority, the Americans routed the British. What was left of the British force fled back to the north, but when they reached the bridge over the Hudson, they found it under the control of the Americans. On October 17, Burgoyne surrendered.

With their victory at Saratoga the Americans not only doomed the British strategy of splitting the northern colonies, they also proved that they were capable of defeating a large regular army, at least under favorable conditions. Most important, it convinced the French that the revolution had a chance of success, and they agreed to an alliance in February 1778. The French had already been providing weapons and supplies on credit; now they began to send them in quantity. The arrival of new fusils greatly improved American firepower.

EUROPEAN CONTRIBUTIONS

Equally important was the arrival of several experienced European officers who undertook the enormous task of transforming the Continental Army from a militia into a regular army. In 1775 the Continental Congress

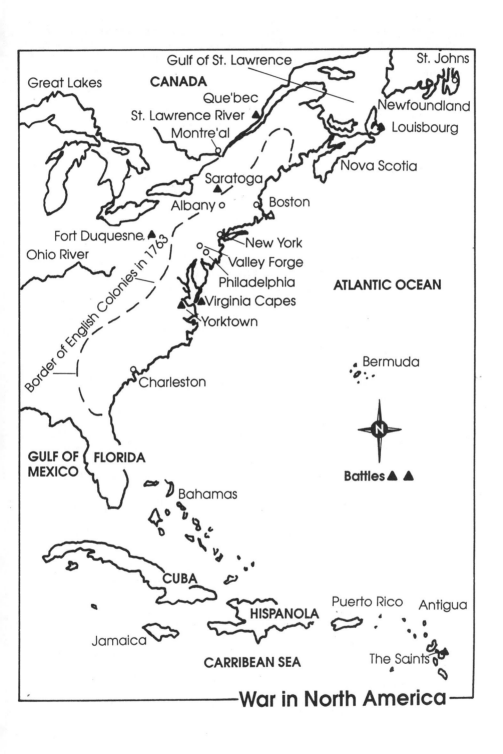

Gulf of St. Lawrence   St. Johns

CANADA

Great Lakes

Que'bec

St. Lawrence River   Newfoundland

Montre'al   Louisbourg

Nova Scotia

Saratoga

Albany o   Boston

Fort Duquesne   New York

Ohio River   Valley Forge

Border of English Colonies in 1763

Philadelphia   ATLANTIC OCEAN

Virginia Capes

Yorktown

Bermuda

N

Charleston

Battles ▲ ▲

GULF OF   FLORIDA
MEXICO

Bahamas

CUBA

Puerto Rico   Antigua

HISPANOLA

Jamaica

The Saints

CARRIBEAN SEA

War in North America

had combined the many colonial militias into a national army and had named George Washington as its commander in chief. In its first two years, the Continental Army did fight better than could have been expected of militiamen, but it was incapable of holding strategic locations against the British regulars. Washington recognized the need for a well-drilled army in order to win the war.

Although a number of former British officers served in the Continental Army, it was largely a group of continental military men who provided the expertise in drill that transformed it. They included a number of Frenchmen such as the marquis de Lafayette; two Poles, Thaddeus Kosciuszko and Casimir Pulaski; and the German barons Kalb and von Steuben. Von Steuban was the most important of these foreign officers. A veteran of Frederick II's army, he came to America in 1777. During the desperate winter of 1777-78, while the Continental Army was starving at Valley Forge in Pennsylvania, Steuben imposed Prussian drill and discipline on it. But he had to admit that American soldier were different from those of Europe. When European soldiers are told "do this, and they do it," he said; but in America, "I am obliged to say 'this is the reason why you ought to do this' before the Americans do it."[1] By spring, Steuben's drill had made them into a far better force.

The final victory for the American independecne depended heavily on European intervention in the war. After Britain declared war on France following the alliance with the Americans, France persuaded Spain to declare war on Britain a year later. Britain also declared war on the Netherlands in 1780 because of the large quantities of war goods the Dutch were selling to the Americans. The support of the foreign powers persuaded many bankers to lend money to the Continental Congress.

In 1779-80, the war on land was a see-saw affair. Both sides had successes, and both allowed good opportunities to slip away. As a result of the protracted maneuvering of those years, the British decided to consolidate a large force at the mouth of the Chesapeake Bay in order to control that vital waterway. Washington and the French general Rochambeau, commanding 8,000 elite French troops in Rhode Island, agreed to transport nearly all their available manpower to Chesapeake Bay in hope of trapping the British there.

THE BATTLE OF YORKTOWN

Any prospect of defeating the British in the Chesapeake required the service of a strong fleet. The fledgling American navy throughout the war was largely a privateering fleet. Since 1763, France had been putting great effort into rebuilding its fleet. By 1778, while still inferior overall to the British fleet, it was capable of defeating the British under favorable conditions. George Washington well recognized how badly a powerful fleet was needed to control the coastal waters, and asked the French king for one. Louis XVI agreed and in 1781 dispatched Admiral de Grasse to America.

In August, de Grasse's fleet arrived in the Chesapeake and, after unloading 3,000 soldiers, blockaded the bay. A month later a British attempt to break the blockade failed, largely because the British flagship flew two conflicting signals at the start of the battle. The British captains, not wishing to face a court-martial for violating the battle instructions, followed the line-ahead signal and refused to close with the individual enemy ships. Shortly after the Battle of the Chesapeake, the American and French forces arrived from the north. On September 28, 1781, 9,500 American and 7,800 French soldiers opened the siege of Yorktown, where General Cornwallis had 8,000 men behind hastily built fortifications.

Rochambeau, in an amazing act of cooperation, placed himself under Washington's command; the coordination between the two armies and the French fleet was exceptionally good. The French brought in siege pieces by sea, including the new Gribeauval guns, which were mounted on a semicircular track on which the guns could swivel nearly 180 degrees. On October 9, the siege guns opened up on the British fortifications. Assaults by allied troops took several outlying redoubts, and a large British sortie was easily thrown back. On October 17, Cornwallis realized that the game was up and surrendered. The loss of his army was the final blow to a British government already badly divided over the question of making peace. Peace negotiations began in July 1782, and the Peace of Paris was concluded the next April.

Before peace was made, however, one more major battle was fought. It was a naval encounter in the Caribbean, called the Battle of the Saints from the several small islands near Guadeloupe where it occurred in April 1782. After Yorktown, both the British fleet with thirty-six ships and the French of thirty-three ships had gone to the Caribbean for the winter. Under orders to find and destroy the French fleet, Admiral Rodney found it between Dominica and Guadeloupe. After several days of calm, the winds picked up enough to allow the fleets to form the line-ahead. The battle began with the two lines sailing past each other firing their broadsides in the conventional manner. The wind shifted abruptly to a direction that disordered the French fleet while having less serious an impact on the British. Gaps quickly appeared in the French line. Rodney, in violation of the battle instructions, took his flagship and six other ships through one of the gaps, while the rear division went through another gap. As the British ships sailed through the French line, they fired broadsides in both directions at the bows and sterns of the French ships, which were not able to respond. Five French ships, including Admiral de Grasse's flagship, were captured. Rodney's victory established cutting through the enemy line as an acceptable tactic for the British navy and began undermining the rigid tactics of the battle instructions, which continued through the naval battles of the French Revolution, and culminated at the Battle of Trafalgar in 1805. The British victory, however, did not affect the peace negotiations, which took into account the British defeat at Yorktown, but not their victory in the Caribbean six months later.

CONSEQUENCES OF THE AMERICAN REVOLUTION

It is difficult to avoid the conclusion that for all the valor of the American and French armies, the American victory depended above all on the fact that the long voyage across the Atlantic made sending and supplying a large army in America too difficult for the British. They were never able to transport enough manpower to make quick work of the rebels, as theoretically they were capable of doing. When France entered the war, the task of transoceanic logistics was made far more difficult. It became impossible to continue the war at a cost acceptable to the British Parliament, where there had always been a strong peace party. In short British seapower, which had made the American Revolution possible through the conquest of Canada, failed during the War of American Independence.

The enormous differences between Europe and North America, which were obvious to most military men, obscured the implications of the new developments in the American Revolution, and like the American Civil War it had little immediate impact on military thinking in Europe. The vast distances and the small forces involved in America required a different style of army than found in Europe—more mobile, less dependent on supply depots, less likely to be forced into a formal battle unless both sides badly wanted it. The battles that were fought were small in comparison to those of the recent wars in Europe. Another major difference was the almost complete absence of fortifications in America, which permitted the easy and wide-ranging movement of forces that marked the war. Other differences included the limited amount of artillery in the war and the negligible presence of cavalry. Few European officers could have thought that there were any lessons to learn from the war in America.

More predictive of the future was the effective use of irregulars, who disrupted the British forces, cut their supply lines, and in general cost the British a great deal in casualties, supplies, and morale. Their style of warfare, called in Europe "little war," required a soldier who was self-reliant and capable of acting as an individual, or at least in a small group, rather than as an automaton in the "long thin line." It also put greater emphasis on marksmanship with firearms, although large-scale dependence on marksmanship awaited standardized rifled firearms.

Perhaps the most important development in the American Revolution was the appearance of what can be called a citizen army. Only part of the manpower that fought for the American cause was made up of the regulars in the Continental Army. The majority were irregulars who only took up arms when a British force was in their region. Such militia-type forces were certainly not new to this war, for many wars in the past had seen militias in action. Since 1600, however, they had been little used in Europe. Most military men of the eighteenth century regarded well-drilled regulars as the only acceptable military force, and could not conceive of using any other type. But there were some officers who thought otherwise.

Even before the American Revolution began, a French officer, the Count Guibert, had written in 1772 about the enormous potential of such armies. Like so many military theorists before him, Guibert looked to the Roman citizen-soldier as the ideal. The legion had travelled lightly and quickly as it campaigned, unlike the slow, cumbersome armies of his time. Guibert also recognized the bloodiness of Roman war and argued that war should not be fought as it was in his era, with armies acting as if they were in leg irons. His citizen-soldiers would inflict and suffer heavy casualties, down to the last man, if necessary, in pursuit of victory for their just cause. One element of the early Roman army that Guibert did not mention, but that had reappeared to some degree in the American army, was a style of discipline that combined the discipline created by drill with that produced by patriotism. It created a soldier who fought with both zeal and discipline, essentially the modern soldier.

Guibert, however, did not expect that his ideal army would ever appear. He believed that the peoples of Europe were too corrupt to become austere and vigorous again. He died only a year before such an army did appear during the French Revolution. The appearance of armies with citizen-soldiers and drill-imposed discipline on a much grander scale during the Napoleonic Wars is regarded as the origin of modern warfare.

NOTE

1. Quoted in Christopher Duffy, *The Army of Frederick the Great* (London, 1974), p. 210.

Suggested Readings

The works listed below were chosen because I found them useful in writing this work, they are in English, and they should be available in most college and university libraries.

1. GENERAL STUDIES OF MILITARY HISTORY

Larry Addington. *the Patterns of War through the Eighteenth Century*. Bloomington, Ind., 1990.

Robert Andersen. *Oared Fighting Ships*. London, 1962.

Carl Brockelmann. *History of Islamic Peoples*. London, 1952.

The Cambridge History of Islam. 2 vols. Cambridge, 1970.

The Cambridge Medieval History. 10 vols. London, 1926.

Hans Delbrück. *History of the Art of War*. 4 vols., Westport, Conn., 1975-85.

R. E. and T. N. Dupuy. *The Encyclopedia of Military History from 3500 B.C. to the Present*. New York, 1977.

John Fuller. *A Military History of the Western World*. 3 vols. New York, 1954.

Oliver Hogg. *Artillery: Its Origins, Heyday and Decline*. London, 1970.

Michael Howard. *War in European History*. Oxford, 1976.

James Hughes. *Military Architecture*. New York, 1974.

Archer Jones. *The Art of War in the Western World*. Urbana, Ill., 1987.

Bjorn Landström. *The Ship*. Garden City, N.J., 1961.

William McNeill. *The Pursuit of Power: Technology, Armed Force and Society since A.D. 1000*. Chicago, 1982.

John Nef. *War and Human Progress*. Cambridge, 1950.

The New Cambridge Modern History. 14 vols. Cambridge, 1965.

Robert O'Connell. *Of Arms and Men: A History of War, Weapons, and Aggression*. Oxford, 1989.

Richard Preston and Sidney Wise. *Men in Arms*. New York, 1970.

Charles Quigley. *Weapon Systems and Political Stability: A History*. Washington, D.C., 1983.

William Reid. *Weapons through the Ages*. London, 1976.

Oliver Spaulding, et al. *Warfare: A Study of Military Methods from Earliest Times*. Washington, D.C., 1939.

Sidney Toy. *A History of Fortification 3000 B.C. to A.D. 1700*. New York, 1955.

Martin Van Creveld. *Technology and War From 2000 B.C. to the Present*. New York, 1989.

Quincy Wright. *A Study of War*. London, 1965.

2. THE GREEK PHALANX

Frank Adcock. *Greek and Roman Art of War*. Berkeley, Calif., 1957.
J.K. Anderson. *Military Theory and Practice in the Age of Xenophon*. Berkeley, Calif., 1970.
Donald Engels. *Alexander the Great and the Logistics of the Macedonian Army*. Berkeley, 1978.
Arthur Ferrill. *The Origins of War from the Stone Age to Alexander the Great*. London, 1985.
Victor Hanson. *The Western Way of War: Infantry Battle in Classical Greece*. New York, 1989.
Herodotus, Xenophon, and Thucydides. *Greek Histories The Complete and Unabridged Historical Works*. New York, 1942.
William Pritchett. *The Greek State at War*. 4 vols. Berkeley, Calif., 1971-85.
William Tarn. *Alexander the Great*. 2 vols. Boston, 1056.

3. THE ROMAN LEGION

Frank Adcock. *The Roman Art of War under the Republic*. New York, 1963.
Julius Caesar. *Eight Books of Caesar's Gallic Wars*. New York, 1891.
Roy Davies. *Service in the Roman Army*. New York, 1989.
Henry Parker. *The Roman Legions*. New York, 1958.
Chester Starr. *The Roman Imperial Navy*. New York, 1960.
George Watson. *The Roman Soldier*. Ithaca, N.Y., 1969.
Graham Webster. *The Roman Imperial Army*. New York, 1969.

4. THE FALL OF THE ROMAN EMPIRE

Thomas Burns. *A History of the Ostro-Goths*. Bloomington, Ind., 1984.
John Bury. *Invasion of Europe by the Barbarians*. New York, 1963.
Arthur Ferrell. *The Fall of the Roman Empire*. London, 1986.
Edward Luttwak. *Grand Strategy of the Roman Empire from the First Century A.D. to the Third*. Baltimore, 1976.
Otto Manchen-Helfen. *The World of the Huns*. Berkeley, 1973.
William Patterson. "The Archers of Islam." *Journal of the Economic and Social History of the Orient* 9 (1966); 68-87.
Omeljam Pritsak. *Studies in Medieval Eurasian History*. London, 1981.
E.A. Thompson. *History of Attila and the Huns*. Westport, Conn., 1975.
Edward Thompson. *Romans and Barbarians: The Decline of the West*. Madison, Wis., 1982.
Flavius Vegetius. *Military Institutions of the Romans*. Harrisburg, Penn., 1960.

5. THE BYZANTINE AND ARAB EMPIRES

John Barker. *Justinian and the Later Roman Empire*. Madison, Wis., 1966.
Clive Foss. *Rome and Byzantium*. Oxford, 1977.
John Glubb. *The Great Arab Conquests*. London, 1963.
Cyril Mango. *Byzantium: The Empire of New Rome*. London, 1980.
Georgije Ostrogorsky. *History of the Byzantine State*. Oxford, 1956.
V.J. Parry and Malcolm Yapp. *War, Technology, and Society in the Middle East*. London, 1975.
Denys Pringle. *Defense of Byzantine Africa from Justinian to the Arab Conquest*. Oxford, 1981.
John Pryor. *Geography, techology, and war: Studies in the maritime history of the Mediterranean 649-1571*. Cambridge, 1988.
Andreos Stratos. *Byzantium in the Seventh Century*. Amsterdam, 1968.

6. THE EARLY MIDDLE AGES IN WESTERN EUROPE

Bernard Bachrach. "Charles Martel, Shock Combat, the Stirrup, and Feudalism."
    Studies in Medieval and Renaissance History 7 (1976); 42-75.
Bernard Bachrach. *Merovingian Military Organization 481-751.* Minneapolis,
    1972.
John Beeler. *Warfare in Feudal Europe 730-1200.* Ithaca, N.Y., 1971.
Phillippe Contamine. *War in the Middle Ages.* New York, 1984.
Norman Daniel. *The Arabs and Medieval Europe.* London, 1975.
Patrick Geary. *Before France and Germany.* Oxford, 1988.
Geoffrey Hindley. *Medieval Warfare.* New York, 1971.
H.W. Koch. *Medieval Warfare.* London, 1978.
Gwyn Jones. *History of the Vikings.* Oxford, 1984.
Karl Leyser. "The Battle at the Lech, 955: A Study in Tenth-Century Warfare."
    History 50 (1965); 1-25.
Charles Oman. *The Art of War in the Middle Ages AD 378-1485.* 2 vols. London,
    1924.
Lynn White. *Medieval Technology and Social Change.* Oxford, 1962.

7. FEUDALISM

Claude Blair. *European Armor 1066 to 1700.* London, 1958.
R.A. Brown. *The Normans and the Norman Conquest.* London, 1969.
R.A. Brown. *Origins of English Feudalism.* London, 1973.
Georges Duby. *The Three Orders: Feudal Society Imagined.* Chicago, 1978.
Charles Ffoulkes. *Armor and Weapons.* Oxford, 1909.
François Ganshof. *Feudalism.* New York, 1961.
Charles Haskins. *The Normans in European History.* New York, 1943.
Charles Hollister. *Anglo-Saxon Institutions on the Eve of the Norman Conquest.*
    Oxford, 1962.
Charles Hollister. *The Military Organization of Norman England.* Oxford, 1965.
David Howarth. *1066: The Year of the Conquest.* London, 1977.
J.F. Verbruggen. *The Art of Warfare in Western Europe during the Middle Ages.*
    Amsterdam, 1977.

8. HOLY WAR IN THE MIDDLE EAST

Thomas Archer. *Crusades: The Story of the Latin Kingdom of Jerusalem.* Lon-
    don, 1894.
James Brundage. *Richard Lion Heart.* New York, 1974.
Ronald Finucane. *Soldiers of the Faith.* New York, 1983.
Vladimir Minorsky. *The Turks, Iran and Caucasus in the Middle Ages.* London,
    1978.
John Norwich. *A History of Venice.* New York, 1984.
Zoe Oldenburg. *The Crusades.* New York, 1966.
Donald Queller. *The Fourth Crusade.* Leicester, 1978.
Steven Runciman. *A History of the Crusades.* 3 vols. Cambridge, 1951-54.
Kenneth Setton. *A History of the Crusades.* 5 vols. Madison, Wis., 1969-86.
R.C. Smail. *Crusading Warfare 1097-1193.* Cambridge, 1956.

9. CASTLES AND SIEGECRAFT

Bernard Bachrach. "The Angevin Strategy of Castle Building in the Reign of Fulk
    Nerra, 987-1040." *American Historical Review* 88 (1983); 533-60.
Robin Fedden. *Crusader Castles.* London, 1957.
Henry Hazard. *The Art and Architecture of the Crusader State.* Madison, Wis.,
    1977.

John Patrick. *Artillery and Warfare dring the Thirteenth and Fourteenth Centuries.* Logan, Utah, 1961.
Derek Renn. *Norman Castles in England.* London, 1918.
Sheila Sancha. *The Castle Story.* London, 1977.
A.H. Thompson. *Military Architecture During the Middle Ages.* Oxford, 1912.
Eugene Viollet-le-Duc. *Essay on the Military Architecture of the Middle Ages.* Westport, Conn., 1977.
Philip Warner. *Sieges of the Middle Ages.* London, 1968.

10. WAR IN THE MIDDLE AGES

John Baldwin. *The Government of Philip Augustus.* Berkeley, 1986.
John Gillingham. *Angevin Empire.* Leiden, 1984.
Ronald Nicholson. *Edward III and the Scots.* Oxford, 1965.
Sidney Painter. *The Reign of King John.* Baltimore, 1949.
Ralph Payne-Gallwey. *The Crossbow, Medieval and Modern.* New York, 1958.
Eduoard Perroy. *The Hundred Years War.* London, 1951.
Michael Prestwich. *The Three Edwards: War and State in England 1272-1377.* New York, 1980.
Michael Prestwich. *War, Politics and Finance Under Edward I.* London, 1980.

11. THE END OF THE MEDIEVAL MILITARY

A.D. Alderson. *Structures of the Ottoman Dynasty.* Oxford, 1956.
Franz Babinger. *Mehmed the Conqueror and His Times.* Princeton, 1978.
C.J. Beckingham. *Between Islam and Christendom.* London, 1983.
James Chambers. *The Devil's Horsemen: The Mongol Invasion of Europe.* New York, 1979.
Herbert Gibbon. *The Foundation of the Ottoman Empire.* London, 1918.
John Gillingham. *The War of the Roses.* London, 1981.
Anthony Goodman. *The War of the Roses: Military Activity and English Society 1452-97.* London, 1981.
John Keegan. *The Face of Battle.* New York, 1977.
David Morgan. *The Mongols.* New York, 1986.
Richard Newhall. *The English Conquest of Normandy 1416-1424.* London, 1924.
D.M. Nicol. *The Last Centuries of Byzantium 1261-1453.* New York, 1972.
J.J. Saunders. *The History of the Mongol Conquests.* London, 1971.
Peter Sugar. *Southeastern Europe Under Ottoman Rule 1354-1804.* Seattle, 1977.
Barbara Tuchman. *A Distant Mirror.* New York, 1978.
M.G.A. Vale. *Charles VII.* Berkeley, 1974.
M.G.A. Vale. *War and Chivalry.* London, 1981.
George Vernadsky. *The Mongols and Russia.* New Haven, 1953.

12. THE FIFTEENTH CENTURY: PIKES AND GUNS

F.M. Bartos. *The Hussite Revolution 1424-37.* New York, 1986.
W.Y. Carman. *A History of Firearms.* New York, 1955.
Carlo Cipolla. *Guns, Sails and Empire.* New York, 1965.
Frederick Heymann. *John Zizka and the Hussite Revolution.* Leiden, 1969.
H.J. Hime. *The Origins of Artillery.* London, 1945.
Howard Kaminsky. *History of the Hussite Revolution.* Berkeley, 1967.
Paul Kendall. *Louis XI.* New York, 1971.
Joseph Needham. *Gunpowder as the Fourth Power: East and West.* Hong Kong, 1985.
Joseph Needham. *Science and Civilization in China.* Vol. 5, Cambridge, 1986.
Richard Vaughan. *Charles the Bold: the Last Valois Duke of Burgundy.* London, 1973.

Richard Vaughan. *Valois Burgundy*. London, 1975.

13. WAR IN THE RENAISSANCE
Ernle Bradford. *Shield and the Sword: The Knights of St. John*. New York, 1973.
Antony Bridge. *Suleiman the Magnificent, Scourge of Heaven*. London, 1983.
E. D. Brockman. *The Two Sieges of Rhodes 1480-1522*. London, 1969.
J.R. Hale. *Renaissance War Studies*. London, 1983.
J.R. Hale. *War and Society in Renaissance Europe*. Baltimore, 1985.
J.R. Hale and Michael Mallet. *The Military Organization of a Renaissance State: Venice c 1400 to 1617*. Cambridge, 1984.
R.J. Knecht. *Francis I*. Cambridge, 1982.
Charles Kortepedes. *Ottoman Imperialism uring the Reformation*. New York, 1972.
Niccolò Machiavelli. *Art of War*. Indianapolis, 1966.
Roger Merriman. *Rise of the Spanish Empire in the Old World and in the New*. 3 vols. New York, 1918.
Charles Oman. *A History of the Art of War in the Sixteenth Century*. New York, 1937.
Peter Paret. *Makers of Modern Strategy: Military Thought from Machiavelli to Hitler*. Princeton, 1976.
Frederick Taylor. *Art of War in Italy 1494-1529*. London, 1973.
George Trease. *The Condottieri: Soldiers of Fortune*. New York, 1971.

14. NAVAL WAR IN THE MEDITERRANEAN
Jack Beeching. *The Galleys at Lepanto*. New York, 1982.
Ernle Bradford. *The Great Siege*. London, 1961.
Ernle Bradford. *The Sultan's Admiral: Life of Barbarossa*. London, 1969.
Fernand Braudel. *The Mediterranean and the Mediterranean World in the Age of Philip II*. 2 vols. London, 1973.
John Guilmartin. *Gunpowder and Galleys*. Cambridge, 1974.
Andrew Hess. "The Evaluation of the Ottoman Seaborne Empire in the Age of Oceanic Discoveries." *American Historical Review* 75 (1970); 1892-1919.
Andrew Hess. *Forgotten Frontier: A History of the Sixteenth Century Ibero-African Frontier*. Chicago, 1978.
William Rodgers. *Naval Warfare Under Oars: 4th to 16th Centuries*. Annapolis, 1940.
Alberto Tenenti. *Piracy and the Decline of Venice 1580-1615*. Berkeley, 1967.
Armin Vambery. *Hungary in Ancient, Medieval and Modern Times*. London, 1987.

15. THE RISE OF THE ATLANTIC FLEETS
Ernle Bradford. *The Story of the "Mary Rose."* New York, 1982.
Charles Boxer. *From Lisbon to Goa 1500-1750*. London, 1984.
Charles Boxer. *The Portuguese Seaborne Empire 1415-1825*. London, 1969.
John Guilmartin. "The Guns of the Sanctissimo Sacramento." *Technology and Culture* 24 (1983); 559-601.
David Howarth. *The Voyage of the Armada: The Spanish Story*. London, 1981.
Michael Lewis. *Armada Guns*. London, 1961.
Michael Lewis. *The Spanish Armada*. Batsford, 1960.
Colin Martin and Geoffrey Parker. *The Spanish Armada*. New York, 1988.
Garrett Mattingly. *The Armada*. Boston, 1959.
John Parry. *The Age of Reconnaissance*. Cleveland, 1963.
Peter Pierson. *Commander of the Armada: The Seventh Duke of Medina-Sidonia*. New Haven, 1989.

334   Suggested Readings

16. THE SIXTEENTH CENTURY

Frederic Baumgartner. *Henry II King of France*. Durham, NC, 1988.
David Buisseret. *Henry IV*. London, 1984.
Andre Courvisier. *Armies and Societies in Europe, 1494-1789*. New York, 1979.
Christopher Duffy. *Siege Warfare: The Fortress in the Early Modern World 1494-1660*. London, 1979.
Henri de La Croix. *Military Considerations in City Planning*. London, 1972.
Howell Lloyd. *The Rouen Campaign 1590-1592*. Oxford, 1973.
William Maltby. *Alba*. Berkeley, 1983.
Geoffrey Parker. *European Soldiers 1550-1650*. Cambridge, 1977.
Geoffrey Parker. *The Military Revolution: Military Innovation and the Rise of the West, 1500-1800*. Cambridge, 1988.
Simon Pepper. *Firearms and Fortifications: Military Architecture and Siege Warfare in Sixteenth-Century Siena*. Chicago, 1986.

17. THE DUTCH REVOLT

Charles Boxer. *The Dutch in Brazil 1621-1654*. Oxford, 1957.
Maury Feld. *The Structures of Violence: Armed Forces and Social Systems*. London, 1977.
Pieter Geyl. *The Revolt of the Netherlands 1559-1609*. London, 1958.
Jonathan Israel. *The Dutch Republic and the Hispanic World 1606-1661*. Oxford, 1982.
Geoffrey Parker. *The Army of Flanders and the Spanish Road 1567-1659*. Cambridge, 1972.
Geoffrey Parker. *The Dutch Revolt*. Ithaca, N.Y., 1977.
Geoffrey Parker. *Spain and the Netherlands 1559-1659*. London, 1979.
C.V. Wedgwood. *William the Silent*. London, 1967.

18. THE THIRTY YEARS WAR

J.H. Elliott. *The Count Duke of Olivares The Statesman in an Age of Decline*. New Haven, 1986.
R.J.W. Evans. *The Making of the Habsburg Monarchy 1550-1700*. Oxford, 1974.
Golo Mann. *Wallenstein: His Life Narrated*. London, 1976.
Herbert Langer. *The Thirty Years War*. Poole, Dorset, 1980.
Geoffrey Parker. ed. *The Thirty Years War*. Boston, 1984.
F.M. Redlick. *The German Military Enterpriser and his Workforce*. Wiesbaden, 1964.
Michael Roberts. *Gustavus Adolphus: A History of Sweden 1611-1632*. 2 vols. London, 1953-58.
Michael Roberts. *Gustavus Adolphus and the Rise of Sweden*. London, 1973.
Michael Roberts. *Essays in Swedish History*. London, 1967.
Michael Roberts. *The Swedish Imperial Experience 1560-1718*. Cambridge, 1979.
Martin Van Creveld. *Supplying War: Logistics from Wallenstein to Patton*. London, 1977.
C.V. Wedgwood. *The Thirty Years War*. London, 1938.

19. THE NEW MODEL ARMY AND NAVY

Maurice Ashley. *Oliver Cromwell and the Puritan Revolution*. New York, 1958.
J.R. Jones. *Britain and Europe in the Seventeenth Century*. New York, 1966.
George Clark. *War and Society in the Seventeenth Century*. London, 1958.
C.H. Firth. *Cromwell's Army*. London, 1963.
David Howarth. *Sovereign of the Seas*. London, 1974.
Paul Kennedy. *The Rise and Fall of British Naval Mastery*. New York, 1976.
Peter Young. *The British Army 1642-1970*. London, 1976.

20. THE WARS OF LOUIS XIV
Douglas Baxter. *Servants of the Sword: French Intendants of the Army 1630-70*. Urbana, Ill., 1976.
David Chandler. *The Art of Warfare in the Age of Marlborough*. London, 1976.
David Chandler. *Marlborough as a Military Commander*. London, 1973.
John Childs. *Armies and Warfare in Euorpe, 1648-1789*. New York, 1982.
Jock Haswell. *The Battle for Empire: A Century of Anglo-French Conflict*. London, 1976.
Derek McKay. *Prince Eugene of Savoy*. London, 1977.
Geoffrey Symcox. *The Crisis of French Seapower 1688-1697*. The Hague, 1974.
John Wolf. *Louis XIV*. New York, 1968.

21. WARFARE IN THE EARLY EIGHTEENTH CENTURY
Christopher Duffy. *The Military Experience in the Age of Reason*. London, 1987.
Christopher Duffy. *Russia's Military Way to the West: Origins and Nature of Russian Military Power*. London, 1981.
Christopher Duffy. *Siege Warfare: The Fortress in the Age of Vauban and Frederick the Great 1660-1789*. London, 1979.
Robert Massie. *Peter the Great: His Life and World*. New York, 1980.
Robert Quimby. *The Background of Napoleonic Warfare: The Theory of Military Tactics in Eighteenth-Century France*. New York, 1957.
John Stoye. *The Siege of Vienna*. New York, 1965.

22. THE WARS OF FREDERICK THE GREAT
Gordon Donaldson. *Battle for a Continent Quebec 1759*. Garden City, NY, 1973.
Christopher Duffy. *The Army of Frederick the Great*. London, 1974.
T.N. Dupuy. *The Military Life of Frederick the Great of Prussia*. New York, 1969.
Lee Kennett. *The French Armies in the Seven Year War*. Durham, N.C., 1967.
Gerhard Ritter. *Frederick the Great*. London, 1968.
Maurice de Saxe. *Reveries or Memoires on the Art of War*. Westport, Conn., 1971.
Jon White. *Marshal of France: The Life and Times of Maurice Comte de Saxe*. Chicago, 1962.

23. TO THE FRENCH REVOLUTION
Geoffrey Best. *War and Society in Revolutionary Europe, 1770-1870*. Oxford, 1986.
R.A.   Bowler. *Logistics and the Failure of the British Army in America 1775-1783*. Princeton, 1975.
Jonathan Dull. *The French Navy and American Independence*. Princeton, N.J., 1975.
Don Higginbotham. *Reconsiderations on the Revolutionary War*. Westport, Conn., 1978.
Don Higginbotham. *The War of American Independence*. New York, 1971.
Ronald Hoffman. *Arms and Independence: The Military Character of the American Revolution*. Charlottesville, Va., 1984.
Piers Mackesy. *The War for America, 1775-1783*. Cambridge, 1964.
Peter Paret. *Yorck and the Era of Prussian Reform*. Princeton, 1966.
John Shy. *A people numerous and armed: Reflections on the military struggle for American Independence*. Oxford, 1976.

Index

About the Author

FREDERIC J. BAUMGARTNER is Professor of History at Virginia Polytechnic Institute and State University, Blacksburg, Virginia. He is the author of *Henry II King of France*, *Change and Continuity in the French Episcopate*, and *Radical Reactionaries*. He has contributed articles to *Sixteenth Century Journal*, *Journal for the History of Astronomy*, and *Annals of Science*.